Living

How Black Britain Performs Its Past

Steven Blevins

MINNESOTA

University of Minnesota Press
Minneapolis • London

Excerpts from *Lara* in chapter 4 are reprinted courtesy of Bernardine Evaristo and Bloodaxe Books, Northumberland, UK.

Published by the University of Minnesota Press
111 Third Avenue South, Suite 290
Minneapolis, MN 55401-2520
http://www.upress.umn.edu

Printed in the United States of America on acid-free paper

The University of Minnesota is an equal-opportunity educator and employer.

21 20 19 18 17 16 10 9 8 7 6 5 4 3 2 1

Library of Congress Cataloging-in-Publication Data
Names: Blevins, Steven, author.
Title: Living cargo : how Black Britain performs its past / Steven Blevins.
Description: Minneapolis : University of Minnesota Press, 2016. | Includes bibliographical references and index.
Identifiers: LCCN 2015039887 | ISBN 978-0-8166-9714-4 (hc) | ISBN 978-0-8166-9716-8 (pb)
Subjects: LCSH: Arts, Black—Great Britain—21st century—Themes, motives. | Arts and history—Great Britain—History—21st century. | Blacks—Great Britain—Intellectual life—21st century. | English literature—Black authors—History and criticism.
Classification: LCC NX543 .B578 2016 | DDC 700.89/96041—dc23
LC record available at http://lccn.loc.gov/2015039887

LIVING CARGO

Contents

History Unhoused

Performing the Life of Human Bio-Cargo

History is housed: in the archive and on the street; on the body and in the home. This book is about *un*housing the past; about opening up archives and drawing history out; and about the opening *out* that occurs when history goes public. *Living Cargo: How Black Britain Performs Its Past* is also about the social, political, and ethical demands such openings (up and out) make on public and private lives; and about the publics and counterpublics that are produced when history is on the move. My contention is that when history is unhoused, when it travels—narratively, visually, performatively—its movements help bind people together, as surely as its institutional enclosure helps keep them apart. Less abstractly, this book is about the black public cultures of postcolonial Britain; the particular historical resonances that join together many disparate communities in the UK under *and beyond* the banner of the nation; and the transnational circuits of exchange—economic, social, political, affective—that take British colonial history for a ride. In short, this book is about the ways in which history is *unhoused* when narratives, performances, and exhibitions of the colonial past, once consolidated in the archive, are constellated for public culture.

Over the last two decades the *archive* has come to name a dominant critical idiom in the academic humanities, a shorthand for capturing the interplay between the vast storehouses of records, documents, and artifacts held by state institutions, civic organizations, and private associations, on the one hand, and the ideologies, discourses, and rationales that determine how these items are accessed, disseminated, received, read, and interpreted, on the other.[1] But when the archive is under lock and key—or when placed on lockdown by the state—history is housed. When scholars retreat to the archive as an intellectual enclave, history remains housed. Through surreptitious policies of institutional enclosure, the archive is claimed as occupied territory, a regulated scene of colonial domestication, or a manicured setting for the ongoing civilizing missions of nation and empire. And yet, as Anjali Arondekar concisely puts it, "The archive still promises."[2] Like Arondekar, recent critics have acknowledged the countless ways in which this "archival turn" challenges the hierarchies that have long governed which archives matter and which do not, or which documents count as "evidence" and which do not, as well as broader assumptions about what "counts" as an archive at all. In the feverish drive to restore the past through the promise of the archive, however, we run the risk of forgetting other forms of collective memory, modes of historical consciousness, and practices of history making. In its capaciousness, the archive strives to subsume the past. Yet the lesson of the archive remains the same: history can be housed but never fully contained.

At the same time, when academic movements advance too smoothly, when theoretical trends rise and fall too swiftly, scholars run the risk of sanctioning a different kind of historical amnesia, a kind of critical "forgetting" that, as Diana Taylor reminds us, often accompanies the introduction of the new.[3] In the rapid development of transnational theory and globalization studies—two primary optics for apprehending the contemporary world—scholars too often ignore the historical conditions and material exigencies that determine how one lives in the present, conditions and determinations that persist in dialectical relation to the enormous creative potential for the transformation in social life today. When valuable theoretical innovations are abandoned, when vital critical interventions are dismissed, when important movements in creative expression are ignored—all in the name of staying current for currency's sake—precious intellectual resources are wasted. Over the past two decades, the commitment to history generally and materialist critique in particular, once central to both postcolonial theory and cultural studies, has been all but forgotten, and the enormous body of pioneering critical and creative work in these fields seems to have disappeared. But what are the consequences of forgetting the colonial and postcolonial prehistories of global neoliberalism?

One outcome has certainly been a tendency toward presentism in scholarly accounts of the global, scholarship valorized by the neoliberal academy and conducive to, if not explicitly geared toward, housing the past. Material history is deemed retrograde or made redundant—shelved, archived, housed—as modes of analysis suitable for apprehending the immediacy of transnational "flows," the intricacies of networked societies, or the intensity of global markets. As a conceptual frame, the transnational too often privileges the fast tempos of contemporeity, the empty homogenous time of the global "scape," and the spatial synchrony of networked exchange over the sonorous diachrony of materialist critique. In their eager presentism, transnational and globalization studies are subsumed into their own objects of analysis. Conducive to the same economic forces they had once set out to critique, these new marketplace methodologies now too often authorize the institutional quiescence and the political quietism global capital demands, and history is deemed inconsequential to the complex economic and social transactions operating within transnational space.

In order for such flows to be understood within the context of contemporary global geopolitics, however, they must first be apprehended as articulations of long historical structures, institutions, and relationships.[4] Thinking along the axes of synchrony and diachrony is crucial to comprehending current transnational migrations, social imaginaries, and public cultures. "Transnational" remains an empty signifier when unaccompanied by a sustained but situated historical-materialist analysis. But to think transnationally in any intellectually honest and substantive way demands that one think historically; conversely, to think historically necessitates thinking transnationally. I find it not only useful but imperative that we return to the theoretically inflected historiography associated with an earlier moment in black British and postcolonial cultural studies: precious resources, as I suggested earlier, that now run the risk of being eclipsed, if not erased, by the presentist orientation of the "transnational" as a critical idiom. Thus, rather than simply viewing the transnational as a viable aperture for comprehending the present, *Living Cargo* is principally a postcolonial project that treats the transnational and global (as well as the national) as long historical constructs open to critical interrogation.

To be sure, *postcolonial* itself has never functioned adequately or unproblematically as a chronotope for periodizing colonial relations that developed and dispersed across time and space, certainly not along the axes of before and after its prefix implies; as a theoretical field, however, the postcolonial continues to offer an invaluable chrono*trope* for figuring the reflexively situated *turn* in practices of imminent critique of the colonial, challenging many of the fundamental tenets of Marxist historicism without jettisoning its materialist core. What happens, however, when the postcolonial takes the transnational as its object of analysis? How might the postcolonial reconstitute the transnational as a contested but still useful framework for producing new knowledge of the contemporary, for empowering social agents, or for activating radical forms of collective action? I believe it is crucial at this volatile historical juncture that the postcolonial as critical and theoretical terrain be leveraged to understand the transnational as a long historical formation. While *Living Cargo* argues for the reaffirmation of materialist critique, it also reconsiders the theoretical constitution of the material, and recalibrates our understanding of the material relationship between the social, political, and ethical demands made when history is performed in/by/for public cultures. New configurations of materiality have emphasized the embodied experience of "feeling historical" through aesthetic and synaesthetic sensation—emphasizing touching, tasting, smelling, hearing, speaking, and seeing—as well as affect and feeling.[5] Embodiment has long posed a challenge to ways of thinking about the historical "matter" of materialist critique, but the critical reorientation of aesthetic experience from the conceptual to the affective has had a significant impact on a number of cultural fields and creative practices, including museum exhibition and artistic performance. Here the body is reposed in and as an archive, an artifact among artifacts. Not simply as text to be read, the artifactual body names a site of material entextualization, where one's own embodiment is experienced through wide-ranging and far-flung fragments, traces, and ruins—beautiful remnants and brutal remains—precariously held together in ensembles and assemblages, constellated in embroidered exhibitions and orchestrated performances of the archive.

Such a materialist framework also helps us think about matters of ethical responsibility often abandoned in older Marxist analysis, a critical reframing that proves crucial to confronting the challenges of comprehending the violent consequences of global capital dispersed across transnational space and a structural entanglement that necessarily and unavoidably places us all in a position of obligation to others whose precarious existence underwrites our own. The rise of global neoliberalism has certainly reproduced unequal power dynamics and entrenched economic hierarchies reminiscent of older forms of colonialism and imperialism, creating what is essentially the neocolonial or neo-imperial social order today. In the global economy subjugated knowledges, once deterritorialized, are easily reterritorialized within the circuits of global commodity flows. Postcolonial subjects of postimperial Britain negotiate the question of such reterritorialization in a variety of ways. But, in their own ways, each of the texts I engage—whether literary, visual, or performative—provide quite apposite examples of the way in which various forms of creative expression reproduced within cultural and mass media circuits are also capable of providing the means through which various constituencies can "imagine" a broad matrix of social belonging—global, national, and local.[6] I thus underscore the possibilities opened up by the consolidation of new public *imaginaries* in postimperial Britain. "It is the imagination," Arjun Appadurai observes, "its collective forms, that creates ideas of neighborhoods and nationhoods, of moral economies and unjust rule, of higher wages and foreign labor prospects. The imagination is today a staging ground for action, and not only for escape."[7] At the same time, I am suggesting that such public cultures become most actively engaged and politically empowered when a sense of shared history is activated as an integral component in the machinery of the social imaginary. Creative works such as the ones I discuss intervene in long histories of violence, oppression, and exploitation at the very core of social life—violent histories that comprise a series of rupturing events that occur both within *and* as effects of the *longue durée* of a singular globalizing capitalism, and as such are exigent to the experiences of violent displacement, movement, and migration.[8] The rapid expansion and intensification of conditions of precarity under global neoliberalism pose ethical as well as social and political dilemmas that the postcolonial critic must address. At the same time, however, it is vital that we also acknowledge that the transhistorical and transnational forces that power global markets—and drive the often unwelcome movements of people and unwanted displacements of whole populations—also bring communities of activists and creative producers into collaborative association, social alliance, and political solidarity. Consequently, important relays are formed between cultural producers across Africa, the Caribbean, the Americas, and Western Europe.[9]

In addition to creative engagements in the problems of history, memory, and redress, I draw on theoretical and critical work in the fields of black British and transnational cultural studies, on the one hand, and postcolonial and poststructural critiques of violence, power, and the reordering of the ethical terrain of the postcolonial and postimperial world, on the other, in order to explore how the translation of historical memory and experience into public narratives, performances, and exhibitions within transnational circuits dramatically refigures the social landscape of postimperial Britain. Recent studies, focusing on migrations initiated by upheavals in the global economy and the geopolitical disruptions and displacements they entail, have expressed a spirited interest in nomadic subjectivities and identities, flexible and global citizenships, and, most pervasively, cosmopolitanism, and its corollary, cosmo*politics*.[10] Transnational cultural studies scholars, taking their cue from postcolonial and globalization theory, have begun to describe the material conditions that circumscribe acts of migration and movement in an age in which mobility is simultaneously expanding and contracting.[11] Emphasizing movements and interactions among (rather than between) regions, nations, cities, and communities, a highly interdisciplinary "transnational" cultural studies has rethought older models of nation and state, class and identity, race and ethnicity.[12] Scholars involved in the study of transnational public cultures have sought ways of understanding the ever-shifting terrain of culture and cultural production in the wake of postcolonialism and globalization. Taking its cue from an earlier moment in postcolonial theory, transnational cultural studies concerns itself with the improvisational performances of hybridic identities initiated by transcultural encounters, and the way in which these performances get played out under the new disciplinary and institutional regimes of the postcolonial nation, former imperial centers, and now transnational sites, governmental and nongovernmental bodies, civil institutions, corporations, and agencies. Their analyses of the processes of economic and cultural globalization, which unpack the complicated forms of transnational media and commodity circulation, inform my approach to literary and visual arts production within the public cultures of postcolonial, postimperial Britain. Central to the methodology of transnational cultural studies is the belief that cultural objects are constituted equally by the production, circulation, translation, and consumption in varying reception contexts situated across a variety of public spheres, and that elite and popular political and cultural forms encounter and reinforce one another.[13] At the same time, because the domain of the public sphere, once associated with the nation-state and the rise of civil society,[14] is now understood to exceed national borders, theorists argue for a conception of "public cultures," which designates a matrix of social belonging, transnational and fluid in nature.[15] A public culture is both constituted by and constitutive of the texts, performances, exhibitions, and everyday experiences that circulate in it.

Living Cargo insists that the critical junctures of postcolonial and black British cultural studies remain crucial to understanding practices of global worlding today. My critical practice, then, aims to retain both political and ethical imperatives to social action as it attempts a historically substantive "setting to work" of deconstruction at sites of archival constellation and historical articulation performed in and by the creative works I discuss.[16] In this sense, the book offers both a materialist critique of contemporary creative historiography and engages in a deconstructive reading practice that aims to rethink the intersection of public history and embodied postcolonial subjectivity in the present. To do so I situate the literary, performative, and visual texts I analyze within sites of social action and political conflict as well as the everyday discourses, rhetorics, and practices that mediate the experience of public history. By reaffirming the postcolonial as an optic on globalization and the transnational, I hope to turn attention back toward rich material histories and creative practices that continue to circulate within, across, and between national and transnational public cultures. While many of the creative works I discuss rely at least in part on the institutional archives of state and civil society, they also draw from personal artifacts, common records, and shared stories that survive, narratives that are passed on and passed down in oral traditions, cultural practices, and informal collections disseminated across the African Atlantic. Having combed through the archive—formal and informal, institutional and communal, familial and personal—I have discovered that these artists and writers produce and perform rich and inventive works engaging with critical problems in the making of black public history.[17] I contend that the reterritorialization of the colonial archive has emerged as a dominant, perhaps even *the* dominant, aesthetic practice and political praxis within contemporary black creative expression. Highly performative and critically reflexive, such performances of the archive enact a provisional reoccupation and an improvisational unhousing of colonial and postcolonial history. When the archive is reframed as emergent rather than received as the very emblem of the residual, cultural producers find inexhaustible expressive possibilities through the assemblage of historical traces and temporal fragments consolidated in and by the archive.[18] Once scattered *in* the archive, the beautiful remnants and brutal remains of the colonial past reappear through the performative, counterarchival constellation of public history.

Performing the Past, Periodizing the Present

Unhousing is a performance. That is, unhousing names a particular kind of *enactment* of the archive. Unhousing occurs when the material remnants and affective remains once dispersed across transnational, globalized space are *reactivated* in what Diana Taylor has named a *repertoire* of performative actions and expressive behaviors that draw cultural memory and collective history into circulation.[19] Such performances traffic in turbulent encounters, rely on contingency and convergence, and gain currency through indetermination. They are necessarily provisional and improvisational, and always aleatory. Crucially, as Taylor also reminds us, performances are embodied, and they stage the body as a site of historical traces and violent inscription. But it is at the site of the body that Taylor's distinction between archive and repertoire begins to break down, if not quite collapse altogether. For the body that performs is itself both an artifact and affect of history, both archive and repertoire.[20] Wrought by the forces of history, the artifactual body is marked by and in the archive. The repertoire works in cooperative, even if disjunctive, relation to the archive. When unhoused, the artifactual body performs its archival past. As I argue throughout *Living Cargo,* the public history works performed by the black writers and artists the book addresses not only reactivate historical traces housed by the archive but likewise unhouse the body as an artifact of history. In works that draw on a wide range of aesthetic practices and creative forms across media, such disjunctive performances—critical and reflexive, provisional and improvisational—build upon what was once withheld *archivally* and are now put into constellation *performatively.*

Living Cargo assembles as *its* archive an equally provisional and improvisational selection of creative works by contemporary black writers and artists who reoccupy the archive when they narrate, exhibit, and stage the long and violent history of European colonialism, in particular the history of the transatlantic slave trade and plantation slavery. For reasons I will address below, however, the project remains situated within the British national frame even as it contests the ways in which nation is understood as a singular, bounded episteme of sovereign power. Though I will take occasional liberties with the national frame suggested by the book's subtitle, I continue to focus on those creative producers and cultural practitioners who largely reside in the UK but whose lives and works circulate transnationally. Significantly, the contemporary works I analyze are largely associated with the second and third generations of black Britons living and working in the UK. An interdisciplinary project that moves across a wide field of cultural production, the book is comprised of six chapters and partitioned into three sections. Part I, "History and Human Cargo," is concerned with the challenges posed by long-established biopolitical social imaginaries—the archival, the juridical, the genealogical—to literary and visual form and practices of historical and literary representation, analyzing works by the novelists Fred D'Aguiar (chapter 1) and Caryl Phillips (chapter 2). Part II, "Assembling Human Bio-Cargo," considers the biopolitics of human assemblage in relation to the literary and visual narratives by David Dabydeen (chapter 3) and Bernardine Evaristo, Dorothea Smartt, Inge Blackman/Campbell X, and Isaac Julien (chapter 4) that reflexively constellate the archive into assemblages of their own. Part III, "Exorbitant Life in an Age of Austerity," thinks about the persistence of cosmopolitanism under global neoliberalism, focusing on problems of history and the historicity of fashion and art in the "global designs" of bespoke tailor Ozwald Boateng and installation artist Yinka Shonibare (chapter 5), and urban planning and redevelopment in the city of Bristol (chapter 6), concluding with a discussion of commission artworks by Graham Mortimer Evelyn and Hew Locke. The writers and artists assembled here bring us back to the postcolonial through a new materialist historiography of slavery and the slave trade, a creative engagement with the past essential to understanding the intricate national and transnational circuits that comprise present-day Britain. In their public history work, these artists constellate historical fragments and traces, bodies and communities, affects and sensations, in order to get at the structure(s) of feeling circulating within and passing through the intimate public sphere. In the works I discuss, I show how the archive is reactivated and opened out in order to form alliances, build communities, and negotiate the structural violence and oppression that attends the present. In critical solidarity with this renewed public history, the book reads black British public culture work *as* a postcolonial historiographic intervention into the discourses of transnational belonging and global migration today.

If the black British writers, artists, and performers identified above constitute my archive, cultural theory in its broadest sense is my repertoire. I have always felt more at home ranging across critical landscapes and disciplinary borders than inhabiting them. Materialist critique and textual deconstruction, historicism and political philosophy, performance studies and discourse analysis, queer theory and feminist intervention—each of these methods of analysis makes its way into my own modes of critical promiscuity. Emphasizing the tensions and contradictions implicit in these theoretical frames often seems to me more productive than trying to resolve them, or simply picking sides. But throughout the book, I maintain scrutiny on two broad areas to which they contribute: postcolonial historiography and transnational cultural studies as it arrives through black British cultural critique.[21] I maintain that postcolonial theory continues to offer the most productive optic on globalization and the transnational. By insisting on the ongoing relevance of both postcolonial theory and its underlying poststructuralist critical methodologies, I argue that the contemporary critical and creative approaches to history, historicizing, and historiography at the center of my analysis are reflexively engaged in "doing" and "undoing" the institutionally recognized practices of world-making. On the one hand, the works I discuss are operating within the strictures of institutional public knowledge-work. On the other hand, these historiographic creative practices provide a means for "imagining" the postcolonial for those who often lack access to the institutions and technologies (say, new digital media) of dominant world-making, and aid in establishing the relationship between the local and the global. These works bring out of the archive a coherent, but contingent, nontotalizing, materialist history for new local, national, and transnational public cultures. Here the "post" of postcolonial should be understood as a prefix that underscores rather than effaces the violent colonial histories subtending the present globality. By engaging with approaches held in distinction—the creative and the critical—I offer a uniquely textured account of the ways that formal history and the experience of collective historical memory can collapse into *in*distinction when translated into public narratives, performances, and exhibitions.

What is at stake, many will ask, in reanimating a past that has surely long been buried? In opening old historical wounds? For those who keep up with contemporary British literature, or have attended plays or visited museums or galleries represented by British, especially black British, playwrights and artists, in the turn to the past, and specifically to narrating the history of the slave trade, of slavery in the colonies, or colonial exploitation in South and East Asia, Africa, and the Caribbean, the stakes have been made at times abundantly clear, yet at other times troublingly difficult to comprehend. In many ways this has become my central research question: What is at stake in the turn to history and historical narration in contemporary black British cultural production? And what distinct narrative forms have emerged that give account of this history while also troubling our own modes of historical consciousness? I believe that the stakes are high indeed, not only for literary or cultural analysis but for social history, cultural politics, and public policy today. By engaging critically and creatively with colonial historiography, these artists are not simply opening the history books but are entering into, drawing out of, and performing from quite specific institutional archives, many located in London, Liverpool, and Bristol—cities most associated with the Atlantic system—as well as the more localized archives of daily public and private life. If one of the many acts of violence the archive perpetuates is the idea that history is both obscure and relevant to only a handful of the elite—or best left undisturbed, buried deep in the vaults of the national unconscious—the work of public history shows us that the past is right here before us, a part of us just as much as we are a part of it, indeed that we are agents of it. If the archive houses, such performances of public history unhouse, materializing the past in and as the present, and making the past relevant for—and indispensable to—public discussion and debate.

Paradoxically, the history of black Britain tends to be either well rehearsed or relatively unknown. Before the 1980s, the development of Britain as a multiracial, multiethnic, multicultural nation was generally thought about as a story of global migrations following in the wake of World War II, specifically the postwar exodus from the restless colonies to the imperial metropole, with the *Empire Windrush* serving as its most salient and recognizable emblem. As is well documented, migrations to Britain from its former colonies accelerated rapidly between the 1940s and the 1960s, particularly from South Asia and the Caribbean; what emerged in these decades was a black Britain whose minority status and shared experiences of racial oppression did much to forge a sense of common politics, and in many cases community, despite enormous differences in colonial and postcolonial histories and cultural expressions. Subsequently, the very notion of what it meant to be "British" (or "English") was repeatedly contested and reformulated in the era of decolonization, only to be contested again in the age of globalization.[22] Since the 1970s, however, the history of black Britain has been recast in two longer and broader periodizing frameworks: on the one hand, the emergence of Western colonial modernity and the rise of finance capital founded on a global slave economy; on the other, the premodern "birth" of the British nation itself, stretching back to the arrival of the Roman army in the first century BCE and continuing through the development of seafaring and early modern global trade. For example, while Peter Fryer's influential *Staying Power* focuses on Britain since the sixteenth century, it opens with the Roman invasion in the first century BCE and the earliest historical documentation of African and Asian populations living there.[23] In these long-durational accounts the British Isles become a site of an ongoing and unbroken history of global migrations, and Britain is reimagined as always already "black." Most historians now recognize this longer history of black residence in Britain, and many have acknowledged Britain as ever multicultural, but, like Fryer, they insist on the particular exigencies of modernity in the making and unmaking of the imperial nation. Yet black migration in the postwar years continues to frame the way contemporary Britain is popularly imagined, with an emphasis on the shifting dynamics of belonging and cultural identity in an era of perceived national decline.[24] In order to consider these two trajectories of historicization—what we might call the "long history" of black Britain as a consequence of capitalist modernity and the "late history" of black Britain as an outcome of various postwar settlements—I have focused on the conditions of necessity and possibility for dislocation and migration at population scale. Inasmuch as soldiering on the colonial battlefield and laboring in postwar metropole become critical exigencies for black migration to Britain at the end of the eighteenth century and again after the middle of the twentieth, it is clear once again why thinking about the contemporary biopolitics of migration returns us to the forms of human bio-cargo that made the Atlantic system possible.

My periodizing claim, however, is that a younger generation of black writers and artists, working since the late 1980s and early '90s to the present, have turned increasingly away from the story of postwar migrations, the immigrant experience in Britain and the politics of belonging and Englishness exemplified by the Windrush generation of writers and artists, producing works that instead place these narratives of migration within a long historical context, that *historicize* postcolonial migrations within the long colonial past. They do so predominantly through public and performative creative practices and expressive forms that engage the public in a conversation about the legacy of colonialism—slavery in particular—in the contemporary postcolonial and postimperial world. The shift in cultural dominant I am describing is perhaps most clearly illustrated in the long historical and wide geopolitical reorientations that distinguish Paul Gilroy's *The Black Atlantic* (1993) from his earlier book *"There Ain't No Black in the Union Jack"* (1987), both of which were and remain remarkably influential inside and outside academic circles.[25] In many ways *The Black Atlantic* can be seen as having helped consolidate and constellate the transhistorical and transnational turns sustained in creative works addressing the postcolonial present of black presence in the post-Thatcherite era. I want to suggest, however, that *The Black Atlantic* itself represents the structure of feeling already gaining articulation in new work appearing under the banner of *Sankofa*. Another way of figuring this decade of critical and cultural transition might be to situate it between the establishment of the small, independent black arts film and video collective Sankofa in 1983 and the global release of the Burkinabé filmmaker Haile Gerima's feature *Sankofa* in 1993 (the same year as *The Black Atlantic*) with financial backing from the UK, the United States, and Germany, as well as Ghana and Burkina Faso.[26]

My periodization of postcolonial Britain thus differs from earlier scholars in that I am describing a creative turn that marks a discontinuity with the thematic concerns of the Black Arts Movement and a rejection of the idea of a black Renaissance particular to the 1980s.[27] While the artists associated with the Black Arts Movement in the UK (which is itself often seen as a belated manifestation of the movement of the same name dating from the 1960s) offered a trenchant critique voice of Thatcherism, it remained tied to the politics of the 1970s as a time of spreading discontent among white working-class Britons that facilitated Thatcher's rather sudden appearance and rapid rise within the ranks of the moribund Conservative Party. The eruption of wide-scale protests, scenes of volatile unrest, and full-throated (if not long-lasting) insurrections in urban neighborhoods across the country—St. Pauls in 1980; Brixton, Chapeltown, Handsworth, and Toxteth in 1981; Brixton, Handsworth, and Toxteth again in 1985, along with Broadwater Farm and Peckham—brought the politics of multiculturalism, which had unified *black* as a social signifier across more subtle racial and ethnic divisions, largely to a close. To be sure, many black writers, artists, and performers responded to the riots of the early to mid-1980s with powerful, largely gallery-based works; but for others the riots—and subsequent dissolution of black British as an inclusive social and political signifier—were exigent to the expression of a new sensibility powered by the quite visible manifestation of historical continuity as violent repetition, the feeling of going through it all over again, of experiencing the past in the present through social forms and state policies that appeared new but represented retrenchment.

Reconsidering the periodization of contemporary black Britain along the lines outlined above will help in understanding the transhistorical and transnational foundations of the current moment in global neoliberalism, which, I am suggesting, is most productively accessed at the critical intersection of black British cultural studies, the development of the postcolonial as a framework for thinking about the British nation, and the study of transnational circuits and global exchanges over the last several centuries of African Atlantic history. Indeed, Margaret Thatcher often operates as a figure of rupture, inaugurating a new era of British hegemony, albeit one with a significantly truncated global reach. The election of Thatcher in May 1979 appears to be both an aggravated symptom and an exacerbating cause of those perilous years of economic transformation and social destruction felt most potently by those pulled into a new, seemingly permanent vortex of material deprivation and by those already emplaced in a structure of racialized social exclusion. Despite her best efforts, Thatcher also figures as an emblem of long historical continuity in a moment of economic and political transition. Creative works engaged in the project of critical, postcolonial historiography began to circulate toward the end of the 1980s, gaining considerable traction by the mid-1990s. The generation of black British writers who gained prominence in the years following Margaret Thatcher's rise to power have been singularly concerned with the long history of European colonialism that shaped—and continues to shape—the present. As a generation, these writers are especially adept at drawing our attention to the emergence of new strategies and technologies of life and death we now identify as biopolitical.

While a number of more recent scholars have offered important surveys of the postwar black British literary scene, only a handful have brought together a study of black public cultures across literary, visual, and performance media.[28] *Living Cargo* distinguishes itself in three key ways: (1) by offering a focused metacritical assessment of the problems of public history and social justice that scholars and artists have wrestled with over the last two decades; (2) by thinking across time and place, situating its archive of contemporary public history work in conversation with the records, documents, and artifacts housed, if not buried, in the historical archives of the eighteenth and nineteenth centuries on which the former draw and with which they engage; and (3) by bringing together a set of literary, visual, performance, and popular texts across both national and transnational spaces and public cultures.[29] The writers and artists I address all broach the exigencies of postcolonial migrations from Britain's former colonies by placing them within the context of the long-durational history of dislocation. The history of displacement they trace follows from the advance of mercantile and industrial capitalism—and subsequently colonialism and imperialism—to the formation of diasporic, transnational publics that emerge within the regimes of neo-imperialism and globalization.

More significantly, *Living Cargo* breaks new ground by offering a materialist historiography of the contemporary routed through the public history work performed *by* and *in* contemporary black Britain. *Living Cargo* surveys the cultural landscape of "postimperial" Britain in order to understand the politics and practices of new migrant, transnational publics in the rapidly changing postcolonial metropolis. I explore postcolonial migrations to Britain after the independence movements of the 1940s, '50s, and '60s, the social practices (and attending cultural and textual performances, exhibitions, and rituals) that emplace the migrant subject, and the consolidation of the new social imaginaries through which both national and transnational subjects come to understand their own belonging to specific (migrant, national, communal, or cosmopolitan) public cultures. I also analyze the forms of cultural expression that foreground the need for justice through an appeal to a public, that is, an appeal made in public and that, in turn, also consolidates various publics. Throughout the book, I consider sites often outside the spaces one usually associates with the public sphere, and locations often obscured from the public sphere, for instance from within the home itself, as well as from positions of homelessness or geopolitical displacement.[30]

By rethinking the "periodization of the present" in relation to—but also beyond—Thatcherism as a national watchword for global neoliberalism, I am able to reconceptualize the historical trajectory and geopolitical pathways of black British literary studies and cultural theory as they travel into the future. I argue that this turn to history follows from the aftermath of the collapse of "black British" as a singular, albeit self-consciously and reflexively strategic, political identity in the 1980s. I demonstrate how this historiographic turn found exigency in the shock-driven marketization of state industry and social services in the Thatcherite '80s, and developed alongside the accelerated financialization of everyday life under New Labour. I contend that a significant number of contemporary black writers, artists, and performers have responded to the social transformations of the 1980s and '90s by demanding a more careful historicization of the present by engaging with the past through quite specific *archival* practices and interventions, often working with, upon, and through materials located in repositories across the UK. Further, the book teases out what Ann Cvetkovich calls an "archive of feelings"—less concrete, perhaps, but no less material—that indexes collective, transhistorical *affect* within contemporary public cultures and social bodies.

Prospects for a Critical Redressive Historiography

What I am describing, then, is an important creative, historiographic turn in black British cultural production and an intervention into the conversation about the future of colonial redress. I name this mode of public history work a *critical redressive historiography,* a reflexive performative stylization of the past that imagines the possibility of historical justice in the face of its undeniable belatedness and insufficiency.[31] The concomitant development of modern law and modern commerce ground these problems of historical redress in quite material ways. Although typically conceptualized at the intersection of law and economy, and associated with those remedies made available through the application of the law, often in its most reductive form as economic calculation and monetary restitution, *redress* has historically functioned elsewhere—ethically, spiritually, even medically—as paradigm and practice of active intervention directed as a future "to come," in Derrida's well-known formulation.[32] Reclaiming redress from the juridical imaginary—from the framework of law and economy—is part of the critical historiographic project I am describing. It is also a project with which I am in solidarity. I add the expression *redressive,* then, as a modifier for the critical public history work characteristic of this moment in black diasporic creative expression, both transnationally and in the British context specifically. Interrogating the law as a biopolitical apparatus articulated in careful coordination with economy—neither reducible to the other—through a wide range of state, civil, and private practices of governmentality, is a crucial first step in understanding the ways in which calculation is instrumentalized to capture and secure value in the long history of modern human bio-cargo. Looking at the juridical imaginary as a broader framework for accepting the norms of economic and legal calculation as a framework of everyday sociality, however, helps us identify and understand the more complex and paradoxical forms of worlding through which the biopolitics of colonial slavery is extrapolated into an expansive arena of sovereign command and normative order operating at "home" and in the colonies. The creative works I discuss throughout *Living Cargo* foreground the biopolitical—a descriptive term not necessarily shared in their formal vocabulary—as a site for redressive action, and eschew the overly abstract (if not platitudinous) forms that debates about the unpalatable history of slave-trading and slave-holding too often take. Rather, they home in on the governing homologies between particularized and localized acts of violence and their historical, institutional, and structural corollaries, expanding the ways in which we might think about redress as a collective well beyond the parameters of legal accountability as economic calculability.

In the contemporary black British cultural field, fictional narratives, visual installations, and performance interventions *stage* these historical remnants, hold together these scattered archival remains, and thus obtain a powerful intermedial role in the production of a vibrant materialist public history. Many of the contemporary writers, artists, and performers I consider create for an increasing global and fluid media market, producing the commodities that feed the "market in postcolonial objects."[33] Others, however, lack the kind of cachet needed to gain entry into global circulation and therefore remain in relatively minor positions in relation to the market. These artists combine their concern for the present with a careful historicization of the colonial past by drawing upon quite specific materials from a wide range of institutional and cultural archives. While these works unhouse the history of displacement and exploitation that so powerfully shapes Britain as a postcolonial nation, they also leverage the publicness of their performances for collective empowerment and community enfranchisement. Indeed, these creative responses to the past dislodge violent colonial and postcolonial histories from their particular sites of encounter and archivization and bring them into mobile national and transnational public imaginaries. *Living Cargo* interrogates the politics of these new transnational public cultures in transit across global terrain, and demonstrates how embodied experiences of publicness—through the performance, exhibition, and circulation of literary, visual, and performance texts—assemble provisional and improvisational platforms upon which problems of history and social justice converge. Although theoretically engaged, the book remains attentive to the ways in which the exhibition and circulation of visual, literary, and performative texts brings history into public, disrupts and reformulates both contemporary British and transnational social imaginaries, and opens up new spaces for the critique of violence and the appeal for justice crucial to the work of public history. Such performances of the past enact the *un*housing of this introduction's title, an unhousing that endeavors to restore history and historicity to public culture.

The book focuses on the particular way in which the history of slavery and the slave trade enters into both the British and the transnational public imaginaries through works that bring the history of slavery and its trade into public view. That said, I do not want to confine these texts to the generic category of the neo-slave narrative, which remains a problematic designation more generally, but I am also thinking about the kind of public history work such texts perform (or help perform) and the current social, political, and economic exigencies that drive the turn to history in contemporary black British culture work. While my analysis underscores the critical and theoretical problems surrounding the production and reproduction of violence within colonial, postcolonial, and neocolonial regimes, it also theorizes the persistence of a reparative ethos of responsibility at the heart of postcolonial creative and critical practices. At the same time, I interrogate the investment of various neoliberal social institutions in their own efforts to remember and commemorate the history of slavery.[34] Such corporate, state, and civic organizations attempt to co-opt public history through commemorative events that serve as opportunities to consolidate a very marketable set of historical tropes in order to establish their own lucrative multicultural street credibility. By investigating the ways in which contemporary black British narrative performances of migration and displacement dislodge these violent colonial and postcolonial histories from their particular sites of encounter and archivization, I offer a nuanced account of the politics of new transnational public cultures in transit across the global terrain.

Modern Human Bio-Cargo

My approach to thinking about the prospects of a critical redressing historiography begins by establishing and interrogating the points of conjunction and departure between black British cultural studies, postcolonial historiography, and theoretical debates over the politics of "life itself" as a matter of modern biopolitics.[35] Building upon the reassessment of biopolitics as a critical framework, *Living Cargo* develops the notion of "modern human bio-cargo" as an unsettling concept-metaphor apposite for characterizing the arrogation of particular human lives into global commodity circulation that marks the rupture of both the West and the non-West into colonial modernity. I use the term *bio-cargo* rather than the expression *human cargo,* common in the eighteenth and nineteenth centuries, in order to ground human enslavement and trafficking to the development of colonial biopolitics and to situate the slave system within the story of capitalism not simply as a matter of economics but as a fundamental element of modern political economy (see Figure 1). At the same time, the expression is intended to underscore the ease with which the tropes of economic trade and financialized exchange are deployed in the language of social life—and social death—under capitalist modernity, and to remember the terms inherited from the past that link the designation of "black cargo" in the eighteenth century to forms of "human trafficking" today.[36] As might be imagined, doing so entails drawing together a set of theoretical positions (and personalities) held in perpetual tension with one another—less a coordinated intersection than an agonistic cul-de-sac, around which reside, say, Jacques Derrida and Michel Foucault, Edward Said and Gayatri Spivak, Stuart Hall and Paul Gilroy. Here I want to focus attention on the line of my argument that extends from Foucault and his posthumous interlocutors, Giorgio Agamben and Achille Mbembe. Although his work remains intellectually contentious, Foucault consistently tried to imagine ways of conceptualizing European history from within its own political discourse but without simply accepting or perpetuating the conceptual framework and critical vocabulary that grew out of and carefully shaped how Europe came into existence as a discursive order. How is it that a society comes to regard a life as human? And why? What are the consequences for having done so, for both those forms of life brought within this conceptual enclosure and those forms of life relegated to some conceptual outside, however variously construed? It should go without saying that these are important questions to ask, and that any response will be distinctly historically determined. The works my book addresses draw together both the abstract, even metaphysical, question and its most concrete, grossly material, historical responses that circulated alongside the bodies of the enslaved from at least the later half of the eighteenth century. They do so, I want to suggest, as a way of insisting on the continued persistence of the problem of designating life as human and staking a claim on the imperative to reconsider both particular ways of responding and the terms of distinction themselves.

Bio-cargo describes a disposition toward life itself that is always already a disposition toward disposability and death, which is then played out in

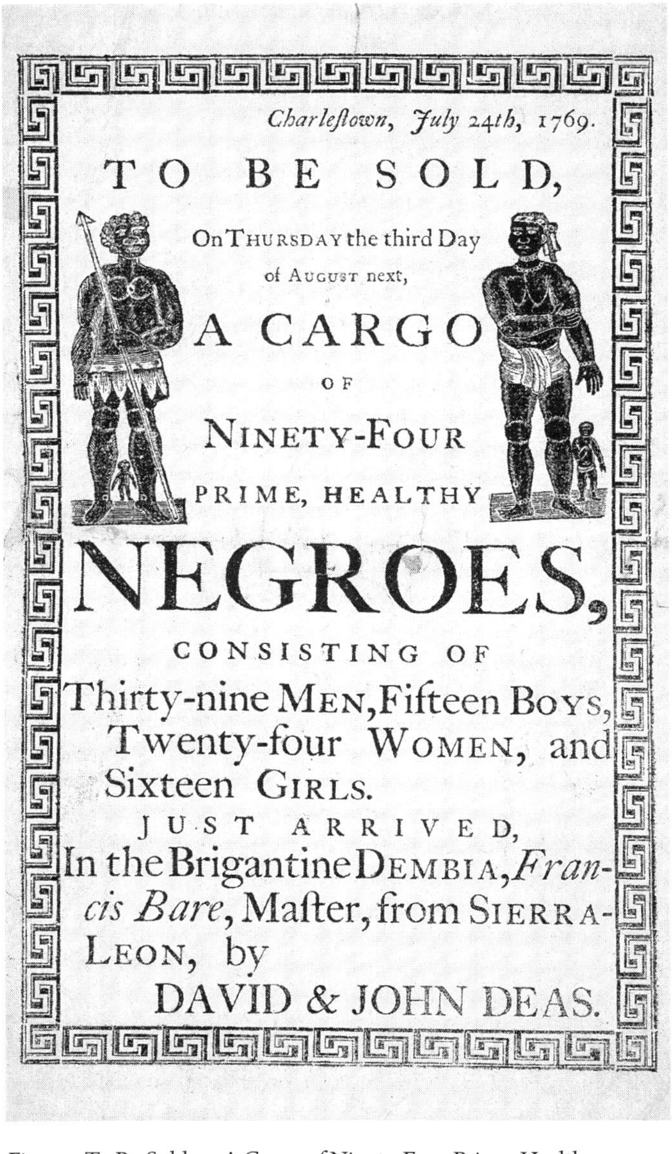

Figure 1. To Be Sold . . . A Cargo of Ninety-Four Prime, Healthy Negroes. *Advertising broadside, Charleston, South Carolina, 1769. Courtesy of the American Antiquarian Society, Worcester, Massachusetts, USA/Bridgeman Images.*

the technologies of capitalist production and accumulation. One is made bio-cargo when one's life is placed at the absolute disposal of the market, when the market decides who must live and who can die, and toward what ends. Or, as in the case of slavery, who must live as movable property, when that life will be allowed to die as fully exhaustible labor-power, and when that life must be killed to secure bio-cargo itself as an instrumental disposition. The former often happens out of sight if not entirely out of view; the latter spectacularly, within public view even when that public is limited to other items of bio-cargo, if bare life can be said to form a public at all. Through the cooperating systems of bio-cargo and the juridical imaginary, we discern a unique, modern form for constituting the human, for determining their disposability, for rending the sociality and ecology of other life-worlds, and for governing on both the micro- and macroscale. In fact, the denial of legal personhood or moral humanness served as one of the necessary conditions for turning people and populations into fungible commodities. In this sense my insistence of the "human" within the expression is strategic, designating the haunting humanness that will always live on.[37]

But bio-cargo is also a condition from which life takes flight, a point crucial to understanding the historiographic turn in contemporary black British creative historiography. By grounding the continuing significance of human bio-cargo as a critical concept, I offer two brief examples that come readily to mind. The first comes from the American artist Hank Willis Thomas, whose *Absolute Power* (2003) was included in the artist's multimedia and photography series *Branded* that opened in New York at the Jack Shainman Gallery in 2006 (see Figure 2). Here Thomas marries two iconic images. The first, more explicitly identifiable for contemporary audiences in both the United States and globally, is the distinctively abstract shape—a description no less appropriate for hazarding a contradiction—of the Absolut Vodka bottle, a design leveraged in the company's decades-long and spectacularly successful advertising campaign, which began in the early 1980s and continues through today, making it perhaps the longest-running trademarked advertising campaign in commercial history. The second is an almost equally, if more implicitly, recognizable historical citation of the infamous series of diagrams of the slave ship *Brookes,* a powerful graphic illustration of the violently abstracting logic of economic calculation, which were reproduced ubiquitously in campaigns to abolish the Atlantic slave trade of the late eighteenth and nineteenth centuries. The

Brookes drawings, however, have achieved a popular revival in artworks and illustrations over the last two decades, as activists and artists return to the iconic shapes of the slave ship and its human cargo—housed on the suffocating decks below—as an accessible emblem of modern human bio-cargo that continues on in different forms today.[38] Thomas emphasizes the durability of cargo as a way of thinking historically about the housing and transport of black bodies and the ongoing arrogation of black cultural life into global commercial networks as objects of consumption and disposability.[39]

My second example comes from the Palestinian artist Mona Hatoum, who entered London in 1975 from Beirut, where her family had been exiled

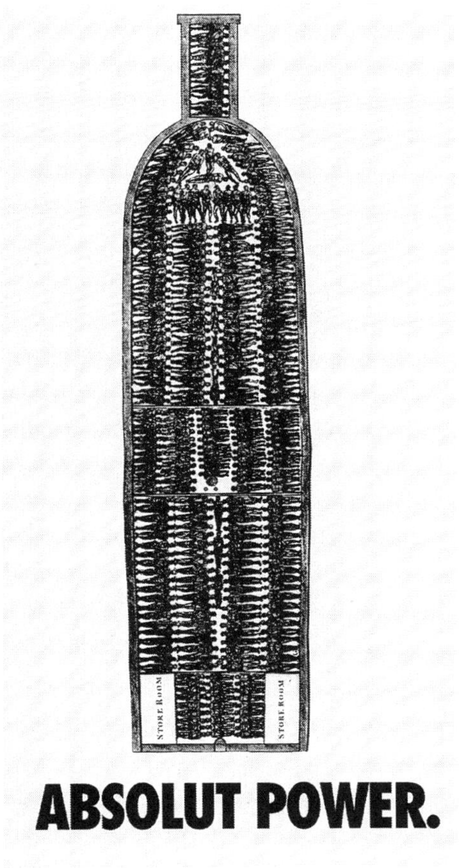

Figure 2. Hank Willis Thomas, Absolute Power, *2003. Inkjet print on canvas. Dimensions variable. Courtesy of the artist and Jack Shainman Gallery, New York.*

after 1948, arriving shortly before the outbreak of the long civil war in Lebanon. Hatoum's large-scale installation *Light Sentence* (1992) synthesizes and thematizes the relationship between form and content in the housing and transport of the dispossessed and the displaced, emphasizing institutional sites of biopolitical disposition and human lives rendered disposable as objects of what I am calling human bio-cargo.[40] Like many contemporary artists working in multimedia installation, Hatoum exposes the institutions of art themselves as sites likewise predisposed to modern biopolitics. Although much of Hatoum's work indexes colonial and postcolonial biopolitics in far more abstract ways than the examples cited above, they are nevertheless equally visceral. *Light Sentence* is comprised of dozens of one-by-one-foot wire storage lockers stacked six high in two long parallel rows (see Figure 3). A single, 100-watt household light bulb positioned in the middle of the structure travels slowly up and down, casting shadows along the gallery walls that remain in constant, unsettling motion.[41] While the lockers resemble stacks of small cages, the architectural form of the installation as a whole is reminiscent of the brutalist aesthetic of the fortress-like tower blocks of social housing that arose in the postwar years. According to Hatoum, "the whole environment [of the gallery space] begins to look like an architectural model of a city lined with the kind of boring, uniform, functional and box-like architecture designed to provide cheap housing for people on low income."[42] At the same time, the light passing through the wire mesh casts moving shadows along the gallery wall, increasing the scale of enclosure from a small box for personal storage to a large cell for human stowage. In a conversation with Janine Antoni, Hatoum describes the uncanny experience the installation evokes, saying, "When you enter the space, you have the impression that the whole room is swaying and you have the disturbing feeling that the ground is shifting under your feet. This is an environment in constant flux—no single point of view, no solid frame of reference. There is a sense of instability and restlessness in the work."[43] In a powerful orchestration of her signature minimalist aesthetic and the selection of austere materials—the hard sensation of steel tempered by the flimsy sensuousness of wire, the glare of the light that dissipates into two dull paths even as it casts dark, imposing staves across the walls—Hatoum ensnares the spectator's own shadow, their own spectral other, in the abstracting logic of the carceral. "When I speak of works like *Light Sentence* . . . as making a reference to some kind of institutional violence," she tells Antoni, "I am speaking of encountering architectural and institutional structures in Western urban environments that are about the regimentation of individuals, fixing them in space and putting them under surveillance." Hatoum's installation formally indexes institutional forms of mass housing of populations deemed materially disposable: prisoners, refugees, the homeless, the socially excluded and economically deprived. At the same time, the installation stages the experience of being housed—as alienated embodiment and uncanny sensation; as a feeling of displacement and dispossession; as an act of capture and entrapment—that defines the life of human bio-cargo.

Any historiography of the biopolitical must begin by looking back at the transatlantic slave trade and plantation slavery as a unique historical site for gaining purchase on the present, and the literary and artistic works addressed in the chapters that follow, like those presented above, here bring us back to the colonial order—and closer to an awareness of the current moment of global neocolonialism—by marshaling materials drawn from

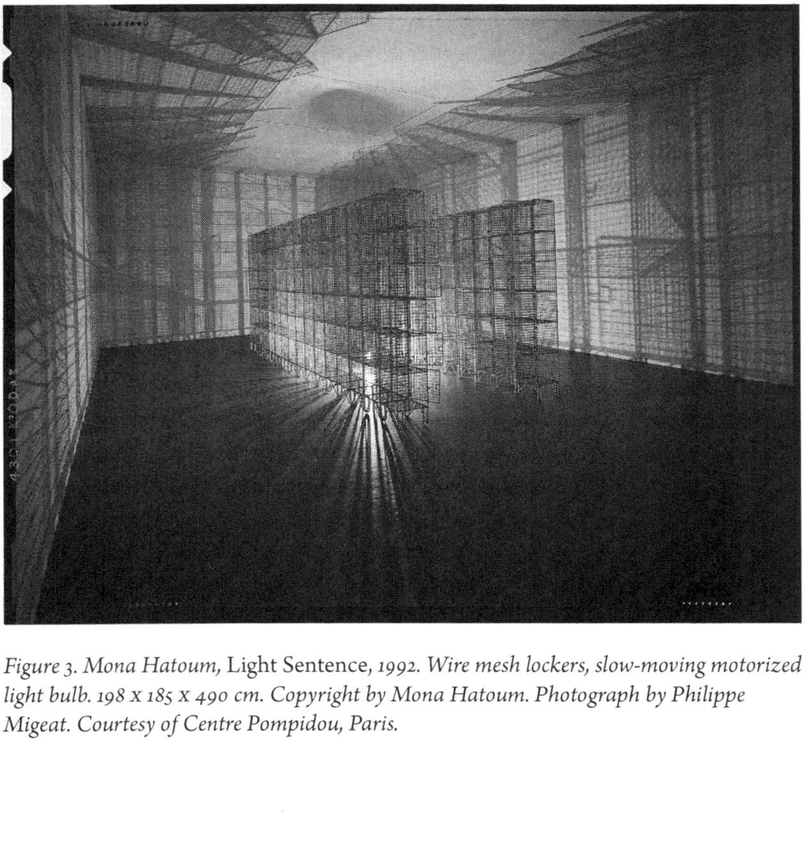

Figure 3. Mona Hatoum, Light Sentence, *1992. Wire mesh lockers, slow-moving motorized light bulb. 198 x 185 x 490 cm. Copyright by Mona Hatoum. Photograph by Philippe Migeat. Courtesy of Centre Pompidou, Paris.*

the archive, and by leveraging the materiality of the archive to produce a "bio-historiography" of human cargo. In these creative renditions, the past—the new bio-cargo, made of African life—points toward a broader, structural biojuridical imaginary governing travel, migration, and population displacement today. As with the politics of the archive, biopolitics operates through the mutually attending forces of dispersion and consolidation. The powerful structural metaphor we inherit from Giorgio Agamben, *the camp*, is inadequate to describe the unremittingly violent mobilizations of bio-cargo whose lineage links the entrenched contingencies of mobility and immobility of the postcolonial migrant back to the slave ship and the plantation system. Paradoxically, if the camp designates the place of absolute stasis—where entire populations of *homines sacri* are cast aside as residual, redundant, and disposable—in their absolute disposability the postcolonial migrant is imagined to be functionally portable and substantively rootless. The history of the slave trade marks the moment when the enslaved, as human bio-cargo, is established as a quite mobile "thing" *in law.* The institutions of law begin to operate *within* this normalizing regime as one apparatus among others deployed for the purpose of social regulation and the instrumentalization of human life.[44] Maintaining an itinerant human cargo whose contingent labor could be redeployed on command became increasingly necessary to the economic and social order of the colonial plantation, the Atlantic system, and ultimately the global order itself. At the same time, as a dispersed bio-cargo, African populations seized into slavery were able to activate new forms of community and belonging, a new social life that ran counter to the imposition of social death. I maintain that the logic of bio-cargo is encoded in the history of postcolonial migrations and that the migrant and migrant communities are treated as the new bio-cargo lodged in the system of what Foucault called the "carceral archipelago."[45]

The juridical imaginary has served as perhaps the principle discursive framework for actuating biopolitical modernity, and it extends well beyond the formal structures of the law itself. Because of the particular kinds of archives available for postcolonial appropriation, current black public history works almost invariably address the vicissitudes of the law when confronted with the systematic appropriation of human life into economic exchange. We see this most strikingly in the "legal fictions" through which governmentality draws the very biological fact of life itself into the fundamental principles and governing logic of globalizing capital. History must account for the function of the juridical imaginary in the material and conceptual liquidation of African lives as they enter the system of transatlantic trade as just so many items of modern human bio-cargo. Further, because the framework of the juridical imaginary is rooted in and routed through biopolitical modernity, I suggest that eighteenth- and early nineteenth-century practices of—and discourses on—slavery in general, and on the slave's body in particular, shape modern ways of worlding still at work today.

Through these two interventions I am able to argue that the unhousing performed by black British culture-work and public history today functions simultaneously as dispersion and reactivation. As the chapters unfold, the concept-metaphors of housing and unhousing gain valence. As tropes, they frame discussions of a variety of contemporary social concerns: migration and displacement; homelessness and exile; detention and incarceration; habitation and occupation; the private home and housing estate; the house museum and gallery space; the fashion runway and the performance stage; the shopping center and the tourist trap. Throughout, the slave ship and the plantation name two competing but often conflated biopolitical logics crucial to understanding the prehistory of contemporary global migrations—one a logic of the traffic and transport of human cargo, the other a logic of the internment and instrumentalization of human bodies. But the slave ship is as much a site of absolute immobilization as the plantation is a location of ceaseless human traffic. Reflecting on the biopolitics of housing and unhousing draws the project into unexpected critical terrain: the economy of signs that subtends the modern ethical, theological, and juridical frameworks of biological life and commodity form; the birth of modern bio-cargo from within the Atlantic cycle of accumulation; the perennial sociopolitical problem of human recognition; the transmission of history as genealogy in its most fundamental biological sense; the erotopolitics of subjection and submission; urban regeneration schemes and the new forms of bio-cargo they produce. Modern biopolitical governmentality was initiated in the colonies, "carried out," according to Betty Joseph, "through a practice of archiving, a systematic circulation, preservation, and recall of written texts that allowed the rule by remote control from London."[46] The colonial archive, Joseph concludes, was never intended as a "repository" for the evidence of colonial rule available for "public scrutiny" but "an instrument of governance" (6). In the chapters that follow, I demonstrate what happens—and what becomes possible—when the colonial archive goes public.

I

History and Human Cargo

· CHAPTER 1 ·

Beautiful Remnants, Brutal Remains

Dwelling on the Melancholy Archive

A Perfect Affliction

The colonial archive in general, and the archive of slavery in particular, is an exceptionally melancholy place to dwell. There one confronts—repeatedly, ceaselessly—a legacy of violence, atrocity, and loss impossible to apprehend but equally impossible to escape. To dwell in the colonial archive feels like mourning, and like the work of mourning it is utterly exhausting. Yet the archive proves inexhaustible. There is no end to the archive of colonial violence. A similar paradox is lived outside the institutional archives of state and civil society: an inexhaustible sense of collective exhaustion—material, political, intellectual, affective—experienced by those who live on in the wake of colonial history.[1] For is it not the case that the endless need to reclaim one's history—to recover the voices of the past or to *be* the voice of collective memory; to represent those who survived and those who could not; to return over and over again to the archive in search of redress or redemption; to endlessly repeat the "work" of mourning—is it not the case that all of *this* should inevitably lead to an inexhaustible sense of exhaustion? Such endless repetition, however, suggests something other than personal mourning, something closer to collective melancholia, related to but not reducible to "Afro-pessimism" as an "intellectual disposition."[2] But might we pause in the midst of our melancholy rumination to ponder who, in fact, makes such demands and why? Whose redemption is being sought and by whom? And whose labor makes whose work of mourning possible?

In the opening prologue to David Dabydeen's *A Harlot's Progress* (1998), a novel set during the height of the transatlantic slave trade in the eighteenth century, the reader encounters a protagonist already in a state of utter exhaustion. Over the course of the novel, that protagonist, who is named (by others) first Mungo and later Noah, refuses the demand to provide his cajoling interlocutor—a certain Mr. Pringle, representative from the Committee for the Abolition of Slavery—a single, coherent, and reliable narrative of his own mortifying enslavement and redeeming emancipation. Mungo will not give in to Pringle's relentless entreaties for a pornographic record of the horrors of the slave ship and the brutality of the plantation; neither will he give up the scandalous details from his years of service in an aristocratic London household; nor will he admit to the singular affair with the infamous prostitute whose reputation had once made him famous; and crucially, Mungo simply will not submit to Pringle's expectation of gratitude for the "charity" of his abolitionist benefactors or acknowledge his "redemption" by the abolition committee itself. Dabydeen seems to anticipate a reading audience not unlike the good-hearted members of Pringle's committee, or the legions of armchair abolitionists Pringle hopes will purchase an advance subscription to Mungo's published account, that is, an audience whose moral outrage is easily satisfied by reading an outrageous narrative replete with immoral deeds and wicked desires ascribed to the peculiar institution of slavery. Both novelist and protagonist alike foresee a readership expecting—indeed, searching for—an astonishing "tale of undeserved woe" told by an intrepid but humble survivor. Inasmuch as Pringle hopes that Mungo's tale might bring "great dividends" to the abolition committee, anticipating readers eager for the moral edification that comes with the story of the emancipation of man by man, the prologue might be said to interpellate an audience more attuned to the dynamics of profit and loss through which the slave narrative operates in abolitionist discourse. For whom, by whom, and to whom is the work of mourning profitable? The question redounds across Dabydeen's novel, implicating readers and writers alike in the contemporary market in fictional narratives of colonial atrocity. For the imagined reader, the novel promises empathetic outrage mollified by a feeling of ultimate deliverance; for the imagined author, it promises a steady flow of royalties should the narrative deliver on its affective potential. Readers of contemporary fiction, now interpellated as consumers of spectacle and atrocity, are placed under reflexive scrutiny and compelled to consider the overwhelming sense of collective exhaustion in which they are both participant *and* precipitant.

Mungo is exhausted from the moment the novel commences. "He is exhausted," the narrator later tells us, by the demand to "confess" placed on him by Pringle and his group of English abolitionists. "He is exhausted," the narrator adds, "by [their] need to repent, by the way they peck at themselves out of guilt and will use him to leech that guilt." "He is exhausted," the narrator repeats, and "he wants them to let him go." The line aches in the rawness of its affect and the impossible simplicity of its demand. "He wants them to let him go," but they will not. Rather, "they will ensnare him in their needs." They will "nail him down" with the "nib of [a] pen," and "he will struggle to wriggle free from [the] page." Mungo is both an ideal specimen and a figure of Christ, trapped in a salvific wish at the center of another's worlding; subject of and to writing, Mungo is the object framed and preserved under glass.[3] Why must Mungo, the novel asks implicitly, be burdened to admit to the sins of slavery? Why must *he* bear *their* guilt? After thirty years of nominal freedom, Mungo remains enchained by a way of thinking, with its own melancholy structures of feeling, which continues to seize upon *him* as a sign of *its* loss, whatever that loss may be. I call this way of thinking the juridical imaginary as a system of understanding that frames our most basic social interactions in terms of the law, of innocence and guilt, conviction or exoneration, punishment and compensation. And I want to argue that this juridical imaginary fundamentally underwrites how the West formulates notions of redress, redemption, recovery, and reparation whether played out in narratives of colonial history, statements of formal apology, benign acts of charity, or courtroom dramas of civil litigation.

Mungo's exhaustion resonates in our melancholy present. Indeed, melancholia might be said to have appeared, in the last decade or so, as one of our moment's most persuasive critical modes.[4] Critical melancholia anticipates the failures that await us in the archive. It is, to cite Hortence Spillers on the psychoanalysis of race, "a perfect affliction, if by that we mean an undeniable setup that not only shapes one's view of things but demands an endless response" to them.[5] And here, I think, such an approach parts ways with any radical political potential that might be located from within so-called Afro-pessimism, giving up on utopia, as it appears to do, as it anticipates an "endless response," as it watches the future vanish beyond the horizon of the now. Critical melancholia admits fatigue—if not defeat—in the face of an impossible justice. Such critical fatigue appears particularly acute when scholars enter into entrenched academic debates over the historiography of colonial slavery. It appears dialectically immobilized—if not demobilized—in response to the irreconcilability of the risks and consequences of representing violence and the agonistic politics of historical memory; the communal need for acknowledging loss and the impossibility of naming the dead; the social value of collective mourning and the limits of routinized public commemoration; and crucially, in response to the inadequate possibilities for historical redress and the exacting demands that even the most normative forms of justice make on all of us for the countless individual atrocities, as well as the singular, systemic atrocity: the trade in human lives. In other words, critical melancholia is bound up in the juridical imaginary.

Few academic quarrels are as contentious as those enacted over the ways in which—and the extent to which—history is commodified and consumed today, and over the consequences of engaging the past at the intersection of the public square and the private marketplace. Consider, for example, the elegantly stylized sentiment of Danny Boyle's celebrated opening ceremony at the 2012 London Olympics. That event choreographed the archive in full distention, both shamelessly self-aware of its own nationalist fantasies and overflowing with the comforting signs of an inflated national history utterly emptied of historical consciousness. By spectacularizing the past, Boyle—along with the army of Olympic organizers, London officials, British politicians, and even the queen herself, each encouraging if not demanding such excess—was engaged in nothing less (and little more) than the fascistic aestheticization of politics that Walter Benjamin so famously warned against. Like the melancholy archive, such packaged events house the past and, as I argued in the introduction, a history that remains housed is not truly performed but merely staged. Conversely, a history that is performed—with the sense of improvisation, invention, incompletion, imperfection, and provisionality associated with theories of performativity—cannot be easily packaged. I worry, however, that in surrendering to the law of repetition that governs the melancholy archive, we run the risk of facilitating rather than disabling the ongoing neoliberal, commercial repackaging of the past for easier public consumption, or adding to the persistence of racial or ethnic absolutisms whose recourse to the past assumes the guise of an ugly triumphalism. If the task for public history work is to open up such packages and to scrutinize their contents, we must begin by unpacking the particular forms through which history is repeatedly commodified, and those articulations of the past that the melancholy archive continues to affirm even in its most vociferous acts of disavowal.

And yet the sense of reflexive unease emanating from much African Atlantic scholarship over at least the last two decades, and its portrayal of an equally melancholy public, is often at odds with the vibrant, provocative, and stirring public history work performed in and by black public cultures today, even as scholars themselves remain active participants in black culture work. While they may at times appear fatigued, they have proven over and over again to be confidently indefatigable. The performances of the colonial archive encountered in the literary narratives addressed in this chapter anticipate the more visible public staging of the archive treated in subsequent chapters. Collectively, these narratives open up creative possibilities by drawing on a wide range of aesthetic forms from both the African Atlantic and Euro-Western traditions, and are much more aligned with what Benjamin valorized as fascism's greatest threat: the politicization of the aesthetic.[6] In many ways, *A Harlot's Progress* is a devastating novel to read, but the wreckage that builds up before us page after page, archive after archive, just might—even if only contingently—compel its audience to turn around and seize the future that begins now, rather than watching it too slip away. Which is to suggest that the novel resists the alluring entrapments of both liberal sentiment and nationalist triumphalism. Although *A Harlot's Progress* might perform the paradox of melancholy exhaustion, what Dabydeen's novel is constellating is something significantly different from and counter to the melancholy archive.

If we go to the archive seeking redress, looking for evidence for historical recovery, searching for just the right example, or a set of examples, which we then collect and claim as *our* archive, what we just might find instead is an unguarded exit that takes us to the street where the archive we have just left is already in constellation in public culture. This chapter brings recent critical and literary turns into constellation with the institutional archives with which they are engaged and from which they also draw from the past: a letter written by a long-dead abolitionist; a sampling of transcripts and records from parliaments long ago recessed and courts long since adjourned; a handful of broadsides, pamphlets, and tracts making the case for and against the economic system of plantation slavery and speculative trade in human lives. This admittedly select and dispersed ("unhoused") archive of old documents, recent fiction, and current trends in academic theory help us to understand the kind of public history work being performed both "then" (largely in the late eighteenth and early nineteenth centuries) and "now" (the late twentieth and early twenty-first centuries). As I begin to explore the manner in which contemporary black British public history work intercedes in the colonial archive, I want to attend in particular to the way the archive enters dynamic circulation in public culture. By drawing together and then dispersing the unraveled stories, fragmented narratives, and frayed images housed in and by the colonial archive, these cultural practitioners improvise new aesthetic forms and innovative historiographies that *un*house the past from the archive of colonial violence. I call this practice a *critical redressive historiography*—critical because it refuses to remain locked in a juridical imaginary that casts redress, recovery, and reparation as matters of economy, equivalency, and exchange. We will never find redress in the archive, but to seek it elsewhere we need the archive. We need the archive to go public.

A Public Sorrow

In late 2006, Prime Minister Tony Blair had an opportunity to stage the colonial archive dynamically for both British and transnational publics, and to do so through a performative call for historical justice and social transformation. Instead, he faxed a press release to the offices of the relatively small, black British publication *New Nation,* "condemning Britain's role in the transatlantic slave trade as a 'crime against humanity' and expressing 'deep sorrow' that it ever happened."[7] The outsized letters of the headline emblazoned beneath an equally outsized photograph of the prime minister, donning an expression somewhere between sardonic comment and derisive grin, underscored the smallness of his gesture: "Blair: My Sorrow at the Slave Trade" (see Figure 4). There are few better examples of sanctioned melancholia than the prime minister's perpetual "sorrow," the one affect universally authorized for public sentiment regarding the history of slavery and slave trading. Above the headline and to the right of a large photo of Blair appeared a canned publicity still from the 1977 American Broadcasting Company's (ABC) adaptation of Alex Haley's controversial 1976 historical novel, *Roots: The Saga of an American Family.* The four black men in the still—chained and crated, but also shirtless, their muscled torsos glistening—cast their cargoed gaze upon the sorrowful Blair. The admonition came two hundred years after the abolition of the trade, in anticipation of a year of commemorative events that would follow. "It is hard to believe," the prime minister wrote, "that what would now be a crime against humanity was legal at the time. Personally I believe the bicentenary offers us a chance not just to say how profoundly shameful the slave trade was—how we condemn its existence utterly and praise those who fought for its abolition, but also to express our deep sorrow that it ever

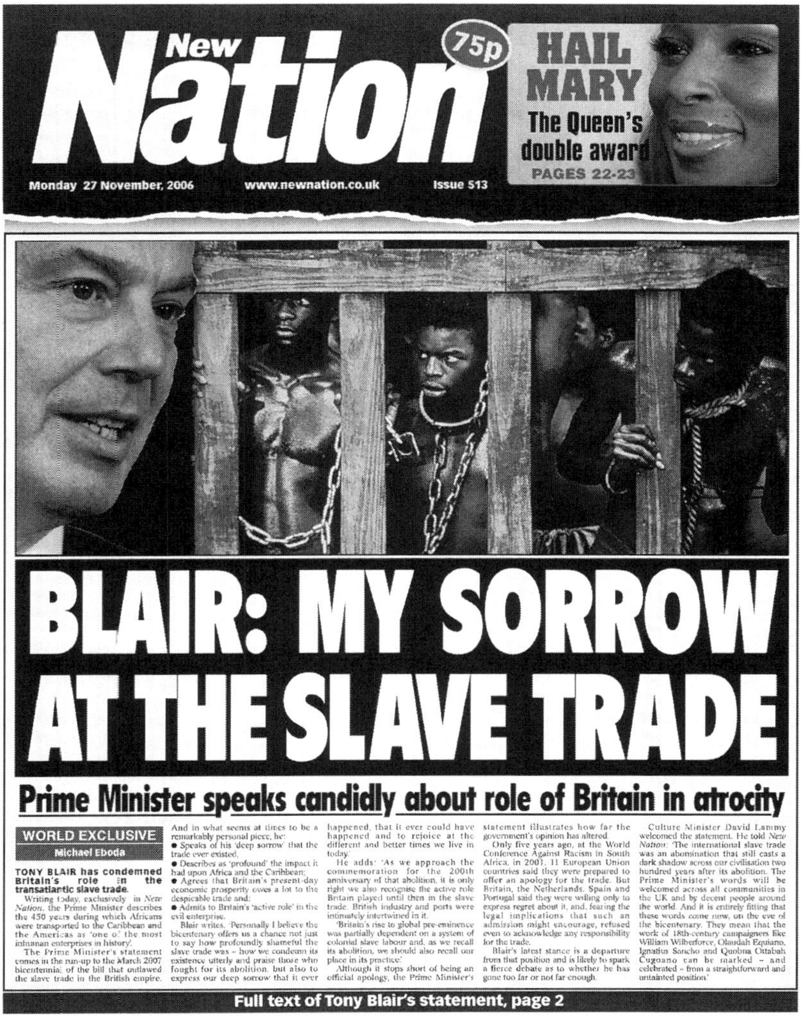

New Nation 75p

HAIL MARY
The Queen's double award
PAGES 22-23

Monday 27 November, 2006 www.newnation.co.uk Issue 513

BLAIR: MY SORROW AT THE SLAVE TRADE

Prime Minister speaks candidly about role of Britain in atrocity

WORLD EXCLUSIVE
Michael Eboda

TONY BLAIR has condemned Britain's role in the transatlantic slave trade.

Writing today, exclusively in *New Nation*, the Prime Minister describes the 450 years during which Africans were transported to the Caribbean and the Americas as 'one of the most inhuman enterprises in history'.

The Prime Minister's statement comes in the run-up to the March 2007 bicentennial of the bill that outlawed the slave trade in the British empire. And in what seems at times to be a remarkably personal piece, he:

- Speaks of his 'deep sorrow' that the trade ever existed,
- Describes as 'profound' the impact it had upon Africa and the Caribbean;
- Agrees that Britain's present-day economic prosperity owes a lot to the despicable trade and;
- Admits to Britain's 'active role' in the evil enterprise.

Blair writes, 'Personally I believe the bicentenary offers us a chance not just to say how profoundly shameful the slave trade was – how we condemn its existence utterly and praise those who fought for its abolition, but also to express our deep sorrow that it ever happened, that it ever could have happened and to rejoice at the different and better times we live in today.'

He adds: 'As we approach the commemoration for the 200th anniversary of that abolition, it is only right we also recognise the active role Britain played until then in the slave trade. British industry and ports were intimately intertwined in it.

'Britain's rise to global pre-eminence was partially dependent on a system of colonial slave labour and, as we recall its abolition, we should also recall our place in its practice.'

Although it stops short of being an official apology, the Prime Minister's statement illustrates how far the government's opinion has altered.

Only five years ago, at the World Conference Against Racism in South Africa, in 2001, 11 European Union countries said they were prepared to offer an apology for the trade. But Britain, the Netherlands, Spain and Portugal said they were willing only to express regret about it, and, fearing the legal implications that such an admission might encourage, refused even to acknowledge any responsibility for the trade.

Blair's latest stance is a departure from that position and is likely to spark a fierce debate as to whether he has gone too far or not far enough.

Culture Minister David Lammy welcomed the statement. He told *New Nation*: 'The international slave trade was an abomination that still casts a dark shadow across our civilisation two hundred years after its abolition. The Prime Minister's words will be welcomed across all communities in the UK and by decent people around the world. And it is entirely fitting that these words come now, on the eve of the bicentenary. They mean that the work of 18th-century campaigners like William Wilberforce, Olaudah Equiano, Ignatius Sancho and Quobna Ottabah Cugoano can be marked – and celebrated – from a straightforward and untainted position.'

Full text of Tony Blair's statement, page 2

Figure 4. Front page of New Nation, *27 November 2006.*

happened, that it *could* have happened and to rejoice at the different and better times we live in today."[8] Shame and sorrow operate here as the two axes of Blair's—and by metonymic extension Britain's—reparative discourse. As has been noted in press accounts, Blair's statement appeared as a concession to black activists in Britain who had been demanding a platform of historical redress that included, but was not limited to, a formal apology acknowledging slavery and the slave trade as crimes against humanity whose legacy of entrenched racism and systematic inequality carries that period of colonial violence into the postcolonial present. Remarkably, Blair offered no such apology, just a hesitant declaration of condemnation, a diffident expression of remorse, a congratulatory tribute to the heroes of abolition, and a self-serving opportunity to "rejoice" in the healing passage of time. In his joyful presentism, Blair *addressed* the legacy of the slave trade without offering a vision of how to *redress* it. It is hardly surprising that many viewed the statement's strategic placement in *New Nation* as an especially cynical maneuver, and the competing images that accompanied it no doubt a mocking editorial decision.

In what was seen by many in the national press as something akin to what Marx described as a kind of repetition-with-a-difference in the unfolding manner of bourgeois events—from tragedy to farce—the following summer the never publicity-shy London Mayor Ken Livingstone declared 23 August a formal day of remembrance, one that coincided with the United Nation's International Day for the Remembrance of the Slave Trade and Its Abolition.[9] From the comfort of his government office, the emotive mayor pointed accusingly toward the steel and glass towers of London's financial district and declared, "You can look across there to see the institutions that still have the benefit of the wealth they created from slavery." Reciting a familiar litany of exemplary punishments and acts of atrocious violence, Livingstone twice paused in order to compose himself from the swell of emotion. Through tears, he apologized "on behalf of London and its institutions" for their role in transatlantic slavery, upon which he was embraced by the American civil rights leader Reverend Jesse Jackson. "It was the racial murder," Livingstone emphasized, "of not just those who were transported but generations of enslaved African men, women and children. To justify this murder and torture black people had to be declared inferior or not human. We live with the consequences today."[10] Livingstone's apology was seen in the press as a performative rebuke of Tony Blair and his government for having refused to offer a similar apology the year before, a move

Livingstone had publicly excoriated as "squalid."[11] While the mayor certainly traded in the familiar rhetorical tropes of liberal apology, he went much further than many might have expected by underscoring the *failure* of the liberal state and its institution, emphasizing instead the role of slave revolt and revolution in ending slavery. It would be easy to dismiss both of these state-sponsored and institutionally authorized statements, and the commemorative projects they bookended, as the cynical instrumentalization of the past by Prime Minister Blair's national government and Mayor Livingston's city-state, in an effort to galvanize their respective images and legacies of liberal inclusiveness and multicultural sensitivity. But I want to go in a slightly different direction by reframing their discourse with that of late eighteenth- and early nineteenth-century abolitionism.

To be sure, both Blair's melancholy sorrow and Livingston's tearful admonition fall within a decidedly liberal tradition of redressive thinking in which justice is tethered equally to the laws of the state (as Blair felt the need to remind his readers, "slavery was legal at the time") and the laws of God (represented by Rev. Jackson's embrace). Now consider the following passage from a letter by the renowned English abolitionist Granville Sharp, which circulated broadly in an antislavery tract printed in 1807, the year of slave-trade abolition. Having achieved the abolition of the trade, Sharp is now urging the abolition of plantation slavery itself, and warning of the exacting punishment of "Divine vengeance" that would descend upon the British "state and nation" for what he described as the "national crime" of slavery. Sharp observes:

> We have had repeated public fasts, of late years, proclaimed for the avowed purpose of a general repentance and acknowledgment of our sins (which must surely include our public, or national, as well as private sins) and yet the illegal toleration of Slavery in our Colonies (a disloyal "respect of persons," which the united authority of King, Lords, and Commons never did, nor ever can, render legal . . .) has never once been mentioned as a national crime.[12]

In no uncertain terms, Sharp brought public attention to the limits and failures of British law, and to a judicial and parliamentary order that sought every possible precedent to sustain the institutions of slavery. "The toleration," he concludes, "of unredressed Slavery (. . . i.e. 'without judgment' . . . by Law) in any court of the King's Dominions is a heinous National crime in all Administration of our limited government."[13] One is tempted, anachronistically, to see both Prime Minister Blair and Mayor Livingstone as precisely the kind of national leaders Sharp charges with insincerity in their contrition. Placed next to Sharp's letter, the evangelical zeal of Blair's comments, and his embrace of the tenets of Christian good works as powerful instruments of a liberal sense of social justice, hardly seem surprising, but the *longue durée* of human progress suddenly appears minute. Indeed, like Tony Blair, Granville Sharp had put enormous faith in the liberal right of redress before the law. As a practitioner of law, Sharp is remembered for the many cases he brought on behalf of those Africans living in England whose legal precarity left them forever under threat of return to bondage. Sharp believed that recourse *to* the law was fundamental to the recognition of human life and that the cases he brought to public attention and legal scrutiny might serve as an arena for a broader collective judgment that would eventually overturn the order of slavery. But the frightening possibility (or inevitability) of divine justice remains the guarantor securing secular law: if redress is not granted in the one (in the here and now), it will redound in the other (in a time to come). That is, the liberal tradition within which Blair and Livingstone participate reaches back to the same speculative political theology that had long ago underwritten abolitionist discourse. Accordingly, redress is warranted by the absolute judgment of an absolutely vengeful divine sovereign. To put it another way, redress operates between the immanent particular as a material social demand and the transcendent universal as an equally material divine intervention.

By the end of the eighteenth century, calls for abolition were ensconced in the theological and juridical language of redress. Yet, in contrasting the *general* search for mercy at the hand of God with the quite *specific* "sin" of slavery in the colonies, Sharp draws our attention—in those two qualifying parentheticals ("our public, or national, *as well as* private sins"; and the "'respect of persons,' which the united authority of King, Lords, and Commons never did, *nor ever can,* render legal") to the discordant interests of personal redemption and collective calculation, whether legal, political, or economic. The tension he identifies between the notion of a "national crime" and the claims of sovereign right is perhaps intensified rather than quelled by the call for public redemption. However, Sharp's willingness to imagine the consequences of collective acts of criminal atrocity (in this case ones designated "national") both brought into relief and attempted to efface the distinction between divine and human justice, between the

Laws of God and the laws of man. Thus, the two social scripts—the shared social text from which Blair and Livingston read (2006–7), and the one Sharp articulated two centuries before (1807)—share a strikingly similar vision. But one cannot feel especially sanguine about the prospects of a politics of recognition and responsibility rooted in the Sharpist–Blairist rhetoric of liberal circumspection and national reckoning for collective actions.

It is widely agreed that in order to redress a past wrong one must begin by publicly acknowledging it. But acknowledgment can easily be construed as an end in itself, as a stopping rather than starting point. When narrative history seals off the archive from the project of social transformation in the present it serves as an alibi that sanctions political quiescence. Conversely, narratives of melancholy exhaustion express symptoms of the archive rather than an intervention into it. Storytelling—as either acknowledgment or apology—is never enough; but neither is the endless enumeration of irreparable loss. As we are so often reminded, recounting past wrongs always runs the risk of reproducing rather than repairing social injury. In order to tell stories about the violence of the past that imagine social justice non-normatively—outside the juridical imaginary—one must be especially attentive to the *shape* those stories take, and the way they resonate in form and content with those stories that came before. In developing a historiography that *repairs* rather than *impairs* one must confront whole series of contingencies and contradictions long recognized at the very core of narrative form and practices of signification. Likewise, one must dislodge redress itself from its location in the juridical imaginary. That is, one must unhouse redress from the archive of law in order to reconstitute it conceptually, theoretically, and strategically as a provisional principle on which a transformative public history work might productively operate.[14]

As a particular kind of restorative gesture, historical redress appears already implicated in the fundamental discursive frameworks of Western liberalism crucial to the enshrinement of individual private property at the center of both criminal and civil law. And since property always retains a fungible value, legal remedy becomes an exercise in calculating monetary payout or monetized payback: a social debt repaid through bodily sacrifice. As a normative expression of justice, then, redress is reduced to the command for dispossession through economic forfeiture and/or carceral persecution. When possibilities for redress are constrained by retributive rather than restorative or transformative principles of justice, endless cycles of violence appear inevitable. We can already see the significant constraints the Western juridical imaginary places on how modern societies—including transnational social bodies such as the United Nations or the International Criminal Court—think about possibilities for seeking, offering, or achieving retrospective justice in cases of irreparable and irreplaceable collective loss. While redress aspires to remedy, its historical precursors in the West have fundamentally—that is, constitutively and structurally—entailed the reiteration of some of the worst forms of both material and substantively symbolic violence across long historical periods. Thus is the melancholy logic of retribution writ large across the juridical imaginary.

Reflecting on the consolidation of the word *redress* in the eighteenth century, Stephen Best and Saidiya Hartman have noted that black abolitionist writers like Ottobah Cugoano were keenly aware that the possibility for social remedy was limited by "the governing logic of law and commerce," a subtending logic that continues to frame how we think about retrospective justice today. Cugoano, they argue, "insists that the injury of slavery must be borne, since it cannot be reversed," concluding that "if what has been done cannot be undone, then the forms of legal and social compensation available are less a matter of wiping the slate clean than of *embracing the limited scope of the possible in face of the irreparable,* and calling attention to the incommensurability between pain and compensation."[15] Hartman and Best instruct us that whatever remedy might be afforded by the law—Sharp's faith notwithstanding—the law itself is enmeshed in a logic of economic exchange that projects the ruse of completion, while simultaneously foreclosing any attempt to reach the justice that lies beyond; yet the "incommensurability" between the law and justice does not vacate the imperative to operate in both at the same time, "to calculate with the incalculable," to invoke Derrida's famous expression.[16] This imperative is captured so poignantly in Hartman and Best's phrase cited above, "embracing the limited scope of the possible in the face of the irreparable." And yet, does that line not already, in advance, cede defeat, at least rhetorically? Is it not the very sign of (their) exhaustion? Are we really so paralyzed by the exhausting evocation of the past as melancholic loss that the future can only be anticipated as defeat? I also wonder if the terms on which critical melancholia depend are not themselves so trapped in this juridical imaginary that critics cannot see the other forms in which redress might also be put into play.

Perhaps Cugoano already offers us a much more powerful articulation of redress that goes unremarked but finds its rhetorical articulation in that long, provocative eighteenth-century title for which he remains famous, *Thoughts and Sentiments on the Evil and Wicked Traffic of the Slavery and Commerce of the Human Species.*[17] I read in that title a remarkable caesura between the abstract, normative, and mystified concepts of the first part of the title (sentiment, evil, wicked) and a set of demystifying expressions that name the systematic structure of violence and the scale of social harm (traffic, slavery, commerce, human species) that resonates with my own decidedly unsentimental term of art: human bio-cargo. Cargo was also a term of art for the trade itself, as those many advertisements housed in the colonial archive attest. But there is a second caesura, it seems to me, that is equally instructive. Terms like *evil* and *wicked,* which fail to name anything concrete (or redressible outside of divine intervention), can easily portend the temporization or foreclosure of justice as social action. Following a path laid out by the remarkable critical project of rethinking affect, which has been crucial to both queer theory and postcolonial studies (and an equally crucial site of their overlap), Cugoano's evocation of "thoughts and sentiments" is not only indicative of his historical moment (now an untenable anatomo-cognitive binary) but also suggests perhaps another way into the problem of redress, one that rethinks what counts as the "material" of historical materialism without disavowing materialist critique altogether.

Recalcitrant Recoveries

Critical melancholists offer a hard lesson in archival recalcitrance: that nothing one finds in the archive is truly amenable to recovery, at least not in anything like the fullness of return the word implies; that much of what one finds there points toward the intractably irrecoverable; that the archaeology of what remains can be exhausting, that empty traces can be exhausted, but that the archive itself remains inexhaustible. Scholars of the African Atlantic have long problematized the theoretical and methodological pitfalls of trying to restore through experiments in critical historiography a past erased by and overwritten in dominant history, but critical melancholia goes further: on the one hand, while admitting (to) the (im)possibility of recovery, critical melancholists insistently point to—and point out—the bad faith politics of much of what passes for historical recuperation; on the other, the melancholist obsessively rehearses the reflexive limits of its own politics of redress, often at the cost of political commitment itself. By accepting the conceptual logic of presence and absence on which recovery depends, critical melancholists settle into a state of perpetual mourning. But the same deconstruction that disables the promise of recovery also enables remarkable possibilities for performing the archive by accessing the potential for the inexhaustible iterability—provisional and improvisational—of whatever one finds there. In order to breach the creative and critical barricade that appears to wall off the work of the archive from work of public culture, I want to turn to a few of the archival traces on which Fred D'Aguiar has constructed his novel *Feeding the Ghosts:* not, however, those documents that provide accounts of exceptional atrocities committed on the slave ship *Zong,* which inform the novel's dominant storyline, but a set of objects that record acts of exemplary violence aboard the slave ship *Recovery* on which its plot truly pivots—an archival constellation more volatile in the contest of the meaning and significance of the singular event when it is leveraged into an example.

I arrive at this particular archival constellation by way of another scholar's painful recounting of what transpired on board the *Recovery*—a name that aches with irony—alongside her own melancholy ruminations on the prospects for historical recovery. Midway through Saidiya Hartman's *Lose Your Mother: A Journey along the Atlantic Slave Route* (2007), in a chapter given the provocative and perhaps symptomatic title "The Dead Book," the author tells in visceral detail the story of a single past atrocity: the flogging and death of a female slave at the hands of a slave ship captain. In her arresting account, Hartman describes a nameless girl (Hartman's word), no older than fifteen and suffering from what was most likely yaws (but construed by the ship's surgeon as syphilis), who was stolen into slavery on the West African coast in the late eighteenth century. Although the details of her death are few—and facts of her life before arriving on board the *Recovery* are entirely lost—in the years that followed this girl would "stand" before the British public as an unremittingly valuable *figure* of colonial atrocity. "Of the twenty-one slaves who died aboard the *Recovery,*" Hartman tells us, "and the million and more tossed into the Atlantic, one girl comes into view."[18] Her spectral appearance suggests that the girl both haunts the archival record (as a handful of "facts" that cannot be known for certain) and is conjured from it (imagined with no less certainty). A sick and "recalcitrant" slave, the girl refused to eat, refused to "dance" (for exercise), refused to bend to the will of the ship's captain and crew. In the course of a day, she was hung by tackle secured to the mizzen stay, hoisted above the deck, severely lashed with the cat-o-nine-tails, dropped to the deck, raised again and whipped—first by one hand, and then by the other; next by one leg and then the other—repeatedly until she could no longer walk but had to crawl to the stairs down which she tumbled back into the hold. The punishment was ordered by the captain, executed by the third mate, and witnessed by the ship's surgeon. She died three days later, whereupon she was tossed into the unfathomable sea of history.

As Hartman is keenly aware, in our ongoing obligation to historicize, such a recovery founders on the intractable paradox of what is politically imperative and what is ethically possible. Unable to undo or overcome the problem of violence in the act of storytelling, her own singular narrative recuperation attempts to both reflexively perform and intervene in the violent discursive operations of exemplarity in order to highlight violence *as* a problem of storytelling. On the one hand, her reenactment stages her own creative engagement with the archival record and rethinks her memorable refusal to reproduce the "terrible spectacle" of exemplary violence in the opening pages of Hartman's earlier book, *Scenes of Subjection.*[19] On the other hand, in *Lose Your Mother,* Hartman's critical engagement is overwhelmed by its melancholy attachment to a life that is irrecoverably lost: "Looking at the Atlantic I thought of the girl. There were countless others buried at the bottom of the ocean, but she was the one I had my eyes set on" (136).

The girl had arrived in the historical record through a quite unusual accusation, a charge made against the ship's captain by other officers, which in turn led to a criminal inquiry into the deaths of two African women. She reappeared later in the circulation of a series of tracts debating what the trial of John Kimber demonstrated about the slave trade. As Hartman asserts, "Exceptional circumstances prevented her from simply vanishing into the heap of obscure lives scattered along the ocean's floor: a captain was tried for murder" (138). After Kimber's acquittal, her "case" was then taken up by the British abolitionist William Wilberforce, who publicized the account of her death offered by two witnesses at trial (the third mate and the surgeon) as a means of furthering the abolitionist cause. In Hartman's concise phrase, she became an allegory, a stand-in, an example that could be used instrumentally by either Captain John Kimber of the slave ship *Recovery,* whose name *should not* be forgotten, or William Wilberforce, the Member of Parliament, whose name will *never* be forgotten. For the captain of the slave ship, the girl was an exception, and her actions represented an exceptional form of maritime disorder that posed a risk to his venture.

She represented one seemingly aleatory element of the trade: events like the outbreak of disease or slave rebellion might be predictable in general but difficult to anticipate in the particular. In law, she was both exceptional commodity and singular example: subject to the order of the ship, her refusal to conform—her singularity—legitimized her exemplary punishment. In law, this allegorization—this abstract exchangeability—"dematerializes" the singular body into a fungible signifier that operates like a ghostly commodity.[20] Her body became a trope for colonial violence: for Wilberforce, the violence of the slave trade; for Kimber, the violent response to a threat to the order of the ship; in law, an intractable structural threat to Law itself.

Hartman hopes to undo the way in which, as allegory, the story of the slave is perpetually bound to both commodity and discursive circulation by contesting such seamless narrative exchangeability, and by imaginatively re-creating the singularity of her experience—of rematerializing the past in order that we too, the future public of this narrative, can witness and *feel* the violence of the particular, individual atrocity. "It is said that if you look at the sea long enough," Hartman begins, "scenes from the past come back to life. . . . Looking at the Atlantic, I thought of the girl. There were countless others buried at the bottom of the ocean, but she was the one I had my eyes set on. If only I concentrated hard enough I could see it all happening again" (136). If the slave was made spectral through the poetics of figuration in the tracts that circulated, and the account that Wilberforce presented before Parliament and the public, if she was made to represent the fate of the disobedient offender before the eyes of her fellow captives, if she was made to serve as an *exemplary* token of the ultimate authority of law over its subject, she was also a *singular* instance of the intolerable but abiding cruelty of the colonial enterprise. Hartman acknowledges the manner in which the figure of the young girl materialized within the eighteenth-century public sphere, while cautioning us against the too easy or uncritical appropriation of such specters within our own scholarly efforts to historicize.

By telling the story of the girl *as* a commodity (material and discursive), Hartman hopes to avoid her own reduction of her *to* a commodity circulating in our own historical moment. She does so through a careful chronological disruption that emphasizes rather than effaces the mediations on which narrative rests: beginning with the girl's final moments, Hartman weaves a story of abuse that brings us to the girl's arrival on board the *Recovery* in such a way that we feel the violence of the singular atrocity. Slowly, Hartman uncovers a narrative account that moves back in time to that moment of ultimate rupture—her capture into slavery.

In addition to an assiduously detailed and visceral account of the embodied experience of exemplary punishment, Hartman leverages a narrative mode that underscores the material and affective implications of an implacably incomplete "recovery." She also reminds us that the unfolding atrocity on board the *Recovery* was itself underwritten by a number of prior narratives: of economic necessity, of sovereign right, and of legal authority, all of which validate Kimber's actions. For yet another tragedy of the *Recovery* isn't simply that Kimber was acquitted of atrocious crimes but that he likely was not guilty of any crime at all, at least *by law*.[21] The "dead book" to which the title of Hartman's chapter refers is the ledger typically kept and "sworn to" (authorized) by the ship's surgeon, which serves as a site of historical erasure as much as commercial memory. The book, whose purpose was to attest to the number of lives lost at sea, indicated nothing of the loss of this particular girl. In the criminal case, that no such loss is recorded provided the captain with the greatest evidentiary support for his claims of innocence. On the other hand, in this instance the surgeon refused to swear to the book, precisely because, he claimed in court, it was not a truthful document of the transactions on board the ship.

I want to dwell for a moment in and beyond Hartman's archive, to situate the documents on which she relies with others that are "like" the Kimber trial record. The story Hartman tells is derived, as she acknowledges, from a prior account published at the end of the eighteenth century, *The Trial of Captain John Kimber for the Murder of a Negro Girl on Board the Ship Recovery.* As she also discusses, reports of abuse of slaves on board slave ships traversing the Middle Passage were common, and as commonly did abolitionists like Wilberforce and Sharp appropriate them to the uses of the abolitionist cause. Indeed, there were several versions of Kimber's trial record printed in an array of tracts and placed in heavy circulation in the years leading up to the abolition of the trade in 1807. None of these, it is worth noting, were "official" court transcripts; they each reproduce verbatim the initial indictment, which was printed and made available.[22]

There is another story to be told about the *Recovery,* or another way of telling it, a story about the archive itself and the violence it houses and enacts; about the consolidation of the historical record consolidated from an array of documents and objects once distributed for public consumption;

a story that places Hartman's account into a broader constellation in the public life of history. I am tempted to say that this other story is found in Fred D'Aguiar's *Feeding the Ghosts,* and to some extent it is, but it is really found in the resonance between the objects in the archive, and between the objects in the archive and those that are not; between the institutional archives from which such objects escape and the other archives those institutions cannot capture, or are not interested in capturing. This story is about the production of the colonial archive as the archive of the law, whose machinery is at work long before Kimber is brought to the bar, and continues long after he is free to take his leave, whose machinery continues to produce the trial out in the streets, salons, and coffee houses of the celebrated eighteenth-century public sphere, in the broadsides and tracts that produced and preserved competing versions of Captain Kimber's trial, competing versions of the accused and of his accusers, and sharply competing versions of the two women who were taken from somewhere in Africa and killed somewhere upon the Atlantic. Competing interests, competing purposes, competing characterizations, competing assumptions. In the subsequent chapter, I return to a fuller discussion of this question of competition in terms of the life-making, death-letting, and death-meting enacted at the intersection of law and commerce.

The Trial of Captain John Kimber for the Murder of Two Female Negro Slaves, On Board the Recovery, African Slave Ship was published in London in 1792 by the abolitionist printer Charles Stalker. It includes an appendix that insists on the injustice of the outcome of Kimber's trial, and argues that Kimber's acquittal is yet another example of the failures and limits of English maritime and criminal law. Meanwhile, allies of Captain Kimber, and proponents of the slave trade, likewise published a transcript of the trial, and here it is instructive to repeat two key sections of the long frontispiece title: *Genuine State of Facts. The Trial of Captain John Kimber For the Supposed Murder of an African Girl . . . Of which he was most humbly acquitted, and the Two Evidences for the Prosecution committed to Newgate to take their Trials for Willful and Corrupt Perjury.* This edition was printed by William Lane, somewhat of a hack publisher of vanity books and founder of the popular romance outfit Minerva Press. One should note immediately the variants in the title of the two documents: "supposed murder" of "an African girl" versus the more certain "murder of *two* female slaves." The Stalker edition, however, differs in significant ways from the pamphlet offered by Lane, which aimed at exonerating Kimber from the charge of murder. Lane's purports to be the "genuine state of facts," noting that Kimber was "honorably acquitted" and his *accusers* were then remanded to Newgate on charges of perjury. Here the emphasis is not only on Kimber's acquittal but also on the perjury charges subsequently brought against his accusers, as an act of unequivocal justice before the law.

The Stalker transcript, while acknowledging Kimber's acquittal, does not concede the legal question of the girl's death at the captain's hand but rather suggests such deaths were commonplace, indeed unexceptional, and that the case offers insight into the systemic violence of the trade:

> Whatever the public opinion may be relative to the prosecution carried on against Captain Kimber, who has been (we suppose fairly) acquitted by an English Jury, it was evidently a necessary and a useful measure. It may afford a salutary lesson to those captains of slave ships, and masters of slaves [who] hereafter attempt to commit such horrid outrages as he has been charged with: and it may, from the circumstances here related (for such barbarities have doubtless been often practiced), fill the minds of men universally with horror against the present system: until tyranny shall at length give way to public opinion, and liberty and happiness be restored to human beings. (vi–vii)

As an example, the case now redounds upon the system of slavery itself, from the particular instance to the general structure. The variants in the two documents are also interesting for what they each disclose as well as what they both foreclose. Each is marked by its own gaps and silences, and as Hartman makes so clear, neither is much concerned with the girl whose death motivated the case. The girl is indeed foreclosed, as is that *second* victim, Venus, who is only mentioned in passing in either document, and whose death is excised from the title of Lane's edition of the trial as the charges for her murder were dismissed with the collapse of the case.[23]

The exceptional violence enacted upon the slave's body, as a way of rendering her an example to others, was reenacted before a British public at pains to come to terms with its own intimate relationship to slavery and the trade. While the passage of time might have obscured the extent of the imbrications of imperial center and colonial periphery, the British public of the late eighteenth century had daily reminders that almost all the commodities they consumed were tainted by slavery and the slave trade.

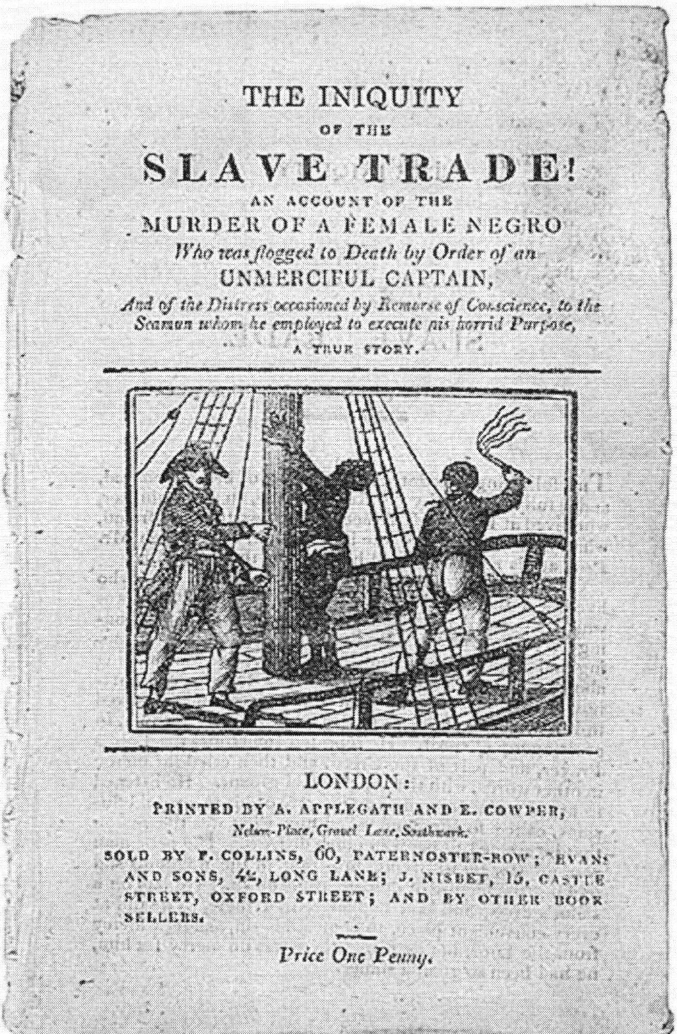

THE INIQUITY
OF THE
SLAVE TRADE!
AN ACCOUNT OF THE
MURDER OF A FEMALE NEGRO
Who was flogged to Death by Order of an
UNMERCIFUL CAPTAIN,
And of the Distress occasioned by Remorse of Conscience, to the Seaman whom he employed to execute his horrid Purpose,
A TRUE STORY.

LONDON:
PRINTED BY A. APPLEGATH AND E. COWPER,
Nelson-Place, Gravel Lane, Southwark.
SOLD BY F. COLLINS, 60, PATERNOSTER-ROW; EVANS AND SONS, 42, LONG LANE; J. NISBET, 15, CASTLE STREET, OXFORD STREET; AND BY OTHER BOOKSELLERS.

Price One Penny.

Figure 5. The Iniquity of the Slave Trade! An Account of the Murder of a Female Negro Who was Flogged to Death by Order of an Unmerciful Captain, and of the Distress occasioned by Remorse of Conscience, to the Seaman whom he employed to execute his horrid Purpose *(1830 [orig. 1800]). Woodblock. Printed by A. Applegate & E. Cowper. Courtesy of Cowan's Auctions Inc.*

Abolitionist pamphlets, like the one pictured below, circulated in the tens of thousands, as did others defending slavery (see Figure 5). Published in 1800, *The Iniquity of the Slave Trade!* is reminiscent of other accounts of exemplary violence, such as those presented in the *Abstract of the Evidence delivered before a Select Committee of the House of Commons, in 1790 and 1791,* circulated widely in the last decade of the eighteenth century.[24] This particular pamphlet offered the British public an account of the morbid punishment enacted in particular on the female slave—who, as on the *Recovery,* was beaten to death and discarded at sea—accompanied by a particularly graphic reenactment, a narrative no less gruesome and appalling for being somewhat generic. Appended to the end of the tract, it is worth noting, is Robert Southey's poem "The Sailor Who Had Served in the Slave Trade" (1798), commemorating both the slave's death (and as such the atrocity of slavery itself) *and* the sailor's redemption.

The account of the exemplary violence that appeared in both *The Iniquity of the Slave Trade* and Southey's poem recalls the transcripts of the earlier trial of John Kimber, which was itself captured in horrifying detail in Isaac Cruikshank's famous and far more lurid rendering of the abuse (see Figure 6).[25] In both, the figure of the slave appears as simultaneously the target of exemplary corporal violence and an object of ethnographic display. We know that these kinds of images, and the stories they captured, served equally the supposedly righteous principles of the abolitionists and the prurient appetites of the English public. Hortence Spillers long ago argued that the exceptional violence of capture into slavery degendered those who were enslaved, an assertion that might at first appear at variance with the examples above taken from the historical archive. But what Spillers understood so astutely is that when women are captured, enslaved, and rendered an item of bio-cargo, they are deprived of gendered subjectivity but retain their functional biological sex. Reduced to the status of female flesh, they are then made available as a crude repository for the bodies of men. "A female body strung from a tree limb," Spillers painfully observes, "or bleeding from the breast on any given day of field work because the 'overseer,' standing the length of a whip, has popped her flesh open, adds lexical and living dimension to the narratives of women in culture and society. This materialized scene of unprotected female flesh—of female flesh 'ungendered'—offers a praxis and a theory, a text for living and for dying, and a method for reading both through their diverse mediations."[26] By emphasizing the way in which the bodies of African women operate as exceptional sites of white male domination, we can begin to see the powerful ways in which the spectacular displays—first on the slave ship and the slave plantation in the colonies, and then in narrative and visual circulation for avid audiences "back home"— of exemplary violence contributed to fixing race by undoing gender as applicable categories in law. Indeed, the bodies of enslaved African women appear as exemplary figures for acts of *speculation* across a wide range of registers—from practices of looking that secure economies of the gaze, to acts of ideational apprehension that ground taxonomies of human life, to acts of accounting and measure of prediction that subtend calculations of value. That the term *species* initially derived from the same etymological root as *speculation* to denote a coin or form of money only underscores the relationship between the language, representation, figuration, on one side, and the philosophical, scientific, and economic foundations of racism as the primary principles in the making of modern human bio-cargo.[27]

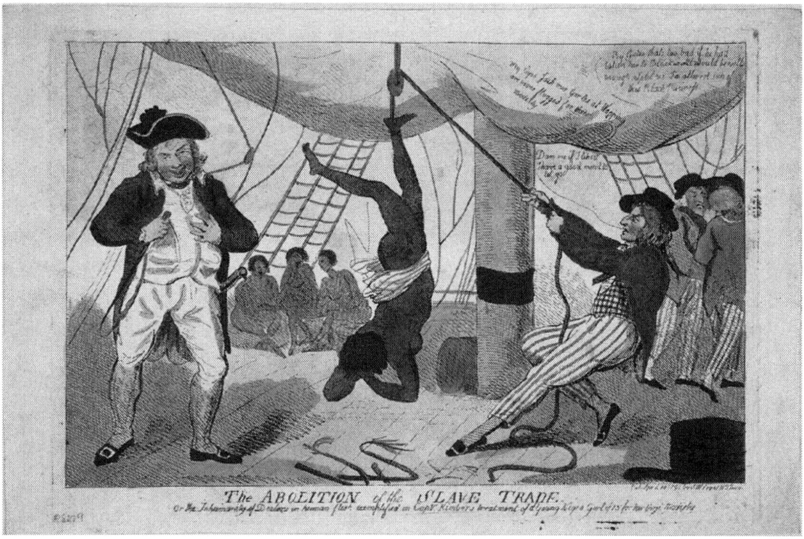

Figure 6. Isaac Cruikshank, The Abolition of the Slave Trade; or, The Inhumanity of Dealers in Human Flesh Exemplified in Captn. Kimber's Treatment of a Young Negro Girl of 15 for Her Virjen Modesty *(1792). Courtesy of Library of Congress, Washington, D.C.*

Scattered Speculations

Fred D'Aguiar's *Feeding the Ghosts* "weaves" rather than conflates the violent events that transpired on the deck of the *Recovery* with the more infamous atrocities committed aboard the slave ship *Zong,* and to do so it "constellates" the varying and contradictory accounts preserved in the archive. The reading that follows turns on the ambiguities implied by those two incompatible tropes: the weave and the constellation. My analysis also turns against the somewhat attenuated attention given to the novel in the final chapter of Ian Baucom's *Specters of the Atlantic,* an otherwise breathtaking meditation on the case of the *Zong* as an aperture through which the history of the long Atlantic cycle of capitalist accumulation opens up before our very eyes. While *Specters of the Atlantic* offers a painstakingly detailed study of the significance and consequences of three coincident historical eruptions into capitalist modernity—the global expansion of European maritime trade; the development of the colonial economy founded on the Atlantic system of slave trading and the use of slave labor in the Americas; and the emergence of formal insurance markets and the rise of finance capital by the early eighteenth century—Baucom's primary critical intervention developed as an indictment of speculation as the governing logic of modern capitalism. *Specters* also provides a sweeping survey of the historical archive, and a trenchant analysis of the legal claims made by the owners, investors, and insurers of human bio-cargo; his assessment of contemporary black British literary historiography is unable to read these works as anything but a melancholy response to the historical archive and the unending circuits of commodity exchange in which it is ensnared. Rather, the notorious deaths of 132 women and men captured, enslaved, then discarded at sea from the deck of the slave ship *Zong* serves as an aperture into the eighteenth-century trade in human bio-cargo that facilitated an explosion in high-risk and high-return financial speculation, expansion of insurance markets, evolution in actuarial reasoning, and the ways in which these developments helped to "fix" legal redress in forms of monetized reparation; "justice," like human bio-cargo, circulates in an economy of exchange values. The image of the *Zong*—comprised of the specters of those discarded at sea and those abandoned to the market—would, or at least should, forever haunt the British public imaginary.

The legal battle over who would bear the financial cost of those deaths, the *Zong*'s investors or the insurers against whom they had filed claim, framed the case as a matter of the unrecoverability of property, not the irredeemability of human life; and justice construed as the adjudication of risk and dispensation of loss, made possible by the careful application of the law.[28] Baucom rightfully worries that the same actuarial logic, financial speculation endemic to maritime trade, also underwrites the narrative frameworks available to talk about reparative justice in the present, in which the loss of one human life, or the loss of a numerable few, is meant to represent the loss of innumerable others, in which value is ascribed to making those lives count through the lives of those who can be counted, in which some kind of gain is made possible through the representation of loss. If social justice is reduced to a question of value, organized by and applied through the rules of contractual exchange, then irreparable human losses run the risk of being seen as redeemable through a system of representational—even monetized—equivalence. In such an order of justice, life is rendered symbolically and economically fungible. To be sure, unraveling the particular forms of loss from within a sea of atrocity, to make the singular stand in for the general (if not universal), is to draw the claim for justice into a circuit of exchange. Baucom, however, indicts broadly any form of representation that gains through the evocation of loss. Like their eighteenth-century abolitionist predecessors, contemporary narrative historiographies of the black Atlantic risk effacing the singularity of any particular atrocity by demanding that it function *as* an example; in which each atrocity be construed as atrocity *as such;* in which every evocation of loss adds narrative value by suspending the singularity of each particular event of atrocity, and thus compounding the speculative interests in the figuration of exemplary violence.[29]

Feeding the Ghosts provides something like a "poetics" of exemplarity through which narrative singularity is also continuously performed, as the novel interrogates the form that justice takes under the demands of juridical abstraction and economic calculation. The novel is divided into three sections bracketed by a prologue and epilogue. Each part offers a distinct narrative form: an omniscient third-person account of the disposal of those 132 bodies over the three days the *Zong* is adrift at sea; a second third-person account of the court case that pitted the investors against the insurers, which underscores the role of evidence and testimony at the core of juridical reason; and a first-person retelling of the event by a fictional lone survivor, one of the 132 who lives on as witness to the atrocity. The prologue and epilogue, however, provide a *poetics* or heuristic through which we might consider reflexively the act of reading creative historiography. That is, these bookends make a critical and ethical demand on the reader that I would describe as redressive. Here D'Aguiar emphasizes the singular nature of this particular execution of extreme violence. As with Hartman, the exemplary punishment of a female slave, who likewise refuses to acquiesce to the perverse will of a vicious captain, sets up a narrative of recovery and redemption that stages rather than assumes the processes of loss and gain that Baucom finds so deeply problematic. Once again, through "exceptional circumstances," a slave ship captain was put on trial.

In the novel, Captain Cunningham, the fictional name given to the historical figure Captain Luke Collingwood of the *Zong,* is not held criminally accountable for the 132 human deaths he ordered, but he must justify in a civil action the "necessity" of throwing 132 items of cargo overboard, each represented by one of 132 marks in his ledger. Each mark denotes a loss of property; each one points to a financial, rather than human, investment whose value was protected by an insurance policy. Each life is reduced to an actuarial calculation. Through this reflexive historiographic narrative, D'Aguiar juxtaposes the conceptual abstractions that enact violence within the law and corporeal affliction and somatic sensation experienced on board the slave ship. He does so in order to stage the long-standing problem of representing atrocity without ethical reduction or economic reification. The poetics of exemplary violence D'Aguiar deploys obliges us to imagine in quite material ways the process of disposing of 132 bodies across the bow of a slave ship. Thus the novel does not merely represent violent atrocity but multiplies particularity and extends exceptionality in the passage of singularity to exemplarity, a process the term *abstraction* is inadequate to describe.

In a novel rich in poetic description and figurative language, the central trope for historical memory is the sea itself, which serves as a heuristic for reading both the material and affective past. The figure of the somatic sea makes such materialization possible. Here I quote a rather long passage from the prologue:

> The sea is slavery. Sea water boils in its own current. Salt gives
> the sea the texture of fabric, something thick and close-knitted,
> not unlike the fine dust of a barn seen floating in a shaft of light.
> Sea receives a body as if that body has come to rest on a cushion,
> one that gives way to the body's weight and folds around it like

> an envelope. Over three days 131 such bodies, no, 132, are flung at this sea. Each lands with a sound that the sea absorbs and silences. Each opens a wound in this sea that heals over each body without the evidence of a scar. Two hundred and sixty-four arms and 264 legs punch and kick against a tide that insists all who land on it, all who break its smooth surface, must succumb to its swells, tumbles, pushes and pulls. Water replaces air in 131 of these bodies. . . . Salt washes the wounds on those bodies instilled by the locks, chains, masks, collars, binds, fetters, handcuffs and whips of the land, washes until those wounds belong to the sea. . . . Sea refuses to grant that body the quiet of a grave in the ground. Instead it rolls that body across its terrain, sends that body down into its depths, its stellar dark, swells the body to bursting point, tumbles it beyond the reach of horizons and gradually breaks fragments from that body with its nibbling, dissecting current. Soon all those bodies melt down to bones, then the sea begins to treat the bones like rock, there to be shaped over time or ground to dust. Sea does not stop at death. Salt wants to consume every morsel of those bodies until the sea becomes them, becomes their memory. So it is from the sea that all 131 souls are to be plucked. From a sea oblivious to time. One hundred and thirty-one dissipated bodies find breath in the wind skimming the surface of the sea and howl. Those bodies have their lives written on salt water. The sea current turns pages of memory. One hundred and thirty-one souls roam the Atlantic with countless others. When the wind is heard it is their breath, their speech. The sea is therefore home.[30]

History is sustained—but also reworked and worked over—in this passage by a fluid chain of both tangible and abstract metaphors and metonymies: sea, fabric, dust, cushion, envelop, on the one hand; wound, scar, grave, and page, on the other. Each trope inscribes or "entextualizes" the material violence enacted on the human body plunged into the ocean. These are bodies that have already experienced unimaginable violence through the application of quite material devices of torture and constraint: "locks, fetters, chains, masks, collars, binds, fetters, handcuffs and whips." The sea becomes a geography of death, "oblivious" to the time of corporeal disintegration, as the synecdoche of the body withers into its own oblivion: from flesh to bone to dust to memory, indeed "pages of memory," another "dead book." The passage is likewise oblivious to the time of reading, as one is compelled to linger over the novel's opening pages, whose unbound figuration binds us to the materiality of atrocious violence and horrific death. Here D'Aguiar stuns, arrests, delays, and provokes. If the novel functions allegorically, its metalepses—its uncontainable metaphoricity, and metonymic or synecdochal representationality—allow its allegory to operate asymptotically, refusing an easy parallel alignment between its multiple planes of meaning. Such metaleptic repetitions of the singular occasion of violence, according to Baucom, extend transversally across time and space, within the hauntological structure of historical memory. For Baucom, then, historical memory relies upon a system of substitution that turns the singular event into a fungible commodity while the commodity form itself enables the translation of the past into reified social relations today. I am arguing, contra Baucom, that narrative and figurative exchanges need not collapse back into the logic of the commodity form. By challenging traditional allegory's representational parallelisms, *Feeding the Ghosts* resists subsumption into an economy of pure exchange values. On the one hand, the necromantic sea becomes a site of inscription and an archive of atrocity. But "sea"—without an article—names the subject of inscription, suggesting that the sea is also an *agent* of archival knowledge. At the same time, as a metaphor of counterarchival power, the sea erases as much as it encases. It is a force of entropic dysfunction within the archive. As a figure of history, sea describes both a place and a process—a synchronic archive and a diachronic machine.

It is that one subtracted body, the one that resurfaces and endures as the singular trace of the atrocity—no longer 132 lives lost, but 131—who drives the dominant narrative strand, and in so doing stands as both a subject in and witness to history.[31] The single and singular survivor provides a counterhistory through which we can better imagine the act of confronting the material violence of human expropriation and disposability, as well as the ever-present possibility (or potentiality) of disruption, disorder, and opposition that exemplary violence produces. D'Aguiar gives this figure of disruption a name, Mintah, and it is she who confronts the limits and failures of dominant historiography. Like the girl on the *Recovery,* Mintah is the emblem of disobedience, the agent of disorder whose exceptionality leads to an act of exemplary violence, not simply as a figure of atrocity but as a singular instance that stands beside itself in a sea of criminal atrocity, the exception who occupies a space both within and outside the 132 Africans thrown overboard from the *Zong*, each of whom also bears a singular occasion of 132 acts of violence repeated over three days. But the bodies that lie beneath the surface of the sea, the bodies that form a submarine network that subtends the vast web of social relations above, are appropriated for a *maripoesis* of loss and gain that guarantees, insures, underwrites every possible social relation, every possible accounting of the past, and every possible fantasy of the future. To do justice within this system of exchange is, of course, to traffic in ghosts.

While the singular might be rendered useless to the logic of capitalist accumulation, it remains haunted by the imperative to represent. In the simultaneous disclosures and foreclosures of the secret buried but lurking beneath the surface we see workings of a cryptographesis simultaneously encoding, decoding, and recoding loss and gain, or loss as gain. As an example, the singular at best teeters on the edge of, and at worst collapses back into, an economy of exchange values, precisely because the singular cannot be contained as itself but must signify beyond itself—as representational excess or surplus—and beyond its use within the circuits of capital. As an exception, the example tropes—doubles, trebles, extends in perpetuity—its own singularity. When singularity is sustained and rendered incalculable, the example shows its own ultimate undecidability; through the example one "calculates with the incalculable," but in forms so perverse to the regulation and calculation of meaning on which capital relies that speculation itself scatters across the horizon of the future.

In a sense, then, I have been arguing *for* exchange and speculation, against the shadow of critical melancholia and against what I see as dominant trends in African Atlanticist criticism. Rather than assuming the homology between capitalist speculation and critical speculation, I have tried to articulate their convergences and divergences. To be sure, much dominant history and even critical historiography has been blind to the dilemmas of narrative and figurative exchange, and of the complications generated by the use of the example. Although I largely agree with the diagnosis, I continue to believe that as a figure the example offers a more complicated form and a more ambivalent register of meaning. However, I have not yet made a convincing case that exemplarity makes possible other, more perverse constellations of meaning that, if not exempt from, cannot be reconciled to a logic of exchange value on which the capitalist economy rests. I want to conclude this chapter, then, by asking what it would take to release the example, which remains fundamental to narrative historiography, from one system of speculative exchange (legal, economic, discursive) while maintaining its place in another (redress, justice, futurity). Can the singular example resist subsumption into the logic of exchange value? Does not precisely such a figure appear in the single and singular survivor of atrocity, the one who refuses to yield to the will of the captain, who refuses the demand to give testimony, or who refuses to be reduced to *the* figure of enslavement, of exemplary violence, even as she stands as an example of it? As we saw at the beginning of the chapter, in Dabydeen's *A Harlot's Progress* such a figure arrives in recalcitrant relation to the name Mungo (among others); in D'Aguiar's *Feeding the Ghost,* she is called into being as Mintah.

The deployment of Mintah as an example is crucial to the formal structure of *Feeding the Ghosts.* We see this first in the exchange and exchangeability of names, a development within the novel that responds thematically and structurally to the violent erasure of names from the history of slavery. Once again, Giorgio Agamben's description of the relationship between the singular and the exemplary is useful here; for by standing beside itself the example not only sustains its singularity but also proliferates or disseminates singularity; it sustains both its singularity *and* its own exceptionality. But the example also acknowledges the ultimate undecidability that makes the demand for justice an impossible decision that must be rendered nonetheless. The singular, in its exemplary form, marks out and makes visible the *in*calculable. It is the ghostly margin of economic calculation that haunts historical representation but also as a temporal catachresis, a bewildering indeterminacy and contingency within historical representation.

Unlike the girl on board the *Recovery,* Mintah's disobedience is precipitated by an already unfolding atrocity, as the captain and first mate begin to dispose of those slaves deemed unlikely to yield a suitable profit. She responds by naming the atrocity itself and by naming one of the perpetrators of it: Kelsal, the first mate and the one name she knows. From deep within the hold of the ship she calls out his name, repeatedly, "Kelsal!" Hers is an act of Althusserian interpellation that names Kelsal as a guilty criminal accomplice in the conspiracy he is charged to carry out. Hearing his name called out from an unknown source, as if it were emitted by the *Zong* itself, Kelsal is unnerved and ultimately enraged, hailed not as the first mate on board a cargo ship but as a mass-murderer. As Kelsal reports to Captain Cunningham, "The woman knew English and had been shouting his name in a manner to provoke him but, more importantly, one that was likely to incite rebellion in the other slaves" (29–30). The act of naming the crime and identifying the criminal from the ghostly margins of the ship provokes the exemplary acts of violence used against Mintah, but by giving a name to the perpetrators of atrocity she also challenges the authority vested in the officers of the ship as the very figures of the law itself.

Acts of exemplary violence described in the text represent the way in which the order of the ship and the order of capital work together to reassert and reinsure the law once it has been challenged. For Mintah, however, the exemplary violence borne by her own body is redirected outward toward Kelsal, in the fervent repetition of his name:

> His name burst out of her eyes and ears and nose and mouth. Her pores sweated his name. He seeped out from under her fingernails, from the ends of her hair. She saw herself taking hold of his hands, and she shouted his name at those hands for the offence of beating, for the offence of holding a living body and slinging it over the side into the uncaring sea, and the flesh peeled from those offending hands and the little offending bones of the fingers and wrists splintered shattered, crumbled and blew away. She shouted his name again, this time to his face, until his skin peeled off and his flesh and the bones in his face disintegrated followed by the rest of him. (38)

As the epistemological counterviolence of naming injustice redounds upon Mintah, she becomes the exemplary object against which law-affirming violence must be directed. "Reason was suspended by him when a black body said his name," the narrator says of Kelsal, "and he saw it as impudence and sought not a fair punishment to bring redress, but revenge" (37). It is not unproblematic, reading these two passages, that Kelsal and Mintah seem to stand in for the split between reason and embodiment, perhaps one of the West's most persistent and reductive tropes. On the other hand, D'Aguiar is resolute in ascribing a more productive subject-constituting power to such somatic inscription. Rather than seeing Mintah as pure embodiment, he suggests that she both leverages embodiment and withholds it. Strikingly, Mintah's fantasy of disintegration (a fantasy repeated throughout the novel through the conflicting tropes of wood and sea), of the pulling away of skin and bones, describes the process attributed in the prologue of the novel to the ravenous sea: "One at a time the sick were grabbed and bound if they fought. The sea was hungry. One at a time they were thrown in. The sea could not wait. It climbed over the side onto the deck. . . . The captain peered into my face as if it was his ledger." Adrift along the famished road of the transatlantic slave route, she too must eat, if only by the force of law: "They fed and watered me by forcing a funnel down my throat. I was not my name. I was not my body. I became my own secret, lost somewhere. Time stood still in my veins. . . . Time rusted in my joints. . . . Time became a funnel fed into me. Time turned me from my left to my right side. Time wiped me clean" (215–16). Time and history, inflected through the violence and violation of the funnel, appears as invasive and erosive somatic processes, engines of useless accumulation and evacuation.

Through the violent exchange between Mintah and Kelsal, D'Aguiar gestures toward the often narrow line between redress and revenge, and the possibility of their collapse into *in*distinction once punishment and law are evoked. For the captain and crew of the *Zong*, Mintah was a threat to the ship's order, a disruptive and insurrectionary figure whose disposal protected against a slave revolt on board. Later, in the second part of the novel set in Lord Mansfield's courtroom, First Mate Kelsal emphasizes the threat she posed to the smooth operations of the ship: "She was quiet on the *Zong* up to the moment the disposals began," he tells the court. But his testimony continues:

> I admit she was not physically sick like the others, but her sanity was questionable, and once insane an African is useless as labour since he does not respond to orders or punishment. The temperament of the mad infects the others into similar disregard for authority. This was her condition when I had her ejected from the ship. In my view her mind was unsuited to a life of servitude. She would forever be a thorn in the side of authority. Her manner would spread dissent among the slaves and disrupt the workings of a plantation. (158)

For Kelsal, there is little difference between the physical infection sweeping the ship and the insurrection mounting below deck. Both are contagious, both malicious. In the inverted logic of capital, labor is useless if it is inured to discipline, if it refuses to yield to the whip, to bear the exemplarity of the violence enacted on it: "She had been warned, beaten, chained, gagged and here she was again, as impudent with his name as before. She was a fine specimen, would fetch a good price in Jamaica, but he couldn't countenance her another moment on this ship" (47). If one justification for slavery had been the unique suitability of the African to hard labor, Mintah again was exceptional—unsuited, useless, dangerous. And in the inverted logic of insurance, only her death could produce value, could make her recalcitrance productive to capital. In the end, Kelsal asks that Mintah too be thrown overboard, like the 131 other slaves suffering from the affliction of declining profitability:

> The captain nodded his assent and made a rapid, reluctant stroke in his ledger. She is not sick, he thought, though she is enough of a nuisance to cause trouble on this ship. His honest ledger had a stroke for Mintah. He recorded her among the sick and infirm whose presence on the *Zong* had jeopardized the health and safety of everyone else. Their judicious disposal as damaged stock would preserve the rest and merit a claim for their loss against the underwriters. Insolence was a sickness. Stubbornness too. Behaviour liable to fuel discontent and promote an insurrection among the slaves was the worst sickness of all. Even his mind, untrained in legal matters, could comprehend this easily, could argue it with facility in a court under English law, if the need ever arose. He could foresee no such need. (48)

With each body thrown overboard, we are told, "Captain Cunningham marked the strokes in his ledger and nodded with satisfaction" (38–39). For three days bodies are disposed over the bow of the ship, and for three days Cunningham holds tight to his ledger, accounting for every loss and legal contingency—"if the need ever arose"—which of course it did. "Over three days he carried out a careful sorting of sick from healthy. The captain's ledger attests to the fact that he witnessed the disposal of every piece" (166). Ultimately, the evidence confronts necessity, and the limits and contradictions of the law unfold in the court case that Collingwood could anticipate but not foresee. Accounting and exchange work at the level of narrative arrangement and in its figurative orchestration: the exchange of a body for a stroke in a ledger that is, in turn, exchanged for monetary reparations already anticipated through actuarial agreement; the exchange of names that both expresses injustice and enrages violence; the exchange of evidence and testimony that then circulates through the public sphere and into debates in the House of Commons.

There is another narrative, however, that develops obliquely, overwritten by the testimony presented at trial—by the very force of law itself—manifested in the courtroom drama of the middle section of the novel: Kelsal and Mintah have exchanged names once before, when a sick and debilitated ship's mate seeks refuge at a Danish mission wherein Mintah resides. This is the prehistory exigent to the eruption of violence on board the *Zong*. During the trial Kelsal begins but fails to testify to his previous relationship to the slave who could read, write, and speak English, and who called out his name from below deck. In the final pages of the novel, long after the conclusion of the *Zong* trials, Mintah does provide such an account:

> I was one of the children who took turns to watch over him and mop his brow and empty his waste and feed him. He opened his eyes and did not know his name or where he was on earth. I had to teach him. "Kelsal!" I said, "you are Kelsal."
>
> "You are Kelsal?"
>
> "No! You! You are Kelsal! I am Mintah!"
>
> "I am Mintah?"
>
> "No! I am Mintah! You are Kelsal!"
>
> "Kelsal?"
>
> "Yes! Kelsal!"
>
> Why was I shouting? Because he seemed to be lost. The fever seemed to knock the common sense out of him so that I was him, he me.
>
> He was soon on his feet, and repairing the building around the fort. What a slow worker! He watched me walk past him at a safe distance and said my name and I said his as if our names did not belong to ourselves, not since we had exchanged them when he was hot and stupid. . . . Then one day he walked out of the fort, without so much as a goodbye, and into my future. (195–96)

The singular exchange of names suggests the possibility of an economy of care and mutuality that contrasts with the earlier interpellation in which Mintah's hailing of Kelsal anchored him firmly to the economy of calculation and exchange value. Indeed, caregiving, as women are ever reminded, is almost always subsumed into an economy of forced labor extraction. On the other hand, the power of Mintah's question "Why was I shouting?"

resides in its anticipation of a future that has already been narrated. Thus, her prophetic answer, "Because he seemed to be lost," is just as much an ethical and spiritual judgment as a physical or economic one. But if we imagine that the economy of the mission is the obverse of that of the slave trade, are we not once again in the precarious region of allegory? After all, historically, such Christian missions were deeply imbedded in rather than at odds with the system of Atlantic trade. This is, indeed, one of the ironies of the narrative; the structure of colonial violence had already been reappropriated for affective gain. Thus, through the contingencies of history and orchestration of European trade, two names are uttered by the remaining African slaves crammed into the hold of the ship, that of their tormenter, Kelsal, and that of their savior, Mintah—one echoing the other; one ever the specter of the other. At the same time, as an "encrypted" instance of singular knowledge, the relationship between Kelsal and Mintah stands outside the evidence admissible into law; its affective indemonstrability renders it immaterial to the law.

So too is the introduction of one final piece of evidence: a written account of the *Zong* composed by Mintah herself in the days she spent hiding among the nonhuman cargo of the ship. Against the evidence of the ledger, in D'Aguiar's fictional account of the trial, though obviously not in the actual trial records, stands Mintah's book—her testimony of what transpired in those three days of mass execution—which she has clandestinely slipped to the cook's dull-witted assistant, Simon, and he has presented to the court as evidence against the investors in general, and Captain Cunningham in particular. As a counterarchive of the event, however, Mintah's book itself "stands in" for the witness who cannot be present to give an account. At the same time, as evidence of the operations of actuarial calculation and economic necessity, her account is deemed inadmissible. Placed next to the evidence of the Cunningham's ledger, the material artifact that registers the truth of necessity, Mintah's account of the events of those days, and of the motivations and determinations for the execution of atrocity, could carry no force of law. Because she is a slave, her testimony, whether spoken or written, would have been effectively immaterial. "There was the captain's ledger, evidence in black and white and a clause to match concerning the action. How could the insurers not concede defeat?" (138). Confronted with Mintah's book, the investor's attorney must "re-establish the authority of the evidence of the captain's ledger" (143) and remind the court of the letter of the law, of the broad discretion it gives to the captain of the ship in the management of its cargo, and it is for the captain to decide what necessity entails: "'All this was there in the ledger, every fact and act scrupulously recorded for just such an eventuality as this: its disruption by insurers whose sole wish always seems to be that they should benefit from a venture and never have to suffer the consequences if their speculation went awry'" (144). Another "dead book," Mintah's account is presented as counterevidence to the ledger in support of the interests of the insurers, and thus within the logic of exchange subtending the law. But for the reader it likewise stands in for the testimony foreclosed by both the law and the structure of historical narration itself. D'Aguiar suggests that even if the slave's testimony had been heard, or even if it could be recovered today, it is both literally and figuratively *immaterial* before the law.

Law and economy—assured through acts of exemplary violence—play on and profit from the distinction between the material and the immaterial, determining what counts and what does not, who is counted and who is not. Under the actuarial logic that yokes the law to the interests of commerce, the legal dispute over actions taken aboard the *Zong* comes down to a matter of math: "As counsel for the insurers, Mr. Wilkes had completed his calculation of the *Zong*'s claim. The mathematics displeased him" (139). Ironically, on the side of the insurers is the indictment of calculation and insistence on the limits of necessity, the determinate outside of speculation, for "mathematics notwithstanding, there was something not quite right about the circumstances of the claim" (139). The captain's ledger might have indicated the spreading sickness, or might have fabricated necessity, but it does not explain how the slaves fought against their disposal, or whether his actions fall within the parameters of the law. The ambiguity and ambivalence of the law, its capacity to be an instrument of capital, shows up the violence of its determination of means and ends. As a problem for determination, the force of law heralds the specter of necessity and the vicissitudes of exceptionality. For the investors, the "'captain set in motion certain measures that curtailed that disaster, contained it, reversed it'" (144). Meanwhile, Wilkes, the insurer's attorney, argues that the captain's actions generated "'not a fairly won profit from a gentlemanly endeavour, but a profit wrung from a crude interpretation of the law. A law intended to protect ships like the *Zong* from disaster'" (140). Here, however, Wilkes himself gets caught up in a web of contradictions the law cannot tease out when he adds:

> A just ruling would throw out this claim for seeking to exploit the law. What does that law say? It states quite categorically that any measure deemed necessary by the captain can be taken to protect his stock from further loss or damage. It must be admitted that this measure was *extreme.* Not at all necessary. And indecent. . . . It will never be known how many slaves might have recovered from their ailments and gone on to fetch a decent profit at auction. How many men, women and children might have lived or even died from their symptoms, will never be known. Why should this be so? Because the law allows it. And because the captain decided to invoke that law for his own gain and *not* out of necessity as the law maintains. . . . The action itself is so drastic it clearly indicates a concern not for the preservation of stock but of profiteering from the law. (140–41)

For the insurers, trying to carve out a space of protection from within the law, a space that insists on an interminable speculation, a ruling for the investors would stand as a precedent that undermines the very operations of speculation itself. For the investors, equally invested in those same operations, necessity and decision underwritten by the insurers themselves insure their profit. Drawing on the scant remains of the historical archive, *Feeding the Ghosts* provides a reflexive indictment of the logic of calculation, exchange, and necessity at the heart of the law and at the core of the narrative form itself.

Expiation

The final chapters of *Feeding the Ghost* are set in 1833, the year of nominal emancipation for slaves held in the British colonies. This section offers a long reflection on two dominant motifs developed in the narrative but prefigured in the prologue: sea and wood. These chapters recast the events of the three days aboard the *Zong,* and they narrate the weeks, months, and years that followed, as Mintah is taken first to Jamaica and then to Maryland, where she was sold. Eventually able to "purchase" her freedom, Mintah assists runaway slaves making their way to the North in their own search for freedom. Here another kind of calculus emerges, an ethical calculus that indicts the law of profit: Mintah counts each of those conveyed to the North as exemplary figures of those she witnessed tossed into the sea. She then doubles that number to designate her minimal ethical responsibility: “For every one thrown to the sea I multiplied by two in Maryland when I acted as guide” (209). Two hundred and sixty-four bodies transported to freedom, two for every one killed on the *Zong;* two for every mark in the captain's ledger. Mintah then returns to Jamaica to live out her remaining days within the discomforting earshot of the sea. She reclaims her father's craft as a woodworker, a skill she almost lost in the genealogical rupture of colonialism and slavery that carried her from her family. In Jamaica she survives by carving and selling wooden trinkets and figurines to travelers crisscrossing the Atlantic. But as in Maryland, she also puts her skills to use making a singular memorial to those lives lost on board the *Zong,* by producing a set of figures carved in an act of ethical calculation made beyond the laws of exchange value. The wood effigies she carves but refuses to sell or relinquish, indeed hordes within her home, each represent a life lost at sea:

> My hut is full of the things I have made and couldn't bear to part with. Objects stacked in corners of my hut making it even more cramped. I call my house my hold. It is crowded with pieces of wood. The shape of each piece is pulled from the sea of my mind and has been shaped by water, with water's contours. People say they see a figure of some kind, man, woman, or child reaching up out of the depths. They love what I do with wood but cannot keep such a shape in their homes. Such shapes do not quench a thirst. They unsettle a stomach. Fill the eyes with unease. I keep them in my home like guests who will not leave and whom I eventually cannot bear to part with. . . . There are 131 of them. A veritable army. And I have been working on another for months now. . . . I have plans for ten more after that. (208–9)

Mintah's hut replicates the “hold” of the ship while simultaneously representing a kind of ethical recovery; these figures are held in the archive but withheld from circulation; the past is both sustained and displayed but cannot be assimilated or incorporated into commodity form; history unsettles, disturbs, makes demands; the form that our obligation to the past takes resembles, to evoke another idiom borrowed from Derrida, absolute hospitality.[32] The logic of her archive also replicates the structural logic of the example I have been advocating: the singularity of the multiples that stand together by also standing beside themselves in an army that occupies, to repeat Agamben's elegant phrase, "the empty space in which its undefinable and unforgettable life unfolds." The ghastly and ghostly shapes of these uncanny effigies both represent and sustain the singularity of each individual criminal atrocity within the larger atrocity aboard the *Zong*. But their haunting affectivity all but guarantees that they are incapable of circulating as commodities, since potential buyers "cannot keep such a shape in their homes." These fetishes exhibit a kind of purely hewn materiality that forecloses commodity form and its logic of fetishization. They accumulate in Mintah's hut until they are eventually destroyed, along with Mintah herself, in an act of self-immolation by an all-consuming fire. The novel ends with the kind of divine expiation imagined by Granville Sharp with which I began, and by Benjamin, and later Derrida, in the centuries that followed.

The singular, the exceptional, and the exemplary: three ways of standing out and standing alone. But they are not interchangeable, though they are often exchanged in the myriad forms that history takes as it is translated and transferred across the seas and through the centuries. The singular is buried in the example, the exceptional in the exemplary, and the exemplary in the singular. Each haunts the other; each often obliterates the other. The singular, the exceptional, and the exemplary are all violent principles; each one enacts violence on the other, as well as on the past, on the present, and on the future. The exemplary is also a way of "standing in," and as such it is subject to the most violent of figurative displacements. D'Aguiar, like Hartman and Baucom, provides an insistent reminder that exemplary violence is ever the instrument of the law and the law of economic calculation, and both offer a powerful example of what I have called a critical redressive historiography. Are these writers thematizing modes of exchange outside the logic of capital? Absolutely. Are they imagining potentiality beyond the possibilities afforded by the law and the laws of determination? Of course. But I am arguing, further, that their works stage the politics and poetics of exchange in a way that repositions the archive as an exemplary site of entry and of opening up. If this new historiography must work—like its predecessors—from within the archive and from within the problem of violence (poetic, exemplary), it must do so by challenging its own structures of exchange, not by suspending speculation but by exacerbating it. The archive remains the future of colonial redress. Such a history, once unhoused, holds transformative possibilities. One cannot escape the violence, but one can still aspire to justice.

· CHAPTER 2 ·

Living Rough

The Disposition and Dispensation of Aleatory Life

Carceral Assemblages

The history of modern human bio-cargo does not begin or end with colonial slavery, but the Atlantic system proved crucial to the initiation and expansion of strategies of capture, containment, and conversion of human lives into living chattels, and the introduction of new methods of transfer and networks of exchange capable of efficiently and profitably organizing the movement of money and merchandise and the transport of property and populations, whether through capture and enslavement or through the social prescriptions of custody, detention, or internment. The institution of colonial slavery eventually cohered into a biopolitical system that carried entire African communities from inland villages to coastal slave factories and from slave factories to cargo ships harbored offshore; the consignment of hundreds of people in yokes and restraints of the ship's hold, and their conveyance, shackled and manacled, from the stowage decks to the weather deck above, resulted in a callisthenic routine of disciplinary life. These individuals were transferred from slave ship to auction block, then transported from slave auction to slave plantation, from one plantation to another, or to other sites of enclosure ranging across the colonies and "back home" in the colonial metropole. As older forms of capitalist accumulation adapted to changing global conditions, newer forms of human bio-cargo emerged, along with new sites of assemblage: slave factories, slave ships, and slave plantations find corollaries in present-day labor colonies, refugee settlements, and prison camps as well as the extension of their carceral logic into many new human enclosures. Increasingly, these latter are seen not simply as visual analogues of earlier modes of confinement but as historically continuous homologies, that is, not merely formal equivalents but structural derivations.[1]

Few writers have plumbed the historical depths of systemic violence of carceral systems as insistently as Caryl Phillips. Since the early 1980s, in both fiction and nonfiction—in dozens of novels, plays, essays, and interviews—he has recalled acts of atrocity and the atrocious events that play out in state, civil, and private institutions that authorize and execute the capture of human life through technologies of modern human bio-cargo. In the opening section of *Higher Ground* (1989), an unnamed "factor"—the person who negotiates the transport and sale of slaves from the African interior to slavers anchored along the coast—is cast into the dungeon of a slave fort on the late eighteenth-century Gold Coast as reprisal for interfering in the rape of a woman kept as a sexual slave. In the second section of that same novel, set at the height of the American civil rights movement in the 1960s, Rudi Phillips is incarcerated for having, in his words, "tried to liberate some bread from a liquor store"; he is placed in solitary confinement and his unduly long sentence is extended indefinitely due to his refusal to submit to the order of the prison.[2] Likewise, in *Cambridge* (1991), Olumide—whose name is changed to the eponymous Cambridge—is stolen into slavery, subsequently emancipated, then recaptured and resold into slavery through the machinations of a ruthless sea captain and later executed for the murder of a vicious plantation overseer.[3] Beginning with a mournful elegy to the African diaspora violently displaced through capture and enslavement, *Crossing the River* (1993) recounts three distinct stories of personal and collective abandonment set on three continents and over three centuries, each linked to the rupturing force of colonial slavery.[4] *Foreigners* (2007) tracks the fortunes of three historical figures: Francis Barber, who was Samuel Johnson's personal servant and lifelong companion in the eighteenth century; Randy Turpin, the 1951 world boxing champion; and David Oluwale, a Nigerian who immigrated to Leeds in 1949 and whose brutal death in 1969 at the hands of two police officers led to an outcry by black activists against police brutality.[5]

Much of Phillips's fiction shares two formal features. First, they draw together multiple narratives—each discrete in plot, setting, character, and voice, and each utilizing a variety of literary techniques and creative forms—into a single fictional work, most often as a novel.[6] Second, these dispersed narratives find articulation within the long history of colonial modernity, fragments of an irrecoverable "total" history driven by, but also in excess of, the economic forces of capitalist development. While Phillips is reflexively aware that historical narratives of colonialism, slavery, and the slave trade run the risk of aestheticizing the violence that has practically come to define the African Atlantic—and thus unwittingly and uncritically restaging acts of atrocity as spectacles of public entertainment and objects of pornographic consumption—he is equally concerned with the ways in which the agents and institutions of global modernity continue to shape the present through the orchestration of violence historically rooted and formally situated, a condition that cannot go unacknowledged or unaddressed. As discussed in the preceding chapters and addressed again in the next, the primary foundations of the Western social imaginary—law and economy—originate with acts of exception and exemplary violence embedded in systems of exchange that remake human life as modern bio-cargo. By surveying Phillips's prodigious body of historiographic fiction, I will show how the problems of law, economy, and exchange find critical articulation in the creative practices that distinguish black British writing in the post-Thatcher era. His experiments in narrative form offer more than simply reflexive turns and "meta" gestures associated with the "post" of both the postmodern and postcolonial; rather, they express formally the difficult critical terrain across which a redressive historiography must navigate. The implicit formal devices Phillips deploys in his fiction, I argue, compel readers to take their places on the stage of exemplary violence; assume their positions as the object-spectators of such pornographic events; consider their own positions in the economy of violent exemplarity; contemplate the manner by which the exceptional abuse of one person or entire groups of people are performed before the devouring gaze of others; and situate themselves at the very site where colonial violence is staged, stylized, and even accessorized in the circuits of exchange in which the life of human bio-cargo is lived.

For the women and men who broke out of one system of biopolitical enclosure, individually and collectively, who eventually found their own passages to a designated and circumscribed freedom, other forms of human disposability would await: new and surreptitious arrangements of forced labor, new schemes for scaled relocation of target populations, new strategies of social abandonment. By the end of the eighteenth century, new philanthropic organizations, such as the Committee for the Relief of the Black Poor, were established to aid those "blacks in distress," many of whom had been transported to Britain as domestic servants with ambiguous legal status; others had come to England in the aftermath of the American Revolution, having been promised their freedom in exchange for loyalty to the Crown. Philanthropy itself developed into a system for planning and executing a variety of projects to dispose of the "teeming" populations of urban poor through forced immigration, including thousands of black women and men no longer held as slaves now targeted for "repatriation" to West Africa. By the mid-nineteenth century, charitable organizations would be regarded as an essential part of polite civil society. Philanthropy, however, offered yet another mechanism in the manufacture of human bio-cargo, a social apparatus geared toward managing populations, including free black populations, left destitute in the wake of rapid urbanization and a brutal industrialization. Under the guise of "good works," projects of philanthropy effaced their dependence on and attendance to the structural violence on which the law itself relies. Operating under the banners of charity, benevolence, altruism, goodwill or good works, philanthropy expresses a variety of structural failures of modern capitalism and its reliance on colonialism and the plantation system economy, but philanthropy also names another site of articulation in which civil society colludes with the state in the extension of biopolitics into those groups otherwise abandoned by both the market and the law. Philanthropy, in other words, retains its own carceral logic through which it operates as a disciplinary regime in the process of social normalization. In a historical period in which sovereign authority is increasingly qualified, the power over life disseminates well beyond the state, to a variety of local, national, and transnational civil institutions, benevolent societies and corporations.

Consider the opening section of Caryl Phillips's novel *Crossing the River*. Set between 1834 and 1842, "The Pagan Coast" tells the story of Nash Williams, an educated black American who was born into slavery on a Virginia plantation; unexpectedly emancipated by the plantation's owner, Edward Williams; and "repatriated" to the new settlement of Liberia through the aid of the American Colonization Society. In a series of letters to his former master and "spiritual father," Nash vacillates between celebrating the freedoms Liberia promises for freed blacks—the valorization of a life lived outside debt, the rewards of Christian industry and good works, the unrealized potential for material abundance—and describing the poor conditions of the settlement, the declining prospects for the emergent colony, and the material scarcity threatening their very existence. Nash asks repeatedly for Edward to resupply the carefully enumerated provisions he needs to keep his struggling smallholding and mission school running. In the five letters that comprise much of the section, Nash likewise seeks acknowledgment of the worthiness of his endeavor, Edward's responsibility to its success, and Edward's promises to Nash himself. His pleas often ache with the increasing desperation of his requests and the seeming inconsequence of such trivial items:

> Dear Father, perhaps you will please send me one bonnet and an umbrella, if you please. And some cloth to make one white frock, as there is none to be found in this country. These things will not prove difficult for you to get, for there is plenty in America and nothing here. Can you please send some valuable books, such as history, and a dictionary, and writing paper and quills and steel pens. Also flour and pork, and other articles you may think will be of service to me, including a hoe, an axe, some trowels and some hammers. If you, or any of your kind family to whom I am already under so many obligations, shall send anything for me, it shall not be misplaced charity, for provision is scarce.[7]

Within this brief passage we get a sense of the complicated oscillation between basic material want and vital affective need, both of which continue to accumulate as the letters unfold. Indeed, between the first four letters—which largely recount the progress and setbacks of the colony, reflect on the promises of liberty and the perniciousness of slavery, and praise both God and Edward himself—Nash makes at least eight direct appeals for compensation and requests about four dozen quantifiable material items and a number of more general ones. In short, Nash's letters to his "Beloved Benefactor" stage the demand for redress.

Through the enumeration of specific material items, which also gesture toward the obligations renounced in the wake of Edward's undisclosed and therefore incalculable moral failings, *Crossing the River* recasts a now familiar claim to the irredeemable historical debt that follows from the irreparable injustices of colonial slavery. By recounting his losses, needs, and wants, Nash indexes those historical accounts yet to be settled. His acts of material, ethical, and affective accounting underscore the consequences of leaving one's debts in arrears even as it reinforces the paradox that such debts can never be fully repaid. In their tone these letters infer a complicated series of affective exchanges between Nash and Edward that, in effect, leaves Nash stranded in a sense of debt: an affective debt that now undercuts, but also underwrites, the material exchanges of/as property that continue to bind them to one another. That is, through their evocation of material scarcity and affective deprivation, the feelings of loss and sense of abandonment, Nash's letters enter into a complicated economy of debt, reparation, and redress in order to lay bare not only the unjust material circumstances under which Nash continues to labor but the displaced and dispersed affective conditions that tie the language of charity to the problem of inheritance. For his letters go unanswered and his repeated appeals for help unheeded, the reader ultimately discovers, because they were never received; they were, in fact, withheld by Edward's wife in her attempt to disavow the perverse truth of mutual, if uneven, affection: ambiguously sexual and paternal. Neither his philanthropic spirit nor abolitionist ideals can account for his decision to exile Nash to the precarious new settlement in Liberia; rather, Edward is motivated by the will to banish his own violent past to the colonial periphery. Edward's Christian charity relies upon, even as it disavows, the ambiguities of philanthropy as a function of biopolitics and the valences of exemplary violence that order and secure the system under which life as human bio-cargo is made possible.

Crossing the River opens and closes with a mournful evocation of African complicity in the transatlantic slave trade, as a father laments that in an act of "desperate foolishness," he has sold his three children to the captain of a slave ship. Allegorical in a Jamesonian sense, the brief proem and coda serve as an interpretive key for understanding the historical transcoding that binds the three otherwise discrete narratives scattered over time and across the diaspora but persist in the political unconscious.[8] Having "jettisoned" his children "at this point, where the tributary stumbles and swims into the sea," the father confesses, "Soon after, the chorus of a common memory began to haunt me." As he continues to describe his profound sense of loss and feeling of guilt, time expands to encompass a broader historical scale and the personal traumas of a father and his children is recast as the moment of rupture into the long history of the African diaspora forever evicted from home:

> For two hundred and fifty years I have listened to the many-tongued chorus. And occasionally, among the sundry restless voices, I have discovered those of my own children. My Nash. My Martha. My Travis. Their lives fractured. Sinking hopeful roots into difficult soil. For two hundred and fifty years I have longed to tell them: Children, I am your father. I love you. But understand. There are no paths in water. No signposts. There is no return. To a land trampled by the muddy boots of others. To a people

> encouraged to war among themselves. To a father consumed with guilt. You are beyond. Broken-off, like limbs from a tree. (1–2)

The names of the narrator's three children—Nash, Martha, Travis—will reappear as the names of the novel's protagonists in each of its three sections, set respectively in early nineteenth-century Liberia, the late nineteenth-century American West, and mid-twentieth-century Britain. Although the African father, whose lament frames *Crossing the River,* is situated in the distant past—at the site of collective trauma and a moment of historical rupture—he foretells the fate of his lost children and in the novel's concluding pages anticipates a bleak future lived in diaspora. In a brief epilogue the narrator offers an expansive historical vision expressed in fragmented images and staccato phrases presaging horrifying events unfolding over the centuries to follow, events that now comprise our past. But like Benjamin's angel of history, in the final lines of the novel the father realizes that there is no going back, no way of undoing what has been done, just an appeal, a demand, a haunting: "A guilty father, always listening. There are no paths in water. No signposts. There is no return. A desperate foolishness. The crops failed. I sold my beloved children. . . . But they arrived on the far bank of the river, loved" (237).[9] As the voices of his children shout out to him from the future, so too do they call upon us from the past. The redressive imaginary Phillips offers rests upon the reader's response to this call.

Phillips has suggested that historical redress resides in the prospect of meeting one's obligation to the past by facilitating social transformation in the present, paving the way for new possibilities in the future. In an interview shortly after the publication of *Crossing the River,* Phillips asserts that as a writer,

> you do become aware of the possibility of being somebody who can identify a history and perhaps do something about redressing the imbalance of some of the ills and falsehoods that have been perpetuated by others about your own history. Beyond that, I think a writer really has a responsibility to at least acknowledge that he was produced by very specific social circumstances. . . . One shouldn't feel a guilt for one's history and one shouldn't feel ashamed of one's history, one should just take responsibility for it.[10]

Phillips has endeavored to satisfy his own obligation to history by bringing into focus those margins of the past—those marginalized and made vulnerable through systems and practices of inclusion and exclusions endemic to colonial modernity—that survive into the present and trouble the production of dominant historical knowledge. At the same time, he holds onto the possibilities afforded by a careful archaeology of those archives and archival practices that serve the interest of dominant historiography, placing them in relation to those other modes of historical feeling almost always violently effaced. His narrative strategy is most often one of imitation, but in a mode that postcolonial scholars have long understood as also disruptive.[11]

Phillips appears ambivalently committed to and agnostic about his historical sources. On the one hand, he recognizes the profound unreliability of their accounts; on the other, his creative practice endeavors to stage the subtle ironies and unnoticed paradoxes that were ultimately so destructive to so many. His loyalty to the archive performs an utter *dis*loyalty to dominant history. In *Cambridge,* Phillips borrows from a nineteenth-century public account of an Englishwoman's voyage to the Caribbean to attend to the plantation over which her father has served as an absent landlord. Mrs. Carmichael's widely circulated travel journal, *Domestic Manners and Social Condition of the White, Coloured, and Negro Population of the West Indies* (1833), Maria Nugent's *Lady Nugent's Journal of Her Residence in Jamaica from 1801 to 1805* (1839), and Monk Lewis's *Journal of a West Indian Proprietor* (1834) serve as the bases for Emily Cartwright's narrative.[12] Like Emily, Lewis had inherited an estate in the Caribbean, and also like Emily he at first imagines that his sojourn there will help ameliorate the conditions of slavery. In the second section of the novel, Phillips provides a narrative account of Cambridge's experiences in rough imitation of Equiano's *Interesting Narrative.* A third account is afforded by a fragment of "official" documentation of Cambridge's crime and subsequent execution, which is modeled on a variety of legal and personal accounts of West Indian slave laws and criminal cases.[13] Quite strikingly, Emily's narrative rarely intersects with Cambridge's; they are almost opaque to one another. Yet their respective accounts demonstrate through their tenuous connections the ways in which multiple historical accounts (dominant and minor) do not always line up.

It is within the context of the nonaligned that Carmichael, Lewis, and Equiano recount such radically different experiences of life lived in the colonial periphery—the variant gendering of the circumstances of Carmichael's journeying out to and Lewis's long residence in the Caribbean; the racialized condition of enslavement that Equiano is captured (and recaptured) within but struggles mightily against—disjunctures that necessarily reverberate throughout the novel. Phillips emphasizes such historical conjunctions and disjunctions, as well as the circumstances that give rise to them and consequences that follow from them, as sequencing events in the long history of capital and attendant operations of biopower. In reading across Phillips's literary career I am primarily concerned with the historical moments that Phillips is self-reflexively bringing together through the imitation of these older narrative models and forms. I have emphasized the circulation of these various historical tracts and pamphlets in order to think about how Phillips adopts a set of formal strategies drawn from eighteenth- and nineteenth-century sources—whether Mary Carmichael's journal or John Newton's ship's logs—as a way of bringing history back into the public realm, such that the exigencies of our contemporary moment of neocolonial displacements is likewise unhoused through the circulation of his innovative narrative forms.[14]

Here I want to turn to those novels in which Phillips explicitly returns to those representative late eighteenth- and early nineteenth-century treatises on slavery before and after the abolition of the trade cited above, which all insist on recounting the legacies of violence that are not as easy to erase as the property and criminal laws that enabled them. My discussion of Phillips will move between legal, economic, and theoretical discourses within which colonial violence, and the plantation system in particular, extends to the biopolitical order as such, a regime of power still operating today. Yet, as much as Phillips draws from the historical documentation of the history of colonialism, slavery, and the slave trade, the narratives are not reducible to a pastiche of these prior forms. Phillips's concern for the conditions of present-day diasporic subjects, and for opening up possibilities for their future (despite his famous recalcitrant pessimism), speaks through these historically grounded narratives.[15] Thus, I am not simply interested in outlining Phillips's particular historical sources, many of which have been acknowledged by Phillips himself or identified by scholars in the field.[16] Rather, I am interested in thinking about how those documents in circulation in the nineteenth century, and the issues and debates they publicize, provide the foundation for his formal innovations. Phillips's metafictional and metahistorical concerns are ever in direct conversation with those earlier discourses. That is, I will compare briefly the form of these older documentary narratives in relation to the forms that Phillips adopts form them. In doing so, I hope to underscore not the sourcing of historical documents or testimonies but how the conditions of narrative form itself circumscribe possibility for confronting injustice in the stormy seas of capitalist accumulation and development, as well as the biopolitical order that underwrites the lives of these narrative subjects.

Carry-ons and Throwaways

Cambridge provides an apposite context in which to return to that line of thought in Giorgio Agamben that links the operations of biopolitics to the exercise of the law, a relationship that finds its most material instantiation in the rise of the "camp" as a system and structure or the ordering and organization of discreet populations. The camp, which serves as a spatial metaphor for the structured manifestation of the carceral logic fundamental to modern biopower, remains a powerful model for thinking about the historical relationship between dominant models of exclusion, isolation, and control, from the dungeons of the slave factory to the corporate prison.[17] The logic of the camp organizes our relations to social space as such, and it is extended to infinite arrangements of internment, detention, imprisonment, whether in the forms of urban planning, immigration law, sentencing guidelines, or the regulation of working conditions and labor migrations. The utter abjection of human life that underwrites the operations of the camp expresses the inimical logic of biopolitical modernity, wherein the decisions forged in the crucible of economic calculation, and in the name of capitalist development, find material instantiation in an array of populations deemed absolutely disposable. If the camp has come to represent the topological outcome of the application of biopower in a seemingly endless array of forms across the globe, it is also the point of encryption and inscription of the logic of the state. Such sites of archivization are posited precisely through what Colin Dayan describes as "the sorcery of the law," which is "most instrumental when most fantastic and most violent when most spectral."[18]

Caryl Phillips has long endeavored to describe such scenes of social life performed within the structure of social death, and he has insisted on a structural homology between multiple historical sites in the exceptional instrumentalization of human life. The opening prologue of *Cambridge,* for instance, highlights the economic arrangements that motivate the various actions in the novel, and the manner in which these economic arrangements find form in the technologies of biopower. The prologue itself is something of an "apology" for the narrator of the first part of the novel, Emily Cartwright (whose name we only discover much later in the novel), explaining her unwanted, arranged engagement to a much older man, a wealthy friend of her father. In other words, the novel opens upon a decidedly economic settlement between men: in her view, Emily has been auctioned off, in what we are implicitly asked to imagine is a gender analogue to slavery. The brief prologue gives an account of this conventional familial pact, which sets the terms of her narrowly circumscribed agency as a woman, even as a woman of considerable wealth. Yet, by traveling abroad to the colonies, Emily retains considerable authority, as the narrative that follows lays bare. By removing Emily to her father's West Indian plantation, Phillips underscores the economic determinations of all social relations that will dominate in the novel—between father and daughter, husband and wife, master and slave—and as the novel unfolds the language of race and blood becomes increasingly central to these determinations.

Because *Cambridge* provides a polyvocal narrative of individual sacrifice and social obligation, economic speculation and ethical decision, all within the confines of the slave plantation system, it seems to me an apt text to pursue in this consideration of the biopolitics of human cargo. Phillips is quite explicitly interested in both public and private articulations of power, social administration and governmentality, domesticity and property management, and bodily discipline and social regulation—all regimes of the biopolitical. From the opening prologue the language of the novel draws the reader's attention to the normalizing and disciplining technologies that link the duties of the eighteenth- and nineteenth-century bourgeois woman to those of the slave within the broad canvas of the era's social order. Describing the contingencies that bring Emily to the Caribbean in the first place, the speaker—gliding between a third-person voice and interior monologue—informs us that her father has decided "that she should travel to his West Indian estate and on her return marry Thomas Lockwood . . . a fifty-year-old widower with three children as a mode of transport through life" (3). Emily is entirely aware that by being "offered"—like a bargain or a bond, not a gift—to a man "ably provided for" but twenty years her senior, the marriage would not only guarantee her own mode of "transport" but also "insure [her father's] own future" (4). The language emphasizes the role that women served in the entire domestic economy and the significance of that domestic economy to the broader social economy that "bonded" the generational transfer of wealth through the wedding band (contract), a system of exchange carried out with the subtlety of "the rude mechanics of horse-trading," Emily observes (4). Moreover, the rhetoric suggests the translation of the institution of marriage for its earlier, feudal form into a modern biopolitical one, not only safeguarding one family's fortunes by buying and/or selling into that of another but also securing the social order and population as such. Emily's father flippantly jokes about "resid[ing] under the auspices of a 'petticoat government,'" but Phillips want to make sure that the reader is thinking about the overlapping and converging articulations that bind the governance of the household to the governance of the state and drawing the domestic sphere into a new type of public one. No matter how structurally entangled are the public and private within the order of modern capitalism, when the old lines are crossed and distinctions blurred they must be forcefully, if anxiously, reestablished; thus her father's nervous comment about the tyranny of a "petticoat government."

The derisive reference to the frightening specter of a "petticoat government" is not a throwaway; the expression can hardly even veil the growing alarm, since at least the eighteenth century, over rapidly changing technologies of state and civil authority and who will, and more importantly, who will not, have access to it. Emily's father seems to understand the new authority Emily can claim when she arrives in the West Indies and how such empowerment is unlikely to be ceded upon her return. It might be worth noting that Monk Lewis had, with an equally anxious derision, dismissed an incident of insubordination by a group of enslaved women at his Jamaican estate as a "petticoat rebellion."[19] The line of distinction between a petticoat government in the home or a petticoat rebellion on the plantation fades quickly in Phillips's novel, from the moment Emily arrives at her father's estate. Ultimately, Phillips wants to draw our attention to the same overlapping and converging articulations that bring the plantation system into the biopolitical system, beginning with those articulations that appear of the human body: "The truth was she was fleeing the lonely regime which fastened her into backboards, corsets and stays to improve her posture. The same friendless regime which advertised her as an ambassadress of grace" (4). On the one hand, she names the instruments of bodily discipline, invented for the purpose of "improvement." On the other hand, she places them at the center of marriage as a sex-gender system, but she does so in the language of the state; marriage is imagined a regime and Emily its ambassadress, a posture, of sorts, she will occupy on her arrival abroad. Phillips evokes the disciplinary "shaping" of the commodified female body, while simultaneously analogizing the slave's bondage.[20] Later, on board the merchant ship that will take her to the West Indies, Emily describes the straps used to "lash" her onto the "narrow plank" that serves as a bed (8). By describing those lashed into their uncertain beds, the novel asks us to also imagine those shackled in the hold of the slave ship. Analogy, though, is inadequate as a term of comparison; rather, Phillips seems to be *homologizing* the relationship between middle-class women sold into marriage and forced into domestic labor and the slave stolen into servitude and bound to plantation labor. That is, the comparison is not simply of like kind but of a common structural foundation. Biopolitics, as a social operation within capital, names such a structure. In the reading that follows I will develop the idea of biopolitics in a way that underscores the discursive knot of gender, sexual, and racial politics through which colonial governmentality is made possible.

The first section of *Cambridge,* after this initial prologue, recounts Emily Cartwright's voyage to her father's West Indian plantation, and her planned three-month stay on the island. But it begins with a detailed account of her Atlantic crossing, and of the death of her "lady's maid," Isabella. Emily is appalled by the conditions on board the ship, which she describes as "a perfectly chaotic world of men and freight," commanded by a captain who is "no doubt the veteran of much trafficking" (7). Once again, Emily recognizes her place in economic terms, as yet another item of cargo in transit across the Atlantic. Determined to record her observations of both the voyage and her months on her father's plantation in a journal, which we are presumably now reading, Emily hopes to provide "a better account for the use of my father what pains and pleasures are endured by those whose labour enables him to continue to indulge himself in the heavy-pocketed manner to which he has become accustomed" (7). She is keenly aware not only of the arrangement of the slave plantation economy but also of the heated debates between abolitionists and colonialists around the turn of the nineteenth century about the brutality of slavery and of the systemic delinquency brought about by landlord absenteeism on these Caribbean estates; she is also aware of the manner in which these debates circulated in tracts and lecture tours, both of which she hopes to capitalize upon:

> Perhaps my adventuring will encourage Father to accept the increasingly common, though abstract, English belief in the iniquity of slavery. It is these days heard abroad, and argued with much vigour, that the lordship over one's own person is a blessing far beyond mere food and shelter. However, to many of these *lobbyists,* slavery is simply a notional term to be equated with whatever propaganda they have read in prose and verse. It is therefore unsurprising that despite the outcry raised by their communal voices, there remain many persons scattered throughout our kingdom who inwardly cling to their old prejudices, and secretly mourn over actual or designed reforms. (7–8)

The passage is striking in the number of issues contained if not conflated within it—about absenteeism, the delegation of authority to an overseer, the circulation of abolitionist tracts ("propaganda in prose and verse"), the reforms of the 1820s (which helps date the narrative to about the third decade of the nineteenth century), among others. If the passage reads as a little too didactic and self-conscious, it is because Phillips is imitating the style of such pamphlets, or demonstrating the way in which Emily's attitudes have been shaped by the rhetoric and discourse of these debates in broad circulation at the time.

Phillips is quite self-conscious in weaving such historical debates into his narrative, yet the style of discourse is ascribed as an "authentic" aspect of Emily's voice, as she tries to establish her own authority—authority as a narrator, as a landowner, as a woman who is asked (quite inexplicably) to oversee her father's estate. Indeed, the passage's didacticism resonates with Phillips's historical sources, such as Mrs. Carmichael's *Domestic Manners in the West Indies* or Monk Lewis's *Journal of a West Indian Proprietor.* At the same time, Emily's journal is marked by its similarity to popular "sentimental" works of its time, for instance in the way that her saccharine evocation of Englishness is set in contrast to the colonial exotic as she quotes from Henry Nelson Coleridge's *Six Months in the West Indies, in 1825*: "O my country, I have no pride but that I belong to thee, and can write my name in the muster-roll of mankind, an Englishman. If thou wert ten times more cloudy, and rainy and bleak, I should still prefer thy clouds and thy storms to the spicy gardens of the Orient" (8).[21] Throughout the narrative, Emily vacillates between expressing her extreme class privilege (disappointed that Isabella's illness leaves her without a servant, prevailing on a cabin boy to bring her morning tea) and exhibiting her uncritical class awareness—treating Isabella as servant one moment and dearest friend the next. There is a privileged complacency to Emily's description of the violence she confronts, whether it is the violence of the sea, the death of her trusted servant, or the fortunes of the sailors aboard the ship. Consider, for instance, the jarring ambivalence of Emily's appreciation of "nature's new delights," as she refers to her experience of marine life and maritime travel:

> The sailors caught a dolphin, the heavenliest creature that goes upon fins, but attempted to do so without the traditional spear. A line was fastened to the stern and baited with salt-pork, but the dolphin is a large and powerful fish. Through a natural fear that this graceful beauty might break the line and flee, the decision to toss the spear was taken. This goddess of the deep was soon wrestled onto the deck where her bright colours were observed and admired, that is until the loss of blood caused them to fade and the cook made ready to prepare her for dinner. (14–15)

Such complacency will turn to utter disdain later in the novel; but here, at the beginning, we already see that Emily has a striking capacity to express emotional pain and longing, but then to regain almost instantly her sense of adventure and pleasure. On another occasion, after the death of her "beloved" Isabella, she claims, "Tropicus has indeed revealed to us a new world, the beauty of which has gone no small way to mollifying the pain which is daily lacerating my heart" (15). But in a mere couple of days (for the reader a mere page), the deceased Isabella has been affectively forgotten, and reduced by abstraction into another disposable commodity, and their relationship rendered purely economic: "I have grown accustomed to bathing myself, and executing other tedious duties, for there is nobody on board to whom I might turn and offer employment. I long to arrive in the islands, where I shall engage a servant to take up where Isabella left off" (16). She shows a similar ambivalence about the fate of those slaves stolen from Africa, writing first, "Of late I have thought much of this ocean, whose breast has supported many a ship heavy with slaves. The torn roots of these *children of the sun* has occasioned the stain of *the institution* to mark first their native soil, then bleed across the waters to deface the Americas." In the next breath, however, she appears to have entirely forgotten such slaves: "There will be much to discover on arriving in tropical America, but I am engaged to spend only a three-month sojourn. I am therefore set apart from those projectors who visit the West Indies to either make or mend their fortune" (16).

Indeed, as a cipher for the most common views of colonial landowners, Emily poses considerable challenges for the reader, who must negotiate the jarring between what she reads in Emily's narrative and what she knows about colonial history. Upon her arrival at her unnamed island destination, which she characteristically describes as "entering a dark tropical unknown" (22), the narrative begins its long account of life in the West Indies, again drawn from the historical sources of Lewis and Carmichael, among others. Hers is a narrative attentive to the details of island and plantation life, told through a voice at increasing ease with conventional discourses of race and racial stereotypes she had earlier criticized. Readers no doubt cringe with discomfort as her racist commentary unfolds. Consider, for instance, the following exemplary remark: "The negro brought with him a water melon whose taste I could not suffer. It had about it a Shylocky taste of raw flesh" (17). In this instance, the evocation of one of the most long-standing of black stereotypes is matched by an anti-Semitic one still in circulation if centuries out of date—where the prejudices of *Othello* meet those of *The Merchant of Venice.*[22]

The stereotypes of black depravity and criminality that emerge in fact point toward but also obscure the way that race functions within the biopolitical order. That is, Emily's rhetoric naturalizes her opinions about the slaves and free blacks residing on the island but functions in the narrative as a reminder of the role that racial discourses played in the consolidation of the colonial system. Emily supposes, for instance, that the house slave Stella's assertion that she did not know her father because he was sold off to another estate is perhaps "her *black* way of disguising some greater embarrassment" and that the "mixed" paternity of Stella's own children demonstrates that "negro relations would appear to have much in common with those practiced by animals in the field, for they seem to find nothing unnatural in breeding with whomever they should stumble upon" (36). Such attitudes obscure the biopolitical order of the plantation that restricted marriage between slaves and saw the brutal sexual abuse of female slaves by male overseers and owners. This view of sexual and genealogical license is reinforced by Stella's desire to be called "Aunt Stella," a promiscuous use of familial title that disturbs Emily's sense of propriety (36). Yet Emily comes to see Stella as her most reliable servant, and like Isabella earlier, comes to imagine her as a loyal friend: "Stella's loyalty is, I am led to understand, typical of her people. It would appear that Mr Wilberforce and his like have been volleying well wide of the mark, for the greatest fear of the black is not having a master whom they know they can turn to in times of strife. The knowledge of who and where one's master is affords the black status." She adds a moment later, "The blacks are so well aware of the comforts that are to be enjoyed under *massa*'s rule, that many, particularly those beyond the prime of life, will never accept manumission" (37). The narrator blinds herself to much of what transpires on her plantation and in her own home. Disavowal becomes the most prominent mode through which Emily recounts plantation life.[23]

The narrator's observations, of course, place the inhabitants of the island, both black and white, colonizer and colonized, under her gaze, with all the implications this brings with it. As Homi Bhabha insists, colonial discourses, like those ventriloquized by Emily, depend upon assertions of fixity (racial, cultural, historical) in constituting or representing the other. But at the same time, fixity creates a paradox by requiring rigidity or stability of the dominant order, on the one hand, and the threat of "disorder, degeneracy, and daemonic repetition," on the other (and on the part of the other). The stereotype is the dominant strategy of fixity, which likewise demonstrates this paradox: it is a form of knowledge that is always "already known" but must be "anxiously repeated," such that we are once again in the terrain of ambivalence and disavowal. "For it is the force of ambivalence," Bhabha tells us, "that gives the colonial stereotype its currency: ensures its repeatability in changing historical and discursive conjunctures; informs its strategies of individuation and marginalization; produces that effect of probabilistic truth and predictability which, for the stereotype, must always be in excess of what can be empirically proved or logically construed."[24] Indeed, the stereotype is the ruse of biopolitical discourse. For example, Emily is simultaneously attracted and revolted, aroused and repulsed, by local dress, especially that of the slaves. What she experiences upon her arrival in the colony is the ambivalence produced by both an epistemological and an ontological break, one that simultaneously marks an entirely new way of being and a rupture in her capacity to comprehend. And yet it is through the colonial episteme that Emily recounts her experiences on the island, complete with quite recognizable stereotypes of the unclean, savage other in need of proper training. By linking the role of racial stereotypes to the need to produce "probabilistic truth" and the necessity of biopolitical "predictability," as Bhabha suggests, I want to emphasize the way in which biopower manages economic and social risk through the body of the slave. Biopolitics applies strategic "truths" that in turn authorize the production of colonial knowledge.

The discourse on race and colonial society is wrought through the language of the visual, where all one need do to discern the "truth" of the slave or the slave population is to *look*. Emily is encouraged to observe at every turn, and indeed the stated purpose of this account is to provide her observations. By the end of the novel it is clear that observation, and the entire epistemological apparatus of empirical accounting, will unravel. Emily draws our attention precisely to the epistemological undercurrent of her observations, and of all such narratives of colonial life in circulation among an English public. As a narrator, Emily contrasts and then conflates observation and explanation, emphasizing the metonymic logic through which the public came to understand plantation life. The narrative emphasizes the logic of dissemination through which reportage operates. "Under the guidance of Mr Brown," Emily tells the reader, "I was able to observe all the tools, utensils, and instruments employed in this industry, but it not being the season I was unable to see the process in full operation. However, Mr Brown's explanation was so thorough that not only do I feel confident that I might explain the mysteries of this process to any stranger, but I am persuaded that I must myself have observed it in action!" (83). The thick description provided by writers like Monk Lewis and Mrs. Carmichael treated such partial observations as a complete explanation and imagined that their limited understanding of a local process could provide them with a view of the "full operation" of colonial life. We can easily imagine which implements Emily might have seen, and those she likely did not in fact see, as well as those instruments of torture she did not want to see. Nor were those colonial adventurers, upon whose accounts Emily's narrative is based, especially self-aware or critical of the episteme through which their narrow observations were translated into discursive knowledge. Phillips is metacritically drawing the reader's attention to the paradox of reportage as a form. We see the slip from observation to knowledge early in the novel in Emily's short trip from the shore to the plantation. Here she is subject to "a short but edifying lecture" that recounts the fate of the native Carib Indians who "had to be dispatched" because of their refusal to be subdued by Europeans engaged in their civilizing and economic mission, and who are described to Emily in the most savage terms, as "fierce, superstitious and vengeful, ready to vent their anger on any and everything, animate or inanimate," who "displayed an implacable opposition to correction," and who refused the "improvements of civilized life" (24). That the indigenous population was deemed unsuitable for modern economic life reinforces Emily's belief in the need for careful and rigorous biopolitical regulation of that population imported to take their place.

The Artifice and Artifacts of the Law

Throughout the first section of the novel, the narrator emphasizes the management of plantation life and worries over the decline of the colonial economy. Mr. McDonald in particular warns Emily of the growing problem of absentee planters, and contrasts the attitude of the French, who consider the island colonies their "homes," to the English, who see their residence as a temporary exile or who rarely, if ever, visit their overseas properties. "These men of the privileged pigmentation, who eschew the slightest labour as not only painful but degrading, have of late begun to exhaust their scant credit in England, transferring their holdings to the jurisdiction of agents, managers, overseers, and book-keepers. They are now happy to see their properties maintained in any way, so long as they continue to reap a small reward while some profit remains" (50). Because economic contingency rests in part upon those unpredictable determinations of the population and the variability of society, biopolitics can be viewed as a technology of risk management. The aleatory economy is, the narrator suggests, perhaps ultimately at the mercy of social entropy. Thus, as Emily continues to listen to Mr. McDonald's warnings, she comes to see not only the danger of absenteeism but also the immanent collapse of the colonial plantation economy itself:

> According to Mr McDonald the day of profitable exploitation of West Indian sugar is in its eventide, due in part to trading restrictions, and in part to the new age of industry dawning in England. Thus, fewer men of caliber are wont to appear in the tropics, and the dire consequences of abandoning control to others are everyday visible. Throughout the region places once of honour and trust are being gradually filled by mediocrities and scoundrels. Multiple office-holding has apparently become commonplace and is being carried out to extravagant lengths, as self-created lawyers,

> self-educated physicians, and venal merchants carry the day. The good doctor swears that at any moment the legislative and administrative organization of our own island is likely to collapse, and he is sure that there can be few local estates not now hopelessly entangled in debt, and indeed he insists that many are probably mortgaged beyond their real value. (50)

McDonald unwittingly describes almost precisely the situation on Emily's estate: her father is an absentee landlord, receives a "healthy annual income" from his property, but has also borrowed heavily against it to finance ventures back in England, and Emily does in fact remind him of this. Nonetheless, McDonald asserts that "absenteeism [is] the primary cause of social breakdown, for just as one could not run a school without a headmaster, or a monarchical system without a monarch, one could not hope to run these tropical possessions without commitment to responsibility at the highest level" (51). The problem of the management of the colonial plantation, then, is treated as an extension of the problem of imperial sovereignty. The "mistreatment" of the slaves, he maintains, is due to the mismanagement of economic affairs by men in "the lower orders," those "degraded," creolized whites and recent working-class immigrants from abroad who view the slaves as there merely to provide for their own ease and comfort. The failure of this new managerial class, McDonald suggests, is in their inability to comprehend the broader economic and social order, in which the colonial plantation serves economic interests back in the metropolis.

But for all the aspersions on the character of the white population living in the West Indies, what is striking about the narrator's account of these discussions is the way in which Phillips has turned, almost didactically, to the most prominent points made by both pro- and antislavery proponents, catalogued in the many pamphlets, tracts, speeches, and accounts of slavery produced and circulated at the time. Consider, for instance, the tenor of McDonald's sentiment toward African slaves: "Constant association with an inferior race will weaken the moral fibre of a white man and debase the quality of his life. A mere glance should be sufficient to convince an observer that the West Indian negro has all the characteristics of his race. That he steals, lies, is witless, incompetent, irresponsible, habitually lazy, and wantonly loose in his sexual behavior, is apparent to even the most generous of those who would take *sambo*'s part. It is only the dread of corporeal punishment which keeps these incorrigible thieves in order" (52).

The attitudes of these planters offer, really, a primer on colonialist discourse of the eighteenth and nineteenth centuries circulating in the print media. That McDonald's is the language appropriate to the plantation is suggested in the original tracts that underlie Phillips's historical reckoning. It is, therefore, not surprising that Emily's narrative should turn to the issue of miscegenation, the physical manifestation of social mixing that so alarms McDonald. This time Emily paraphrases rather than quotes him: "the clearest evidence of West Indian moral turpitude was to be found in the social evil of miscegenation, a practice contrary to the Anglo-Saxon nature, and one that gave rise to a sub-species of hybrid. . . . The female offspring invariably take the name of *housekeeper* and in turn become the mistresses of white men, while the male offspring merely drag out an existence as scarcely tolerated spaniels permitted to lick the feet of their masters" (52). What is striking here, and throughout these passages describing plantation life, is the way in which social practices that emanate from colonial law and social practice are either naturalized or seen as an example of the agency of Caribbean blacks.

Like McDonald—and like Phillips's source, Mrs. Carmichael—Emily recounts the systemic management of the island population, both white and black, through the most typical colonial idioms, in particular through the language of racial purity. She notes that with the abolition of the trade, "there are littered about these shores fewer and fewer Africans," and that now "the great majority are *creoles*" (38). Once again evoking the specter of social decline and economic entropy, Emily tries to recover the potentiality of a productive creolization. "One important advantage of this *creolization* of the negro," she explains, "is that the pure African has a far greater tendency towards madness and eventual suicide" (38). Emily, indeed, describes the island slaves in the discourse of animal husbandry and domestication, and dwells on imagined weaknesses or supposed propensity toward crime:

> Unfortunately, I have heard several reports, some indeed furnished by negro servants themselves, that the black is addicted to theft and deceit at every opportunity. The average negro would not feel out of place in London's infamous thieves' kitchen of Seven Dials. His thievishness is more than a match for all the laws that can emanate from any parliament, and even when apprehended in the act the black will invariably fly into a passion if you refuse him the

> honour of being able to take up the book and swear to the truth of what he knows to be false. This prevalent knavery is considered by many negroes to be no crime so long as it passes undiscovered. So adroit are they in this that the shame lies in their being apprehended rather than in the act itself. Sad to say, this pilfering habit is apparently engrafted onto them by elder negroes, who consider the teaching of ingenious theft a most necessary part of their parental duties. (39)

The language of "engrafting" is a curious discursive shift from other places in the novel where Emily speaks through the language of blood and race science. Here the stereotype of black criminality passes pedagogically from one generation to the next, but the trope used to describe the genealogy of black criminality links it to husbandry and the notion of "management." The passage also points toward Cambridge's narrative in the next section of the novel, and the account of his residence in England.

The story of colonial exploitation and extraction is told as a narrative of the biological fitness of one race to toil and another to govern, of one class to work and another to rule. Racial "suitability" is treated as economic fact. So convoluted is economic and racial discourse, however, that one might be inclined to describe it as a discursive anarchy, a discourse gone awry. It is at that point where this evolving racial discourse and the interests of the biopolitical order do not quite meet that the most pronounced element of contingency is seen—the threat from within biopolitics itself. Indeed, there is something about the excessiveness of race itself as a discursive bodily configuration and the language of economic surplus that meet in Emily's description of plantation intemperance, indulgence, and immoderation of all the islands' inhabitants. At the same time, Emily's arrival on the island is an enormous source of disorder, just as her refusal to marry disrupts her father's economic arrangement with Lockwood. Emily herself recognizes the possibility of her own disruptive presence on the plantation: "I insisted that the circumstances of my being on the island could not, of course, be permitted to unseat the established system of discipline which secures the labour and obedience of the slaves" (121).

In her attempt at producing a publishable pamphlet or convincing lecture for an insatiable English market, Emily produces a kind of proto-ethnography of the slave communities, emphasizing those aspects of the social order most intimately linked to social reproduction and political containment. While she shows little interest in understanding the lives of Africans before their arrival in the Caribbean, she tracks the fate of those slaves who arrive with almost prurient interest in detail. She describes their auction on the island dock quite tangibly, and acknowledges their fate once auctioned to a merchant or landowner. She exhibits a typical fetishistic interest in the way in which the slave was marked as property and either castrated or preserved for reproduction: "Some owners have a fancy for maiming their African slaves, some branded them, pulled out some teeth, or wounded them a little with shot, while others wished them whole in order that they might *stud* the stock" (40). The emphasis again is on the slave's status as chattel, as the ultimate instrument in the reproduction of the colonial order. Emily likewise depicts the order and organization of field labor and the subsistence allowances given to the slave "by law," which, she adds, "reliev[es] the estate a little from the heavy burden of feeding as well as clothing them" (40). She describes the disciplinary arrangement of field slaves, the system of overseers and drivers, and a "head driver," "who carries with him the emblem of his rank and dignity, a polished staff upon which he can lean." She deems him "the most important personage in the slave population of an estate" (40–41). "Ideally," she adds, "he should be an athletic man of respected character, clean in his person and habits; if possible a *creole* long used to field-work, one marked out for his sobriety, patience and general civility. Most important, he should always show respect towards white people, and suffer no undue freedom of conversation or indulgence in trivial humour from those beneath him. A negro-man such as this must indeed be difficult to acquire" (41). The irony, of course, is that Cambridge exhibits all of the qualities identified in the first sentence and none in the second. Cambridge has also repeatedly refused the "honor" of serving as head driver; thus, like Emily, he has become an agent of disorder, an emblem of the contingency of order as such. Indeed, the irony deepens when Emily witnesses the use of the cattle-whip by Mr. Brown:

> As they began to march I made note that male and female were naked down to the waist, and I could often observe where the application of the lash had sculpted a hideous pattern of weals upon their broad backs. The *children of the sun* are mortals, and accordingly possess their share of failings and must endure the crack of the inhuman whip. But its use must be judicious, for there can be little more offensive to the human spirit than to observe the

> cattle-whip being inflicted with all the severity of vindictive malice. This, I must admit, I was unfortunate enough to witness, the villain bestowing the rope's-end being none other than Mr Brown. (41)

The reversal of positions, in which Mr. Brown becomes the villain, and the slave the wronged party, undoes the discourse Emily has presented of the propensity of blacks for criminal behavior, and the assertion that the use of the whip should be judicious. This is also the reader's introduction to the titular character, Cambridge: "This coarse man [Mr. Brown] had before him a black Hercules of a brute who far outweighed and outspanned him. They stared at each other, their hatred undiluted, but the grey-haired *blackie* displayed no hint of trepidation at what might follow" (41). But Emily herself seems not to feel much trepidation, as her eyes remain transfixed by the black Hercules, in a combination of desire, sympathy, curiosity, and horror. While she notices that "his fellow field-workers trudged on toward the village, reluctant to turn their heads for fear of what they might witness," she likewise notes that "not for one moment did I doubt that their pounding hearts were not with their refractory fellow negro," adding "and if I am to be honest I would have to add that theirs were not the only hearts whose sympathies leapt instinctively to this poor unfortunate. And so Mr Brown raised and cracked his cattle-whip, and in a moment down dropped the aged black upon his knees. But still he stared up in defiance, his dark eyes bright in the sun" (39). All Emily is told is that the slave, Cambridge, has a history of insubordination and is frequently punished with the whip.

Earlier I discussed the way in which Phillips draws on Mrs. Carmichael's *Domestic Manners,* and indeed the first part of the narrative is a detailed iteration of these "manners," of both the planter and the slave. As I have shown, the narrative works its way through the various topics of interest to an "ethnography" of the plantation, of the habits and practices, modes of life and being in the world, which the narrator is attempting to ascertain, in order to convey this knowledge to her father for the "improvement" of the estate. Because of this narrative structure, the novel appears didactic, if not entirely mechanistic. One is tempted to focus entirely upon these "manners" as they reproduce the colonial discourse of the time and bring that discursive history into the present, indeed as they help demonstrate the way in which that older vocabulary of race, gender, and sexuality is reproduced in our own present moment, clearly one central part of Phillips's project. But Phillips is not simply trying to reproduce a "sense" of history, or link the colonial discourses of the past with neocolonial ones today. Rather, I have been arguing that such narrative afterlives, and the capacity of writers like Phillips to intervene in the practices of narrative historiography, reflect a critical move toward an "ethical spectrology," to use Bishnupriya Ghosh's expression. The postcolonial turn toward history is simultaneously a turn toward ethics, a turn that stages the materialization of the phenomenological (embodied, corporeal) encounter with the technologies of biopolitics. Such encounters emplace the colonial/postcolonial subject as the exceptional and exemplary outside entrapped within the paradox of the law.

Such a juridical paradox underlies the central plot of the novel, the death of Mr. Brown at the hands of Cambridge, but it also resounds throughout each of the book's three sections. Emily has not been on the plantation long before she witnesses and records the legal paradox of the slave. At first Emily describes the lashing of Cambridge with the cattle-whip by Mr. Brown as an "unnecessary savagery," but she amends her initial reaction to provide an explanation to her imagined readers. Corporeal punishment, she is told by Brown, is necessary for managing the ongoing risk of slave rebellion; punishment works in concert with other legal apparatuses to ameliorate the deficiency in numbers between white and black. "The fear was insurrection, and discipline became the chief and governing principle on every estate," Emily explains (59). Yet Phillips seems keen to lay bare the cooperative relationship between discipline and regulation at work both in the law and in the extralegal practices of plantation governance. For example, Brown mentions the "deficiency laws" that formally established the proportion of free whites to enslaved blacks that must reside on a single plantation. (The "appropriate" ratio would have been 1:35.) However, Brown tells Emily, "these deficiency laws proved difficult to regulate, for Caribbean emigration was equally difficult to promote"; and thus, "the numbers of negroes in proportion to whites was not only growing, but the quality of whites was rapidly falling" (59). Cambridge is seen by Mr. Brown as the central threat to the precarious order he has maintained. He tells Emily, "[Cambridge] is the chief trouble-maker of the estate. He steals, lies and provokes others to acts of minor rebellion which must be quashed at once." The cattle-whip functions as an emblem of the plantation overseer's absolute authority to exact whatever form of punishment he deems appropriate for securing order. "[Mr. Brown] insisted that punishment, varying in severity according to the master's disposition, often called for the use of the whip" (59). Notably, it is the "master's disposition" rather than the action of the slave that determines the severity of the punishment, a disposition that was guaranteed by colonial law. "For all his surliness," Emily explains, "Mr Brown knows well how to manage the negroes, and does so from what one might term *ground level* rather than by dispensing his justice from on high" (63). The narrator suggests that the criminal, civil, and/or common laws of England represent precisely that position from on high unsuitable to the management of the colonial outpost. The law of the plantation, of "justice" at the ground level, is the rule of colonial biopolitics in its juridical and extrajuridical instruments. And the management of the slave population entails the reassertion of need for exemplary violence that ever secures biopower. Emily is reminded again and again of the "constant apprehension of revolt" and that "such eruptions occur with frequency and are met with equally fierce suppression, the latitude of punishment being curtailed only by the desirability of avoiding permanent injury to valuable stock" (62). Further, the management of risk and contingency demands biopolitics capable of guarding the aleatory event or singular individual. As in the previous chapter, the problem of the singular and the exemplary appear within an unpredictable social order.

Cambridge draws our attention to both the legal and extralegal forces that govern plantation society. Emily describes a system of inter- and intraplantation mediation and a set of local statutes that replace the institutions of law operating back in England. Emily also recognizes that this local system clearly does not work in favor of the slaves, though she still characterizes it as "just." The summary nature of justice, in both its legal and extralegal forms, is most explicitly expressed through the relationship between Brown and Cambridge. Cambridge is both a pious and a kerygmatic Christian, whose commitment to divine justice and political liberty places him in conflict with the order of the plantation, in particular with Brown. Cambridge has refused to labor as a driver of other slaves, and he intercedes on behalf of other slaves when conflict or need arise. Although, as I said earlier, the plot line that develops around this figure is almost oblique to Emily's narrative (she sees Cambridge brutally whipped early in the novel and only speaks with him once), the second, much shorter, section of the novel is told in Cambridge's own voice and is modeled on the well-known slave narratives of the period, in particular Equiano's *Interesting Narrative.* We know from Emily's account that Cambridge kills Brown, and that he is summarily hanged for Brown's "murder," but Cambridge himself provides us with a quite different account, placing his confrontation with Brown at the tail end of a long list of personal injustices and atrocious treatment experienced over the course of his lifetime.

I describe the division between the discrete narrative fragments provided in the first two sections of the novel by Emily and Cambridge—and the "official" court documents provided in the third—as a reflection of the difference between a depiction of the broader biopolitical order (Emily's account) and the individual who is disciplined and normalized within it (Cambridge's narrative). Both underscore the continuities and discontinuities between the operations of civil society and the application of the law, and both provide an account of the particular relationship between the black population bound into a social and civil system that at the same time reduces that population to bare life. As such, *appearance* itself becomes what is at stake in such a relationship of the exclusionary logic of biopolitics: the ability to appear before the law, or the capacity to be seen or recognized at all, intersects with the problem of one's physical appearance—that is, with the markers of race, whether through skin color, dress, or custom. At the same time, physical appearance is variously depicted as rooted in nature and entirely economic. For Emily, a disorderly physical appearance draws into question the very notion of a "negro civility" (105). She describes both slave and free blacks on the island through the common association of racial "taint" and bodily cleanliness, where civility itself enters into a discourse of blood. "Most of the sooty tribe have embraced dully the belief in their own degradation and inferiority, and clearly this is the greatest impediment to their making progress," Emily assumes, adding that the "desperate tendency to despise their own race and colour is one of the ugliest consequences of their miserable condition" (105). For Emily, such abjection precedes rather than produces their "dirty appearance" (106). The "taint" of black skin and the impoverished state it naturalizes equates the taint of skin with that of blood and the black race with moral turpitude. The threat of this black taint means that colonial society must be diligent in maintaining clear boundaries between white and black. Because creolization and miscegenation are imagined to pose the greatest threats to social order, and because the processes of hybridity are also necessary for social reproduction, colonial governmentality must ever operate within the paradoxes of law and the ambivalence of biopolitics.[25] Seemingly aware of such contradictions, throughout the novel Emily characterizes the colonial West Indies as a narrative of social decline.

At the same time, Emily's narrative expresses the syncretic mixing of discursive formulations. Her account of the trial of a slave in the extrajudicial "slave-court," for example, is utterly convoluted, laying claim to both the execution of justice and the inadequacies of the legal process, to both the benefits of formalities of law and the disadvantages of judicial procedure, which she describes as "the often laborious and time-wasting process of quiz and counter-quiz, and artful cross examination punctuated by theatrical appeals to the passions" (106). Criticizing the inequalities between testimony offered to the black slave and the free white, Emily asserts that a "formal system of law whereby any offender, irrespective of colour or quality, is meted out just punishment, seems not to have taken hold on this island" (107).[26] The convolution of colonial discourse, and the violent system of exploitation it serves, is likewise figured in the conflict between Mr. Brown and the prior plantation overseer, Mr. Wilson, a conflict that precedes Emily's arrival. Mr. Wilson is mutinously forced out of his position precisely because he is unwilling to exercise what Brown believes to be the "proper" control over the field slaves: Brown considers Wilson far too judicious in his use of the whip. While Wilson is described as a "just" manager, Brown is defined by his brutality. Emily acknowledges this, saying, "Although Mr Brown is a good *cane-man,* fear, not debate, is his method of government" (124). Yet Cambridge intrepidly goes to battle against him. The deaths of Brown and Cambridge follow in quick succession in Emily's narrative, and she says little about the incidents of either, except that Cambridge killed Mr. Brown in unclear circumstances and was quickly executed: "And now the negro is hanged from a tree, no longer able to explain or defend his treacherous act. The white people of this island dispatched him as a summary warning to any other negroes who might consider such a mutinous path" (128). We then come to discover more specifically that Wilson was exiled for defending a black victim of a crime against a white criminal. Wilson's reappearance seems to function in the narrative as a counterdiscourse to that provided by Emily. Indeed, the conversations they share emphasize the relationship between the colonial system of law and the appropriate management of the plantation.

Here I return to the figure of *homo sacer,* Giorgio Agamben's expression for bare life that resembles but is not quite reducible to Colin Dayan's legal slave. Neither condemned to death nor protected from it, *homo sacer* names the exceptional figure who can be killed but not sacrificed, who represents an ambiguous existence outside-in the law—that is, completely outside its protection but fully within its reach—whose death is neither ordered nor ordained but simply allowed.[27] I have already shown how Phillips, in the prologue to *Cambridge,* underscores the cooperating axis of the domestic life and civil society. Indeed, Emily explicitly describes her life back in England as "a life sacrificed," and she dreams of her life on the island as one of adventure and freedom (113). In fact, Cambridge appears as the figure of *homo sacer,* the one who dwells in such the no-man's-land of the law, the one who can be killed but not sacrificed. And yet his execution serves as the very emblem of exemplary violence sanctioned by the law and carried out under the authority of the law.

If Cambridge appears to serve as the exceptional figure of bare life in his encounter with the exemplary violence of colonial biopolitics, perhaps a more singular attribution of the moniker *homo sacer* should be reserved for the person whose very representation the narrative finds impossible to account—the "obeah woman," Christiania. And if the conflict between Mr. Brown and Cambridge frames one way of portraying the exercise of biopower on the colonial plantation, the encounter between Emily and Christiania reminds us of the extent that biopower penetrates the domestic scene. It is, after all, the latter's infiltration of the colonial household that the former finds most utterly intolerable. The house slave Stella, of course, is responsible for mediating much of their interaction. When Emily arrives on the plantation, she finds Christiania seated rather than serving at the table, a social gesture that causes Emily to "tremble with indignation" (73). Between Stella's defense of Christiania and Christiania's own recalcitrance, Emily imagines a "conspiracy of black womanhood against white" at work in her own household. Emily views Christiania merely as Mr. Brown's "concubine," and while she is willing to accept the sexual arrangements between white overseer and black slave, which she assumes is consensual, she refuses to submit to its consequences. The conspiracy of black womanhood is, for Emily, a decidedly sexual one, generated by all the stereotypes of black femininity the reader has come to expect from her: "I was also aware that the highest position on which a sable damsel could set her sights was to become the mistress of a white man. They seek unions with planters, overseers, book-keepers, doctors, merchants and lawyers, and when their beauties fail, they seek similar positions for their daughters, knowing that success will assure them of a life of ease and prestige among their own people" (75). Emily at first dismisses the notion of obeah—the practitioner of which can "deliver persons to, and retrieve them from the clutches of, their enemies"

(74)—but when Christiania begins a nightly ritual outside Emily's window, she is immobilized by fear, a fear that reunites her with her deathly experience of an Atlantic crossing:

> Disconcertingly, the emotion of fear is becoming increasingly familiar to me. These past nights the sensation has seized me again, causing me to recollect the prior occasion on which I felt such trepidation. After the death of Isabella at sea, the demon made his last assault. As these alarms continued to threaten me in my impotence, I feared I should soon be reunited with my dead companion. And now this devilish fear has reasserted itself its power, but this time I find myself adrift, not on threatening waves, but upon an ocean of negroes who care little for my fears. (89)

Emily neither understands nor accepts the practices of obeah, but they nonetheless hold powerful emotional sway over her, causing her to see herself as yet another item of human cargo sacrificed upon the sea of the colonial enterprise. The irony that Phillips develops here is that no matter how much the narrator tries to understand the order and arrangement of the plantation, the mechanisms of its organization remain obscure to her, as it must have to those readers of colonial travel accounts of the West Indies. Nor does the narrative, in any of its sections or multiple voices, provide any definitive or total perspective. Cambridge will later claim that Christiania is his own wife, who was forced against her will into a relationship with Mr. Brown. Christiania is herself never given a voice, but her ritual practices outside Emily's window suggest that there remains, in fact, an unaccountable cultural life whose presence is felt but not explained by the narrative, or by narrative form itself.

Contingencies of Blood

The articulation of the law through the trope of blood, Dayan insists, is fundamental to the way that the law differentially isolates and contains targeted groups, distributing populations into two categories of artificial personhood: "legal slaves" and "civil bodies." Dayan identifies the "civil body" as a person who continues to be recognized as a subject in law, an "artificial person who possesses self and property." The "legal slave," on the other hand, is not recognized as a legal subject but is rendered an "artificial person who exists as both person and property." Both are granted an artificial legal personality, and both are also sacrificed to civil order; but according to Dayan, "civil bodies are governed by one set of laws, and legal slaves by another. . . . They cannot be the subjects of a common system of laws" (4). As legal fictions, the category of legal slave assumes a recalcitrant disposition toward crime and is often racially marked, while the civil body remains unmarked by race, goes largely unacknowledged, and quietly assumes full subjection to the law. The legal slave can no longer be possessed as another's property but, no longer in sovereign possession of a civil body, maintains only a designated personhood that is outside-in the law; subject to its disciplinary regime, the legal slave is situated beyond the protection of the law. Although possession and dispossession of legal personhood are recast in the jurisprudential language of artificiality, for those deemed legal slaves such abstractions govern quite material forms of possession and dispossession. The disciplinary and regulatory authority consolidated in and by the body of the law is achieved and sustained by compromising the integrity of those bodies over which the law commands: possessed by the "spirit of the law," the legal slave is dispossessed of material personhood.

The racialization of legal slaves follows from the long history of racialized slavery. In her important study of eighteenth-century colonial slave codes, Elsa Goveia long ago observed,

> Because the slave was a person, he raised problems of public order, which the police regulations generally were meant to cover. The law was forced to allow the slave some kind of *persona* for the purpose of dealing with him under this aspect of his activity as a special kind of property. . . . In so far as the slave was allowed personality before the law, he was regarded chiefly, almost solely, as a potential criminal.[28]

By the end of the eighteenth century, new laws governing the treatment of slaves in the colonies—most passed locally by island assemblies, a few enacted by the British Parliament—gave statutory substance to the common law practices of policing, disciplining, and otherwise maintaining the populations of enslaved women and men in the British colonies, formally encoding their status as chattel and securing rights of ownership over them. Promulgated under the banner of reform, these statutory laws functioned as a sign of legal restraint for owners and a promise of humane treatment for the owned, but they rarely afforded any realizable productions for those enslaved or recognized the value of emergent black civil society both on and off the plantation. The judicial apparatus was now capable of extending or retracting legal personhood for the purpose of increased commerce and greater profit by the application of racial designations; those who were free were still exposed to "civil death" should they run afoul of the law, but for those who were enslaved a collective "social death," if not guaranteed, was certainly now authorized by law. "In this logic," Dayan writes succinctly, "the law covers you in white skin and the law encases you in black, whether or not the colors can be seen. The law giveth and the law taketh away. The law kills and the law resurrects" (5).

How, then, to reconcile the relationship between the individual who can be killed but not sacrificed and the individual whose public execution serves an exemplary purpose in the consolidation and maintenance of biopolitical order? Both modes of death are outside the law, and both are integral to the sovereignty of law. As the very figure of the living dead, Agamben's *homo sacer* in fact represents the primordial sacrifice to the law itself, a sacrifice already accomplished at the founding of political society: the *homo sacer* cannot be sacrificed because he represents a sacrifice that is not his own but one that initiates civil subjects into the purview of the law itself, a sacrifice that underwrites the extension of the law's protection while it overwrites their ongoing subjection to its rules of conduct and norms of punishment. In this sense, *homo sacer,* like the figures of exemplary violence discussed in the prior chapter, operates within the same conceptual field—biopolitical/necropolitical—that designates and casts out bare life from the sphere of civil society; both signify a sacrifice without sacrifice. It is in this context that I would like to return to Dayan's contribution to colonial history and legal theory in her analysis of the quasi-religious rhetoric through which the slave comes to occupy that position of the sacrifice without sacrifice. In "Legal Slaves and Civil Bodies," she examines the manner by which the body of the slave comes to haunt contemporary jurisprudence through the persistent racialization of crime and the technologies of the prison.[29] For Dayan, indefinite detention and solitary confinement name two such practices of exemplary violence and biopolitical inscription.

Tracing the history of the "artificial person in law," the abstract personality posited by any particular system of law, Dayan lights on a suggestive passage in William Blackstone's *Commentaries on the Laws of England,* in which he speaks of the "natural liberty" that one gives up upon entry into the social contract and civil society, a legal-theoretical fiction that Dayan reads as an inaugural sacrifice to/before the law: "a ritual staged again and again in order to reaffirm the stability of civilization," a forfeiture demanded by the law that forever "haunts" the juridical foundation of civil society (4). The historical form that such rituals of exclusion take can be traced to ancient jurisprudence and the notion of "attainder"—the seizure of the civil rights of the convicted criminal "who, though possessing *natural life,* has lost all *civil rights,*" which finds articulation in contemporary political discourses and legal practices (4). Like Agamben, Dayan looks to the foundations of law in ancient jurisprudence, where "artificial death as punishment for crime entailed a logic of alienation that could extend perpetually along constructed lines of racial kinship" through the notion of "attainder" or "corruption of blood" (4). By considering the relationship between kinship and punishment in earlier historical periods, she is able to account for the introduction of racial markers that led, by at least the eighteenth century, to the criminalization of entire black populations:

> In my pursuit of a conceptual framework for disabilities made indelible through time, I follow the call of *blood,* its meaning and effects, both literal and metaphorical, through three sites of disabling: feudal attainder, the essence of which became "corruption of blood," as punishment for crime, introduced into English common law after the Norman conquest; to its transport to the colonies and its incarnation as the black taint that legally inscribed slavery; to the post-Civil War period, when slaves were reborn as criminals and transplanted into "slaves of the state." I take this circuit of stigmatization as a *historical residue* that turns "metaphoricity" into a way of knowing, that is, acknowledging history. . . . In rereading the claims of civil death into the genealogy of slavery and incarceration, I propose a continuum between being declared dead in law, being made a slave, and being judged a criminal. (6)

In its premodern manifestation, "corruption of blood" in its legal form as attainder, according to Dayan, "probably never had anything to do with ethnicity or biology, but everything to do with taking the attainted person's property to the exclusion of any otherwise rightful heirs" (9). Attainder not only pertained to the individual but could apply to the entire family; attainder comes to designate a heritable property of the family name, a taint that sequesters their property as uninheritable and effectively alienable by the state. As blood began to index nativity, and nativity ultimately translated into a set of racialized properties, the idea of a heritable "taint" was transformed into the fear of racial contamination, with its connotation of filth, disease, depravity, and degeneration. Dayan argues that racial taint was tethered to the law and racial lineage regarded as an "inalienable inheritance" that determined who could be seized as property, and by whom (10). The notion of "tainted" blood precedes, then, the racial discourses that would later correlate racial inferiority and criminal pathology. Legal incapacitation became increasing bound to blood in a new racial genealogy. Under the dominant discourses and common practices that organized the modern Atlantic system of trade and authorized the capture, enslavement, sale, and transport of Africans as human cargo, the notion of racial taint became institutionalized as an essential function of colonial governmentality. Miscegenation emerged as a fundamental problem in the management of plantation society and a powerful source of cultural anxiety. One might recall the enormous unease Emily displays when she describes the multiple degrees of blackness "infecting" the social order of the island, rendering white bodies susceptible to the multiple pathologies of blackness. In the discourses of colonial biopolitics, white blood might cleanse, but black blood certainly corrupts.

By drawing out "blood" as a historical trope circulating within the legal discourse—and by extension what I have described more broadly as the juridical imaginary—Dayan demonstrates how colonial slave law was adapted into a formal jurisprudence, wherein the modern penitentiary "became an alternative to slavery, another kind of receptacle for imperfect creatures whose civil disease justified containment" and an "unsettling counter to servitude: an invention of criminality and prescriptions for treatment that turned humans into the living dead" (15). The instruments of inclusion and exclusion that brought targeted populations within a circumscribed purview of the law—as social agents subject to the law as well as the legal objects of the law—functionally entailed the criminalized blackness tout court, the juridical precursor to the large-scale incarceration of black and ethnic minorities in the post–civil rights era. The "discursive maneuvering" of jurisprudence, Dayan concludes, "sustains the identity of the slave in the person of the prisoner," such that the "legal demolition of personhood that began with slavery has been perfected in the logic of the courtroom" (22). Nowhere are the consequences of juridical contamination by the discourses of blood more irreversibly played out than in the life-meting authority that sovereign power wields over legal punishment, whether in the form of state execution, life sentence, solitary confinement, mandatory terms, or the sanctioned violence that turns the prison into an environment of everyday precarity. The life sentence gains exceptional resonance as a carceral logic now extending well beyond prison walls, sustaining the civil death of entire communities—racial and ethnic minorities, the intractably poor—in perpetuity. Often inverting the spatial logic of the prison, wide swaths of social space are abandoned so that newer, increasingly restrictive, and more impenetrable social enclosures might be more easily managed. Although Dayan explores the way in which the history of "racial taint" continues to haunt the application of the law in U.S. contexts, her analysis is certainly resonant in other national jurisdictions, and certainly in postwar Britain, whether through policies of policing, judicial sentencing, or immigration control.

I conclude by returning to *Higher Ground,* which explicitly compares the body of the slave who experiences social death to that of the felon who suffers civil death, and to the immigrant set adrift in the postwar welfare state. Each of the three sections of this novel is set in some sort of biopolitical "camp": the slave factory of eighteenth-century West Africa in part one ("Heartland"), a prison in the civil rights era U.S. South in part two ("The Cargo Rap"), and a boarding house in postwar London in part three ("Higher Ground"), where a Jewish immigrant who has fled Nazi Germany has been abandoned to a frustrated state apparatus. Each section of the novel dwells on the biopolitical technologies at work in each site. For example, "Heartland" provides a deeply unsettling account of the repeated rape of an African woman sold by her own father into sexual slavery, who is then passed among the men of the fort. It also affords gruesome details about the operations of the slave factory and a harrowing description of its dungeon, into which both the narrator and the woman are ultimately cast. As I discussed earlier, the middle section of the novel recounts the dilemma faced by Rudi Williams, a prisoner convicted for an armed robbery of a convenience store, whose prison detention is extended indefinitely, and whose solitary confinement sends him reeling into madness and ultimately death.

As an epistolary narrative, "The Cargo Rap" chronicles Rudi's descent into madness due to his sustained isolation in solitary confinement. It would be too easy to view Rudi as merely a caricature of the '60s black radical.[30] Rather, his narrative offers the reader a disarming combination of acute honesty, profound self-deception, and perspicacious insight into the order of justice and incarceration. In a letter to a volunteer attorney to his "defense committee," Rudi draws on the institutional form of the criminal dossier to frame his particular crimes and exceptional punishments:

> The alleged crime: At the age of nineteen manchild years I am supposed to have asked a white man, at the point of a .38, to pay some overdue wages. . . . A posse of Feds blew in and for reasons I still don't follow decided to take me alive. They strapped my wrists and ankles to a pole and carried me off to their judicial feast.
>
> The punishment: One to life in a concentration camp of their own choice. (91–92)

The prison industry described by Dayan resonates powerfully with Rudi's narrative, as Phillips self-consciously links together the biopolitics of the camp with the operations of the prison. The criminal bodies of black men's bodies are constituted through the need to secure the biopolitical order. Not only are the "conditions of confinement" "manipulated in order to confirm depravity," they produce depravity and facilitate reproduction of even the most benign inmate as a violent criminal; meanwhile, the conditions of solitary confinement have been normalized and intensified, reproducing the violent criminal as criminally insane (22). And once the "legal slave" has been transformed into the "civil body" of the felon, once the prisoner is deemed "dead-in-law," then the "actual habitats for incarceration, the technological nuts and bolts of brutalization, transform—not just rhetorically but in practice—prisoners into a mass of not just servile, but idle matter" (23).

Higher Ground draws together the strands of argumentation offered above, as they trace the manner in which the corrupting blood work of the law, which translates the concept of attainder into an irremediable racial taint, consigns racialized populations to precarious lives lived under exceptional conditions of confinement, disposability, and violence. "Corruption of blood" might then be reappropriated as a banner for the taint of racialization that defiles the statutory bodies that write the law and the body of jurisprudence that guides the application of the law. Rudi's narrative represents a singular articulation of the deleterious ends of a biopolitics that extends the carceral logic of life sentence, indefinite detention, and solitary confinement to life itself less imprisoned in than abandoned by world. The long historical trajectory of racial jurisprudence and racialized law is condensed and consolidated into the overdetermined course of Rudi's life. As idle matter within the function and execution of the law, absolutely disposable as an object of exchange, he calls out in excess of the law even as he recounts the interests of the law, as do those other characters discussed above: Nash, Martha, and Travis; Emily, Christiania, and Cambridge. While these characters call upon us as legally conscribed objects of idle matter circulating as modern human bio-cargo, they also insists on the singular capacity of modern human bio-cargo to live in excess of their status as the living dead.

• II •

Assembling Human Bio-Cargo

· CHAPTER 3 ·

Compound Fractures

Archival Constellations, Narrative Violations

The Archivist's Archive

The archive conserves but does not restore; it institutes but cannot restitute. The archive is preoccupied by the law and as such participates in—and serves as an instrument for—the juridical and carceral framework of modern human bio-cargo. Housed in the archive, history is framed by the law, indeed incarcerated by it. To unhouse the past requires nothing less than a violation of the law, a breaking-into the archive and a breaking-out of the confines of the juridical. Writing in the context of state violence and endless war, Judith Butler observes that colloquially, "to be framed" is "to be subject to a con, to a tactic by which evidence is orchestrated so to make a false accusation appear true" and "to be judged in advance without valid evidence and without any obvious means of redress."[1] When "framed" in and by the juridical imaginary, one is situated in material relation to the law: on the side of or set against; protected by or exposed to; imprisoned within or banished beyond. To do so the juridical imaginary requires a vast archive strategically available to power. The "frame-work" of the law defines the perimeter around those who are enclosed within its strategies of protection by disclosing those who are merely subject to tactics of its enforcement, achieved in parts through the mobilization of a vast archive of juridical knowledge. But the juridical imaginary is held captive by and in its own prison-house of exemplary violence; its instrumental appearance exposes the boundaries of its power. Confined in and by a classic structural aporia, the law affords a measure escape. "What's at stake," Fred Moten writes in another context, "is fugitive movement in and out of the frame, bar, or whatever externally imposed social logic—a movement of escape, the stealth of the stolen that can be said . . . to break every enclosure. This fugitive movement is stolen life, and its relation to law is reducible neither to simple interdiction nor bare transgression."[2]

Such an occasion of fugitive movement, a breaking-out, is seized in a memorable scene in the closing minutes of Christopher McQuarrie and Bryan Singer's celebrated film *The Usual Suspects* (1995), which I want to leverage as a popular analogue for the discussion that follows of the colonial archive. As the inexhaustibly talkative petty thief Roger "Verbal" Kint (Kevin Spacey) makes his exit from the San Pedro Police Station—having recounted in breathtaking detail the captivating and convincing tale of the drug kingpin and criminal mastermind Keyser Söze—Special Agent Dave Kujan (Chazz Palminteri) reflects in satisfied amazement on the story he has been told. Casually surveying the cluttered bulletin board hanging on the wall of the office he had commandeered from Sergeant Rabin, an object suddenly catches Kujan's eye: a small metal placard bearing the name of the bulletin board's manufacturer, a company named Quartet located in Skokie, Illinois. The name resonates with a minor detail from Verbal's testimony and Kujan's mind races back to an early moment in his interview with Verbal Kint. "You know back when I was in that barbershop quartet in Skokie, Illinois . . . ," he recalls Kint saying with charming nonchalance. The line reverberates with such unanticipated power that Kujan loses his grip on the coffee mug he is holding and on reality itself. His eyes now dart quickly across the miscellany of items haphazardly posted to the board, bits of information and pieces of evidence from countless other criminal investigations being pursued by local police. Kujan realizes almost instantly that every unlikely detail (such as the barbershop quartet in the suburbs of Chicago), which only hours earlier lent Verbal's account legitimacy, authenticity, the sheen of truth, had been gleaned from the papers, documents, clippings, and photographs littering the surface of Sergeant Rabin's bulletin board. Even the ubiquitous coffee mug from which Kujan sips throughout the interrogation has contributed a crucial detail: the singular name on which Verbal's story hangs, Söze's accomplice, Kobayashi. For every time Kujan had lifted the cup to his mouth, Verbal had seen one detail that Kujan could never have seen: the stamp of its manufacturer, Kobayashi Porcelain—that is, until it lay shattered on the linoleum floor, whereupon the name strikes Kujan with anagnoristic force.

Roger "Verbal" Kint, it turns out, has also commandeered Rubin's office and has put it to use as *his* archive. And from this archive—an archive that Kujan too occupies but does not bother to notice—Verbal extemporizes a tale too good to be believed. As fragments of Verbal's testimony flood back into Kujan's memory, two lines repeat over and over again: first, Kujan's bullying demand that Verbal must "convince" him of his innocence by admitting "every last detail" of his criminal life; and second, Kujan's arrogant assertion to Verbal, "I'm smarter than you." The conceit places the viewer of the film in the same position as the special agent: it is only in retrospect, after the story is completed and Verbal has made his escape, that we see the archive constellated before us. The movie concludes with its famous tag line, borrowed from Baudelaire: "The greatest trick the devil ever pulled was convincing the world he didn't exist." Verbal's performance potentiates the archive of the law as a line of flight; he instrumentalizes the law's very frame of comprehension in order to frame the story of his own escape. Kujan's own performance of the law, on the other hand, enacts its frame, shows up its very limits in the shape of blind arrogance. Summoned to appear before the law, Verbal provokes the appearance of the law. Kujan is framed by Verbal because Kujan has already framed himself; and in the blink of an eye, Verbal vanishes from the frame having convinced the law that he did not exist.

The narrator of David Dabydeen's *A Harlot's Progress* says almost nothing to his interrogator. To the demanding representative of the Committee for the Abolition of Slavery, Mungo appears anything *but* verbal. When he finally does speak—to an imagined audience that does seem to include Pringle—Mungo spins a remarkable tale whose extravagant and unlikely details are taken from a vast archive of eighteenth-century social life. Following the novelist's own cues, most critics have described *A Harlot's Progress* as an attempt to "recover" the voice of the African page attending to Moll Hackabout in the second panel of William Hogarth's series of the same title (see Figure 7). At times willfully evasive and often intentionally incoherent, Mungo does not offer a convincing alibi. As the story concludes, however, reflecting upon the embarrassment of detail the narrator has supplied, the attentive readers may experience a moment of astonishment not unlike the one that sent that Kobayshi mug tumbling to the floor: the realization that Mungo's pyrotechnic extemporization adds up to nothing less—*but nothing more*—than a spectacular orchestration of someone else's archive, one organized under the proper name of William Hogarth.[3]

A Harlot's Progress offers a panorama of character "types" most common to the literary and visual markets of Hogarth's time: a rogues' gallery of notorious libertines living on the periphery of social life, among them Clarissa Harlowe and Robert Lovelace, Tom Jones and Benjamin Partridge, Francis Charteris and John Gourlay, and of course the two Molls,

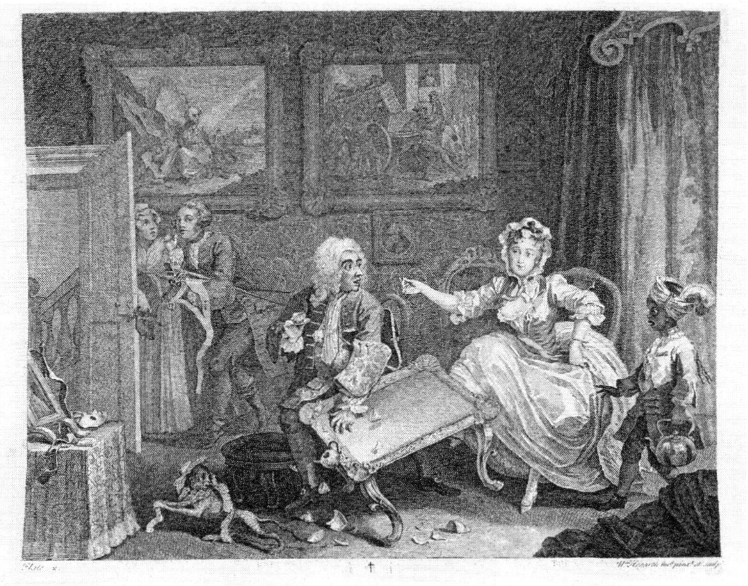

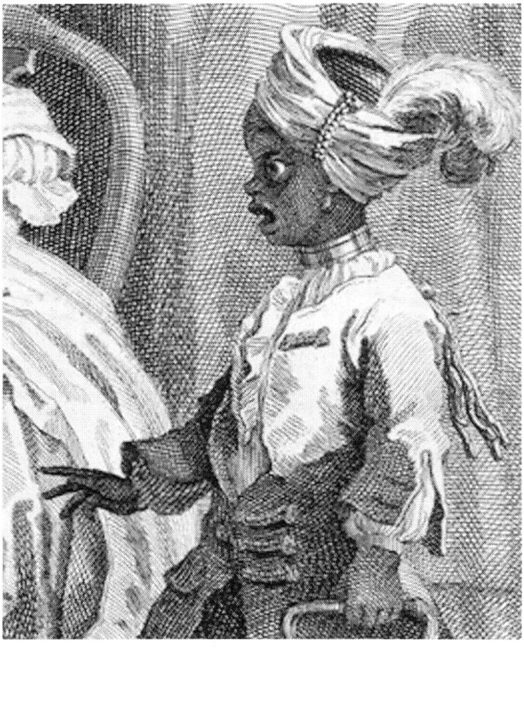

Figure 7. William Hogarth, A Harlot's Progress, *plate 2, 1732. Etching and engraving. Courtesy of La Clé des Langues (Clifford Armion, dir.) and ENS Média (Vincent Brault, photo).*

Hackabout and Flanders; an alliance of upright and uptight propagandists of abolition and benefactors of the dispossessed, including Thomas Clarkson, William Wilberforce, Granville Sharp, and anachronistically Thomas Pringle; a lineup of the agents of the slave trade and executors of plantation slavery such as Thomas Thistlewood, Luke Collingwood, James Kelsall, and John Kimber; and a clutch of celebrated public officials like Lord Mansfield, and infamous ones such as the magistrate Sir John Gonson; finally, an assemblage of Africans whose stories were told, recorded, printed, circulated, and consumed by a salaciously curious, if not sympathetic, reading public—Olaudah Equiano, Ottobah Cugoano, Dido Belle, and later Mary Prince. Two crucial figures among this last group include Ignacio Sancho and Julius Soubise, on whom Dabydeen models the novel's protagonist and the unusual circumstances of Mungo's vicissitudinous life, a critical conflation that stages their troubling incorporation into the aristocratic households of Mary Churchill and John Montagu, Second Duke of Montagu, and Catherine Hyde and Charles Douglas, Third Duke of Queensberry. In Dabydeen's novel, Mungo is closer in appearance and attitude to Soubise, who achieved public notoriety in caricatures depicting him as a "Mungo Macaroni," a fop and womanizer, and later infamy when he fled England just days before the death of Lady Catherine (see Figure 8). Sancho, on the other hand, is remembered as a prominent figure and respected man of letters in eighteenth-century society. Although Mungo's narrative is more closely aligned with Soubise, the household into which he is brought resembles Boughton, the Northhamptonshire country home of Lord and Lady Montagu, whose name is altered to Montagu*e*.

If Mungo represents the "lost object" Pringle is charged to restore, Mungo himself is able to break into and out of the archive by leveraging the abolitionist's frame, breaching its boundaries, plundering its contents, and casting them up into a constellation too unruly to be contained by Pringle's inoperable frame. That Dabydeen is borrowing from Hogarth is made obvious by the novel's title, but the trope of archival appropriation is *diegetic* as well as authorial—Mungo's as well as Dabydeen's—a sly narrative turn that allows Dabydeen to stage the manifold difficulties of narrative recovery identified in the opening chapter. As a character, then, Mungo develops along recognizable metafictional lines, as appropriating author of his own tale, absconding from the archive with more than the figure of a black page child contained in and by the single panel on which he is depicted; also in excess is the litany of similarly pointed scenes of Hogarth's satirical,

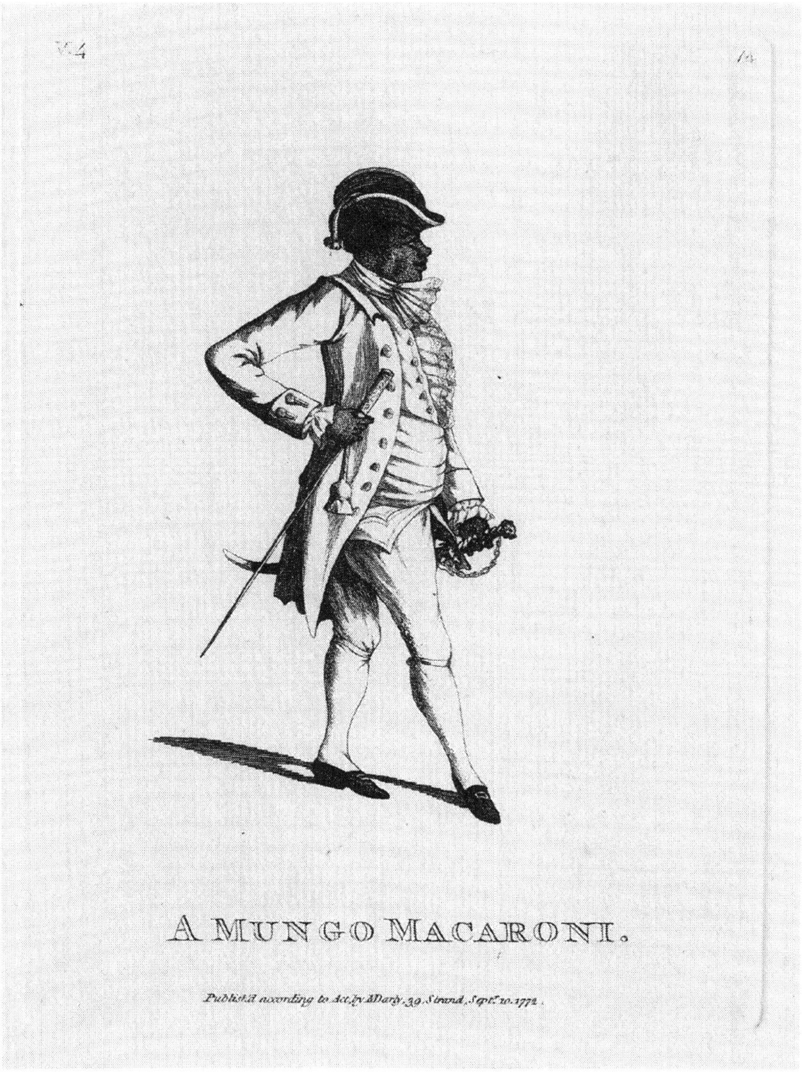

Figure 8. A Mungo Macaroni. *Printed by M. Darly, 1772. Copper engraving. Courtesy of the Lewis Walpole Library, Yale University.*

and often perverse, imagination. As he tries to recall a life his memory can no longer supply, Mungo draws upon the surfeit of details depicted in each panel of Hogarth's series, and in the artist's oeuvre as a whole, as he would have seen it in cheap reproductions circulating en masse in the eighteenth century. Mungo capitalizes on the accredited name of Hogarth, countersigning his singular title. Performing the capacious archive now constellated around him, Mungo extemporizes an account of his life that is as breathless and frenetic as the unusual suspect of *The Usual Suspects.* As a fictional conceit, Mungo's archival performance doubles down on Dabydeen's own narrative strategy, mirroring it, illustrating it, appropriating it, and confounding it. In short, *A Harlot's Progress* delivers a compound fracture to the juridical framework of the archive. The reading that follows attempts to limn the novel's complicated archival constellation even as it recedes *mise en abyme.*

Featured prominently in the second plate in Hogarth's series, a young domestic servant gasps with alarm at the chaos erupting around him upon the unexpected arrival home of his master, who interrupts his unsuspecting mistress still at her trade with another suitor. The servant is a black child whose origins should be familiar: captured near the coast of West Africa; sold on an auction block in the West Indies; and transported to England to serve in a prostitute's household. The enslaved child goes unnamed, his unremarked presence remanded almost but not quite to the periphery of the frame, and mirrored by an excitable monkey along its opposite edge. The black page lends an ironic sense of local "color" to the perverse scene of domestic turbulence. Although the title of Dabydeen's novel alludes to Hogarth's infamous Moll Hackabout, a conflation of Daniel Defoe's Moll Flanders and the historical prostitute Kate Hackabout, the harlot at the center of the narrative is Mungo himself, an eighteenth-century black Londoner with a remarkably storied past: Mungo is captured by slavers in a vicious assault on his African village, chosen as an object of sexual gratification and sadistic abuse by a notorious slave ship captain, placed in a "seasoning house" under the supervision of the petty criminals Betty and Mary, sold at auction in a London coffee house, forced to serve as a fashionable African attendant in an aristocratic household, and finally enlisted to aid a purportedly well-meaning Jewish doctor in a program of euthanizing women suffering the last stages of syphilis, including the prostitute Moll Hackabout. In Dabydeen's hands, however, Mungo also serves as an exemplary figure standing alongside a multitude of irrecoverable, irredeemable others who cannot be remembered.

Beyond his sly appropriation of Hogarth's series, Dabydeen conjures the recalcitrant landscapes of deviant urban life, paraphrasing the social worlds the artist so assiduously and scandalously chronicled. He also draws from a rogues' gallery of notorious libertines living on the periphery of social life, the unruly types that flooded the literary marketplace, parodied in the pages of Defoe, Fielding, and Richardson. To this mix Dabydeen adds an assemblage of Africans whose stories were told, recorded, printed, and circulated in the popular slave narratives of the late eighteenth and nineteenth centuries, voraciously consumed by a salaciously curious, if not always sympathetic, reading public. The novel adopts and adapts these latter "types" as a second "progress" tradition, one that has been especially influential to late twentieth-century African Atlantic writing, such as *A Narrative of the Most Remarkable Particulars in the Life of James Albert "Ukawsaw Gronniosaw," an African Prince* (1772) and crucially *The Interesting Narrative and the Life of "Olaudah Equiano" or Gustavus Vassa, the African* (1789). Both Equiano and Gronniosaw were roughly contemporary with the setting of *A Harlot's Progress,* and Dabydeen draws both biographical material and formal conventions from their examples. As has been well established, the slave narrative may have been less allegorical than the edifying accounts of Christian conversion that preceded them, but they were no less formally contrived.[4] Echoing the ubiquitous prefaces and miscellany that ushered in, "authenticated," and legitimized "true accounts" of enslavement that circulated widely, the opening prologue to *A Harlot's Progress* tropes both historical and contemporary literary markets and frames the demand for retrospection as an instrument of speculation. On a mission to lay claim to the obdurate memory of the former slave, Mr. Pringle's arrival at Mungo's austere lodgings situates the temporal "present" of the novel's setting in a contentious scene of economic narrative recounting and economic accounting. Pringle pursues an archive of atrocity; but he also requires a conversion credited by a sincere confession, and evidence of salvation that, temporized by cycles of iniquity and contrition, he has finally and truly achieved. In order to perform the alchemist's feat of transforming atrocity into gold, Pringle needs a story of redemption. Despite the language of redemption with which, as we will see, the novel trades, as it unfolds, the redressive promise of narrative transaction is implicated in the same economy founded upon gruesome acts of physical violence relentlessly repeated in agonizing superfluity.

Mungo's command of narrative time allows him to gain control over the structures of speculation into which he is cast. An exercise in strategic delay, the narrative leverages the fast time of anticipation against the slow pace of his retrospection, playing fast on the ambivalent tempos of delay: postponement, suspension, repetition. What Pringle receives is a frustrating temporization against which he acts out in the margins of the notebook in which he means to record the slave's narrative. Thus the novel opens with Pringle recording the date in anticipation of the story Mungo will not give him. We are told that Pringle and the abolition committee have been waiting "for months," that they have been "awaiting word" from their intransigent charge. We are told this is Pringle's "third visit," and yet Mungo's narrative still has no beginning. Yet, Mungo reflects, "Still, I delay answering, I mumble and pause, and I pray that he will put my tardiness down to deafness, or to the natural docility of the African who cannot come to a point howsoever instructed by the whip or by the clergy" (4–5). By recording the date, Pringle marks time but also stakes a claim on narrative as an object of exchange whose value is put at risk as Mungo stalls and time is wasted. Mungo, on the other hand, is speculating on the value his story might yield through strategic delay. If Mungo wastes time, Pringle figuratively kills it, violently defacing the few marks he has made in the notebook. Pringle "doodles over the date, drawing a series of ears, some drooping and mutilated, other like the heads of daffodils he had seen at the wayside on his journey to the garret; daffodils bright against the blackened frost of the city, defiant in their proclamation of survival into newness, a new season, a new beginning" (2). The images are themselves, in a sense, archival; one anticipating Wordsworth's perhaps most famous poems, the other looking toward the past and the bizarre story of the War of Jenkins's Ear (1739–46) as a coda to a prior event, the South Sea Bubble (1720). The latter, of course, represents a notorious case of unrestrained speculation and is the subject of a well-known engraving by Hogarth.[5] The wayside daffodils and severed ear enter into Mungo's archival reserve only to return after a long delay as part of his own unlikely story, when Mungo tells how he slices off his own ear as an offering to his horrified mistress, Lady Montague; her refusal of the gift leads inexplicably to his consuming the daffodils resting in a vase at the side of her bed.

In many ways, Pringle's notebook represents the kind of object that might never circulate as a public record, like the ship's ledger in *Feeding the*

Ghosts; but it is also the precursor to a printed work that, like Mintah's diary, offers an affecting account to be passed from hand to hand, promoted by word of mouth, disseminated across an impassioned public culture; or as testimony presented to Parliament as evidence of the atrocity of slavery; but more likely lodged in the archive of colonial violence where a researcher (or novelist) might someday stumble upon it as an example. The archive of such cultural objects is vast, and Mungo's narrative, like the novel itself, activates the object's unrealized potential to manifest spectral worlds otherwise veiled by its commodity form. The "doodles," as he calls them, in Pringle's meticulously prepared notebook feed into Mungo's imaginary writing pad: the date carefully inscribed along the top; a few inelegantly drawn shapes and geometric forms that Pringle sketches while he waits for Mungo to speak; finally, unforgiving scratches and scrawls that violently defile and dismember the date, shapes, and forms as the abolitionist grows increasingly frustrated by Mungo's refusal to speak. But the object itself, Pringle's notebook, remains virtually blank from beginning to end, save for those frustrated marks on the initial page and, tellingly, an outline of potential chapter headings for Mungo's book, another indication of how narrative follows form. Glancing down repeatedly at the pages of Pringle's notebook, Mungo espies the signs of Pringle's boredom, which he spins into a relentless motif of mutilated ears, contorted bodies, and dismembered corpses, a motif to which I will return at the end of this chapter. For the novelist, the dismembered ears foreshadow the narrative that unfolds, but for his narrator, they inspire the way in which his own account is woven into world historical events. Pringle's notebook serves Mungo the same way the bulletin board mounted on the wall in Sergeant Rabin's office serves Verbal Kint: as a place to start. Thus an entire visual field is refracted through an archival improvisation that operates in gap of Mungo's "ruined" memory.

Rack and Ruin

Like the novelist, Thomas Pringle is relentless in his campaign to take charge of another's life; like the novelist, he fabricates what his obdurate archive withholds; and like the novelist, he has at his disposal the published accounts of slavery and the slave trade already in public circulation, formal precursors that provide him in advance both written evidence and a narrative frame in which to situate the testimony of atrocity he will assiduously record under color of its witness. Pringle is the archivist par excellence, as he prepares his notebook to tell Mungo's story in advance, to bend it to the expectations and convention the market has come to expect. Pringle sets down nine "chapter headings," each familiar to readers of Equiano: from his capture in "Africa" and "Voyage to the Americas in Slave Ship"; to a life of "Plantation Labour" and subsequent "Voyage to England with Captain Thistlewood"; then his "Service in the Household of Lord Montague" and the "Purchase of Mungo by "Gideon, a Jew"; he is "Debauched by Service to Moll Hackabout, a Common Prostitute," followed by his "Descent into the Mire of Poverty and Disease"; finally, and crucially, Pringle imagines the "Redemption of Mungo by the Committee for the Abolition of Slavery" (6). Pringle knows Mungo's story because he has heard it all before. What he needs now are examples, just the right details, a bit of color to lend the tale its authenticity, which he will validate in advance, no doubt through the use of some kind of preface, unaware that he has already written it in doodling anger. Pringle may be the agent of archival inquiry, but he too is already subject to the strategies of contravention he deploys. Given the epistemic violence enacted by his chapter headings—or the beheadings, if you will, of his entextualiztion—ultimately, no authority can be made, not by Pringle, not by Mungo, not by Dabydeen, because they are all motivated, in uneven ways and with varying degrees of reflexive acknowledgment, by the market in (post)colonial objects. The African's voice must speak in "broken" English; the African landscape must appear simultaneously scorchingly arid and suffocatingly wet, its climate unpredictable and its environment precarious; its place names must sound convincingly autochthonous (the katran bush, the village of Barambongdodo) and its inhabitants appropriately atavistic, inscrutable, and threatening. But what the market wants most of all is a story of redemption.

Dabydeen's metafictional insistence on fabrication and assemblage demonstrates why "autobiographical" infelicities, such as we find in Equiano, simply do not matter to pubic history, because demonstrations of authenticity, efforts of legitimation, and claims to knowability might themselves be values the archive projects, but they are not the principles by which the archive archives, or by which the law decides what matters, and what does not. Rather, they are values that frame in advance, in anticipation of content, what is authentic, who has legitimacy, and when, where, why, and how something is known. For Pringle, Mungo is deemed unreliable because he cannot remember proper names or the legible markers of place—the exotic flora and fauna Pringle knows the reader will expect—

but Mungo is unreliable because in the frame of the archive projects he will ever remain an object in the archive (bound within the frame of the second plate of Hogarth's *Progress*), never a subject of it. This had already been decided. For his part, Mungo is not quite the obdurate object Pringle takes him to be. Mungo is errant; he withholds, then dissembles; he declares, then disavows; he affirms, then refutes; he carries on, and then gets carried away. What he recounts appears unassimilable to the archive, because it defies the frames of intelligibility, the rules of genre, the principles of exchange. Mungo fails as an example, thus Pringle describes him as a "ruined archive." By repeating Pringle's expression, by characterizing himself as a ruined archive, Mungo emphasizes the relationship between the failure of his memory and the condition of his body. For it is not merely that Mungo refuses to tell. Rather, he insists that he does not remember, that he *cannot* remember, that in fact he has been taught to forget. Although he finds Mungo in "ruins," Pringle continues to believe in Mungo's restoration, even his redemption. The archive can be repaired, fixed, and endowed with knowledge and meaning; the archive can, like a rehabbed warehouse in today's gentrified London, be brought back into use.[6] All he needs is time.

If Pringle is the archivist par excellence, consolidating an archive par exemple, perhaps we might describe Mungo as an archivist *par extraordinaire,* an archivist by chance (to use the French meaning). It is only late in the novel, and notably *not* in the prologue, that Mungo confesses to a massive collection of printed materials "from the journals of the day which," he tells us, he has "saved over all these years to give some meaning to my life." Mungo is an errant archive that both hoards and performs a compendium of singular examples, collected then stored away for some as yet undecided future use. His is an archive, however, that documents the general —the generalized, even universalized—errantry of black life in England, in the Americas, in Africa. His archive gives meaning to his life by providing a set of representations that he can inhabit as his own: "I have, over the years, created an archive of my own morals and manners. I believe no such comprehensive compilation on the Negro exists in one place (though hidden under my bed in no more than two or three fish-boxes, such is the scantiness of our history), and I plan to donate it one day to the Abolition Committee." Ironically scant yet comprehensive, Mungo imagines with a reflexive grandeur a "fine London library" housing "the Mungo Collection," or perhaps "the Noah Collection," "the Barambangdodo Collection," the

"Augustus," or the "Gustavus Collection." Conversely, he thinks, "I plan to sell the archive to supply my small needs, for why should I not generate money from the sale of myself when the sale of the Negro has generated fortunes for foreigners? As a collection of newspaper items, I am a false parcel and counterfeit story but I will pass hands as easily as a forged banknote in the City's markets." And yet, Mungo adds, "I have hesitated out of honour, or perhaps shame, to capitalize my self for only the lewd or the morbid will invest in me. . . . Or is it out of concern for public morals that I refuse to be circulated in the hands of pornographers?" (243–44). What has circulated in the print media is a set of representations framed by assumptions about innate character traits that every African embodies.

The collection Mungo both holds and withholds represents a lifetime of archival accumulation materially secreted away in his garret as the supplement to affective archive entextualized on his own body through the mark of ownership—the double *T* that identifies Thomas Thistlewood as his owner—branded on his forehead. The archive fixes him as an exemplary figure of African errantry, thus the brand that designates Mungo as another's property also represents beyond him: "For what my Negro brethren do," he acknowledges, "is charged on my head" (242). Once again Mungo plays on the mark his body displays, the practice of criminal branding, and the chapter headings inscribed in Pringle's journal discussed earlier. Here are the "headings made years ago [that] remain like stubborn stains," penned by Mungo long before Pringle's arrival:

> "Slave Revolts, "Mutinies," "Runaways," "Suicides," "Infanticides," "Executions by Burning," "Executions by Hand." . . . I have rebelled, stabbed, poisoned, raped, absconded, and sought escape by killing myself and offspring. In return I have been strangled, flogged to death, roasted alive, blown away and lynched. Truly I have made havoc in the hearts and minds of whitepeople, compromising their civility, sharpening their Christian principles to breaking-point. (244)

Mungo's singular collection is nothing less than an archive of exemplary violence. *A Harlot's Progress* shuttles between performances of Mungo's archive and depictions of Mungo *as archive*. Mungo, however, remains situated within multiple circuits of economic and narrative exchange, one item of human bio-cargo circulating in a universe where transactional objects proliferate. Living ambivalently as subject and object in a world of commodities, Mungo enters into transient and transitory scenes of perverse attachments, *de*tachments, fetishistic identifications and *dis*identifications. I want to develop this point, however, by focusing on one formative site of archival violation preceding but also overlapping with acts of exemplary violence that initiates him into the world of human bio-cargo, two events at the center of Mungo's narrative and around which all other stories derive: the "katran bush" located along the edge of Mungo's village but situated at the center of his narrative.

As anticipated, the early chapters of the novel describe Mungo's childhood in a small West African village in the time of colonial terror, a narrative turn that aligns with expectations dictated by the dominant slave narrative form but also an account he will repeat in various, sometime contradictory, ways throughout his tale. In addition to Equiano, Mungo's account appears to draw from a number of eighteenth-century sources, but his initial story concerns his friendship with another young villager named Saba, a "most cruel child" who bullies the other children and whom Mungo is determined to subdue.[7] Mungo is not afraid of Saba but recognizes the inherent weakness masked by his cruelty, a weakness Mungo seeks to exploit in his ploy to overpower him.[8] Mungo conspires to make Saba his slave, which he does through a sudden, unexpected manifestation of violence. "I go up to him," the adult Mungo recounts, "call out his name and when he turn I slap him across the mouth. His hands, once packed with rage, fall by his sides. He is now my slave. I am like death to him" (13). If a single slap across the face appears inadequate to the task of slave-making, it will not be surprising that Mungo repeats the encounter in the following paragraph, already amending his characterization of the intensity of his attack: "A sudden blow," he begins again, "can make you into a slave forever. If you creep up to someone, as I do Saba, and with a quick blow knock all the stuff from his head, words and all, then you make a fresh space where only you can dwell . . . for he is now you and not himself nor no one else" (14). The sudden blow to the head that Mungo administers and Saba receives anticipates the sudden, slave-making abuse he himself receives at the hands of those to whom he is sold and resold, a motif repeated throughout the novel, framing various configurations of those who abuse and those who are abused. "Everything in his head gone, and blood run down his face," Mungo continues. "But heed, to make a slave you have to move quick and lash in one clean stroke, or else he will stay stale, his old self stubborn, and one day will rebel and curse you" (14). Brute force gives way to absolute hegemonic control. "Come to the katran bush with me, I say in a sudden urge, and when he look at me like a beggar look at his sores, I know that I have at last overcome him totally, and will have no pity on him." From this moment on Mungo commands while Saba submits, until "one day," perhaps inevitably, Mungo realizes, "I am bored with him."

As Mungo cajoles Saba toward the forbidden site, he fears the slave's rebellion, "but words come to my mind from somewhere strange," he recalls, "that *I will brook no disobedience,* I am come armed with knives of stone" (14). The voice Mungo hears, or the voice Mungo remembers having heard those many decades before, is of course Thomas Thistlewood's, and he anticipates the reversal that is to come. "Now I remember," he reflects, "but then, in an *uncreated time,* when there were no words, only a small boy there was, driving a bully to his death" (16, emphasis added). Recollecting Saba's name draws out and draws together fragments of memory—his father's death, his mother's sorrow as she prepares her husband's body for transport to its resting place in the katran bush, the rituals that follow, and a scene of seduction in which the women of his village initiate Mungo into the sexual order of adulthood: "Now I remember, and have new words to remember, how beautiful it was, the chorus and the exhibition of shameless painted women. I am brought into manhood. . . . I become the father" (15). Despite the funeral and the ritual, despite his initiation into manhood and the promise of his patrimony—or perhaps because of these things—Mungo decides that his father's death demands a further sacrifice, Saba's sacrifice; "Saba must go" to his father's body inside the katran bush (16): "I push him cruel hard, but he cries, he will not, and his noise is of such distress that I nearly let him free. But we are at the katran bush, my father is waiting, he will have blood, so Saba must obey" (17). But in exchange for this one final "task," should he survive, Mungo will grant Saba his freedom.

This initial scene of violence initiates an escalating sequence of violent events reminiscent of the trajectory of decline shown in abundance in Hogarth's prints and the cycles of sin, remorse, and relapse depicted in the progress narrative and revised by Equiano. Unlike these precedents, however, Mungo does not paint the scene of original sin and ultimate salvation in a steady, consistent—even if intricately detailed—manner. Rather, he gives us multiple, often contradictory, accounts, but accounts whose surfeit of detail, like Hogarth's, resonate with one another and with every other episode in the novel. Indeed, such resonance is produced by the almost inexhaustible, if incoherent, accumulation of detail. The first chapter of the novel begins with Mungo's hesitant remembering of the crime that initiates his narrative of decline, a story in which he at first implicates Saba equally for "wandering in the katran bush." "We make sin there," he continues. "I only know him in the katran bush and in sin, before he went away to become spirit" (12). So vague is Mungo's early recollection that the account is suggestive of sexual rather than ancestral transgression, a suggestion I do not think is negated by other versions and other details later in the novel. Although he begins with the "sin" they commit together, from this sudden flash of memory Mungo recuperates the events that led up to their entry into the katran. The admission of his own sin is simultaneously offered and withheld, and ultimately recast as an enormously consequential violation of society's most fundamental law.

When Mungo forces Saba to enter the sacred "katran bush"—a transgression regarded as a fundamental violation of divine law—the consequences of "a boy's mischief" redound upon the entire village. For the katran bush is sacred land and a forbidden terrain. It serves as a burial ground for the dead and the dwelling place of the ancestors; the katran bush designates the uncertain frontier between life and death, and the opaque borderland of the material and immaterial worlds. The katran bush defines the boundary between one village and the next, a no-man's-land that separates the laws of one social order from those of another, and serves as a buffer zone between the protective spirits of one community and those of its neighbor. Finally, the katran bush houses the law, and the ban on entering the katran bush is the first law from which all others are derived. When Saba returns from the katran bush unscathed, Mungo's belief in the power of his ancestors is severely shaken. Not only had Mungo's own sacrifice not been accepted, but Saba reappears bearing a gourd filled with food "which he has brought back from the plot of dead." When Saba offers the gourd to Mungo "as tribute," Mungo commands that Saba "eat the food of the dead and so commit his life into my service" (18). In trying to establish his own rule over Saba, Mungo's mischief proves nothing less than a law-destroying act of blasphemy.[9]

Both source of law and dwelling place of ancestral spirits encumbered with the task of the law's protection, the katran bush also houses the archive of collective memory. Just as the ancestors defend the village and safeguard the law, so too do they shelter the historical archive. They "guard us,"

Mungo says, “from forgetting the past or seeking the future blindly” (21). When Mungo and Saba enter the katran bush, their ancestors take flight, relinquishing their duty to protect and keep watch over the village and abandoning it to the vicissitudes of the world: “For our ancestors have departed in anger from the katran bush leaving us no defence against enemies of flies, drought, malicious stars, tribes with different scars” (19–20). By forsaking the archive, Mungo laments, the ancestral spirits are “leaving us without memory of past and to a stillborn future” (20). The transgression onto sacred land—against the authority of the ancestors and in violation of its foremost, originary law—opens a breach in the historical archive and a rupture in collective memory. Mungo’s account of the katran bush demonstrates the powerful command this broken line of kinship retains over his present and, in the absence of the collective wisdom of historical experience, his ability to anticipate the future.

If by forcing Saba into the katran bush Mungo has violated the most fundamental sanction of the law, by paying tribute to Mungo with the spoils of his crime—and by consuming that offering at Mungo’s insistence—Saba’s gesture entirely upends the ancestral force of law, who in turn demands atonement. In an act of “useless fury,” Headman scrambles to reassert the law by demanding their sacrifice. He brands Mungo’s forehead with the mark of his crime and abandons him to death, Mungo recalls, “in a deep hole, which me mother is made to dig, . . . for my disobedience has brought sin upon her and the threat of destruction to our village” (19). Mungo must bear the sign of their total dissolution and represent the withering away of collective memory: “My passing will be a sacrifice to gods and ancestors, that knowledge may be restored to our tribe. . . . I am to suffer hunger till flesh loosens from its frame, till all creation is unmade in me” (21). For having entered the katran bush—for having forced Saba too across the threshold of the law, for having broken the law in order to prove his mastery over Saba, and for having offered Saba as a sacrifice to Mungo’s own father’s spirit—not only must he be sacrificed but his infractions entail supernatural retribution and communal punishment: “Saba will die and remain unburied, but this will not pacify our ancestors, though he will be forever entombed. . . . Saba will not seed the future” (20). Neither Mungo’s slow execution nor Saba’s agonizing death, not even “this total banishment from the history of our tribe,” proves “enough to pacify our ancestors” (20). It is, Mungo repeats, a “useless” punishment directed at him by villagers, demanded by law of ancestors. “And if the ancestors are stupid enough to desert us because of a boy's mischief, then let them go uselessly into the dark. What plague of flies, what drought, what enemies have they ever protected us from? The ancestors are weak, they are cowards, they will use a boy's misdeed as excuse to run away and leave us prey to the white hunter who comes with gun (as we have come to name this magic) and torch and chain and cup and cross" (22). Mungo curses their ancestors for foretelling their ultimate uselessness in the face of unforeseeable catastrophe. And as he predicts, without the protection of the law, without the archive of collective memory his ancestors were charged to protect, his community's ultimate annihilation arrives in world historical scale in the form of Captain Thomas Thistlewood, who burns the village to the ground, slaughters his people, and enslaves all who remain. Mungo survives as the sole "witness" to these events, crimes for which—in his mind—he bears sole responsibility and for which he offers a lifetime of penance in the hopes of final expiation. While others are carried away in chains, Mungo is "rescued" from the protective condemnation of the pit—from which he could not have possibly seen the unfolding atrocity he will claim to have witnessed—by Thistlewood himself, a name that serves as the very figure of colonial atrocity.[10] It is also a name that will forever mark Mungo's rupture into order of modern human bio-cargo. Thistlewood becomes a troubling object of Mungo's adoration and a sanctified patronymic for historical redemption. Mungo, Pringle, Thistlewood—survivor, savior, and saint.

Mungo's memory may be imprecise, but its fragmented details are certainly suggestive, refracted, I contend, through the scenes staged on canvas and in print by William Hogarth. Hogarth's oeuvre, as I held earlier, is Mungo's archive; it provides both a narrative structure and an aesthetic form for recalling and recounting the most profane experiences of everyday life, and it provides the motifs that echo in counterpoint from one episode to the next. Like Hogarth, Mungo takes a perverse pleasure in capturing and relentlessly exposing the cruelty endemic across societies and social classes. By staging his memory like a Hogarth engraving, Mungo constellates fragments of both memory and fantasy (fantasies that are, perhaps, remembered as if they were lived). What this constellation of narrative fragments and sensual details begins to orchestrate is a "truth," if you will, that Mungo will never divulge: that he in fact does remember his own name, but he remembers it as another's, for it was Mungo, as Saba, who was forced into the katran bush. Mungo *is* Saba. But Mungo is not ready to remember, any more than he is able to forget. As their existence begins to merge in Mungo's recollection, in the somnolent mist of the katran bush, he is once again returned to the safety of forgetting. "I hear nothing. I open my eyes wide and stare in the direction of his going but see nothing. I tear the mist from my face, but sleeps drapes my eyes, I call out to Saba in panic, I call and call whilst the mist leaks into my mouth like a poisonous sap. . . . Saba comes to my call, just at the moment I go to collapse. The sight of him jolts me back to myself" (17). His existence is sutured to Saba's, but Saba remains a necessary figment, a plausible fiction that rewrites the moment of psychic rupture. "I am glad to see him, and that he is whole, nothing eaten from him, no wound, no torn chest. I am sorry that my father is remaining dead, but still glad for Saba, that he is not flowered into sacrifice" (17–18). Saba returns unscathed, "but wild with grief," his skin "as dull as if the dead had breathed ash upon him" (18). Mungo returns from the katran bush to face an unimagined and unimaginable punishment at the hand of the Headman. But the punishment he receives points to another time and place, another order of violence, and another scene of its exemplarity. Anticipating the scenes on board Thistlewood's vessel, the description of the Headman's rage is recast in the language of slave ship and plantation: "Swiftly it happened, in the space of a breath, though I grew numb after the first blows so that the rest were the useless rage of our village Headman who, between words of chastisement, broke one fresh whip after another against my back, then, yanking back my head so that my forehead faced the sun, pressed a hot stone to it, branding me with a sign of my sin" (19).

When Mungo repeats the story of the katran bush in the following chapter, the entire episode is upended—gone is the admission of the "sin" he makes with Saba, restaged as another's narrative, another who is cast out for disobedience to the law: Rima, who is exiled by the elders because she is unable to reproduce, because she has been rendered useless to men. It is to her story, and the story of women, that Mungo turns: "Whatever the truth, I will be faithful to Rima's account, for she loved me in spite of my sex, abided with me, nurtured me, and even when fatally wounded by gunshot, whispered to me a final blessing. Her mouth ran with blood then, and I will be as profuse in my telling of her story" (28–29). "For these women unfortunate enough to be widowed, weeks of plunder followed, the endurance of the glee of young men . . . too young for war or stalking prey" (29). As soon as these widows show their inability to bear more children, "once their uselessness became evident," they are cast out of the village (29): "The women were marked like jack-jack and sent away to starve or be devoured—in either case a proscriptive sacrifice to the demons of sterility" (30). This is what has happened to Rima. "But even more cruelty was to come, namely the breaking of their wrists, and the pressing of a hot stone into their palms which left the imprint of evil. It was a peculiar sign called *peia* which only sojourn in England made familiar, for my people were ignorant of mathematical formulae. The sign was a matter of superstition, originating from a distant past, when, according to Rima, strangers visited our dreams" (30). Again, readers are reminded that the katran bush is an archive, which he is forbidden to enter: it is an archive of the dead but also the domain of the ancestors who protect the law and thus the fundamental order of the village. Mungo has entered this archive and found there, dwelling among the dead, the white man treading, like him, upon sacred ground. Once they emerge from this archive they will "quicken," come alive, make history. The social world is not, in Mungo's experience, overturned by the exemplary violence of Thistlewood's men but is done so in advance, indeed in anticipation of them, by the encroachments of a child. In this final curse on his ancestors, the accusation of stupidity, weakness, and cowardice, Mungo simultaneously shows up the fault at the heart of the law but also the real dangers of collective historical memory when it is housed in the necromantic archive of the law of the father.

The variant accounts of the katran bush—given reluctantly, anxiously, even excessively by a native informant under enormous pressure to speak—raises important questions about how cultural knowledge operates outside the circuits of local knowledge productions but also within it; about the naïve celebration of tradition imagined to be fixed, authentic, and transparent to representation; and about the way in which colonial history, or the history of Western modernity generally, can be treated as a singular and totalizing narrative for apprehending the non-Western world. Mungo's improvised, fragmented, disordered counternarrative—one emphatically *not* based on the archival record but rather imaginatively speculative—provides a powerful performance of an anticipatory unhousing that points the readers to those countless stories he is yet to tell. While *A Harlot's Progress* depicts countless acts of brutality and instances of exemplary violence that secure the authority of the law, it also stages and restages, differentially, the exceptional event (which stands beside itself as both singular and exemplary) that arises at an unpredictable, spontaneous intersection: Mungo's transgression of the katran bush and Thistlewood's attack on the village, that is, at the intersection of one body of law and another law of commerce. The historical rupture that occurs at the crossroads of the Atlantic, where social existence is liquidated in the production of human bio-cargo, registers at the same time the two forms of violence Benjamin called "mythic" and "divine."[11]

The Captain and the Cash Nexus

Dabydeen has spoken of his appreciation of Hogarth's compositional vision, of the unforgettable characters telling of their own material needs and the extraordinary lengths they must go to satisfy them, and of the artist's capacity to make every person and every object he draws send the narrative off in unexpected directions. In the dense allegories of modern social life—one thinks of the action-packed and information-rich street scenes of *Beer Street* and *Gin Lane,* or the more unsettling *Four Stages of Cruelty*—Hogarth's canvases perform what I have characterized as the exhausting inexhaustibility of the archive. Once housed in the bodies and objects represented on the two-dimensional expanse of synchronous, homogenous time, Hogarth's riveting scenes capture frenetic constellations of social hierarchy, political power, economic interest, class conflict, sexual exploitation, ethical compromise, and moral bankruptcy—a world that is "all about money," in which "the cash nexus replaces human relationships," as Dabydeen recalls in an interview, adding:

> I don't think that anybody who grew up under Thatcher as I did for those fifteen years or so—as a mature person, as it were, not as a child—could not have been affected by this greed that she represented, and the way she placed accountancy and commerce, free market values, and a naked capitalism and privatization at the heart of social and political polity. Everything I've written really, although it might be set in different parts and carrying different characters, is about money.[12]

A Harlot's Progress opens, then, with the cash nexus in which the "gift" of money binds the former slave, Mungo, to his narrative interlocutor, Mr. Pringle. Despite Pringle's recourse to the language of Christian charity, the exchange of money between speaker and listener brings Mungo into—or more precisely, *back into*—circulation.[13] Once "a celebrity of slum and mansion alike," Pringle believes, Mungo's "presence [was] greeted with equal excitement in seedy bagnio or baroque galley. Beggars and nobility were his equal friends, and they flocked to him as he made his entrance to whore house or High Church." Or at least "this much Mr Pringle imagines for his only source of information is Hogarth's portrait of Mungo as a boy-slave to the harlot Moll Hackabout" (4). Mungo, in other words, is already, from the novel's opening pages, presented as a fantasy object manufactured *from* the archive.

The eighteenth-century cultivation of sentiment more than coincided with the development of modern slavery; the "culture of taste" was produced dialectically *with* colonial slavery, as Simon Gikandi has powerfully argued.[14] Captain Thistlewood, however, prefers those premodern forms of sentimental attachment. As a narrator reflexively operating within a cash nexus, however, Mungo refuses to cast Thistlewood as the exemplary figure of evil unabated that Pringle expects and desires. But it is not what Thistlewood does that convolutes expectations about the captain's character, but Mungo's own shifting, often contradictory, characterization of him. For instance, Thistlewood is at one moment deeply caring of the lives in his charge, but such care is at variance to the conditions of their human existence. As bio-cargo, "they were not fully human." More provocatively, however, Mungo frames their condition in a more common framework of Christian salvation, which in turn designates him as the exception:

> They were not human, for none were baptized in the body of Christ, none received the sacraments from Captain Thistlewood's, my father's, mouth. . . . Being heathen, it was inevitable that they would perish in irrelevant numbers. Captain Thistlewood only counted their bodies for human record, for the purpose of the insurance dividends which would be paid for loss of goods once we landed on commercial shores; or for the purpose of calculating quantity of fresh water on board against diminishing demands. [Rather] he tended them not as soulful beings but as sick animals. And when his efforts failed, and they were brought on deck to be disposed of overboard, his face was mulched with sorrow. He was deeply affected by the loss of his creatures. (49–50)

In order to rationalize Thistlewood's actions, Mungo must disavow the captain's own economic rationality and project onto him a confluence of deeply held affective attachments—compassionate, empathetic, and magnanimous—but pitched in the language of animal husbandry that, despite the rhetoric of care and concern, still designates an old technology of "making live or letting die" for economic gain. "The Captain, when he looked upon them, did not behold a scene from hell, for there were not perished souls. He saw animals innocent of crime or sin, animals discharged into his failed care and husbandry" (50). Doubling down on the double-meaning of "husband" as duty to both livestock and wife in the management of the household, Dabydeen not only points us right back to the economic reason underlying Thistlewood's sentiment, in contravention of a premodern model of the technologies of the biopolitical found in the decidedly unsentimental practices of animal husbandry. Captain Thistlewood, Mungo continues, "was moved as fiercely as any decent man is by the sight of undeserved suffering. You, English, inhabitants of a country distinguished for its adoration of pets and charity to the lesser breed, will know the tempest of emotions that overcame my Captain. You have the nightmare of Mr Hogarth's genius, in his series of prints, *Scenes of Cruelty,* to stir you to patriotic rage" (50).

The contradictions in this portrait of Thistlewood stem from Mungo's refusal to see him as someone fully engaged with the system of commerce; rather, Thistlewood is depicted as someone who has disavowed commerce in the name of love. In doing so, Mungo also denies the implicit corollary between the cargo quartered below deck and the cargo quartered in the captain's cabin: "Captain Thistlewood hated the business of death. He hated the classification in his ledger book of Negroes by gender and age (dead males yielding a greater sum in compensation from the insurance company than females and children). He hated the shores of commerce and its citizenry of clerks; soil-bound clerks who showed actuarial contempt for his love of his cargo, for the measureless grief he felt at the suffering of his animals" (50). If he were to render the relationship between the captain and his cargo as purely economic, rather than dutifully paternalistic, then so too might be his own relationship to the captain, with all of the implications about his own life—his own status as life—that would follow: "They were his crew as the slaves below were collectively theirs to dispose of or to husband. Rape was allowed, not only for necessary manly recreation, nor because it calmed their cravings for a shore, but because it promised to increase the stock of slaves. But it had to be a measured act, no lasting hurt done to the females, no excessive violence to exhaust them to the point of extinction. . . . At sea everything had to be managed with care and due control, for their lives' sake and the success of the enterprise" (72). Thistlewood begins to neglect his careful management, so much so has he been transformed by Mungo's love.

By selecting Mungo as the one slave contractually promised him, Thistlewood disrupts what should have been—in that same contractual agreement that bound his captaincy to successful delivery of the ship's bio-cargo—the managed rhythms of economic exchange with the less predictable fluctuations of his desires. Mungo's "fresh body gave hope to Captain Thistlewood, who could dream of new beginnings, and when he took the boy all thoughts of margins and returns which shaped his life disappeared. What does it profit a man to gain the whole world but to lose his life: the words boomed in Captain Thistlewood's mind as he snatched at Mungo desperately as at a raft" (117). Here Mungo appears before Thistlewood as the sign of the captain's own transcendence and a symbol of the captain's own delivery from the sins of the slave trade. In his sentimental rumination Mungo recalls shockingly dissonant memories of Captain Thistlewood's gentle touch and brutal hand, and confesses to the sadomasochistic pleasures of living as the object of another's tortuous affections. Mungo's narrative countersigns one form of exemplary violence—the violence enacted on the bodies of those Africans chained one to another down in the hold of the ship—with another in the intimate space of the captain's quarters. Mungo's tale of the singular love and exceptional pain experienced at the hand of Thistlewood is elevated as an allegory of Christian charity and care that is meant to resonate with the moment of philanthropic generosity exigent to Mungo's confession to Pringle. The assumption of Mungo as an object of desire, however, coincides with the story of Thistlewood's abandonment of the rules of commerce that guarantee the smooth transfer of bio-cargo from initial extraction to final market. Such desires run counter to the fundamental principles of stewardship and husbandry that organize everyday exchanges between captain, crew, and cargo. Ironically, the methodical, disciplinary organization of the trade appeals to Mungo's sense of order, precision, and structural harmony, but Thistlewood's abrogation of his duty to command by following the command of his desires, while securing Mungo's survival, disappoints his own love of ideal form. Disheartened, Mungo tells us,

> I had thought that, in being captured by Captain Thistlewood,
> I had escaped the ramblings of Rima and the confusions of my

> past. The world of logic was promised, the logic, however cruel, of slavery. I envy Mr Pringle his quest for tidiness, but the truth is otherwise. Captain Thistlewood's resolve collapsed, and with it the triangle of commercial interests that fixed Africa to the Americas to England. And the globe too within the triangle, one so perfectly defined. All because of a weakness that inheres in love. (110–11)

Mungo, at least as the retrospective confessor of his tale, is disillusioned by Thistlewood's "love," not simply because it is exercised through extraordinary acts of physical abuse coupled with aberrant practices of Christian worship but because such love runs counter to the very promise of enlightened modernity to return him to the ancestors that abandoned his village—not the ancestors driven out by his own violations of the law but the Greek refugees that made a home somewhere in the West African bush and introduced civilization before the civilizing mission of Thistlewood and his ilk:

> Consider the fate of Captain Thistlewood. He was master of a slaveship, perhaps the most perfectly designed of sea vessels, for every inch of deck needed to be plotted to maximize the cargo. Every inch of sail needed to be measured to take advantage of the winds, given the perishable or rebellious nature of the cargo. When you ferry spices or rum or cloth across the seas, you can afford a little slackness here and there, but the Negro trade demands a precision, nay, a patriotism worthy of Newton's computations that have given England such a reputation for genius. Or consider the perfection of Mr Dryden's couplets, which give new order to the English page where before there was the rudeness of rustic or regional expressions. . . . It was such perfection that Captain Thistlewood betrayed because of his love for me. (Mr Pringle will call it a perversion.) (111)

Mungo describes Thistlewood as a careful and conscientious slaver, "keeping scrupulous distance between his reason and his actions," who raped not with abandon but with the very minimum of violence so that "the slaves remained slaves, as undamaged as possible" (111). Likewise, Mungo notes the captain's scrupulously measured use of the whip: "Even though his actions sometimes maimed or killed a slave," Mungo assures us, "he made sure to put his conscience to rest by compensating the owners for the unforeseen loss" (112). Ambivalence and contradiction abound in Mungo's characterization of Captain Thistlewood. He embraces the notion that he can enact his own recovery of the captain's humanity, but he also narcissistically imagines the power he himself once held over the unredeemed slaver, which in the end leads to Thistlewood's fall and the perfect geometry of law contravened. As a legal frame, political exercise, sexual entanglement, corporeal relation, the "cash nexus" that chains Mungo to Thistlewood also binds the captain to his slave.

Critics have noted Dabydeen's reluctance to demonize the merchant sailors and sea captains who participated in the transatlantic trade. Dabydeen has himself criticized literary works that take a reductive approach to representing individual "perpetrators" of violence. Thomas Thistlewood—who attacks Mungo's village, slaughters and/or captures its members, and sets sail for the West Indies with a new cabin boy at his disposal—is not a "round" character by any means. Thistlewood is nothing more than a projection of Mungo's own narrative desires; he places Thistlewood at his disposal, and disposes of him by professing admiration of his captor and an almost mutual role in the civilizing of one another. The reversal of their positions of power is not aimed at rescue and recovery but at Mungo's own seizing of control—over his narrative, his memory, his agency. Thistlewood, characterized at first as an emblematic product of the Scottish Enlightenment—deliberative, calculating, reasonable—is undone by Mungo's astonishing and captivating presence. Thistlewood is ensnared by love:

> All such equanimity was lost when he allowed himself to desire me beyond reason. . . . He saved me, singled me out from the tribe as a special creature, and taught me Christianity. He beat me manfully but only to resist his growing love for me, his collapsing heart, which, as each day passed, weakened him to the condition of woman. I came to possess him, even as I yielded to him, and the coinage of his speech became rare, when once it dwelt on trade. He told me, in fits of distraction, of an antique world where beasts rolled in imaginary freedom, as if the age in which we actually lived was so regulated that the love he bore for a Negro youth was unlawful; the love that transformed him from master to an aspect of woman. (112)

Should the reader wish to visit Thistlewood, Mungo proposes, one would find him "retired to his home in Hampstead," where he would greet us "in the modest voice of a woman" (112–13). By feminizing the captain, however, Mungo does not attempt to masculinize himself, nor is he ever ashamed at his own feminization, whether in the coming-of-age rituals of his village, his sexual objectification by the captain, or the countless abuses that render him the "harlot" of the novel's title. It might have been easy for Dabydeen to depict Thistlewood along the lines of those damning portraits found in abolitionist testimony; the archive is rife with examples. But the novel refuses to participate in the conventions of abolitionist propaganda, with its often single-minded focus on the slave ship captain as the embodiment of absolute cruelty, any more than he would reproduce the proslavery cant that portrayed the captain as arbiter of sound reason and economic rationality, often at the cost of a classist disparaging image of the seaman from a lower order. Dabydeen is neither concerned with damning figures like Thistlewood or redeeming figures like Mungo, nor with reclaiming a universal humanity sacrificed at the altar of human bio-cargo.

Reckoning

I conclude at the nexus of beauty and violence: exemplary, sacred, sublime. The orchestration of the colonial archive that reproduces the scandal of aestheticized violence in Mungo's narrative brings us back to Hogarth and to Hogarth's own aesthetic criteria: fitness, symmetry, proportion; variety, intricacy, quantity; the relation of parts and wholes; the play of simplicity and complexity; and his famous curving "line of beauty" and serpentine "line of grace." Hogarth's exercise in aesthetic idealism is recorded in his *Analysis of Beauty,* whose two illustrative engravings serve Mungo much like the bulletin board serves Verbal Kint (see Figures 9 and 10). "My figures," Hogarth writes in the introduction, "are to be considered in the same light, with those a mathematician makes with his pen."[15] Hogarth's modern and humanistic association of ideal form and the mathematic sublime parallels—and reinforces—the correlation Mungo espouses between religious piety, moral perfection, and the sacred geometry he claims as a filial inheritance reaching back to an ancient, ancestral civilization. The most significant and complex formal trope for Mungo's singular aesthetic obsession is the Greek letter π, a figure connected with the golden ratio and the 3:4:5 triangle. A symbol of elegant, if inscrutable, perfection, the letter π

figures the syntagmatic slide from sacred geometry to moral perfection to ideal form: *pi—peia—pietà.* Both a mathematical constant and an irrational number, pi represents the elegance of geometric shape, the beauty of ideal form, and the terror of infinite calculation. Pi marks a mathematic sublime that yokes the exercise of exemplary violence to the aestheticization of pain and torture. In a remarkable irony, pi expresses—in the form of an absolute abstraction—the exhausting inexhaustibility of mathematic calculation itself. Pi represents the perfect symmetry of the circle, but its expression is anything but symmetrical—the never ending, never repeating string of digits whose final calculation will forever elude us, as it will the array of supercomputers that are now (at this very moment, no matter when this moment occurs) applying the iterative algorithms that drive the number's computation toward greater and greater precision, but never to achieve anything more than proximity, even as its perfection recedes further into

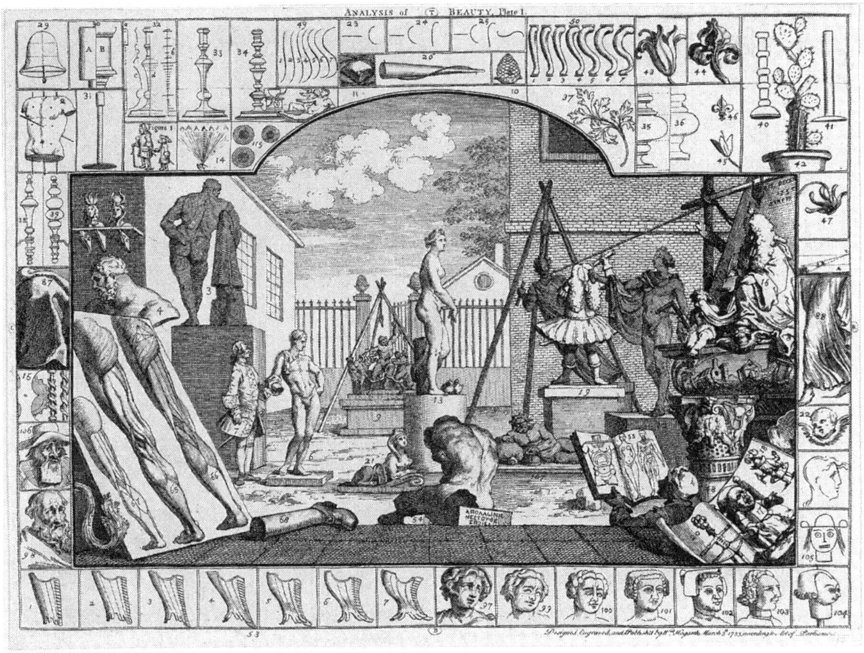

Figure 9. William Hogarth, Analysis of Beauty, *plate 1, 1753. Etching and engraving. Courtesy of La Clé des Langues (Clifford Armion, dir.) and ENS Média (Vincent Brault, photo).*

the digital horizon. Pi functions as one sign among many others that constellate to form one of the novel's most significant narrative motifs: the geometry of human relations under what I have called bio-cargo.

Recall that in the prologue to *A Harlot's Progress,* having carefully written out the date, Pringle awaits Mungo's beginning by "doodling" along the edges of the otherwise pristine notebook. He begins by drawing overlapping geometric shapes, initiating a motif in which pi functions as a sign of perfection. But as his patience wears thin, Pringle defaces these shapes, transforming the page into an anticipatory scene of violence. Mungo describes the page once again at the end of the novel. After Pringle has left, Mungo picks up the piece of paper on which the abolitionist had doodled: "He draw circles and squares and triangles all muddle and mess up. The points of the triangles poking and stretching and deforming the circles which trap them, like bumps on the shaved head of Bedlam folk" (226). In

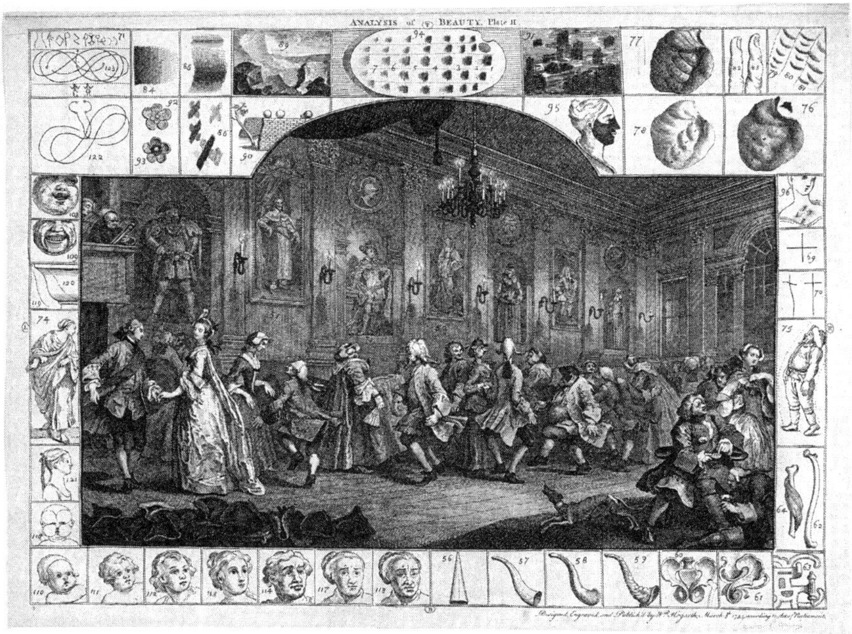

Figure 10. William Hogarth, Analysis of Beauty, *plate 2, 1753. Etching and engraving. Courtesy of La Clé des Langues (Clifford Armion, dir.) and ENS Média (Vincent Brault, photo).*

the clean, symmetrical, arithmetic forms in which he once found comfort, Mungo now sees physical deformity, human monstrosity, and demonic malevolence. "Why they all deem me bringer of disorder," he wonders, "why they watch me and only see an egg hatching in themselves, the shell break, a red beak show and then the body too blasphemous for print?" (226). If pi is a sign for what cannot be fully represented, it also serves as a narrative alibi for Mungo's unrepresentable story, for the traumas he cannot remember and the experiences he refuses to disclose. The story of pi is an alibi for the physical mark of his subjection—the symbol branded into his forehead—the double *T* linked across the top, its serifs forming an almost perfect (but not quite) *TT*. Two perfectly parallel lines intersect at perfectly perpendicular single segments bent at both ends. How that mark came to rest on Mungo's forehead is, in fact, the story he is loath to tell. Rather, he gives a multiplicity of accounts, and while one of them resonates with the historical truths about the slave trade the reader, like Pringle, has come to expect, others are of such implausibility as to be easily dismissed.

The initial chapters of the novel give an extraordinary counternarrative to the typical primitivizing discourses of sub-Saharan Africa found in countless generic travel narratives of the period, such as "Adamson's *Voyage to Africa*," which, Mungo explains, he "perused in England" (41).[16] But it is simultaneously another story of a civilizing mission, this one about a group of ancient Alexandrian Greeks, an unlikely band of wayward explorers who, wandering lost in the West African bush, establish a settlement and introduce the wonders of Euclidian mathematics to Mungo's ancestors. In Mungo's version of the well-known Kisra legend, which resonated with the colonial Hamitic hypothesis of early West African civilization (in the story of Kisra, after a Persian army that had conquered Egypt in the seventh century, converting the majority of the population to Islam, were expelled by the Byzantines, they traveled westward through the Sudan and eventually to West Africa), their ancient forebears are symbolized by the *TT* bestowed as an honor upon his forehead. In other versions of this tale, Mungo recounts the fall and assimilation of Alexandrian society into his own, a fall that recodes the symbol as a sign of evil Mungo is born with, and an omen that forecasts the destruction of his village. From the opening of the prologue to the closing of the final chapter, geometry offers Mungo a soothing form through which to reckon violence. Mungo bears both the curse of Ham and the mark of Cain, a conflation that overdetermines the threat he represents.[17]

For Mungo, even the chaos of nature is tamed through the symmetry of shape—the gracefulness of right angles, the formality of a perpendicular convergence, the certainty in knowing that two parallel lines will never meet. Repetition, pattern, contour, and assemblage: each gives meaning and purpose to the aleatory events, contingent episodes, and dissonant voices that surround him. If the laws of geometry afford a means of organizing his thoughts—ordering events, anchoring him in time and place—they do so only, ironically, in retrospect, in the retelling. Indeed, the elegance of pi as a mathematical constant, which names the inexpressible ratio of the circumference to the diameter in a circle, masks its status as an irrational number, that is, irreducible to a simple fraction. (Is it any wonder that the basic mathematical proof of its irrationality relies upon reductio ad absurdum? Or surprising that this technique would be called the "method of exhaustion"?) As an irrational, transcendental number, its computation has neither pattern nor end. The circle cannot be squared.

The principles of geometry inform the way in which Mungo calculates a wide range of relationships, from those expressed in the natural world to the social bond that both attaches and detaches mother and child. Mungo's body runs parallel to his mother's; they are forever bound together and kept apart by a mathematical law that secures the all too rational distance between them. If the constancy of space places them in an unalterable parallel, the ratio of their measure proves (or proves to be) their incommensurability. Geometry makes comparison possible. When Mungo compares the English and African landscapes, he initially draws them in contrast. The English pastoral is first accessed through the cheap prints that decorate Captain Thistlewood's cabin walls. "You who live in England in manicured gardens," Mungo initially asserts, "you who have melodic names for nature—rills, meadows, groves, spinneys and purling streams—cannot appreciate the dreadfulness of the bush. It howls eternally, like a soul condemned to the habituation of fallen angels" (31). In contrast to the images of the English countryside, beneath which Mungo submits to the symmetry of the captain's desire and his faith, the idyll of Africa recedes from his memory, replaced with allusions derived from the classical (and neoclassical) aesthetic tradition. Only later, through figurative repetition and narrative recursivity, will these two landscapes begin to mirror one another, until finally they come together in the story of Betty's childhood in York, a tale of original sin that almost parallels Mungo's own. But initially, from the vantage point of colonial knowledge production, the African bush "is Satan's kingdom, Hades, the Inferno, the Realms of Pluto, the Underworld. Our native word for it is *peia,* an obvious corruption of the Greek *pi,* which we also signify as TT" (31). It is a story of social decline that will be repeated throughout the novel, in which the Greeks—like those modern European colonizers depicted in popular tales of tropical adventure—succumb to the corrupting pull of the archaic African landscape:

> It was the bush—its insects, its animals, its rank vegetation, its baneful noises, its human eyes gleaming from behind dense foliage—which drove the Greeks to massacre. Legend has it that they speared, hacked, skinned, bonfired and otherwise harassed to death thousands of folk. Whole species of tribes and animals were made extinct. . . . Legend does not yield such detail, so you must excuse me if I seek to embroider my tale but fail in the process, for no English words can describe the perfection of the Greek tribe. . . . They painted, they philosophized. They engaged in speculation on geometry. They measured the relationship between shapes and planes. They codified these in an abstruse algebra. (31–32)

The Greeks, according to Mungo, brought pure knowledge to Africa; they tried to forge a hybrid civilization of learned Africans, but "the initial excitement of penetration gave way to torpor and exhaustion. The African mind stubbornly refused the ecstasy of abstraction. The new tribe, born out of the processes of extinction, became extinct in turn. Bush reclaimed its territory, overran the mural and the fort" (32). Ultimately, Mungo concludes, "they disappeared, leaving the longest memory of our tribe" (33). In the legacy passed down through generations, the "Greeks became the demons of sterility," and Mungo their resurrected spirit who augers the approaching catastrophe. "Some germ of Greek civilization survived the suffocation of bush and blacks to flower on my forehead centuries later. I am certain that I am an imprint of a lost tribe of Greeks, for how else can I explain the sign of *Pi* inscribed on my forehead. . . . I was a harbinger of a new darkness, a new sterility" (33). If his mark feels eerily familiar, it is because the story of his own sin is a retelling of Cain's murder of his brother Abel. The mark of Cain is conflated with the sign of calamity, the coming *Maafa,* and it is symbolized by pi, *TT.* "In a moment, in the space of a gunshot, all that they owned and were ceased, all the efforts over all the ages that made them a tribe with its own scars. I bore on my forehead, in the briefest of marks, all the evidence that once we were. The Headman carved my forehead with the sign of evil: I was to be banished out of sight and memory of our tribe, but what heathen foolishness! He was dead, and all of them, our homes wasted, the fields overrun, all signs of husbandry disappeared. It is as if we had made nothing, except the mark of sin upon a boy's forehead" (59). Initially, Mungo says he was born with the mark of pi, the same mark branded upon the palms of women banished from the village because they could no longer reproduce. Later he describes it as a sign of his punishment and exile for having lead Saba into the katran bush and to his death. Later still, in a coming-of-age ceremony carried out by the men of the village—which we are now told preceded the earlier ceremony of women—the mark on his forehead signifies his entry into manhood.

In the first story, Mungo was "born with the sign of evil" upon his forehead; in the second, pi is the mark of his punishment and exile; in the third, it symbolizes his coming into adulthood. Yet another, a fourth, account of the scar identifies it as the brand of Captain Thomas Thistlewood—*TT*—that tags Mungo as Thistlewood's property:

> One day with a kind hand Captain tie my limbs and stuff my mouth with cloth. He light the coal pot, put a brand in it and when it shine red he raise it to my head. I faint with the shock and when I wake I faint once more with the smell of my own burnt flesh. Captain care me for days and days, rub oil in my skin to cool it and wet me with kiss, till I grow well, and then he fetched glass for me to see how he mark my forehead, TT, and his voice is love as I gaze at the strange bites, and he tells me soon Cross will join Cross when the flesh heal and stretch, and that I am now in life, and will be in death, his own. (66–67)

If the earlier accounts of his scar reinforce the stereotypes of a savage Africa, with its primitive rituals and superstitious beliefs, the latter resonates with what we recognize as the brutality of the slave trade and the cruelty of its beliefs about property. If we are expected to adjudicate the truth-value of Mungo's contradictory narratives, we are tempted, I would suppose, by our contemporary values and assumptions, to favor the latter rather than the former—to assume the scar as the work of colonial rather than indigenous violence. That it is Thistlewood's mark is reinforced by Betty's recognition of the sign as well as its significance: "'Ah, you have been mastered, I can tell,' she laughs. . . . 'You are Thomas Thistlewood's creature, from the mark on your forehead, so you have no feeling. He is famed throughout the profession for breaking nigger boys like you'" (107). At the same time, Mungo continues to offer the story of the Greek ancestors as a counternarrative to Betty's assertion. He proves his knowledge of finance and his facility with numbers by calculating a range of possible outcomes from Betty's soap scheme, factoring in a set of contingent variables. He names Euclid his forebear, and applies the laws of geometry to his understanding of human relationships: because "'parallel lines will never meet,'" so too "'the godly and the savage are one, but will never meet'" (107). "'Colour divides us,'" Mungo continues, "'though we meet, as a circle curls within a triangle wanting to meet its three points but it cannot, for the three points are locked by lines that will not slacken, nor will the circle acquiesce but will round and round in stubbornness'" (108). Two parallel lines intersecting another at a perfect perpendicular angle, the *TT* on Mungo's forehead represents the sublime beauty of pain and suffering when sameness and difference meet: "When Captain Thistlewood was a frenzy of maneuvers, not knowing where to begin, faced with a bewilderment of pleasures, so many modes of entry, so many possibilities of hurt, it was Mungo who became the still point from which a perfect arc could be drawn: the still point from which lines could radiate at perfect angles" (108). But for Betty, his knowledge is merely proof of his "necromancy" (122). His calculations, not the mark on his forehead, serve as a sign of his wickedness. Fearing Mungo's knowledge, Betty demands that he reveal its source: "'I was born with it, I inherited it from the Greeks,'" he tells her, pointing again at the mark of pi on his forehead. To which she replies, "'That's Thistlewood's mark. All it means is that you've been breached and made accustomed to men. It is his way of signalling to men with special tastes that you are a special boy'" (123).

It is following his struggle with Betty that Mungo begins to recollect, however unreliably, what transpired aboard Thistlewood's ship. As he "slips into unconsciousness," Mungo sees a vision that "makes him cry out in bewilderment, yet perfect understanding":

> His mother is pinned to the slaveship's boards, her body rigid as the body of a compass. Then she is freed. Sans legs, sans arms, she spins by her neck like a gentleman strolling happily to his Club twirls his pocket-watch by its chain. Freed from her neck, she lands

> beside him, but his hands are fastened in iron, he cannot angle them towards her. They lie together like parallel lines, like the figure 11 in a ledger book, his fixed price which cannot be changed, not by the subtlest negotiation with a Trader, not the vulgar entreaties of a slave-mother as her child is sold away from her to another plantation. She offers a grass-bangle and an egg to the Trader, but is rejected. She rushes into her hut, brings out a wood carving of Zain, protector of travellers, presses it into his hand, but the Trader, furnished with his own compass and quadrant flings it away into the wasteland. (123)

The geometry of loss replaces the more familiar economy of loss. The two accounts of his mother's fate run in parallel, bend toward one another asymptotically, but they can never meet, can never intersect. So too is physical reconciliation foreclosed by the rule of geometry that reigns on the deck of the ship and in the market in human cargo: "Nor can he meet his mother's body. Parallel lines cannot meet, just as a seller and bidder cannot agree a price. He knows the geometry of death from the circles and the lines his mother makes in the slave-hold, the marks Captain Thistlewood makes in his ledger book" (124). Suffering and loss and death constellate before us through mathematic signs and symbols culled from account books, school primers, and that curious artifact of aesthetic philosophy penned by Hogarth, resonating with the one sign permanently branded on his forehead, the one Pringle anxiously tarries over in his notebook, the one that binds him to Thistlewood, Lord Montague, Gideon the Jew; the one that connects Mungo to his mother but prevents him from ever again intersecting with her body; the one that links him to Rima then conveys Rima into Betty and Mary and Lady Montague and Moll; the one that draws Saba into the signifier "Mungo" and Mungo into "Saba." *Pi—peia—pietà*: figures lined up but in misalignment, characters on deck but sliding across it. Imagine them as a sequence of mathematical signs arrayed in an endless, inexhaustible signifying chain whose meanings do not cohere, whose significance can never achieve reckoning:

$$\top \; \perp \; \cap \; \equiv \; \approx \| \, || \; \nparallel \; \ni \; \not\ni \; \pm \; \pm \; \pm$$

The top and the bottom, conjoined and isometric, equivalent and parallel, divisible and incomparable, in membership and dismemberment, and so on. At the risk of turning the mathematical sublime into the mathematically banal, might an exercise in constellating the symbols of calculation help us begin to unlock the uncanny geometry that yokes the contortions of the body with the twisted logic of capitalist exchange? Or the irreparably damaged life of human bio-cargo within the punishing torts authorized under the perverse sign(s) of the law? For doesn't the $\cap$ that assures Mongo's $\equiv$ with the $\not\ni$ body of his mother or the $\not\ni$ body of his village also signify the fundamental $\parallel$ entailed by an exacting $\nparallel$? Are these not the terms the novel has been tarrying with all along? Inasmuch as the symbols of mathematics signify relationships between the known, the unknown, and the unknowable—or between calculation, the calculable, and the incalculability of the absolute and infinite—it is unsurprising that the vocabulary that gives us the mathematic sublime (whether π or ∞) should align with the ideal shapes of aesthetic form. Has Mungo not spoken all along, and eloquently so, of something like isomorphic congruence of commodified and financialized life as it unravels into a fundamental incongruence?

A Harlot's Progress is a novel about concurrencies and convolutions of story and history, about the contortions and coincidence of the colonized body and the colonial archive awash in aestheticized violence. It is at this point that I want to suggest that Mungo—diegetically—is drawing upon not just Hogarthian aesthetics but on the arrangement of bodies depicted in the two engravings included in *Analysis of Beauty,* which turn out to be riddled with contorted bodies, mutilated torsi, and dismembered limbs, which Hogarth uses as benign illustrations for his argument, which I reconstellate here (see Figure 11). Hogarth's descriptions are as perversely violent as his depictions. Consider the following: "In order to my being well understood, let every object under our consideration, be imagined to have its inward contents scooped out so nicely, as to have nothing of it left but a thin shell" (36). "The most perfect idea we can possibly have of a sphere," he later adds, "is by conceiving an infinite number of straight rays of equal lengths, issue from the center, as from an eye, spreading every way alike; and circumscribed or wound about at their other extremities with close connected circular threads, or lines, forming a true spherical shell" (36). To which he adds, "I would desire the reader to assist his imagination as much as possible, in considering every object, as if his eye were placed within it" (37). In one extended example, Hogarth draws the reader's attention to a dismembered torso pierced through by an angled line, which appears as figure 2 on the first plate of the two engravings: "It represents the trunk of a figure cast in soft wax, with one wire passed perpendicularly through its center, another perpendicularly to the first, going in before and coming out in the middle of the back, and as many more as may be thought necessary, parallel to and at equal distances from these, and each other; as is marked by the several dots in the figure.—Let these wires be so loose as to be taken out at pleasure" (37).

The placement of many of Hogarth's illustrations along the margins of two larger, almost narrative, scenes reminds us of the doodles scrawled in the margins of Pringle's notebook at the beginning of the novel, which is also shot through with the language of geometry that will come to organize its gruesome depictions of violence: "'Put this in your book, Mr Pringle,'" Mungo says to himself, thinking of Moll: "'In the months or years I

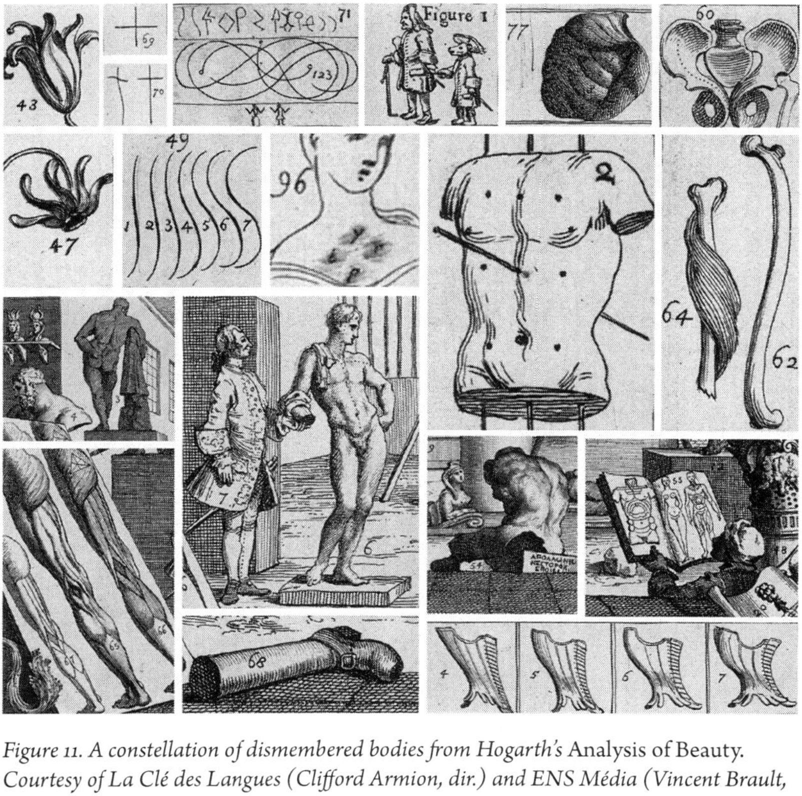

Figure 11. A constellation of dismembered bodies from Hogarth's Analysis of Beauty. *Courtesy of La Clé des Langues (Clifford Armion, dir.) and ENS Média (Vincent Brault, photo).*

stay with her I never know her, for her smile was like a rip in my own eyes'" (184). By recalling Moll, Mungo recollects a long line of women whose identity slips and slides into and across one another but whose particular experience of a violent end resonates with the images and aesthetic detail offered by Hogarth. From Moll to Betty to Rima, the reader is once again transported with the narrator back on board the ship and back to his mother's side. The material implications can be traced through the following string of narrative entailments (⇒):

> Rima, who was all my mothers, died at the very moment she gendered me, and all my life in England I have sought to remake her from the glimpses I have had of women's nakedness. It was not prurience which made me peep at Moll's sleeping form, as you will come to hear, but a fitful yearning for my mother's form, one cloaked in the gloom of time past. And if my hands become stained with ink as I now compose this tale for you, it is because my mother beckons me through this cloak; her frantic silent gestures compel my pen to describe her suffering. I write for Moll, not for Mr Pringle's money. I write for Rima, who was all my mothers. (45)
>
> ⇒
>
> I was catapulted from her lap with such force that all memory instantly emptied from me. . . . Each word I write now is freighted, each mark of punctuation a port and anchorage, for I have skimmed along surfaces for too long and the distant bank that is my death looms. I would have reached there happily in an easeful ignorance, but Mr Pringle's probing has forced me into consciousness, as his ancestor's gun which murdered Rima forced me into birth. . . . And I was delivered onto a ship frantic with blood and the moaning of women. (46)
>
> ⇒
>
> She had on blue clothes, ruffled like the waves of the sea, little nips here and there like the beaks of fish, Captain Thistlewood's care of all living creatures making him empty us overboard as meal. I can tally too the nature of her body. . . . Yet all the cargoes of Empire but a trifle compared to the effort that went into her creation, the centuries and centuries of constant progress, the harbouring of the seed to ensure purity of race and lineage,

> the gradual accumulation of riches and reputation, like a stately ship starts from rude forest, a mansion from rude stone. (184–85)

⇔

The final section of the novel offers a spectacular orchestration of the motif of pi and all that it represents: mathematic sublime, compositional symmetry, geometric precision, religious piety, moral perfection, aesthetic ideal. Mungo's line of beauty runs through the syphilitic bodies, disfigured faces, dismembered torsos, eroticized corpses. If pi holds together an unachievable transcendental idealism, the figure of Moll materializes the all too realized exercise in the exemplary violence enacted on the bodies of women when they were forced to assume the sign of the harlot. While Moll only appears in the novel's final pages, her presence has echoed throughout. Through Moll, the novel's dominant motif constellates into a powerful reflection on the failure of recovery, redemption, and salvation: "To look at her," Mungo insists, "was to look upon perfect form. Greek in the grace and symmetry of its conception" (265). Yet there is a profound *asymmetry,* an aching dissonance, in his depiction of Moll as both a standard of beauty (and a universal equivalent for all the women Mungo "collects") and the life she represents, simultaneously trapped within her own material conditions and imprisoned in the ideal that frames Mungo's sublime fantasies. For Moll is at once his "fair Alexandrian," enslaved—like himself—in a savage, "cannibal region called London"; and like Mungo, she is "plundered and vandalized beyond remembrance of her origin" (266). Throughout the novel, Mungo has performed his own feminization. He has placed himself within a circle of women and described himself as the true harlot at the center of the narrative. Now Moll's salvation—as the restoration of ideal form, the recovery of feminine perfection—depends solely upon him, as had Thistlewood's. "I was determined to restore her, to reawaken her mind to the genius of our ancestors, the traces of which we bore within ourselves" (266). Unable to revive her, however, recovery must come through the merciful end of her suffering through the intercession of a classical rather than Christian god: "I reverted to Hippocratic oaths, invoking the name of Zeus" to "transform her into a flower, nightingale or creature of divinity" (269). It is a prayer he comes to regret, fearing that such "blasphemy" will result in her being taken away, "and put in her place Mr Pringle and then Mr Hogarth" (269). Here Moll's illness serves as a counterpoint to Lady

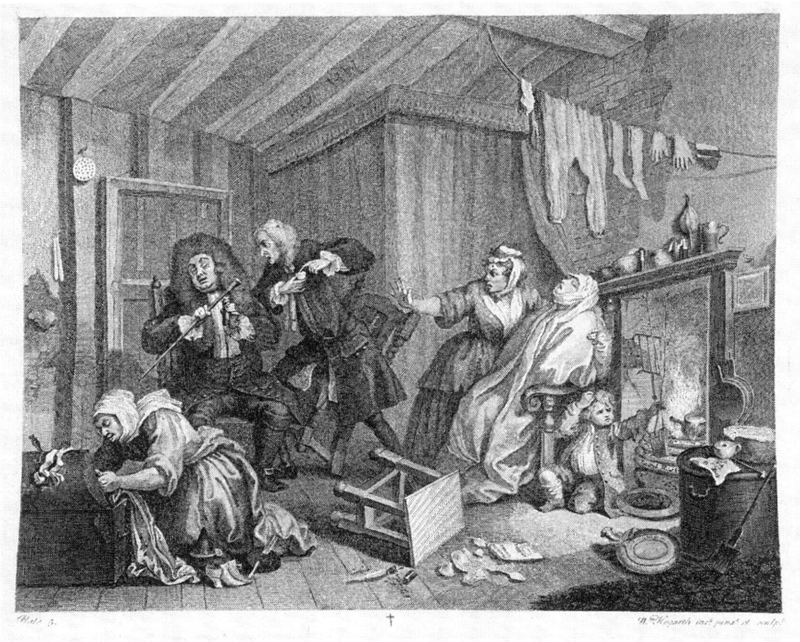

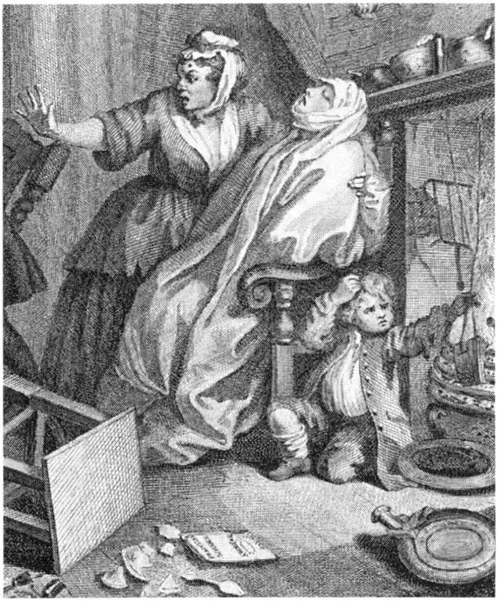

Figure 12. William Hogarth, A Harlot's Progress, *plate 5. Etching and engraving. Courtesy of La Clé des Langues (Clifford Armion, dir.) and ENS Média (Vincent Brault, photo).*

Montague's in the preceding chapters of the novel, as well as his mother's in the earlier chapters. But the image of Moll wrapped tightly in a blanket comes from Hogarth's representation of her in the last panel of his series. Hogarth's image resonates so powerfully in Mungo's mind that it frames, indeed overwhelms, any other memory he might have retained (see Figure 12).

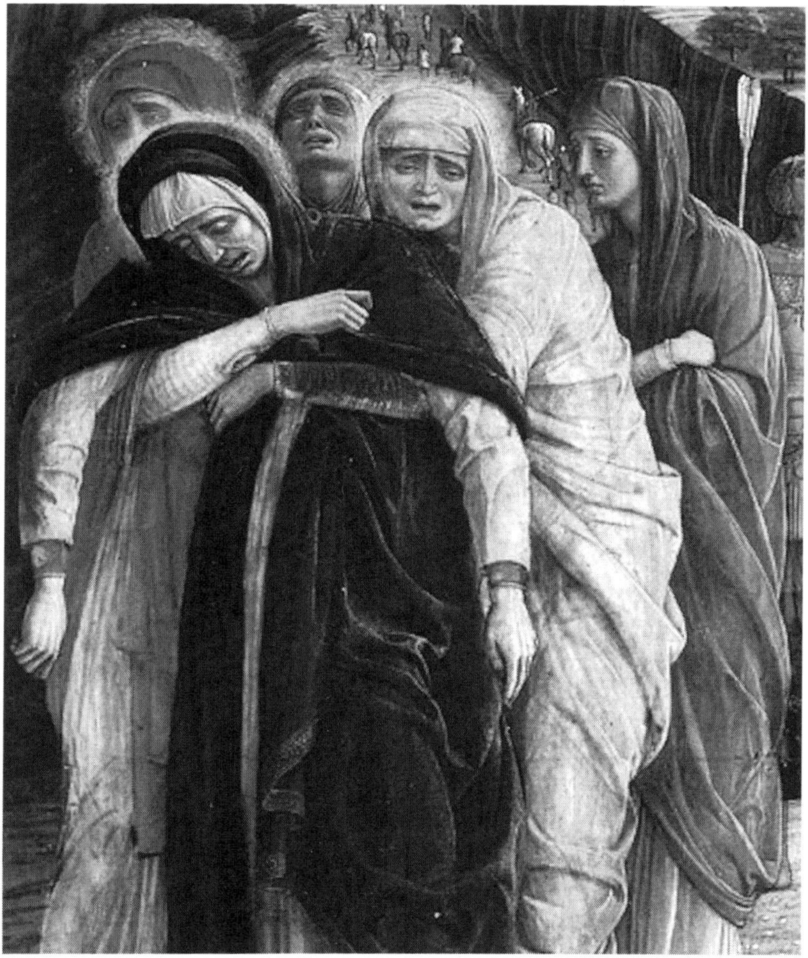

Figure 13. Andrea Mantegna, The Crucifixion *(detail), 1457–59. Tempera on panel. 76 x 96 cm. Courtesy of the Yorke Project/Wikimedia Commons.*

The image of Moll draped by a blanket also evokes the figure of Mary holding a dying Christ in the pietàs Lord Montague collects (see Figure 13). Mungo/Perseus's description variously idealizes the body shrouded in that blanket, concealing "the proportions of her beauty," which he will later uncover "against her will," and in order to gaze upon and bathe her body—eroticizing her corpse. At other times, her body is depicted as ravaged, "like a heap of barren soil." Moll's "decline" goes "unseen" beneath the protection of her blanket, but he can track her illness by the "green blotches" that "suddenly appear on my skin. . . . They were the outward signs of her decay, which I bore on my own flesh." When he strips Moll to bathe her he finds her gaze transfixed by *his* diseased body, a "patchwork of green like areas of the desert." "For the first time I marvelled at strange growths my skin nurtured," Mungo confesses. "Skin that was the curse of my race, bringing slavery upon us, was now a harvest so plentiful that even my planter-father would have been astonished at me." Her body is "unblemished." It achieves perfect form, even though disease "raged within her." In the end, it is "the helpless beautiful body of a harlot," rather than the mark of his sin made by either the village elder or Captain Thistlewood, that confronts him as a sign of his crimes. Despite her outward perfection, Moll's body continues to represent Mongo's own harlotry. Their lives appear in parallel, side by side like Mungo and his mother, whose bodies could never again meet. But unlike the story of atrocity on Thistlewood's ship and the dismemberment of his mother's body, he concludes Moll's story in consummation, conjuncture, and concurrency: "Although there was not the least sign of impurity about her, I still bathed her as a means of cleansing myself of the desire I felt for her. . . . After I had done with it, I lifted it out of the tub with remorse as final as that of the apostle as he lifted Christ's corpse from Calvary" (266–70). No longer locked into the otherwise unrepresentable figure of torture expressed by | |, nor bound to *TT;* no longer living a life of π nor the elegant serpentine line of beauty, in the closing evocation of Mantegna's pietà, Mungo's story ends in *chiasmus,* a simple *X,* a compound fracture.

· CHAPTER 4 ·

Blood Pressures

Queer Inheritance and Intimate Affiliations

Blood Works

Perhaps no sign for life is as intimately connected to the work of death as that of blood. If not universal, it is at least one of the most widely recognized and extensively deployed cultural tropes, stretching across a broad social geography of cultures. To outline the figurative significance of blood to the enclosure of family or the crises of filiation, even in a single historical context, would prove both exhausting and inexhaustible. As I have shown in previous chapters, blood figures into a variety of interlocking social imaginaries—racial and national, theological and juridical—and crises, panics, persecutions, and pogroms that follow. Genealogy, then, names yet another articulation of the biopolitical, in which love, desire, intimacy, and pleasure are captured and enclosed by power in critical sites of consolidation. Home and family become settings for the unrelenting violence of racialization: fantasies of mixing, fears of corruption, and notion of taint are codified in the law of attainder and miscegenation, regulations controlling human reproduction, policies explicitly intended to tear families apart. Racialization casts blood into perpetual crisis; thus as a matter of blood, genealogy becomes a conveyance for racialized violence across generations.

This chapter pursues the matter of blood in the context of the nonreproductive and nonnormatively productive as it considers possibilities for imagining queerer genealogies in a series of literary, visual, and performance works by Bernardine Evaristo, Dorothea Smartt, Inge Blackman (aka Campbell X), and Isaac Julien, each exploring queer existence at the intersection of family life and public history. While the first three chapters emphasized the death-letting and death-meting functions of biopower, here I focus on life-making in the reproduction of life as human bio-cargo against which new claims on the genealogical are made by those most likely to be dismissed from its ranks, excluded by factors of blood. As a coordinated biopolitical apparatus for biological regeneration and genealogical reproduction, blood work remains volatile, available for contingent and improvisational reappropriation. Blood *loss* is restaged through performances of filial belonging as blood*less*.

While earlier chapters addressed the simultaneous operations of recovery and erasure of the history of modern bio-cargo from the archives of colonial atrocity, here I focus on the ways in which a series of creative performances of the archive by queer-identified writers and filmmakers apply counterarchival pressure to genealogy as sanguineous belonging in their pursuit of an intimate public history.[1] The chapter develops through a synthesis of two approaches to thinking about genealogy that are attentive to its role in the transmission of life as labor and property: First, I review the cultural anthropologist Elizabeth Povinelli's interrogation of structures of intimacy, kinship, and belonging that fall both within and beyond what she terms the "genealogical imaginary," a framework in which "the symbolics of genealogy encompass all the conventions and languages of the body, its reproduction, and the means by which goods and materials, rights and obligations, move through these corporealities as markers of inheritance."[2] Second, I discuss the medical sociologist Melinda Cooper's study of what she calls "surplus life" in late twentieth-century biomedical technologies and emergent global bio-economies, wherein "the realms of biological (re) production and capital accumulation move closer together, [and] it is difficult to think about the life sciences without invoking concepts of political economy—production, value, growth, crisis, resistance, and revolution."[3] Working in distinct critical terrains, both Povinelli and Cooper challenge how we think about issues of legal and conceptual personhood, the traffic in particularized human life, and biopolitics of global neoliberalism at the turn of the millennium. By drawing Cooper's critique of the political economy of modern biotechnology into Povinelli's concern with the social meanings that accrue under the sign of the genealogical, one can observe more clearly how the precarious status of surplus life is situated in relation to the unsteady framework of the family tree.

As possibilities afforded by emerging biotechnologies open into the already freighted terrain of genealogy, a number of pressing questions arise: How do developments in biomedical technology—from blood-typing to DNA mapping—reorient notions of genealogy and attending ideas of heredity and heritability implicated in biological reproduction and social regeneration? How might genetic genealogy impact the role that ancestry—already fraught with the challenges of legitimation and integrity—

plays in the consolidation of collective history or the orchestration of social belonging? When the objects of human cargo take the form of discrete pieces of biomatter, whether as cell lines or DNA strands, are we still in pursuit of the family tree? Does the so-called democratization of genealogy alter how it functions as either a biopolitical or historiographic technology? If the primary purpose of genealogy is to organize the inheritance of property and reproduction of social order, how does genealogy operate symbolically and materially for those with no property and very little social power? Finally, given the ways in which the family tree erases key constituents, especially those whose forms of social belonging are nonnormative and/or go unrecognized, can the family tree suture such precarious collective identities or does it only rend them apart?

The blood work of modern human bio-cargo, which proved essential to the development of the colonial slave trade and plantation slavery, continues on in the simultaneous emergence of new regenerative technologies and rise of global neoliberalism. To a significant degree, the "biotech revolution" subtends the "neoliberal revolution," to use Cooper's expressions, assuring the economic hegemony of a postindustrial Global North in the aftermath following the relocation of heavy industry to the Global South (3). "To be responsive to the intense traffic between the biological and the economic spheres," as Cooper insists, one must also be attentive to the history of bio-cargo from the macrobiology of the human body to the microbiology of organs, blood, cell lines, and DNA strands. By drawing together an inquiry into the development of privatized regenerative biotechnologies and critiques of neoliberal political economy, one begins to see more clearly the way in which capital seizes the technologies of the body in the production of new forms of human bio-cargo. The relationship between neoliberalism and biotechnology—operating at both the micro- and macrolevel (from DNA strands and cell lines to tissues and organs to bodies and populations)—stands at our end of the historical continuity between the African slave trade and plantation slavery as early forms of modern bio-cargo and tissue economies today. Reframing Povinelli's discussion of the modern genealogical imaginary in relation to new tissue economies that treat life as surplus, I develop more fully the racialized biopolitical orchestration of abject bodies of human bio-cargo through a consideration of blood, organs, tissues, cell lines, and DNA strands as a way of historicizing the African Atlantic slave trade and plantation slavery as the West's first modern tissue economy.

While the selection of literary, visual, and performance work discussed below is not in any obvious way about contemporary biological sciences, these sources nevertheless offer a way into the genealogical predicates that underwrite both the blood work of the family tree and the bloody orchestration of surplus biomatter. I then turn to a discussion of Bernardine Evaristo's novel in verse, *Lara,* which retraces the divergent ancestral lines of its title character, whose intimate archive of domestic life is unexpectedly routed through the colonial histories of German, Irish, and African diasporas. The two sections that follow consider the poetic cycle *Samboo's Grave* by Dorothea Smartt and the short film *Legacy* by Inge Blackman (Campbell X), both projects of queer archival recovery that unfold at the intersection of familial belonging and public history. In the final section I turn to another film and video artist, Isaac Julien, whose film *The Attendant* imagines counterfamilial forms of queer filiation among groups of care-giving and pleasure-seeking men in a world troublingly emptied of women. All four artists are concerned with the way in which normative and nonnormative forms of belonging are differentially enabled or disabled through material and discursive conditions of reproduction and regeneration; all worry that dominant practices of archivization remain a threat to the viability of precarious life experienced by those caught in the circuits of modern human bio-cargo; they are all reflexively aware that performances of public history remain profoundly entangled with, even when at odds with, the blood work of global biocapital; and for all four, the familial archive, whether housed by the state or in the home, remains crucial to performances of collective memory as public history. The line of analysis I follow aims to show how queer intimate public filiations simultaneously disrupt genealogical reproduction and produce new forms of social aggregation that cross the national, racial, and sexual lines of descent predicated on blood. It centers on forms of filiation organized around the antigenealogies of belonging that *begin within* but *depart from* the framework of blood: through a house that reorients, a grave that reconnects, a ritual that reembodies, a lash that remembers.

Before I travel down the already circuitous path set out above, however, I want to take a detour—from the outline of the chapter and the national context of the book, though within ambit of my topic—in order to examine a stunning (if melancholy) performance of genealogical thinking, one committed to both the fulfillment of the family tree and the promise of the genetic map.

Blood Counts

The interest in genealogy often appears as a melancholy obsession. And if compulsive repetition is a harbinger of melancholia, the sheer volume of Henry Louis Gates Jr.'s output in the many and varied iterations of his PBS series *African American Lives,* the show that transformed the academic star into a media celebrity, suggests that even the most successful and self-fulfilled are susceptible to the captivating call of blood.[4] Indeed, the colonial history of blood—material and figurative—troubles the project of consolidating a black genealogical imaginary central to Gates's celebrated show. In it, the world's most recognized black scholar wades into the rugged terrain of genealogical reconstruction through painstaking research in the biohistorical archive and crosses into more contentious fields of medical technology that have opened up the biogenetic archive of DNA. With the advent of "genetic genealogy," evidence of familial descent housed in the human genome is traced through heritable markers encoded in the helices of individual DNA. The science journalist Claudia Kalb sums up the incredibly high stakes that DNA claims on the contemporary genealogical imaginary, writing, "Our blood holds the secrets to who we are, and increasingly, individuals, families and research scientists are using genetic testing to tell us what we don't already know."[5] Perhaps it is not surprising after all that Gates's perennial pursuit of family trees should strike recognizable notes of melancholia: insatiable longing endlessly repeating. *African American Lives* and the surfeit of books, videos, articles, websites, and sequels that followed is something of a melancholy performance of genealogical exigencies reaching back into the 1970s. "Like 130 million other people," Gates confesses, "I watched every episode of Alex Haley's *Roots* when it first aired in 1977. And like many other African-Americans, I have yearned ever since to trace my own roots, to identify where in Africa my own ancestors came from, what tribe they were part of."[6]

That Gates himself describes the search for his own ancestral roots as a decades-long "yearning" that became an "obsession" returns us in short order to the observation with which I began. As he goes on to describe the internalized feelings of loss and the "generations of doubt and fear" that follow the erasure of African life from the archival record and the foreclosure of black identity from structures of social belonging, Gates foregrounds the insurmountable historical fact of African Atlantic slavery and collective rupture into biopolitical modernity:

> Slavery was a carefully conceived effort to rob our people of all family ties and the most basic sense of self-knowledge. Slave owners didn't want their slaves building family trees. They didn't want them to marry or maintain deep, abiding relations with their mothers and fathers, their grandparents or their siblings. They wanted them to feel no bonds of kinship, especially to Africa or to other Africans. Why? Because a family unit is a bond—and an extended family is a larger bond—and out of such bonds, loyalty and resistance are built. And the last thing in the world slave owners wanted was resistance from our ancestors who were slaves. Slave owners wanted our ancestors to think of themselves as nameless objects of property, plain and simple, like a chicken or a cow.[7]

Gates describes powerfully the enduring practice of familial disruption, collective dispersal, and historical erasure that for centuries helped structure the system of African enslavement. By identifying racism as an enclosed ideological framework, he directs critical attention away from the historical movement of capitalist development as the overdetermining force of colonial slavery. Gates mistakes the violent practices of racism (material and discursive) that secured the system of slavery for the primary violence of capitalist accumulation expropriating African lives for the purpose of economic gain through what I have called modern human bio-cargo, the making-property of life itself. That is, genealogical disruption and dispersal was one practice among many others in the management of populations in the African Atlantic system of colonial governmentality that stretched from the west coast of Africa to the Americas and beyond, a vital distinction to make in order to track the shifting forms of structured violence that shape the historical legacy of colonial slavery to our own moment of global neoliberalism. The assault on African cultures and identities cannot simply be reduced to European racism, which operated as a biopolitical strategy for capital accumulation and development, but racism was one way in which capitalism could articulate with the particular conceptual logic of heritability on which the Western genealogical imaginary rests.

While the experience of profound longing, whether individual or collective, should not be discounted, critical attention must be paid to the ways in which the melancholy desire for a family tree or genetic map is reproduced within the market logic his series explicitly embraces, available for leverage by private interests, including the commercial interests of big bio, big media, and big-name authors. Once the site of an impossible recovery, genealogy itself finds recovery through an almost divine intervention, the "magic" of science. Genetic mapping takes over "when the paper trail ends and we have exhausted our sources," providing "a key to unlocking our African past" and reclaiming "something that our ancestors from Africa brought with them that not even the slave trade could take away: our distinctive strands of DNA."[8] Unable to replace the family tree, genetic genealogy offers something better, an inviolable archive, a past that need not be recovered because it could not be stolen in the first place. The promise of the DNA is nothing less than inalienable self-possession. The dangerous supplement of a dangerous supplement, genetic science and the genealogical imaginary wrap around one another as the double helix of a new archival aporia: the unimpeachably sacrosanct cultural memory of oral histories and family Bibles versus the unassailable "magic" of science; what is passed down through generations versus what is passed down through strands of DNA. It is not hard to imagine the point at which conflict between the genetic and the genealogical trumps their complementarity. By identifying and quantifying markers of genetic difference within variant articulations of the human genome, individuals are particularized and localized, then reified and commodified in a recycling genomic neoliberalism.

For those of us more politically paranoid than critically melancholic, the genetic laboratory is haunted by the blood-soaked specters of scientific racism, and the project of DNA mapping reproduces many of the underlying assumptions of that imaginary. Genetic heritability, for instance, reasserts the historical connection between blood and property, and renews discourses of racial purity that haunt the genealogical imaginary, securing human reproduction as a crucial site of self-regulation and social control and situating family life under the same hermeneutic of suspicion whose legacy has yet to be fully challenged. Reporting from the National Geographic annual Family Tree DNA conference, Kalb describes the fervor with which some pursue the science of the family tree as an outlet for their own anxious belonging: "The genealogy garb was everywhere. Most notable: double-helix ties and pins with haplogroup logos." Conference attendees "raved about the new frontier of DNA testing" and were "spellbound as scientists presented arcane PowerPoints with daunting DNA lingo"; participants spoke anxiously of "nonpaternity events," a "polite term for an affair, which might have muddied the lineage"; or of surnames lost as families "daughtered out."[9] Having stumbled across an unacknowledged "paternity event," Toni Coleman recounts her grandmother's exclamation on her discovery: "'Toni, you little devil. You digging up all kinds of dirt. You done stirred up an old hen's nest.'"[10] The family's secrets might have been news to Coleman, but they appear not to have been for her grandmother. So while she finds the information provided through DNA testing interesting, Coleman learns a much older lesson in finding ones roots. "One thing I do know," she concludes, "based on the family history I've recently learned, is that I haven't spent nearly enough time talking to my grandmother about other secrets she has locked up and about clarifying and sharing the history my eldest relatives do know." The implication resonates with concerns that other critics of DNA testing have voiced: rather than complementing extant genealogical knowledge, archival and genetic research might come to displace, replace, or even erase the oral histories that have survived the passage of genealogical time. DNA mapping shores up an exclusively heteronormative vision of the family, while the family tree is anchored at the roots of biological descent.

In her review of *Faces of America,* Gates's follow-up to *African American Lives,* Alondra Nelson expresses concern for the way the show participates in bodily spectacle, emphasizing the dramatic reactions of the show's celebrity participants to the "surprising reveals" of "unanticipated results," which must stand in for the challenge of legibility posed by strands of DNA.[11] The show, she worries, trades in the disclosure of scandal, as when Gates informs the popular social sciences journalist Malcolm Gladwell that one of his maternal ancestors, "a free woman of color" living in Jamaica, was also a slave owner. "If the findings of conventional genealogical research produce fireworks, the results of the DNA analysis generate shock and awe." Lacking any social or historical contexts, such news can, as it did for Gladwell, be experienced more as a "burden" than as liberation. While DNA mapping encourages some to question the perceptions on which notions of identity and belonging depend, for others genetic testing produces new fantasies of belonging. More worrying, DNA mapping can likewise upset prior genealogies and familial histories, exposing counternarratives of intimate premarital relations, infidelity, and/or sexual violence; as one participant reported, "DNA blew up a family legend," while another had grown up as an African American only to be told that he had "no African blood at all." Following a year of soul searching, that participant came to the conclusion that his racial demystification revealed another aspect of his identity: "Before the test, 'I was unequivocally black,' he says. 'Now I'm a metaphor for America,'" reducing his identity to a homogenous trope of national identity. Empirical science undermines oral history as a system of encoding kinship or defining familial belonging. But family histories are often carefully honed to productively suture the fissures opened by the kind of material and epistemic violence that Gates had characterized as crucial to sustaining the system of slavery. The difficult search for an intact family tree satisfies different personal and collective desires and orchestrates knowledge for quite distinct affective ends. "It is clear," Nelson concludes, "that we fully inhabit a 'genealogical society'—to use the anthropologist Elizabeth Povinelli's phrase. The fruits of the unearthed family tree—historical coherence; redemptive narratives of migration and assimilation; intergenerational social mobility—are unevenly dispersed."

Genetic genealogy is well suited to the biopolitics of contemporary life: privatized, monetized, commodified, and integrated into the ubiquitous apparatuses of the security state. Such connections are easy to discern when the complexities of genetic science find expression through the tropes of the law, as when Gates evokes two common but problematic analogs for explaining how DNA mapping works: as a kind of fingerprinting and as a form of paternity testing, both reminders of the social deployment of race science. DNA testing draws science, medicine, and biotechnology in general into constellation with the law, facilitating the speculation on biological pasts and reproductive futures as matters of criminal law and civil tort. For populations already targeted by aggressive state and civil policing, or historically vulnerable to the most outrageous enactments of institutional biopower, even the most benign mentions of medical testing or anodyne projects of genetic mapping produce unintended historical resonances. The concern has not gone unnoticed by Gates's critics. As Troy Duster remarks:

> The very technology that tells us what proportion of our ancestry can be linked, proportionately, to sub-Saharan Africa (ancestry-informative markers) is the same being offered to police stations around the country to "predict" or "estimate" whether the DNA left at a crime scene belongs to a white or black person. This "ethnic estimation" using DNA relies on a social definition of the phenotype. That is, in order to say that someone is 85 percent African, we must know who is 100 percent African. Any molecular, population, or behavioral geneticist is obliged to disclose that this

> "purity" is a statistical artifact that begins not with the DNA, but with a researcher's adopting the folk categories of race and ethnicity. With the demonstrable skew of the incarcerated population over the last few decades along social categories of race, African-Americans need to be particularly sensitive to the use of phenotype as the starting point for understanding genotype.[12]

It is not difficult to see how the business of DNA testing is apiece with the market in biomedical technology that Cooper argues is co-emergent with the new technologies of economic speculation under neoliberalism.

Cooper's observations would certainly explain why Gates's *Ebony* article reads more like advertisement than reportage, in which he endeavors to "sell" genealogy as belonging: "I would urge anyone who is interested to try and trace their family back to Africa, through genealogical research and DNA testing. There are several tests available, and each is surprisingly inexpensive, often less than a pair of designer sneakers."[13] As Gates continues one can almost visualize the television commercial that might accompany the sales pitch: "Yet learning even these bare facts can be enormously satisfying. Receiving the results in the mail, and sharing them with your family and friends, is one of the most exciting experiences an African-American can have. I know it has been for me, and for my friends such as Oprah Winfrey and Chris Tucker." And in a sidebar that accompanies this *Ebony* article, Gates elaborates on these "surprisingly inexpensive" consumer packages: "FamilyTreeDNA has joined The Inkwell Foundation to form a new company to offer one-stop shopping so that you can have your DNA analyzed (their 25-marker test costs about $189) and your family tree traced (prices start at $699). AfricanAncestry.com offers lower-resolution DNA tests for $349 each, RootsforReal.com charges $300 for its low-resolution tests and National Geographic offers lower-resolution tests for both sexes for about $99 each."[14] Offering a carefully crafted sales pitch, Gates plays up the shared sense of connection produced not only by recovering the names and histories of individual family members or the markers of a broader network of genealogical belonging but also by creating a connection both with the past and with family and friends in the present. At the same time, Gates evokes other potential affects produced by genealogical discovery: "Of course, it can be painful. When one discovers the identity of an ancestor who lived as a slave, one necessarily is forced to relive the brutal details of the slave past, a past that our ancestors experienced not as we do through history books or films, but in their everyday lives." While recognizing the potential for negative affect, Gates reaffirms such feelings as both redemptive and expiatory: "But I believe we must get past this pain. If we are to move forward as a people, we need to be able to understand where we came from. We need to get ourselves grounded, and the process starts by grounding ourselves in our own family's extended past, our own genealogical 'invisible network,' like that cell phone ad says."[15] Ultimately, Gates's project is as much about harnessing new technologies, biomedical technologies in particular, to a commercial venture targeting a quite particular market of black middle-class viewers of PBS and readers of publications like *Ebony.* That is, despite the unquestionably good intentions that motivated the *African American Lives* series, it also certainly endeavored to produce consumer demand and provide just enough consumer satisfaction to melancholically perpetuate the desire for greater and greater genealogical knowledge. "This process is so nourishing," Gates concludes, "because it can enable a person to feel the inimitable sense of connection, of belonging that can *only* be found by unearthing the branches of your family tree, *your very own roots,* roots that extend back through the slave past directly into the verdant soil of Africa."[16] One can hardly be surprised that what Gates has also nourished is an industry in genealogy that stretches from television to print to the Web and to the online companies that, for a price, will sell you your very own roots.

As a pervasive and productive knowledge grid, the family tree, Povinelli reminds us, organizes many of our most materially consequential social arrangements—familial and national, legal and civil—such as the transferability of citizenship or the heritability of property, to name just two. "Why does the recognition of peoples' worth," Povinelli wonders, "of their human and civil rights, always seem to be hanging on the more or less fragile branches of a family tree? Why must we be held by these limbs?"[17] Povinelli worries about those forms of connecting and belonging that are incapable of signifying within systems or discourses that do not account for what cannot be positioned on the genealogical grid or family tree, with its "icons for sex and sexual relationships" and "heterosexual reproduction," icons of which we are all quite familiar: the diamonds, circles, dashes, bars, and lines that designate only heterosexual kinship relations. The introduction of biogenetics into the already troubling framework of the family tree poses particularly acute concerns for those whose sexual identities, expressions, or practices have been poorly served by the latter and unlikely to thrive under the biopolitical regime of the former. The family tree neither registers nor explains their non-iconic filiations (there are no pink triangles linking people here) on the familial, communal, or national plane. As Povinelli explains, "There is no standard icon for 'intimacy,' 'desire,' or 'love'" on the typical family tree.[18] And like any genealogical grid, the genetic map will likely appear as yet another site of failure for queer or otherwise non-normative sexual minorities, as the heterologic of the family tree remains rooted in its reformulation of genealogy.

Blood Streams

Love and intimacy might appear unlikely apertures through which to see the historical contours of colonial slavery and the intractable violence that organizes the regulation of modern human bio-cargo. Engaging public history as an act of intimacy, or with a lover's attentiveness the affective past, however, may yet prove productive in reorienting the politics of belonging toward a more inclusive future. At the same time, scholars within the Anglo-American academy have brought considerable attention to intersections of colonial and postcolonial histories with matters of affect, embodiment, and intimacy in the experience of time and place as disjuncture and disorientation. In turning toward Bernardine Evaristo's *Lara,* I want to move from human bio-cargo in its most biomedicalized forms back to their prehistory in an older genealogical imaginary, one consolidated *in* and suited *to* the rapidly globalizing capitalist economy and the Atlantic cycle of exchange made possible through and sustained by the trade in human lives, a system evoked in the very name of the family home in which the novel's protagonist resides, *Atlantico.*

Lara takes an unusual approach to the genealogy of black migrations to the UK not unlike what I have just described. By underscoring the unlikely, deeply contingent historical "pressures" that brought her own parents together, she is able to follow lines of flight inimical to the rootwork of a singular identity. *Lara* recounts a much broader and continuous history of modern human conflict and in particular the ruptures that activate new lines of genealogical flight, grafting together a family tree that constellates a network of contingent belonging that crisscrosses Ireland and Germany, Nigeria and Brazil, before coming to rest, but only momentarily, in twentieth-century Britain. For Lara's great-great-grandmother Emma, that genealogical line runs through the Irish famine; it doesn't end there but continues diachronically through the long history of English-occupied Ireland and the anticolonial struggles consequential to her family's relocation to London. The novel unfolds through a sequence of mostly single-page, narrative poems, producing a chorus of first- and third-person voices: some poems are spoken by a cast of central characters as they describe social worlds or recount significant events that both consolidate and disrupt those worlds and whose lives are drawn together by a set of unlikely circumstances, ultimately merging into a single (singular) family line. For Louis, Lara's great-great-grandfather, a German émigré, the line tracks his difficult passage to England in the years just ahead of World War I into a new period of anti-German, anti-immigrant xenophobia that erupts in its wake. The novel, then, at first appears as remarkably mappable, both geographically and genealogically.

While there is no world map tipped into the binding of the book, there is, in fact, a family tree printed ahead of the novel's prologue and opening epigraph.[19] By reflecting on the role that this particular family tree plays in the novel—as a graphic paratext that "maps" dispersed and disjointed narrative moves; as a framework for articulating normative forms of belonging, reproducing, or remembering; as a measure of archival recovery the narrative itself can never fulfill—we might productively situate Povinelli's critique of the genealogical imaginary even as the symptom of its persistence confronts us from the very first page, a knowledge grid the author, perhaps, freely participates in or cannot quite break free from. Regardless, its presence insists that the reader ask in advance of the narrative proper: Who is identified and how are they represented? What visual icons assert connections and what familial attachments do they secure? What connections appear effaced and what intimate relations are occluded? Or simply, who is placed on and who is left off the family tree? As we have come to expect, privilege is given to the filial bond over other familial relations (brothers, sisters, aunts, uncles, cousins, etc.) and nonfamilial ones, even when such relations are presented and developed in the narrative, and disappear altogether. The family tree performs narrative blood work: on the one hand, it reproduces an iconology meant to guarantee the legitimacy of the bloodline and secure the regeneration of property wealth through the reproduction of the family as blood relation; on the other, it provides a stable epistemology for identity as rootedness. When the genealogical imaginary compels Lara to follow paternal bloodstreams from London through Lagos and Rio and her ancestral villages of the Amazon basin, the novel offers a counternarrative of reverse migration, reversing the flow of blood, at least symbolically.

The epigraph that follows the depiction of the DaCosta family tree jars us out of one naturalized familial metaphor and into another, from the family tree to the river of time: "However far the stream flows, it never forgets its source." While the old metaphor is commonplace—indeed structuring, framing—in the context of the Western genealogical imaginary, the second harnesses to it a quite specific figure of ethnic and linguistic (what once would have been called tribal) identification, but one even more ambiguous as a marker of belonging. If the family tree promises the security of historically rooted autochthony, the stream portends the contingency of routed, "autopotamic" existence. That is to say, between the family tree and the epigraph, we see the tension between the emplaced and the displaced. If the tree serves as a metaphor for embeddedness in the land, the stream represents life as water in motion. But moreover, the stream is a metaphor for one kind of descent, just as the branch represents another, with the "source" figuring the ancestral (parental, familial, communal Africa) as equally secured, stable, productive. (I'll elide the difficulty one gets into when distinguishing the singular trunk and the dispersive system of roots.) What secures, in the latter case, appears a matter of remembering and forgetting—those perennially dominant themes of the literature of diaspora. Although the proverb suggests a single stream with a single source, both the geography and iconography of rivers emphasize its many branches and tributaries, its multiple sources; its continually shifting topography; sources that are new, sources that dry up and are renewed.

Lest we imagine anything romantic about the metaphor of the seed, or of seeding, the prologue offers us a horrific scene in which a Brazilian slave master "deposits" his seed into the mutilated vagina of a house slave. As with select poems throughout the novel, the opening identifies its setting in time and place above and to the right of the opening lines, reminiscent of the genres of reportage—letters, journal entries, or newspaper articles. The prologue opens the novel in 1849 Brazil. The exact location is not given, but the setting in 1849 certainly complicates those dates most familiar to readers of British accounts of slavery, whether slave-trade abolition in 1807, the legal abolition of plantation in 1834, or the formal end of the period of apprenticeship in 1838. Thus, the reader must confront the historical continuity of slavery following its much-celebrated "conclusion" in the English colonies and, through negotiated settlement with other nations, in much of the Caribbean and Latin America in the decades that followed. By 1849, plantation slavery remains central to the economies of Brazil, Cuba, and the United States. In short, the novel insists that the slow, decades-long dismantling of legal slavery across the colonial world remains a significant part of British national history. As the daughter of a Nigerian immigrant to the UK, the title character is unaware of her Brazilian ancestry recalled in the prologue, a critical revelation that happens well into the later chapters of the novel. Still, the prologue's opening lines suggest that ancestral history and familial belonging are less a matter of factual knowledge than a preternatural, embodied, affective way of knowing, being, and becoming. The opening three lines link the setting to the dominant narrative—Lara's pursuit of her family tree, and her quite embodied connection to her family history that precedes her own journey: "Sugar cane, damp musky earth, saccharine vanilla / journeys in from Eighteen Forty-nine, scenting Lara. / Dismembered chords pluck the air."[20] In advance of narrative, a poetics of sensation bears the past of 1849 into the present and into the presence of a protagonist whose own birth in 1962 is still to come. This ambient movement of historical feeling is borne though the senses—smell, sound, touch, taste—and is reinforced by the play between accent and alliteration in juxtaposed hard and soft sibilance: the musky, sugary, saccharine scent of earth and cane journeys into now-time accompanied by sounds whose harmonics are betrayed by the dissonance of their dismemberment.

These opening lines, like the ones that will follow, are as violent as they are soothing, alternating between a narrative account of the vicious rape of Lara's great-great-grandmother with the cruelly ironic name "'Severina / —the scarred one.'"[21] Here the speaker shifts to direct discourse, allowing the enslaved to provide witness:

> "Severina
> —the scarred one. They took me while my boys slept
> my bones had shivered all day, I could barely think.
> When I bent to work I imagined vultures clawing
> my back. When his men came I heard my bones jangle
> like wooden sticks shaking in a bowl. His chamber,
> sunk in the cellars of that great house, kept for us
> women only. There he pierced me with a bayonet
> as I lay on a marble slab, bound. My screams
> ricocheted the walls, he ejaculated on my ruptured

> body but by then I had become the fire of a naked torch,
> until he put me out."

As we have seen throughout the work of creative historiography of African Atlantic slavery, her account emphasizes the condition of her body and the physicality of its dismemberment. The torture that so pleases the plantation owner severs her from her children and from herself, as she is expelled from her own body through a scream that reverberates across time and space, even as its physical sound is concealed by the impenetrable walls of his subterranean chamber. As her voice echoes through the dungeon, Severina projects herself into and *as* the flame of the master's torch as a means of escape from her tortured body. Severina does not die but migrates, conveyed from her ravaged body to a new existence in the Brazilian landscape:

> "Then I jumped a spider,
> crept deftly through the warren of cellars into daylight
> where a bird swept me up. I became that bird,
> circled the fazenda until a baobab seed rooted
> from my droppings."

If the tenuousness of those older genealogical tropes—the figure of the tree or the metaphor of the stream—appear inadequate to express the systemic repetition of rupture, dislocation, and displacement central to the slave trade and plantation slavery, the prologue offers something like a synthesis in yet another deeply problematic trope of ancestry and familial regeneration: the seed.

Yet Evaristo radically redraws the lines of flight followed by colonial and postcolonial migrants that get figuratively emplaced by the constraints of the family tree, no matter how far its roots extend or how broadly its branches stretch out. As Lara's ancestral spirit, Severina is freed from the torture of slavery through the expiating fire of a torch; borne from the brutality of the torture chamber on the precarious back of a spider; ascends to the sky in the sweeping grip of a bird, a familiar she ultimately comes to inhabit as herself; mingles with food she ingests; and emerges revitalized from her own defecate as the fecund remains of a baobab tree. Severina goes from being the subject of violence in being seeded to being the agent of transformation by spreading seed:

"When it broke through the earth
into life, I lived in that tree, grew quickly, saw one
of my seeds planted by my stronger son over my husband
Antonio's dead body, and so it continued. I was carried over
the ocean, burst into life, watched over Baba until
he joined us nearly a century after my death.
So you have it."

The baobab tree itself bears significant and varying cultural meaning. As the tree of life—seeding, spreading, rooting, returning—it organizes the transubstantiation of the genealogical imaginary from the symbol of blood into the family tree. At the same time, the prologue follows a more familiar line of representation. While the poem initially offers a powerful meditation on matrilineality and the lost voice of the maternal ancestor, it concludes transfixed on the surviving patriarchy, Severina's spirit displaced by the "dead body" of her husband and the work of her "stronger son," Baba, who carries on the planting of seed and the cultivation. What of the presumably weaker son, Baba's twin, Gilberto, who appears on the family tree printed earlier but gets no mention here? Kinship may ultimately get incompletely and ambiguously regrafted onto the family tree—pruned of its weaker members—but tropes of regeneration and reproduction remain deeply confounded as they unsettle the transmorphologies of global migration.

Blood Vessels

Dorothea Smartt's *Samboo's Grave—Bilal's Grave* (2008) is a poetic cycle first commissioned in 2003–4 by the Lancaster Lit Fest.[22] Originally, Smartt was asked to compose a single elegy for "Sambo," whose death occurred only days after his arrival in Lancaster in 1736, and who was largely forgotten until he was first elegized by Reverend James Watson in 1796. Indeed, a brass plaque placed on his grave reproduces Watson's poem (see Figures 14 and 15). As part of the initial commission and residency, Smartt worked in the City of Lancaster archives in order to enrich her knowledge of Lancaster's involvement in the trade.[23] Some of the archival materials she found there made their way into her writing and performance.[24] Smartt then developed this work into a public multimedia and poetry performance to commemorate the two hundredth anniversary of the abolition of the slave trade as part of a larger public project sponsored by the Slave Trade Arts Memorial Project (STAMP), which also included the unveiling of a memorial sculpture by Kevin Dalton-Johnson in late 2006.[25] Her multimedia performance included her reading the poems while standing before projected images of materials taken from the city archives within which she researched. In addition to providing the details of Lancaster's history or

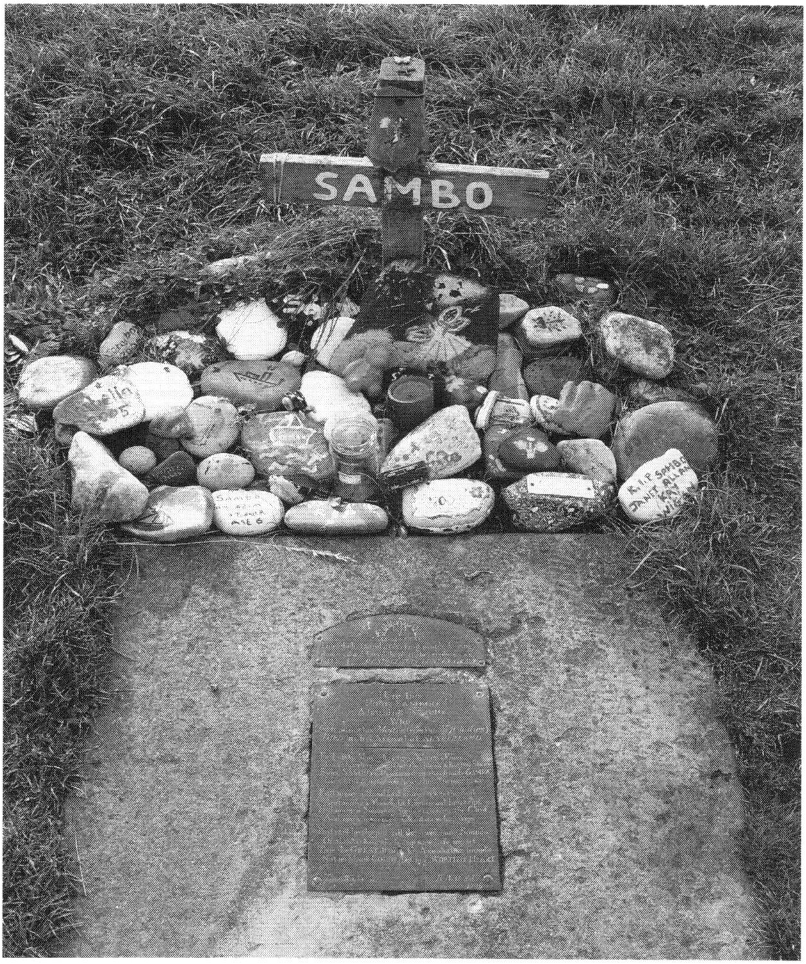

Figure 14. Sambo's Grave, *Sunderland Point, Lancashire, UK, 2007. Photograph by Rwendland. Courtesy of Wikimedia Commons.*

the facts of Sambo's life, she felt an obligation to try to "retrieve" the slave's "voice," as well as those of other Lancastrians represented in the figures of the sea captain, the captain's wife, and the sailors aboard the slave ship en route across the Atlantic triangle.

The double title of Smartt's volume, *Samboo's Grave—Bilal's Grave,* disrupts the epistemic and genealogical lines of historical knowledge that emplace the subject of the poems, the African slave buried on the coast

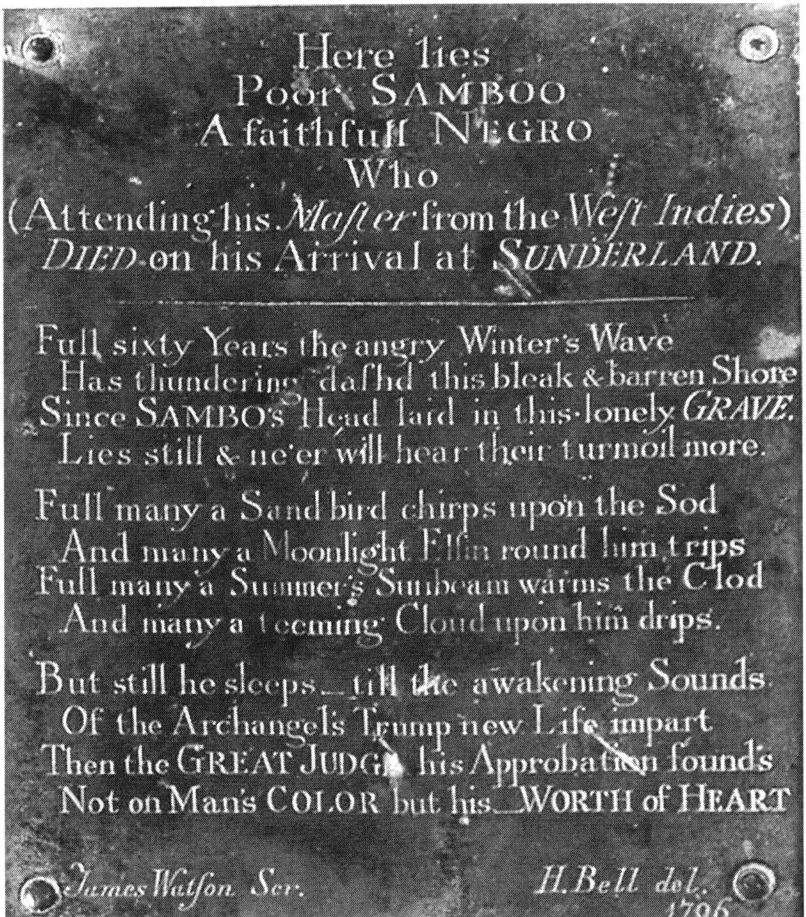

Figure 15. Sambo's Grave, *Sunderland Point, Lancashire, UK, 2007. Photograph by Chris Tomlinson. Courtesy of Wikimedia Commons.*

of England, by replacing the racist nomination, which is spelled variously Sambo and Samboo throughout, with a traditional Muslim one, a name that itself carries a quite significant meaning within Islam. Smartt's Bilal is named after Bilal ibn Ribah, the revered figure in the Qur'an chosen by Muhammad to sing the *muezzin,* or call to prayer *(adhan)*—a tradition itself often passed down from father to son. On the one hand, the tradition operates within a system of patriarchy with its received modes of genealogy, and therefore potentially reinscribes the very logic of the family tree that I argue the text/performance likewise resists. On the other hand, through renaming, Smartt offers a strategic *imaginary* genealogy as a way of translating the unknowable and incalculable into the knowable and calculable, while still holding onto the spectral excess or beyond that remains outside either calculation or knowability. Thus, Smartt sustains both names—the one that is marked on the grave, and therefore recognizable, and the one that is erased *by* the grave and from history.

Smartt both adopts and adapts the elegy form, turning to the African praise song as another poetic tradition, one in which the poet need not be afraid of being critical. She imagines her voice as an extension of the griot's (storyteller or praise singer) own, through which other voices gain entry and provide context. While composing the sequence and working in the archives, she thought about where Sambo most likely would have come from and what his name might have been. Using ship manifests and logs, she determined that he very possibly came from the Sene-Gambia region of Islamic West Africa by way of Barbados, the Caribbean island on which she herself was born. Smartt used the information gleaned from the city archives to construct a plausible fiction of Bilal's transport from Africa to a West Indian plantation and then to the Lancaster port. She was also influenced by David Dabydeen's work on Hogarth's blacks, and imagines that Bilal might have been brought from Barbados as a gift for the captain's wife, as was a common practice among the aristocracy and emergent bourgeois in the eighteenth century.[26] Through her experiences of dreams, visitations, and hauntings, she imagines an alternative or supplementary history to that found in the archive. These other ways of knowing, she insists, are vital to gaining access to the past that is erased by the archive. At the same time, Smartt captures the futility of those acts of remembering and commemorating she is commissioned to provide. In "Bringing It All Back Home," for instance, she confronts "questions, questions from either / side that foul us for answers / the how and the why ultimately defeating us / with shame, with anger" (20). As one example of historical disavowal, Smartt emphasizes the role that Quakers themselves played in the trade. While most people think of the Quakers as the movers and shakers of abolitionism, in the early eighteenth century, Quaker merchants in Lancaster, called "grocers," governed the development of the slave trade: "'Grocer'? You were a slave trader! / And everything has its price, / and denial is only debt / with interest to be paid" (20). Smartt nonetheless insists on the imperative to remember and to historicize in an honest but creative manner that rejects the euphemistic narratives of the past.[27]

Through the spectacle of her performance, Smartt highlights the metonymic-synecdochal structure of historical narrative. In "Sambo's Elegy? No Rhyme No Reason," Smartt draws our attention to the mediating role the poet performs in seizing the past. In fact, Smartt suggests, history demands an entire array of mediations and mediators, including the body itself. For her, the poet functions as a spectacularly embodied, somatic interface for her audience. At the same time, Sambo's buried remains, or even the grave marker itself (placed on the site sixty years after his death and paid for by visitors to the site), mediate affectively a history inaccessible within the traditional archive. Indeed, the brass plaque placed there also served as a protest against the slave trade at the height of abolitionism, reminding us of the ways in which the image of the abused body of the slave circulated in antislavery discourse. Her elegy, which must be read as a response to Watson, is written in both the voice of the slave and that of the poet, thus unsettling both the question of authorship and the tension between "speaking for" and "speaking about" that always attends both the elegiac form and subaltern history. In retelling Sambo/Bilal's experience of the Middle Passage, Smartt deploys the strategies of representational exemplarity and singularity discussed in chapter 1. That is, she represents the slave at Sunderland Point as both a particular—indeed peculiar—instance in the long history of violence committed on the body of the slave and as a stand-in for the general condition of the slave en route across the Atlantic. This account is bookended, however, by the authorial voice struggling with how to write the past and while waiting for the grave, or for the remains interred there, to speak. In the final lines of "Sambo's Elegy?" the speaker implies that the story she has told came to her through a dream, suggesting a paradoxically portentous history—as fleeting and ephemeral as it is ominous and spectacular. It is also a transferential history that operates through the vicissitudes of psychoanalytic dreamwork.

In "My Calling," on the other hand, Smartt acknowledges the strategies of silence and withholding we have come to expect in postcolonial narrative practices that attend to the recovery of the past. Once again, it is Bilal's name that is at stake. When asked his name by a shipman, he is immediately interrupted after uttering only the first syllable, Bil; thereafter he is either called simply Sambo or Samboo, or he is called Bill—"'Right you are, young Samboo, / Bill it is.'" But Bilal does not correct the shipman. Rather, he explains, he "keep de source / of m'smile / hidden," as he quietly acknowledges to himself, "yes, I is my / father, the muezzin, son; I is / Bilal" (35). The violence of indifference and indistinction (he could be called either Bill or Sambo by the white sailors on the ship; it simply did not matter), like the exemplary violence that operates *through* distinction and exception, is met with Bilal's own compelling refusal to acknowledge any markers of distinction. He is simply one Sambo among countless others. Indeed, he concludes the poem, proclaiming, "My true-true / name / is a secret / I keep from those / that would de- / file me" (35). The sly, emphatic doubling of the word "true" prompts the reader to suspect that Bilal is holding his secret from the listener and—given Smartt's conceit as poetic medium, as the embodied mediator of lost voices—from the poet and her audience as well, a lyrical turn that concedes the impossibility of recovery without ceding to the disabling melancholy of the archive, and a poetic turn in keeping with narrative strategies for staging the limits of historical recuperation within the framework of the archive leveraged by each of the writers discussed in previous chapters. The double meaning of "de-file," to which the line break draws our attention, suggests that irreparability is a sign for, as well as consequence of, the violence of the archive as an act of physical abjection. Recognizing this, the speaker refuses to name himself in a way that might reproduce the structural defilement that is enacted when one is filed away in the archive of colonial violence. To organize his narrative under either name—to file it under B for Bill or S for Sambo—would violate the principles that govern the archive; that his account must be cataloged—the foundational imperative of the archiving archive—forces the otherwise imminent structural aporia into the crisis of deconstruction.

In conversation, Smartt admits it is not clear what the average person in the UK knows about the manner and extent that slavery benefited Britain or how it utterly transformed the British landscape along with the nation's global economic position in the eighteenth century. She acknowledges that the history of slavery and the slave trade are not adequately integrated into

British historical imaginary in such a way as to "make it everybody's business—as it *was* and *is*," she emphasizes. Smartt describes Britain as a "culture of denial," with all the psychoanalytic connotations the word evokes. Thus, the conceit of the opening poem, "Bringing It All Back Home," is to have Sambo speak *through* the poet but also to speak *back to* the conscience and consciousness of the present, and to do so *from* one of the most powerful figurative sites of repression, his grave. In his lines, the speaker recognizes himself *as* a figure—one who might be "filled" with meaning, a vessel for the "tears" and "regrets" of his audience. As an emblem of slavery, however, he is also one who disrupts the smooth operations and history of both local and national "pride." Indeed, Sambo describes himself as the "tick in the eye / of Lancaster Pride. The stutter / the pause, the dry cough, shifting / eyes, that cannot meet a Black man's / gaze" (20). But as with any psychoanalytic understanding of denial and repression, shame and guilt are recast through a somatic response manifested in the very locations of sensory reception and articulation: the mouth, the eyes, the throat, and the voice.

To be sure, Smartt's poetic cycle serves as an indictment of Lancaster public life whose local superstructure, if you will, rests upon an economic base sustained by the slave economy abroad. "Pillars of the Community" resembles a concrete poem, with a lean, abstract shape that arranges its terse, two-word descriptions into three columns that arise discordantly from two foundational plinths, forming the teetering pillars of the title. Here Smartt figures this economic and social arrangement in three columns that represent the "lows" of bare life rendered through and around the "highs" of economic calculation. In one column, "high seas," "high finance," "high command," "high church," "high profit," and "high class" each rest upon "low life." In the next, "high tea" is served at "high ground" to those of "high standing" in a "high society" that is "high riding" on "low life" (22). Here is a series of popular catch phrases denoting class privilege, which extend down and across the poem's concrete shape. But the shifting terms on one side of these two-word expressions trope a certain *kind* of life—the "high life" that goes unnamed—in which the social elevation of one class is assured through the social abjection of another; for the former, "high" remains a fixed qualifier for a series of signifiers that stand in for the initial "life" that goes unnamed (the expression "high life" goes unsaid) but also figure the transportation of resources across the colonial world—including the transport of low life as human bio-cargo—and the transfer of wealth from the colonies to the British metropole. Thus, the metonymies cycling through the poem figure the cycle of capitalist accumulation that secures "high life." Meanwhile, "low life" remains the same, neither term having access to mobility beyond the life of modern bio-cargo. The poem's fractured vertical linearity belies the economic hierarchies and uneven social relationships across "ranks" that are often erased in the language of horizontal circulation and networked flows. This is the fundamental social relation on which "high life" depends and on which the "pillars" of "high society" profit. Meanwhile, "Shipshape & Lancaster-Fashion" draws our attention to another underclass rarely addressed in discussions of the slave trade, the sailors who labored aboard merchant ships.[28] The poem stages the brutality hierarchies that govern relations at the bottom end of "low life," among the dispossessed and disposed, where "sailors singing a sea-shanty blues, / homesick, danced on the decks, above / the deep choral undertow of African / voices rolling below" (18) The poem speaks of the "terror of the submerged Africans," bringing to mind both the slaves in the ship's hold—submerged below the waterline, as it were—and those slaves who did not complete the passage, who were tossed out to sea, either dead or dying, without value, and who form the "submarine network" I discussed in chapter 1. At the same time, the poem addresses the psychological imperative to forget one's participation in atrocity. The slave ship, like the colonial system more broadly, survived, thrived even, on the principles of denial and disavowal, where "sailors shared a drunken haze / of rum-pint after rum-pint to soothe / them into forgetting our Maafa" (18).[29] It is with stinging irony that Smartt recognizes that forgetting is achieved through the consumption of the product of the slaves' labor—the rum itself. By identifying the drinking of rum as the means of forgetting, the poem implies that history is ingested and that the body itself houses the past through consumption. The sailors drink the rum the slaves produce, but in trying to forget their own suffering they also forget that of the enslaved, a description of capitalist consumer practices Marx understood well. It would be easy to say that consumption and ingestion work as powerful metaphors for our relationship to the past, or to others here in the present, except that these terms strike me as more than simply metaphorical, but rather phenomenological. Here the body serves as a quite literal repository of the past.

Samboo's Grave—Bilal's Grave figures the body itself as an archive of submerged history in which the past manifests as bodily symptoms. This is perhaps made most explicit in "The Captain's Wife's Story," where Smartt portrays the psychosomatic response to the slave trade experienced, as the title suggests, by the wife of the sea captain who has brought Bilal to England. Following a visit by an "agent from a plantation tied to my husband's ship," the speaker recounts, "the dreams came and my soul's light / dimmed into dis-ease that poured out in fainting- / spells and anonymous pains in my body" (27). If her symptoms began with the ingestion of the dinner served to the "West Indian guest," they persist through her inability to digest the intimate knowledge of slavery this "plantation agent" brings with him. Once again, in this poem experience is mediated through the objects associated with the trade. In addition to the food, there is the "chiming of our crafted Gillow's clock" in which she can "hear his ship's bell toll" and through which she herself will "enter an underworld / inflicted with anxiety and guilt" (27). The poem suggests that shame and guilt disperses through the invested community and is disseminated by way of the intimate contacts and affective relationships to the people and objects that have "touched" the slave's body, as in the repetition of the image of the captain's hands, "the same / hands that strip the Negro of his flesh, / prise open, dig the enslaved's wounds, / stroking them with briny waters for discipline" (27). The captain's wife's story, then, is also one of a submerged somatic history linked to practices that disseminate across both space and time: "The ship–my husband's ship–moored in blood / dispersing merchandise into the Lune for our local / grocers' trade in slaves, merchants and seamen / spilling onto the quayside, fertilizes / the terrors of my nervous condition" (27). Smartt's imagery is in equal measure sexual and violent, implying that the violence of the colonies—in particular the sexual violence of the colonies—cannot be contained through the silence surrounding life "out there." The captain's wife receives that violence into her own body through the traffic that "bring[s] it all back home" (20).

If "The Captain's Wife's Story" describes the housing of colonial affect, the climax of the sequence, "The Present Arrives," depicts its unhousing. By working together the voices of the captain and his wife, the poem recounts the presentation of Bilal as a "gift" for the captain's wife and of her angry and terrified refusal of him. *"Get that thing out of here!"* she screams, or at least according to the captain's narrative (43). Her account differs, however, and Smartt suggests that readers not interpret her reply as simply a common expression of eighteenth-century racism but as a more complex reaction that continues from "The Captain's Wife's Story" earlier in the sequence. For her, Bilal is an emblem of the trade she both despises and profits from, and that is a source for her physical "dis-ease." Her symptoms manifest the affective response she feels when it (plantation slavery) or he (Bilal himself) is "brought home": "This black-skinned boy, / eyes wide and white on me! / *Take it out of my sight,* I whisper. / *It is blinking!"* (43). To have her gaze returned by the slave, whose presence is no longer spectral but fully embodied, is more than she can endure. *"What gift is this that hurls me into your present?"* she asks. Smartt plays on the word "present" as both gift and marker of time, and the "your" of the question seems to double the "you" of her address: her question is addressed to both her husband and the audience, the present of 1836 and of 2007. "My insides run against me," she tells the reader, in response to Bilal's gaze, which arrests her in *her* present and in *his* presence, while "a gust of sugary saliva rushes my mouth, / my avoidance defeated and suspicions alive" (43). She expresses the ambivalence—suggested in "sugary saliva"—that Homi Bhabha describes as at the very foundations of the racism of colonial discourse.[30] Her salty-sweet saliva, as somatic productions, here maps onto avoidance and suspicion as psychic operations of colonial ambivalence.

Throughout, *Sambo's Grave—Bilal's Grave* emphasizes the play between what is revealed and what is withheld, what can be known and what can only be imagined. Smartt describes her own experience of working in the Lancaster archives as one of intimacy, where "touching" the materials in the archive produces a powerful somatic affect—an experience shared, I should think, by most anyone who has handled such materials. The aura of the archive, it would seem, appears to be alive and well. But given the vicissitudes of archival knowledge production I described earlier, perhaps we should say alive but ill, or ailing. In his aptly titled *Archive Fever,* Jacques Derrida argues that the malady of the archive is itself psychosomatic, that is, both unconscious and fully embodied.[31] For him the archive designates both the feverish impulse to collect and the compulsion to repeat. Derrida is especially interested in the archive of bodily violence—the marks on the body that denote subjection to religious law and historical conflict—as a set of "impressions" that in turn convey the *historicity* of inscripture as past, present, and future in the dialectic of becoming: "How can one think about this fatal repetition," Derrida ponders, "in its relationship to memory and the archive? It is easy to perceive, if not to interpret, the necessity of such a relationship, at least if one associates the archive, as naturally one is always tempted to do, with repetition, and repetition with the past. But it is the future that is at issue here, and the archive as an irreducible experience of the future" (68). Derrida maintains that the archive is not only the site for housing the remains of culture, nor is it solely the discursive formations indexed within those remains evoked in Foucault's *Archaeology of Knowledge*.[32] For Derrida, however, the archive is at once the very site of the institution of law and the place from which the law emanates. The archive both houses and designates a structuring principle and its violent hermeneutic code. The archive, he writes, "is not only the place for stocking and for conserving an archivable content *of the past* which would exist in any case. . . . No, the technical structure of the *archiving* archive also determines the structure of the *archivable* content even in its very coming into existence and in its relationship to the future. The archivization produces as much as it records the event" (16–17). As such, he suggests, the archive structures not only the past but also the present and the future "to come"; it is a structure that structures (both *arca* and *techné*)—a *structuring* structure, one might say. In the compulsion to repeat, however, the archive manifests its own structuring principle: the Freudian death drive. The archive aims to forget. This is its tendential law. Here the archive is simultaneously constitutive of past, present, and future and the very sign of history's own death drive and uncanny spectral form. It is not enough to say that the archive begins where memory ends; memory, like the archive, indeed *as* the archive, itself feverishly forgets.

What I have been suggesting throughout is that Dorothea Smartt is working toward a genealogical understanding of history and of historical processes, indeed of historical necessity. She understands that for those displaced through migration, whether in Britain or in the postcolony, there is much at stake in how the past is archived and how it is remembered. Smartt's commission is a public commemorative history from minor positions, positions almost always effaced in the drive toward those almost instantaneous and economically appropriable acts and edifices of commemoration—not the impromptu or provisional memorials that consecrate the ground of local tragedy, but those state-sponsored or underwritten sites that are suddenly and carelessly appropriated as locations for the consolidation of national belonging, a project committed to quite reactionary narratives of the national genealogy. Performative works like hers dislodge the grid of the family tree by imagining alternative antigenealogies that produce an *intimate* history. Through her performances of the archive, the material artifacts found there are withdrawn and "put to work" in constellation with an immaterial narrative that otherwise could never have been archived in the first place. Such performances are staged in the gap opened up between the archiving archive and those embodied, artifactual counterarchives unhoused alongside but askance to the archive. Smartt's artifactual body, which makes its spectral way into the printed work, offers itself as an archival fact, also standing alongside but askance, appended to material that has been dematerialized, incorporating the discorporate bodies the archive cannot abide and could not contain.

Blood Lines

The artifactual body as discorporate body might offer a useful figure for listening to the disembodied conversations that comprise the voice-over narration of Inge Blackman's short film *Legacy.*[33] In this seventeen-minute gallery-based single-screen video installation, commissioned by David A. Bailey for Bristol's Arnolfini Gallery, the filmmaker returns to her native Trinidad in order to interview her own mother about the history and legacy of slavery on families in the African diaspora. Blackman and her mother are the only subjects in the documentary, and their conversations are conveyed through a series of voice-over exchanges that map onto visual sequences that capture them enacting a variety of ritualized traditions. Influenced by filmmakers like Cheryl Dunye and Isaac Julien, Blackman portrays these rituals through a series of visual reenactments and tableaux vivants by mother and daughter. The film opens with an invocation to her ancestors and a consecration of the land performed against the backdrop of crashing waves and the haunting call of the abeng. As they pour ritual libations upon the sand, Blackman and her mother offer words of homage and supplication in alternating rhythm:

> *Blackman:* I honor my African ancestors, who survived the horror of the Middle Passage and the brutality of slavery.
> *Mother:* Mama, I honor you. I pour these libations in your honor, and please look after me and my family.
> *Inge:* I honor my Maroon and Haitian ancestors, who defeated the slave masters by picking up arms and fighting back.
> *Mother:* Mama, my grandmother, I honor you. I pour these libations in your honor. I thank you for giving me my mother; and please look after my family.

The opening benediction links family heritage to the history of resistance by Jamaican Maroons and their Akan or Coromantee ancestors who organized against colonial enslavement from the protective isolation of the island's central mountains. While the audio track continues the dedication, the video fades in to the women standing alongside one another displaying photographs of Blackman's grandmother and great-grandmother, a spectral materialization of four generations of Jamaican women reaching back to the filial memory of enslavement (see Figure 16). Through the film, Blackman partitions the narrative exposition of these traditional practices from the visual reenactments themselves, suggesting the way in which a history that remains inarticulable in narrative terms might find expression in cultural practices that are themselves articulations of the past. By locating narrative and performance on two discrete filmic planes, the visual and the aural, Blackman offers something like what I have called an antigenealogy that, in this case, descends solely along the maternal axis. In her portrayal of a women's homosociality rooted in historical rupture and genealogical disruption, Blackman treads along an immeasurably thin line between familial intimacy and erotic attachment that always troubles a discussion of childhood sexuality. Now adults, however, mother and daughter reengage those ritualized physical intimacies that combine familial comfort with physical pleasure.

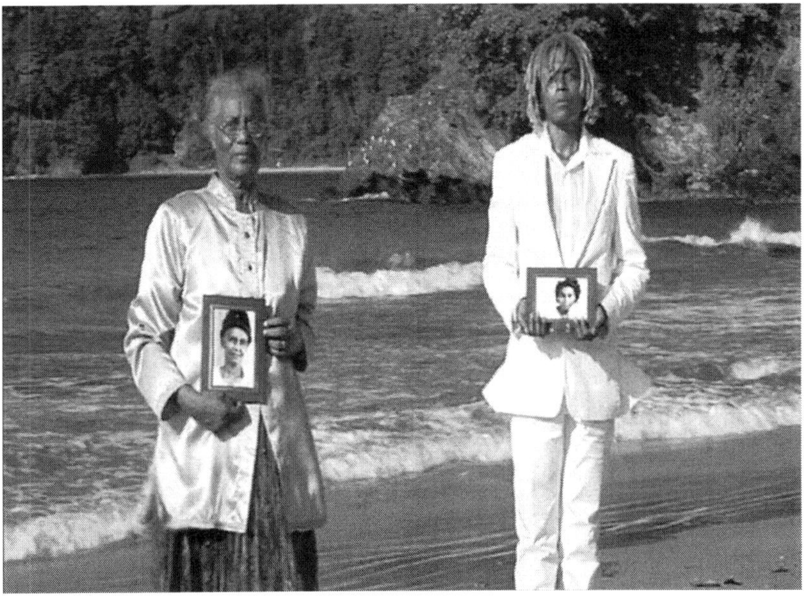

Figure 16. Legacy, *dir. Inge Blackman, 2006.*

Following the inaugural invocation, Blackman's mother—whose voice remains in the disembodied voice-over—addresses the misconception that black diasporic history begins with their capture into slavery and that this rupture absolutely severs them from their African past. On the one hand, she maintains that her own mother "was very adamant that she knew *where* she came from," suggesting that family stories provide legacies vital to the formation of a rooted geographic identity. "She was so very proud," the elder Blackman continues, "of her ancestors coming from the Gold Coast, which is now Ghana." On the other hand, the visual tropes deployed in the film evoke other, ineffable histories performed by and through the body, histories that descend through generations of diasporic women, operate *off* the genealogical map, and cannot be explained by knowledge grids rooted in the Western genealogical imaginary. Such embodied performances set against the disembodied narrative find an especially powerful expression when the two women dance the Kumina, a traditional Afro-Caribbean religious ceremony comprised of music, chanting, and drumming. Kumina was brought to Jamaica by slaves taken from the Congo region of Africa but remains associated with the predominantly Akan community of Maroons with which Blackburn's mother claims heritage. The ritual is intended to call down the spirits of one's ancestors to inhabit the bodies of the living in order to provide them with wisdom and advice. Kumina is often, though not solely, performed during funeral ceremonies and rites of entombment.[34] In the film, while mother and daughter dance and chant in percussive rhythm within a circle of candles on the beach, the mother explains, again in voice-over, that her own mother, as proud as she was, refused to practice African religions and rituals like Kumina, and instead "bent down" to the Anglican Church (see Figure 17). Blackman's mother learned of the practice one night when she "stole away" and watched her grandmother and aunts performing the Kumina. But like her own mother, the elder Blackman does not practice the Kumina nor did she teach it to her daughter, but rather passed down the Christian traditions with which she was more comfortable. For Blackman's white grandfather, her mother recounts, the Kumina evoked fear—in particular fear of confronting the legacy of his own ancestors' involvement in plantation slavery, and of a history that forbade such African practices, which were broadly feared as leading to slave rebellion. Blackman's mother explains that such a legacy of secrecy and fear interfered with the conveyance of traditions from one generation to another, and therefore kept her from teaching her own daughter the Kumina. "We are

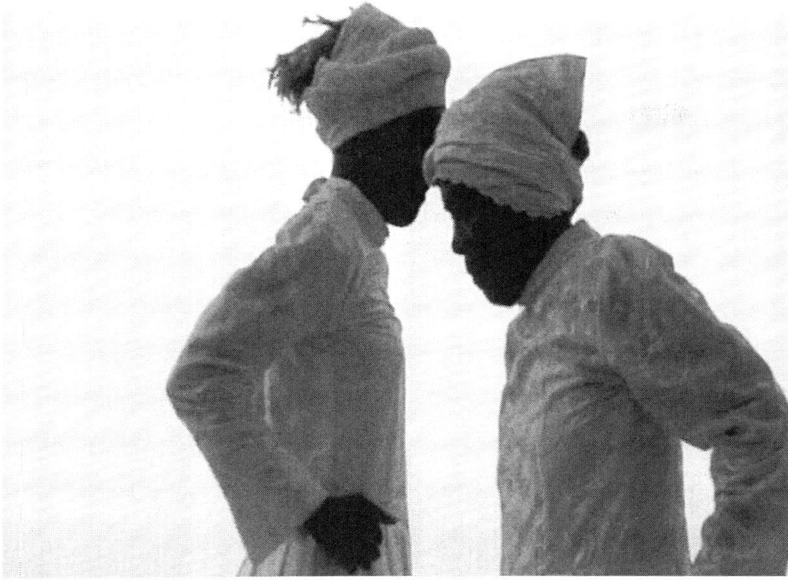

Figure 17. Legacy, *dir. Inge Blackman, 2006.*

still not comfortable with our African traditions," she explains. The film, then, captures the moment in which she finally does, though only at Blackman's urging, while confronting her own uncertain relationship to these traditions.

Although Blackman's grandmother had disavowed African religious traditions, she still honored many other aspects of African Caribbean culture, and like her mother had kept to them. One tradition that gets close attention in the film is the ritualized "bush bath," a tradition of herbal bathing meant to comfort and heal ailing children. In the film, Blackman's mother explains the importance of the bush bath, which Blackman herself doesn't remember ever receiving, while the mother bathes the now-adult daughter. The film implies that this bath, now decades overdue, will allow mother and daughter to heal some of the wounds that held them apart through the years of separation while Blackman herself was abroad in Britain. The intimacy of this ritual, like that of pleating hair and applying oils to the skin, enacts a quite tactile bond between mother and daughter (see Figure 18). As Blackman's mother gently applies oil to her daughter's skin, she recounts the abuse of the slave at the hands of the slave master.

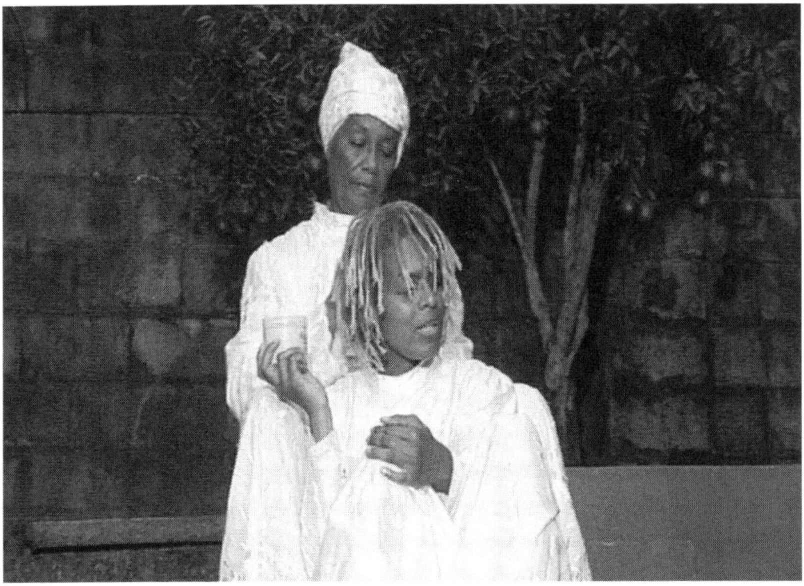

Figure 18. Legacy, *dir. Inge Blackman, 2006.*

Blackman contrasts these acts of bonding to the corporal punishment she received at her mother's hands as a child, another aspect of a local child-rearing tradition common, the mother explains, in her disciplinary culture. When asked why she never hugged or kissed her own children, Blackman's mother responds that this too is part of the legacy of her upbringing, one quite difficult to break. "I do not feel any guilt or shame about it," Blackman's mother responds, "because I love you and I could *demonstrate* my love for you rather than being tactile." These traditions of bathing and hygiene are placed in the context of women's sexuality and the silence and shame that too often interfere between mother and daughter, and the history of sexual violence and the degradation of black women that came out of slavery and the slave trade. Blackman's mother relays her own mother's stories of the way in which women's genitalia were displayed for all to see up on the auction block, and how humiliating this was for African cultures with deep traditions of modesty. In this moment of maternal intimacy they discuss Blackman's experience of corporal punishment as a child and its relationship to the brutal punishments enacted upon the slave. The film then shows them reenacting such a scene in order to account for the "licks" her mother gave her as a child. The visual image that accompanies the voice-over, however, shows Blackman stripped to her waist, kneeling before her mother, who, dressed as a plantation overseer, whips her daughter with a cat-o-nine-tails, Blackman's back bloodied by these licks (see Figure 19). "So you did to me that was done to you. Do you think," she asks her mother, "that could have been a legacy from before? Because I think it's not just the harshness of it and the brutality of it which goes beyond just punishment." Interestingly, her mother has difficulty admitting to the violence of her punishments, saying, "I was sometimes punished harshly, but I would give my children just a few slaps." Mother and daughter disagree on their variant characterizations of corporal punishment, though the mother concedes that she did occasionally beat her children and that this did have an adverse effect on her relationship with her daughter.

Blackman's mother traces the violence articulated both within the black diasporic family and within broader colonial and postcolonial societies by addressing the irony of her own racially mixed heritage, with one set of ancestors brought from Africa to work in the plantations while another traveled from Britain to be their masters. She describes the "joining" of this

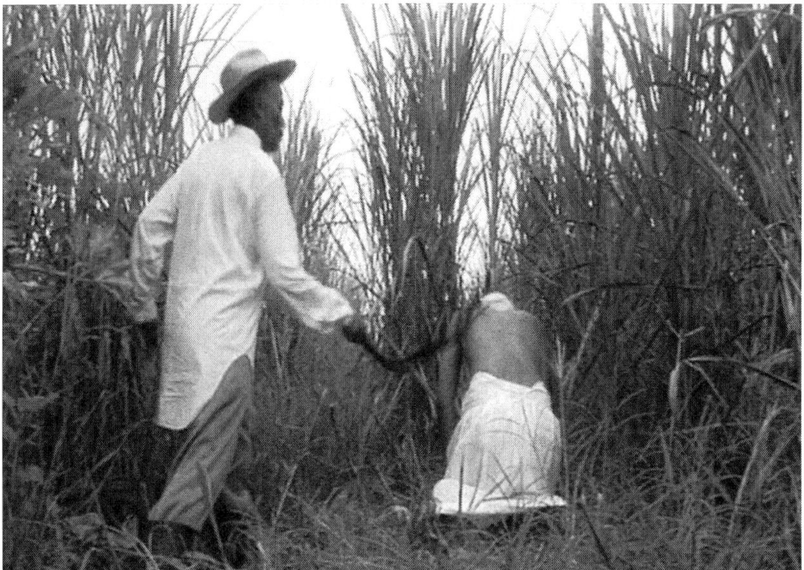

Figure 19. Legacy, *dir. Inge Blackman, 2006.*

history in her own family and recounts the heated arguments, debates, and discussions in her family about the mistreatment of slaves by their British masters. She also notes that while her white father did at times experience "guilt and compassion" about this history, at other moments he was very "self-satisfied" by this history because "he felt that what was done was done for the benefit of the African slaves," an ambivalent set of reactions still common today. She goes on, however, to emphasize that her mother "felt there should be some sort of compensation for the sufferings of the people of the plantation." Although she dwells on her own relationship to her mother, Blackman's sense of kinship is not restricted to a received formula predicated on patrilinearity or heterosexuality; nor does her recourse to the past rely on a narrowly circumscribed notion of genealogy. It may not, then, be surprising that the social bond that links mother and daughter is neither simply a hetero- nor a cultural-normative one; their conversations and physical proximities form a decidedly nonhierarchical filiation. I suggest that Blackman posits women's intimacy as a form of female homosociality, one that is neither prior to nor subsequent to that male homosocial bond that Luce Irigaray, among others, argues subtends the sexual/social contract.[35] Further, Blackman's film demonstrates the way intimacy is forged through touching and caressing as much as through cultural and object exchange.

Intimacy structures the psychic and phenomenological expression of the social body, and of social bodies, and it might form the basis for new historiographic models, perhaps analogous to, or in conversation with, what Elizabeth Freeman has recently called "erotohistoriography," a provocative turn of phrase to which I now turn.[36]

Blood Brothers

In many ways, Isaac Julien's *Looking for Langston* (1989) offers a quintessential treatment of melancholy rumination on the struggle for familial recognition. The film opens, after all, with a wail of sirens more sorrowful than alarming and archival footage of a subway car clattering across an empty Harlem skyline, before fading to the May 1967 funeral of the film's eponymous subject, staged archivally then restaged melodramatically in one of Julien's signature tableaux vivants. Hilton Als, who participated in the film, recently ascribed the filmmaker's interest in the queer recovery of Langston Hughes to Julien's having "so few 'out' ancestors."[37] To be sure, the film constellates an elegant genealogy of black queer belonging whose lineage runs from Hughes to Countee Cullen and Claude McKay to Alain Locke. As the camera pans across the intimate gathering of mourners and pauses above the open lid, we discover, as everyone by now knows, that the casket is occupied by the immobilized but otherwise peaceful body of the still young filmmaker himself. By 1989 far too many young men like Julien had become premature occupants of unexpectedly acquired coffins for hastily arranged funerals. The word *specter* hardly describes the environment of that decade and the one to follow, permeated with the terror and sadness and loneliness and anger wrought by the epidemic. Toward the end of the film, Beauty (Matthew Baidoo), again in voice-over, recites one of Hughes's most poignant if fatalistic expressions of such loss: "I loved my friend / He went away from me / There's nothing more to say. . . . I loved my friend." Julien may have been looking for "out" fathers, but he was also searching for lost brothers.

Be-winged and be-glittered, Julien's club-kid brothers now stand guard over the legacies of James Baldwin and Bruce Nugent, both still fresh in their own graves. The photographs of Baldwin and Nugent held aloft by Julien's angelic intermediaries serve as a sign of his (and our) looking at and searching for heretofore broken filial bonds. More importantly, they allow Julien (and us) to touch—in queer epistolic succession—brothers lost and brothers gained all "linked," as Baldwin is quoted in the film, by their homosexual desire. Julien's meditation stakes a claim on these figures from the past as an act of counterarchival recovery—counterarchival in a more literal sense: in the claim of copyright infringement brought on behalf of the Hughes estate by its executor, George Bass, who tried to have the film stripped of the poet's public voice, presented, for example, in archival footage of Hughes reading his "Weary Blues" accompanied by Charles Mingus and Leonard Feather. Motivated by concern for Hughes's reputation, we might consider Bass's action one of archival and genealogical retrenchment. But since Hughes had no children and Bass had been his secretary, neither the estate nor its executor could escape an inevitable queer failure and the possibilities for other kinds of filiation such failure affords.

HIV/AIDS introduced yet another crisis of blood: a panic over a new deeply racialized queer "taint." By the time *Looking for Langston* was released, gays had long since been banned from "giving" blood, restrictions on seropositive donations only now being eased, though not abolished. The poet Essex Hemphill provided a powerful voice to the uncontainable range of feeling generated by the epidemic, though blood was not the body fluid of gravest concern. Were we to identify the second ritual through which gay men enter into "blood" brotherhood—which likewise "linked" them in their sexuality across racial and class lines—it would be the exchange of semen in the high-risk hunting grounds of public bathhouses, docks, toilets, and parks. Hemphill recites in voice-over his poem "Where the Seed Falls" while on screen James (Akim Mogaji) goes "stalking" in the dark bushes of an isolated graveyard. Hemphill recodes blood sport as a eucharistic consumption of the host. Later we find Marcus (Densil Williams) pulling on a cigarette in a pornographic movie house, while Hemphill intones, "Now we think / when we fuck / this nut might kill," playing on the double meaning of nut as a pointed reminder of the high-stakes pleasure of an anonymous fuck.

Isaac Julien has never shied away from engaging with the complex relationship between racialized and sexualized violence, often playing on historically resonate tropes of master and slave, sadism and masochism, dominance and submission, pleasure and abjection.[38] Elizabeth Freeman has shown persuasively how queer practices of S/M do much more than simply draw upon the visual and technical repertoire of historical violence; they also serve as a way to embody the past through the manipulation of pleasure and pain through slow time. Sadomasochism, she argues, "relentlessly physicalizes the encounter with history, and thereby contributes to a 'reparative' criticism that takes up the materials of a traumatic past and remixes them in the interests of new possibilities for being or knowing."[39] Freeman identifies Julien's short film *The Attendant* (1993) as a work thoughtfully engaged with the interwoven tempos of S/M and historical experience and the racial politics implicated in its practices. *The Attendant* also explores racialized desire within a much longer and more explicitly colonial history of sexualized violence, developing this aesthetic of stylized performance that enters the archive at the intersection of personal pleasure and collective pain to tend and attend to wounds opened up by "historical" exchange. The film reflexively historicizes racialized violence by reenacting scenes of bondage, discipline, domination, and submission *as* sadomasochistic pleasure. As Freeman points out, by restaging the archive as a series of sadomasochistic tableaux, BDSM is presented as a reparative endeavor within the colonization of sexuality. *The Attendant* explicitly links the history of the slave trade to cross-racial queer sexuality and S/M fantasy and practice today.

Like *Looking for Langston, The Attendant* is a meditation on the shared history and iconography of colonial violence and racialized sexuality. The film finds exigency in the cultural artifacts housed in the Wilberforce House Museum, and their relationship to the slave trade itself, as well as the abolitionist movement for which Wilberforce himself is most remembered. Julien has commented on the long engagement with the museum as a site of "pleasure, fantasy, domination, repression, and desire" and "debates over how art is archived in one domain and in another not at all."[40] Julien's museum interventions engage the institutional, museological, and archival complications of the museum space in part through an "aesthetic dialogue" with architectural space. Such a dialogic moment is captured in *The Attendant,* which is nominally set in the Wilberforce House in Hull, in a sequence of low-angle shots of the steps of the museum that project an image of monumental public grandeur and reinforce the tone of dominant and domineering artistic institutionalization. Although the scenes inside the museum are indeed shot at the Wilberforce House, these depict the imposing, classical architecture of the Royal Academy in London, which is, in David Orgeron's phrase, "the ultimate architectural signifier of 'establishment.'"[41] According to Julien himself, "The museum in *The Attendant* is constructed as the historical bastion, the high citadel of colonial artifacts. In this postcolonial moment, it is the black attendant (the unspoken subject/object of most museum installations) who stands guard over the colonial artifacts, nineteenth-century paintings and works of high art."[42] In the film, the gallery is transformed into a stylized, indeed choreographed, space of sensory consumption and fantasy production. As in *Looking for Langston,* the film moves through a series of intimate physical encounters. These acts of seeing and being seen, of hearing and being heard, of feeling and being felt, signal the absolutely embodied forms taken by technologies of recognition and desire; such actions also mark out the progress of its fantasy narrative. Indeed, the attendant's job is to look, to inspect, to scrutinize the museumgoers as they enter into and circulate through the galleries. This brings him into an intimate contact with each of the patrons, a relationship at once economic, disciplinary, and sensual. These intimate disciplinary encounters begin in the film's earliest scenes, such as when the attendant inspects the satchels and gym bags of the museum's visitors for suspicious items, or makes his rounds surveying the patrons and drawing them into an economy of suspicion.

The primary art-historical citation, however, is the inclusion of François-Auguste Biard's painting *Slaves on the West Coast of Africa* (see Figure 20).[43] Accompanying the visual intertext provided by Biard's painting, Julien sets

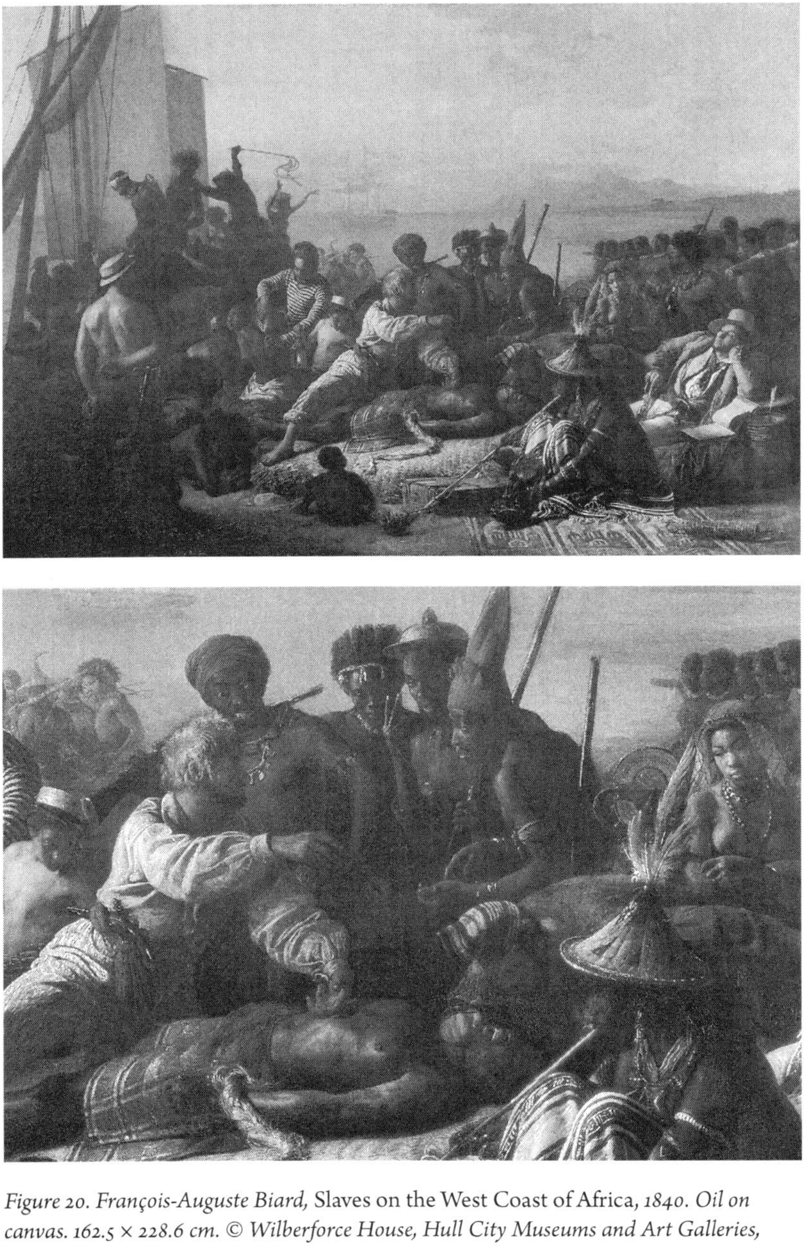

Figure 20. François-Auguste Biard, Slaves on the West Coast of Africa, *1840. Oil on canvas. 162.5 × 228.6 cm. © Wilberforce House, Hull City Museums and Art Galleries, UK/Bridgeman Images.*

the film to the almost liturgical sounds of "Dido's Lament," an aria from Henry Purcell's opera *Dido and Aeneas.* Indeed, Purcell's aria produces something of a counterpoint to Biard's painting, coupling melancholy, longing, and loss, on the one hand, to masochistic enjoyment and the pleasure of sadistic abjection, on the other.[44] Each intertext reinforces the other in two composed but distinct tableaux, one of the slave dying on the shore of West Africa and the other of Dido atop her funeral pyre. Later scenes draw these encounters into the realm of fantasy, as when the attendant, dressed in tux and tails, sings "Dido's Lament" to an audience consisting of the only woman to appear in the film, the museum conservator. Throughout *The Attendant* institutional history is set against domestic, private, or even intimate affective history, but at no point can these competing historical imaginaries be fully untangled. Indeed, it is precisely through the many queer intimacies, including its multiple scenes of S/M, that queer genealogies occluded from the dominant historical narratives haunt notions of legacy and political agency.

Julien draws upon the imagery from Biard's painting in two significant ways: first, as an artifactual object; and second, through reenactment in a series of tableaux vivants depicting scenes of queer sadomasochistic play through which the camera moves (see Figures 21 and 22).[45] Speaking on the controversial appropriation of iconography of Atlantic slavery into the

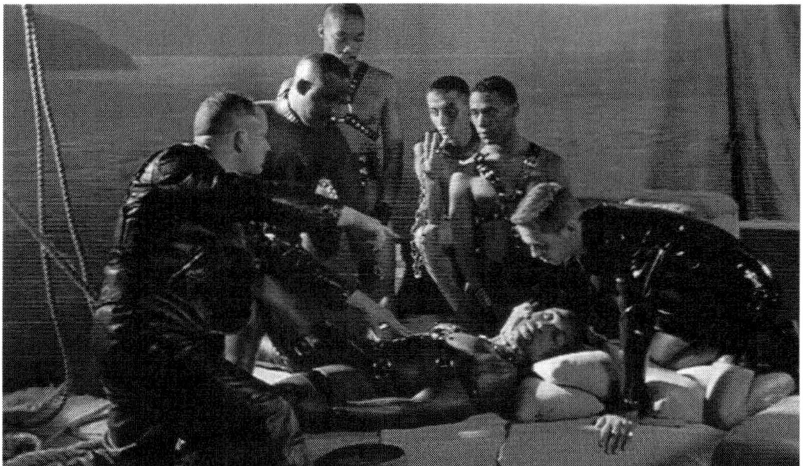

Figure 21. The Attendant, *dir. Isaac Julien, 1993.*

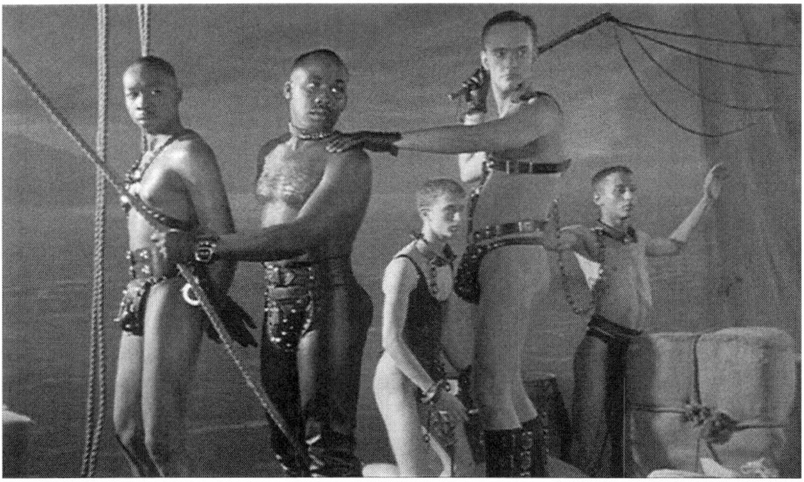

Figure 22. The Attendant, *dir. Isaac Julien, 1993.*

visual vocabulary of sadomasochism, and his inclusion of Biard's painting in particular, Julien writes:

> The painting incorporates several tableaux which visually narrate the history of slavery: the buying and selling of black slaves; black men being whipped by other black men, under orders from the white master; bartering over black bodies. The images in this painting signify, symbolically, the tragic story of enslavement: the fears and fantasies projected onto the Other in the practice of a human brutality aimed, ultimately, at financial profit. *Scene on the Coast of Africa* [*sic*] may have made the white European bourgeoisie question such violent enactments of the "civilizing mission" of industrial capitalist expansion. The legacy of slave imperialism persists, and the world is haunted by its traumatic and ineradicable memory.[46]

On the one hand, the painting provides an institutional, bourgeois history of slavery, and indeed Julien sees the work as a kind of transhistorical depiction of that history allegorized in its several tableaux. On the other hand, Julien also recognizes the possibility of critique the painting might open up to a bourgeois public. Unmistakably, Julien's use of Biard is a self-reflexive questioning of the potential for an artistic intervention into the political.

Slaves on the West Coast of Africa may have demystified the civilizing mission of capitalist development, but the legacy of slavery and imperialism persists, and the painting must also designate the failure, or at least the limits, of art as political intervention. Looking again at the detail from Biard's painting, however, one cannot help but notice the particularly gendered form that violence takes in the scene depicted or Julien's elision of violence against African women, such as the mutilation occurring just to the left and slightly behind the tableau of gendered care in which Julien invests such erotic attachment, a point that underscores the ambivalent relationship between the attendant and the conservator in the film.

Adopting the point of view of the museum spectator, the camera pans across the details of Biard's painting, drawing the violence of the slave market into clearer focus; two later tableaux, however, depict the attendant and visitor themselves in sadomasochistic play, with the visitor and then the attendant wielding the whip (see Figures 23 and 24). By avoiding any spoken dialogue, Julien emphasizes the visual (such as in his use of the painting and tableaux), the aural (as in the lament), and the tactile (as when the attendant finds the bullwhip stashed in the visitor's satchel), each constituting aspects of the sensational fantasy the film explores. Julien writes that, in *The Attendant,* "our gaze is repositioned through the eyes and fantasies of that marginally constructed museum subject/object, the black closeted

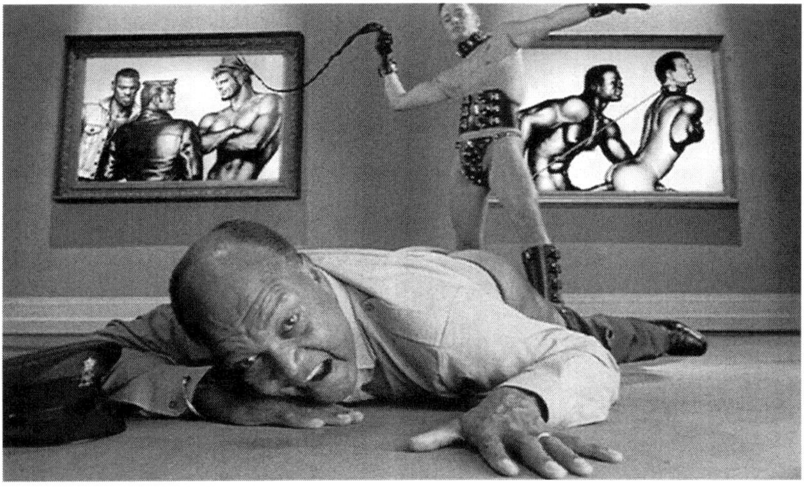

Figure 23. The Attendant, *dir. Isaac Julien, 1993.*

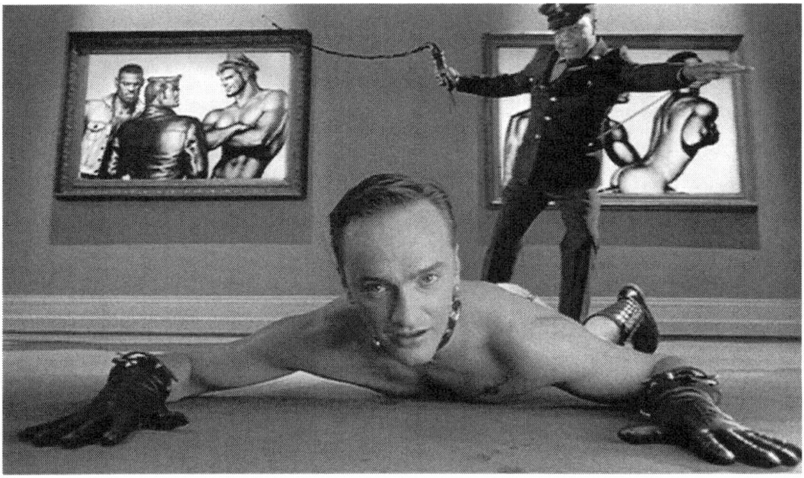

Figure 24. The Attendant, *dir. Isaac Julien, 1993.*

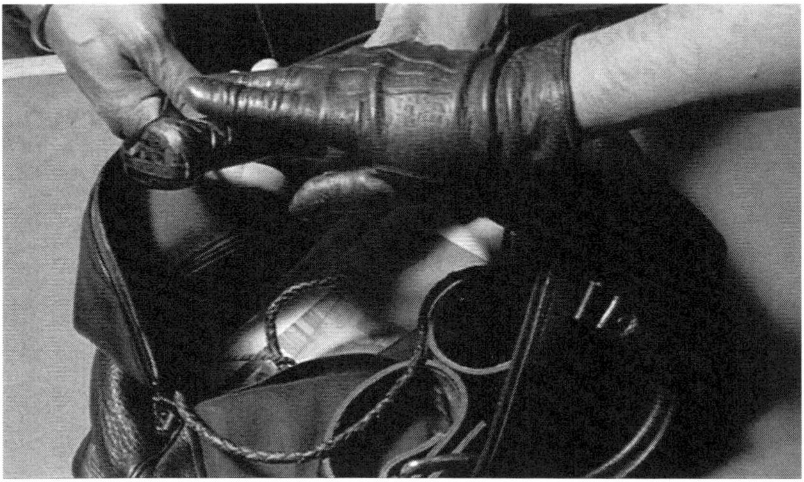

Figure 25. The Attendant, *dir. Isaac Julien, 1993.*

attendant."[47] Looking and listening, then, work in tandem with more tactile sensations, as museumgoer and museum attendant gain a feel for the other through the metonymic handling and caressing of objects (see Figure 25). The attendant and the visitor are thus bound together by these transactional objects and instruments, intermediaries whose historicity likewise links past and present. Sensation and pleasure often rely on such objects, reinforce them, as with the enjoyment the conservator experiences as she listens to the encounter between the attendant and the visitor through the thin gallery wall, an unseen—and unrecognized—aural participant in their perverse pleasures.

David Orgeron, in an otherwise astute analysis of *The Attendant,* tries to imagine the way in which Julien's film "re-members" history but stumbles over precisely the problem that cross-racial sadomasochism poses to notions of sexual agency and intersubjective reversibility. He writes that the fantasy depicted in Julien's tableaux vivants, based as they are on Biard's painting, "allows for 'forbidden' sexuality or pleasure, but at this point is unable to sustain a complete reversal (i.e., black sadism, white masochism). In other words, black male pleasure, at this stage in the fantasy sequence, is envisioned as masochistic and is disturbingly bound to the roles suggested by history."[48] But to simply see sexual reversal along the axes of historical reversal is to fall prey to a decidedly Fanonian imagination of black/white racial pathology, that is, to view history along the axes of the master–slave dialectic. Although Orgeron is correct in seeing the attendant's agency at work in the construction of fantasy, to see history as "revisited and sexualized" is to dramatically underplay the complication that both history and sexuality receive in the film. Orgeron's reading of the decidedly camp renditions of angels and demons playfully encircling both the attendant and the visitor's heads maps psychic intentionality along dominant historical lines, such that the visitor is reductively viewed as the colonial oppressor, while the attendant is the colonial oppressed.

Yet it seems to me that Julien is not satisfied with positing queer S/M as a reproduction in the present of colonial violence per se, but rather he tries to understand the iconographic resemblances in racial and colonial discourses, which is often easily and fetishistically reinscribed in the sexual. Thus, I would question Orgeron's claim that the scene wherein the attendant first exchanges a knowing look with the visitor, a scene in which angels and demons dance about their heads, "reestablishes the two men's relation to the colonial project imagined in the re-created painting—the visitor with his pitchfork-wielding angel is the sadist who occupies the dominant position of the oppressor."[49] The angels and demons are far too ironic for that. The glance that they exchange is not simply one of master and slave, or oppressor and oppressed, nor is it easily seen as two mutually desiring subjects. Rather, I read their glance as a minor precursor to the unfolding of an erotic intimacy that allows them to both touch the past, to feel its powerful hold on the present, and to appropriate that traumatic history in order to reimagine possibilities for an endless series of reversals. According to Julien:

> Although the current images of "whips" and "chains" in the representational practices of s/m have been borrowed from this colonial iconography, the refashioning of these accoutrements (i.e. rubberisation, polished surfaces, latex, polished metal) has transformed them into sexualised, stylised fetish clothing for the queer body. The imperialist slave iconography is appropriated and repositioned. The popular "black," "straight" reading that tries to use the signs of s/m (whips and chains) for neo-colonial racist/sexual practice is an attempt to "fix" these images in time, perpetuating white power and domination.[50]

Might the glance the attendant and visitor exchange function as a form of recognition that both enacts the process of historical memory-judgment-action as well as demands admission and submission as a decidedly reversible transaction? Desire and subjection, fantasy and abjection, run relay through the multiple positions adopted by the attendant and visitor, which is reproduced for the viewer by way of a complicated iconographic genealogy that reaches back through the tableaux to the painting by Biard and the institutional history it organizes and allegorizes.

For Julien, such scenes of S/M both enact and subvert colonial memory, mimic and parody the roles of master and slave once regimented into a fixed racial schema. "Surely in this post-colonial moment," Julien asserts, "black queers should have a choice of acting out the roles of 'slaves' or 'masters' in the realm of desire and sexual fantasy."[51] Must interracial S/M be "moralistically read into the cheap sociology of a pathological, black/self-hating discourse?" Or, he asks, "could not the representation of interracial s/m be read as a practice of a racial and sexual dynamic which, in displaying the codes of a (Fanonian) master/slave dialectic, presents a transgressive simulacrum, one which both parodies and disrupts the codes of societal and racial power?"[52]

It is certainly worth noting, in closing this section of the chapter, that *The Attendant* was also both motivated by and a response to "Operation Spanner," an action taken against S/M practitioners by Manchester police in 1987. In the following months, sixteen individuals were charged with assault leading to bodily harm, while another twenty-six received cautions (by the end of 1990). The defendants pleaded guilty in exchange for reduced sentences but appealed the decision to prosecute to the UK High Court, which affirmed the decision, as did the House of Lords (in 1993), as would the European Court of Human Rights (in 1997).[53] In effect, the Spanner case criminalized any act of sadomasochism that injured the submissive partner, including simple marks like bruises, cuts, or abrasions. Paramount to the film's politics, then, is the current campaign in the UK to regulate nonnormative sex and to gain a legal control of the human body, an interest that certainly reaches back through the biopolitical history of slavery and the slave trade I discussed in the previous chapter. Julien implies that Spanner is also part of a legacy that both archives and erases the colonial past. At the same time, queer activists themselves have been equally guilty of effacing their own complicities with that legacy, either by neglecting nonwhite, noncitizen populations that are imagined as disinterested in matters of sexuality, or by treating nonnormative sexual practices as ahistorical. "Are the questions of race and slavery to remain always in erasure when s/m representations are discussed in white queer discourse, and thus kept in the closet?" Julien wonders.[54] To be sure, the history of colonial slavery haunts practices of S/M, but it is a history to which we must admit and submit precisely *through* the practices themselves, rather than through the policing of them. To do otherwise, Julien suggests, is to yet again place that history under erasure.

Queer feminist historiography provides a critical intervention into the structural frames and operational logics of reproduction and regeneration, opening up the genealogical archive and unhousing histories of kinship, intimacy, love, and belonging. Genealogy provides one possible cognitive map or knowledge grid, which can account for some ways in which collective belonging traveled through diaspora and responded to violent dislocations brought about through the ruptures fundamental to the continuous development of a singular capitalist modernity. But as a product of that same modernity, genealogy cannot render alternative models of kinship and intimacy practiced by those excluded from a socius oriented to capitalist production and reproduction. For women, and queer women of color in particular, much is at stake in how the relationship between genealogy, archive, and law is understood—and not just conceptually, ideologically, or discursively. Material histories appear and disappear through social imaginaries inherited through structures and institutions far more capacious than the family tree. But the genealogical imaginary serves to model belonging across social groups of varying scales, from the nuclear to the national to the one-world family. The persistence of blood as an organizing symbology that links genealogy, archive, and law determines what kinds of families count, what practices of intimacy register, what cooperative actions get authorized, what forms of life are disposable, who gets remade as biocargo. When housed—in the home, by the family tree—history adheres to the rigid lines of genealogy; unhoused, it travels in a line of flight. Unable to fully dismantle the genealogical imaginary, one can nevertheless participate in the antigenealogies that explicitly negotiate with it, whether by reimagining sanguinary lines of descent as emulsive lines of flight or thematizing forms of revision and regeneration splintered from the violent predicates of blood and grafted onto the promise of convivial life.

· III ·

Exorbitant Life in an Age of Austerity

· CHAPTER 5 ·

Bespoke History

Redressing the Past, Tailoring the Present, Fashioning the Future

Agonistic Anachronism

Walking along London's Savile Row generates queer spatial and temporal dissonance. On the one hand, Savile Row feels like a spatial anachronism, a throwback to the Victorian era and the refashioning of ruling-class masculinity into bourgeois style. On the other hand, the Row aches with nostalgia—now on pathetic display in the windows of Henry Poole or Dege & Skinner—whose unhappy consciousness has lost faith with a past it cannot escape. Yet another kind of temporal drag clings to the 1960s retro styles that continue to define Nutters of Savile Row: a time lag that strains against the pull of tradition and the push of newer avant-gardes, idly refashioning irony into earnestness.[1] The ambit of Savile Row is entangled in the affective storm and stress of multisynchronous retrospection. Historically, the Row has always operated in the peculiar slow time of the men's tailor working in the bespoke tradition, "a mysterious and secretive art," according to James Sherwood, in which "the customer is measured by hand, his pattern is cut by hand and the garment is sewn by many hands."[2] The time of hand tailoring is rarified; it is fastidious, methodical, recursive; marked by deferral, hesitation, and postponement. The acquisition of a stylishly refined, well-crafted, made-to-order suit necessitates manifold fittings stretched over weeks or even months. The privileged relationship between a man and his tailor might last a lifetime, and a family's custom might extend across generations. Tailor time is intimate; a time of ceremony and decorum; a time for the laying on of hands. It is a time when the hands of one man, or the hands of many men, are placed ritually upon the body of another; a time when the owner submits to the tools of the worker; and a time when the clandestine society of the guild touches the members of gilded society.

The present cuts through the rarified air of Savile Row with a tailor's precision. In the ever accelerating fast time of the fashion industry—liberalized markets, intensified labor, and fevered consumption—come off-the-peg labels and ready-to-wear designs. Inevitably, the fast time of the sweatshop overtakes the slow time of the tailor shop. The emergent time of fashion remains antithetical to the residual time of bespoke tailoring. On Savile Row, today's fashion emergency presses nostalgia into competition with anticipation and nowness is slashed into narrower and narrower strips of synchrony. Meanwhile, retro style's tightening cycles of recursion vanish *mise en abyme.* If the crunch time of fashion pits today's trends against yesterday's fads, the concentrated presentism of neoliberalism wages war on clothing's own historicity. I begin this chapter with the assertion that material history is housed in the archives of fashion: in texts and textures of textile production; in varieties of fabric and modes of fabrication; in lines and silhouettes of outerwear secretly shaped by undergarments hidden beneath; in garments clandestinely assembled by pieceworkers and wage laborers both near and afar; in ornaments and accessories appended to clothing as decorative base; and in the artifactual bodies on which such attire hangs. In the archives of high fashion, history is housed in style.

Nowhere is the incongruity between the old-fashioned refinement of hand tailoring and the fashion-forward allure of the designer label more evident than in the slick showrooms of Ozwald Boateng, the bespoke tailor turned high-street designer whose eponymous flagship store occupies number 30 Savile Row (see Figure 26). For the last two decades, Boateng has carefully stage-managed the discordance between the slow time of the bespoke and the fast time of ready-to-wear, an elastic performance captured in the elegant convolution of his signature expression, "bespoke couture." Conflating an almost obsolete signifier for gentlemanly sophistication with an exclusive sign of women's vogue, Boateng's coinage attempts to iron out the temporal folds that envelop Savile Row and render seamless the incongruence between the custom-made and customized.

Contrary to his carefully self-fashioned demeanor—cool to the point of aloof—Boateng has an impeccable sense of timing. More than once he has stood at the edge of financial collapse only to rebound at an improbably, if not impossibly, opportune moment. As he doggedly tries to leverage the history of bespoke style into the global circuits of today's fashion industry, Boateng remains unabashed that his designs operate in the empty homogenous time of the neoliberal market.[3] Indeed, his outsized persona

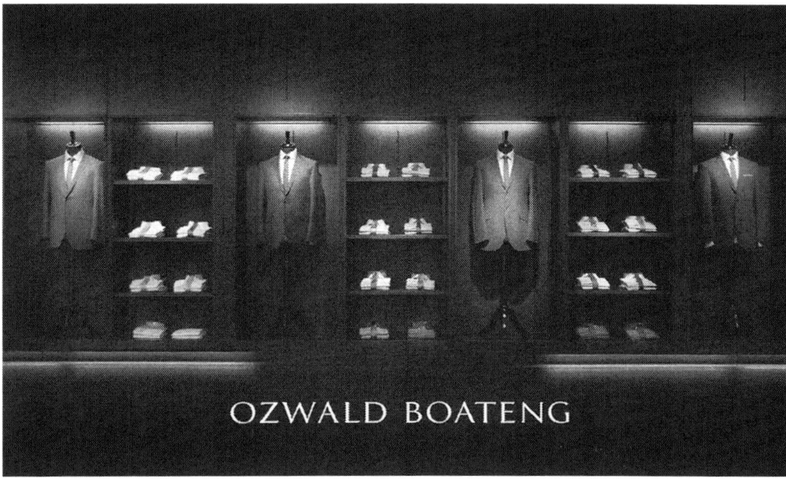

Figure 26. Ozwald Boateng, advertisement, 2008.

and ambitious business model might be said to take an astonishingly hostile attitude toward time and history themselves. Roland Barthes once observed that the "absolute, dogmatic, vengeful present tense in which Fashion speaks" often takes the form and rhythm of the vendetta.[4] In this sense, Boateng's vexed relationship to the discordant historical temporalities that bind Savile Row to the tradition of hand tailoring might be characterized as aggressively and vengefully anachronistic. Although Boateng is nothing less (and perhaps little more) than a product *in* and *of* his historical moment, as a self-acclaimed fashion icon, he is always already "out of time." Here the timelessness of his image competes with the transitory timeliness of fashionability. Or as its affix also suggests, Boateng's anachronism is both out of time and *against* the passage of time itself. Bespoke couture in this sense works as an *agonistic anachronism.*

If the fashionable is, by design, rendered unfashionable in the moment of arrival, bespoke tailoring should have disappeared long ago, a victim of the "vengeful present tense" of the market; and indeed, as my opening sketch of Savile Row implies, bespoke largely endures as a residual emblem of a ruling class long ago eclipsed by the global restructuring consequent to the postwar settlement. Since the 1990s, however, bespoke tailoring—if not quite Savile Row—has made an unlikely comeback. As a refashioned—and in Boateng's case, rebranded—mode of suit making, however, bespoke appears more like a back-formation, related to even as it sharply diverges from its historical precedent. By *styling* empty homogenous time into a market-savvy, anachronistic "bespoke time," Boateng manages the temporal crises endemic to the fashion industry. By *tailoring* anachronistic time through the historical forms and ritualized rhythms of bespoke, he draws upon—and draws out—quite specific moments in the history of colonialism that resonate in our neocolonial present. While the new bespoke remains inimical to historical time—even as it tries to leverage the past into the service of a marketplace that admits (to) no time at all—I suggest that historicity lingers as the bespoke tradition time travels in form and rhythm into the more fashionable if ever vengeful present. I call this vendetta *bespoke history.*

A Hand-Tailored Man

There is nothing inconspicuous about Ozwald Boateng. "Extraordinarily striking, tall and powerfully built, he moves with the confidence and grace of an athlete," according to the *Guardian*'s Decca Aitkenhead, "as if accustomed to commanding attention with physical charisma alone."[5] Lean and graceful at six feet four, Boateng cannot help but stand out in a crowd. His carriage and deportment convey an indefatigable energy and boundless enthusiasm. Details such as these of Boateng's biography have been repeated in the fashion press with such consistency and deference as to appear tailored by his own hand in his own style: trim, elegant, graceful, restrained, with an eye-catching flash of color. Both tailor and tailored, Boateng perhaps cannot help but feel self-satisfied. In an industry buttressed by reciprocal endorsements and mutual adulation, most style writers are happy enough to repeat the authorized script.[6] For many years, media profiles dutifully reproduced Boateng's own rigorously guarded narrative, occasionally adding a touch of reflexive sarcasm for having done so. Aitkenhead, for example, teases her 2012 description quoted above by adding, "If the option of feigning oblivion to his own beauty has ever crossed his mind—which I'd guess was unlikely—it was evidently ruled out."[7] Boateng's own PR-driven persona is honed to near perfection in the three-word tag line appended to his authorized documentary, *A Man's Story:* "Tailor. Icon. Superstar." (see Figure 27). Lacking any sense of irony, the film suggests that for Boateng the line is as sincere as it is aspirational. Following Roland Barthes's suggestion that fashion criticism should begin with an interrogation of the way fashion journalism reinforces the often two-dimensional look of the fashion icon, here I turn my attention to an analysis of Boateng's public persona as it travels in fashion media from aspirational icon to global brand through his "new bespoke" self-tailoring.[8]

Since the 1990s, Ozwald Boateng has been associated with the "new bespoke movement," part of a generation of tailors that set out—following a path cut by Tommy Nutter in the 1960s—to "modernize" bespoke style and resuscitate the tradition of fine men's tailoring. Fashion journalists often struggle to identify the particularly "modern" elements of Boateng's suits, relying again on the tailor's own vague insistence that he combines the old and the new, as when the Style Network fashion critic Robert Verdi tenuously submits, "His suits are the perfect hybrid of tradition and modernity."[9] Suzy Menkes suggests a more exotic mixture of old and new, reversing which elements are modern and which are traditional, when she writes,

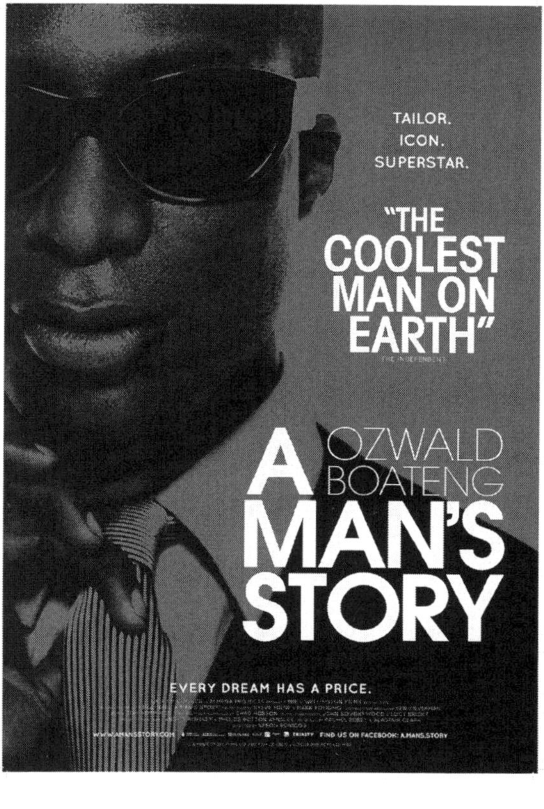

Figure 27. A Man's Story, *dir. Varon Bonicos, 2012. Advertising poster. Virgil Films/ Trinity Filmed Entertainment, Ltd.*

"Boateng is known for his Savile Row-style suits cut close to the body with vivid African colors in the linings or occasional details."[10] Nor does Courtney Colavita elaborate when she asserts that Boateng had "shaken things up on Savile Row by adding details like brightly colored linings"; or that Boateng had "injected" a "designer element" into men's suits; or that the true "departure" comes when "Boateng presents his collection [on] the Paris runway."[11] Reflecting back on his early career, Boateng himself has added a crucial detail to his earlier formulation, telling Aitkenhead, "When I started department stores were either very fashion, or very tailored, so the two never mixed. I mixed it, and they said you're too tailored for fashion and too fashion for tailoring. So I had to move the market. So that's what I did."[12] Boateng's "revolutionary" achievement was branching out into high-end ready-to-wear lines that aspired to a bespoke "look" through a lean, fitted silhouette, colorful linings, and attention to detail. That is, what Boateng had brought to Savile Row was a "bespoke suit" that was *customized* but *not* custom-made.

Boateng's own reflections on the tailoring tradition he variously designs to "shake up," "modernize," or "revolutionize" capture the ambivalent relationship he shares with his profession and the slow time it inhabits: "My perception was that tailoring was this very dusty old thing, but it came naturally to me."[13] His wonderfully archival but anxiously feminizing domestic metaphor suggests that Boateng had come to Savile Row to do a bit of housekeeping, less a "dust-up" than a good "dusting off." Whether there is much new in the "new bespoke" outside its convoluted temporality—which abandoned the slow time of hand-tailoring for the speed of the mass market—it is certainly the case that Boateng has gained his market share of credit for "revitalizing" a moribund tradition. In his own self-mythologizing act of retrospection, when he arrived in the mid-1990s, "Savile Row was a dying concept":

> This was the age of the fashion designer, and tailored suits didn't fit with this new world. But I identified that there was a beauty in handmade suits: I just had to demonstrate this to the world of fashion. And the only way I could do that was by taking the concept of traditional tailoring to Paris, and showing as a tailor, then defining myself more as a couturier for men.[14]

In Boateng's 2006 recollection, the "new world" that is leaving Savile Row behind collecting dust appears to have little to do with the fluctuations in high-end retailing or the market in luxury goods in the 1980s and '90s, or with the devastating legacy of Thatcherism on the production of apparel, in which local manufacturers were shut down and the floodgates opened for the importation of cheaper, mass-produced designer labels from abroad. Indeed, fashion writing almost never discusses the process of manufacture unless it is about the financing of it. Rather, Boateng's is the story of legend, of heroic rescue and herculean accomplishment. Cut loose from the vestiges of the immediate past, the story of Savile Row is recast as yet another tale of the present at war with the distant past, the quarrel of the ancients and moderns writ small.

An admitted admirer of Tony Blair and Gordon Brown, in many respects Boateng's worldview remains remarkably Thatcherite, with its libertarian zeal for the self-actualizing power of personal agency. As he tells Aitkenhead, "'I was brought up in the time of Thatcherism, when it was all about going out and making a success of yourself.' He was a Thatcherite?" Aitkenhead interjects. Boateng's reply: "'Everyone was.'"[15] When asked by Natalie Graham what "lesson" he has "learnt about money," Boateng begins with a redolent reassertion of economic liberalism's most precious tenet: "You have to let money follow its natural flow, by coming in and going out." He concludes, however, with one of capitalism's more intransigent paradoxes, the need to accumulate wealth in order to enter the market to begin with: "Don't try to hold on to it. Once you interfere with the natural flow of money, things go terribly wrong. You are likely to get into debt—and trouble."[16] Modernization—a buzzword repeated incessantly by Tony Blair in his ascendency as Labour Party leader—here appears to have less to do with fashionable style than with the economic logic of the neoliberal market, which binds the accumulation of capital in one sector to the accumulation of debt in another. In this sense, Boateng's resuscitation of Savile Row resonates with Blair's renovation of Labour: rather than rejecting the fundamental tenets of economic neoliberalism, New Labour simply retooled Thatcherism in the more appealing cuts and vibrant colors of the global market.

Boateng's almost overwhelming, if not overbearing, physical presence has certainly contributed to his capacity to brand his own image as a fashion icon. But the "symbolic density" of the icon as both a meaningful trope and an artifactual body, experienced affectively through "magical technologies" and cultural mechanisms as the "hydraulic 'pull' of an embodied encounter," complicates and destabilizes the careful control Boateng wants to maintain over the reception of his own image.[17] In descriptions of Boateng's designs as well as the designer himself, fashion reporters have tended to fall back upon the conventional, sometimes subtle language of the racialized fetish object. In one of his earliest major profiles, back when he was still selling suits out of his studio down at "the ethnic end of London's Portobello Road," *Irish Times* writer Jane Mulvagh opens with her "admiration" of the sensual elegance of "his sassy, bespoke two-piece" suit, in particular the lean, fitted cut of the trouser, which enhances the "masculine leg." So when she writes, "The finesse of its turn and the elongated languor of its gait are employed to the greatest advantage under stove-pipe trousers and those highwaisted jackets which upholster every nuance of the pectorals," it is difficult to decide whether she is describing Boateng's suits or Boateng himself.[18] Mulvagh seems unable to decide what to make of Boateng's style developing "amid the hyper-active clones in ubiquitous baggy and logoed sportswear, " before ultimately deciding that "Boateng is conducting a single-handed battle to highlight good bodies in the nattiest tailoring, and bring suave back to the streets of Britain's capital." In her own pointed mix of metaphors, Boateng's "rapier-sharp tailoring" and "needle-sharp raffishness" have "thankfully" and "emphatically" "ousted the baggy tailoring of the 1980s." One can hardly miss the racial and class inflections of her disdain of baggy, behooded, logoed sportswear, a fashion aesthetic she apparently shares with the bespoke tailor she fetishistically admires, or the "hottest of London's thirtysomething In Crowd" that he "besuits."

Fashion journalists have long picked up on the inherent ambivalence of Boateng's bespoke couture. As far back as 1998, John Walsh, the admittedly portly and reputedly acerbic cultural critic at the *Independent,* wittily describes his first (and presumably only) purchase of one of Boateng's "slimming" suits. "If you're going to splash out on an Ozwald Boateng suit," he begins, "it has to be one of his poster-paint-coloured numbers. He does perfectly respectable charcoal grey business suits with a discreetly coloured pinstripe, but that's not the point. The point is peacockery, flamboyance and showing off—presenting yourself, just for one evening, in a two-piece neck-to-ankle flag of vainglory."[19] Walsh may feel "cool and dashing" when staring at himself in the mirror, but under the gaze of the other, he is sure he "resembled a minor African potentate on his way to a tribal wedding." Attired in Boateng chic, he garners neither the "right" kind of attention nor does he strike the "proper" balance between masculine dash and flamboyant panache—more "king of the fairies" than trailblazing dandy, he quips; more Oberon than Auberon. Unsure whether he comes off as ostentatious autocrat or tempestuous queen, the ideal bespoke client Walsh manages to evoke offers a cross between Idi Amin and Julius Soubise. More niggardly hoary-headed than head-turning spendthrift, Walsh drolly describes how he opted for "eleven hundred quid's worth of schmutter" off the rack rather than sixty-five hundred pounds of customized refinement. Rather, he chides, "Mr. Boateng prides himself on what he calls 'bespoke couture,' as if each suit, in each size, colour and style, had been made specially for each customer." Highlighting the absurd conflation of bespoke and couture, Walsh draws our attention to the incongruity between the unaffordable promise of the fully customized and the inevitable failure of the mass market to deliver, noting the profound *un*suitability of Boateng's elevated style to his mainline business model.[20]

In many ways Walsh's anxiety is not alien to Boateng's own, though they appear to manifest in contrasting ways. Like Walsh, Boateng appears comfortable with public visibility but remains privately reserved, outwardly risky and inwardly risk averse. Reluctant to confront the pitfalls of his own fashionability, Boateng avoids having to wrestle with the dichotomies implicit in both the fashion industry and the bespoke tailoring: between whiteness and blackness, masculinity and femininity, social norms and sexual deviance, working-class beginnings and bourgeois ends. To accommodate the sincerity of his insistence on self-actualization and personal responsibility as authentic elements of manhood, perhaps it would be more appropriate to describe Boateng as hand-tailored rather than self-fashioned. Retaining the dandy's eye for detail in the pursuit of extravagance, the hand-tailored man avows restraint even as he indulges in luxury. There is, of course, another less generous name for such a figure: not the proper dandy but the dissembling poseur. If the dandy exploits the play of the rope, gains balance through the give in the pole—defying gravity and embracing contingency—the poseur recoils from what bends or bows or bulges, terrified of being implicated in categorical uncertainty. The dandy turns categories into repertoires that improvise being and becoming; the poseur renounces identity tout court, anxiously performing nothing more than their awkward discomfort.

In his own act of self-tailoring, Boateng relies on his own brand of fetishized Englishness: "not the typical reserved Englishman," as one interviewer puts it, but an Englishman with a "dose of showmanship." When asked, however, whether his success might be credited to the more flamboyant aspect of his personality, Boateng demurs, "I don't see myself as a showman. I am very passionate about what I do, and, when I do something I feel good about, I am excited to share it."[21] When asked in the same interview about his favorite fashion accessory, however, Boateng demonstrates his tendency to have it both ways: "The keys to my new Aston Martin Rapide," he replies without hesitation, redirecting the specter of effete showmanship onto a more vulgar form of masculine flash anchored in the Englishness of James Bond but linked to the showiness of Will Smith. Boateng has made conspicuous consumption, once supposedly the bane of old-money aristocracy and antithetical to the understated elegance or the seemingly effortless but exacting fit of the bespoke suit, a centerpiece of his brand identity. The banner appearing above Natalie Graham's interview with Boateng in the more consumer-oriented *Daily Telegraph* captures the inescapable sexual ambivalence generated when the architect of bespoke couture hops into a high-performance luxury sedan: "Tailor likes to cut a dash in a fast car."[22] In a single stroke the headline situates Boateng as a tailor who likes to cut, a celebrity who cuts a dash, the iconoclast who now finds himself a media icon, who began his career striking down the old idols of Savile Row only to set himself up in their place. It also situates Boateng as an evasive public figure in hasty retreat—who cuts and runs—a fugitive, perhaps even a runaway slave. Lest this final point seem too much of a stretch, consider John Walsh's description of Boateng's lush, Russia-inspired 2004 fall/winter collection, which both draws together and extends a similar set of tropes: "Dandies would have welcomed the fake-formal, plum-purple velvet jacket with a pinstripe printed on to it. Speed fiends with circulation problems would be pleased to note the new sheepskin coats and biker jackets. . . . If a stern historian might object that Ozwald was throwing together the iconography of four different styles—Cossack, Tsarist, Bolshevik and Soviet, with a dash of James-Bond-villain—there was no doubting his passion for all things Eastern European."[23] Given the unabashed effort and the striking precision with which Boateng tailors his own public image, it remains easy to describe him as a typical modern-day dandy. But the explicitly avowed self-regard and feverish self-cultivation of the dandy contrasts with the designer's guarded discomfort with accusations of inauthenticity his transparent self-regard easily belies. Unlike the dandy, he cannot admit to his own artifice.

Boateng's discomfort with questions of artifice and authenticity are nowhere more evident than in his ambivalent relationship to his own sense of Englishness when forced to confront his experiences of systemic racism.

His refusal to acknowledge the individual damage and collective devastation of entrenched structural racism is certainly one of the reasons he is asked about it repeatedly. If he seems uncomfortable talking about race, when he does, as with all things Boateng, he gives a slim, restrained, "correct" response, with just the right details and just the right amount of embellishment. He also performs the very distinction Freud makes between denial and disavowal: denial is a form of repression that remains fully unconscious; disavowal is a form of repression in which the individual consciously knows what they are saying is not the case but continues to act as though it were so. Boateng doesn't deny racism, but he anxiously repeats its disavowal with steady regularity.[24] The implicit forms that racism takes in its institutional articulation is suggested when the *Daily Telegraph*'s Damian Thompson sets up his interview with Boateng by reporting an unattributed comment by a senior industry insider on one of the designer's many ambitious projects—a joint New York/London men's fashion week—saying Boateng's vision might succeed as long as he "doesn't come on too strong," before adding, "He has rather a lot of attitude."[25] Whether one considers Boateng's particular je ne sais quoi an enviable self-assurance or an unfortunate overconfidence, "attitude," as Thompson points out, is "what some people accuse young black men of having. Savile Row wasn't expecting to make room for a handsome, charmingly stroppy Ghanaian who says 'innit.'" In a rare acknowledgment of racial discrimination, Boateng admits, "Right at the beginning, I'd be ordering material, and it would take twice as long as it ought to," only to retreat from the issue of racism through his own use of the code of "attitude," adding, "I'm not saying it was because of the colour of my skin, but I think some people misconstrued my passion as arrogance." It may very well be this sensitivity to all matters racial that led Robin Givhan to open her 1998 profile by gesturing toward the rhetoric of racialized sexuality that surrounds his media. Opening with the playful but suggestive headline "Unbuttoning Stuffed Shirts: Tailor Ozwald Boateng Shakes Up Savile Row," Givhan evokes that mystical sanctum of clandestine ritual with which this chapter began, the men's tailor shop. Her opening salvo is equally provocative:

> The tailor Ozwald Boateng has crossed the color line. This lanky length of ebony man, dressed in a bespoke suit of deep aubergine, treads through a crowd of fashion devotees who have come to witness clothes as theater. He works the room by simply standing still

> and allowing the curious glances, of which there are many, to linger and turn into stares.[26]

While Givhan herself does not cross any lines here, she is certainly able to draw out the lines that connect Boateng's brand and his branded public persona to the spectacular fetishization of blackness and the primitive theatricality of celebrity or idol worship that elevated Boateng to the status of global icon in the first place. But that particular form of black male spectatorship places Boateng within the genealogy of black dandyism with which he is noticeably uncomfortable. As Monica Miller has brilliantly demonstrated, the figure of the contemporary black dandy is rooted in the history of the plantation slavery and the slave trade, and reaches back to the ambivalent public reception of eighteenth-century black public figures, whether the largely admired Equiano or the popularly caricatured Soubise.[27]

For his own part, Boateng has an uncanny way of performing just the right amount of acknowledgment and disavowal to suggest simultaneously that while racism continues to exist, it ultimately does not matter: "I'm not a black designer with a chip on my shoulder. I'm a tailor who has an incredible love for this place—the most famous street in the world for men's fashion."[28] As with the paradoxes of time, so too with the paradoxes of race: with the right attitude, one becomes virtually immune to it. It is an attitude he hopes to instill in others, as in his 2008 participation in a government program that encourages the community to address "the issues around young black men's underachievement." Under the headline "'Role Models' Scheme to Boost Young Black Men," the *Evening Standard* reported that Boateng would sit "on a panel of judges which will select the new role models in a bid to highlight successful black achievement in areas such as medicine, the law and the arts" in an effort to "offer young people from black and mixed race backgrounds a positive alternative to the culture of 'crime, drugs, guns and gangs' into which some are lured."[29] It would be easy at this point to evoke the figure of the "mimic man" to describe Boateng's appropriation of an indefatigable Englishness, that is, the "handsome, charmingly stroppy Ghanaian who says 'innit.'" No matter how chronically ambiguous his version of Englishness actually is, one should distinguish between the forms of Englishness he projects and the kind of Britishness he represents, as well as the sense of Africanness or Ghanaianess he maintains.

To situate Boateng's uneasy "Englishness" within the colonial entanglements—transnational and transhistorical—let us return to Savile Row and the young Boateng's position vis-à-vis the geography of bespoke tailoring. As several media profiles at the time were quick to point out, prior to the opening of his shop at number 30, Boateng's shop was merely proximate to Savile Row. "To be absolutely pedantic," John Walsh notes with characteristic pedantry, "Mr. Boateng isn't actually on the Row; his address is 9 Vigo Street, just on the corner, opposite Gieves & Hawkes—an appropriate symbol of how he's simultaneously part of the tailors' inner sanctum and at one remove from it."[30] Givhan also found this location noteworthy, writing, "Boateng's shop is just a few yards shy of the intersection. Physically, he isn't quite on Savile Row proper." Yet "mentally," she adds, Boateng "is the modern embodiment of it."[31] Discussing Boateng's self-avowed "love affair with being British" ("his words," she avers), Carola Long agrees that there is potential for forward-leaning contemporary men's fashion to leverage the market in Englishness. "Now, due to the soaring popularity of heritage brands from Burberry to Barbour," she reports, "and a renewed emphasis on traditional craft, the street has found itself in tune with the zeitgeist again."[32] Despite his location's mimicry of the Row, what Boateng did have was a valuable sign of bespoke—as *the* signature tradition in men's British fashion—waiting to be branded on a global scale. As Hadley Freeman slyly acknowledges, "Reference to an Ozwald Boateng suit has become a handy journalistic trope to signify modern wealth and aspiration."[33] Finally, commenting on a confluence of stylish anachronisms, Thompson observes, "Boateng never tires of the juxtaposition of traditional shapes and psychedelic colours: the 18th-century panelling in his office is slathered in damson pink; behind him sits a yellow top hat."[34] If the new bespoke that Boateng epitomizes is not quite a signifier of Englishness as such, it remains a sign of a neo-aristocratic gentlemanliness that lends an air of old money to new by styling empty homogenous time of the fashion market as a timeless anachrony.

Ozwald Boateng is nothing if not resilient; and resiliency, like elasticity, requires a pliant relationship to time. Following the near-collapse of his business in 1998, the tailor had to start over; thus began a period of reinvention that now occupies the center of Boateng's self-mythology—a rebirth carefully recorded and presented for posterity in his authorized documentary. *A Man's Story* (2012) offers a wistful rumination on the tradition of men's bespoke tailoring but also a heroic account of Boateng as the savior of Savile Row. Presenting himself as a product of Cool Britannia—if not its very emblem—he at first appears something of a throwback to an era few viewers are likely to mourn. But in recounting his improbable rise from the ashes, Boateng strives to cast himself into the future. In a ninety-eight-minute performance filmed over twelve years, *A Man's Story* stages ceaseless acts of biographical retailoring in which the most minute yet painstakingly selected details of his past are leveraged to imagine a boundless future: Boateng's autotelic retrospection is placed in the service of his autogenetic speculation.

Early in the film, Boateng speaks about coming of age in the aftermath of the racial tensions of the 1970s and Brixton riots in 1981, a "massive cultural" event depicted through archival footage as a historical and personal moment of rupture. As a break in historical time, according to Boateng, the riots generated two (and only two, apparently) possible responses: to hold the "radical" position, "I'm black and it's a real problem in life," which he doesn't name or characterize; or "I'm black and it's difficult but I'm going to make it work." Boateng adds, "So you have to park colour as an issue and just get on with it." Boateng's comments in the film resonate with a reply to an interviewer in a 2011 profile that appeared in the South African publication *Business Day.* When asked about the challenge of being "a newcomer and black designer entering a traditional English establishment," Boateng dissembles, "I didn't take on my skin colour as an issue. I never allowed it to be a barrier as I knew the importance of Savile Row in regards to its heritage and it being British, and I liked the idea of making an impact on that street."[35] Of the three events that anchor narrative time—the Brixton riots in 1981, his divorce and bankruptcy in 1998, and his second divorce in 2009—only the first is historical, but even this event is rendered mostly via scene setting, indeed disavowed as causally relevant.

Of the modes of retrospective form, few are as quintessential to social memory as the funeral service, so it is perhaps not surprising that in 2003 Boateng participated in the weekly series "It's Your Funeral" in the *Mail on Sunday,* which "invites celebrities to plan their own ideal funeral, exactly as they would wish it to be." As is befitting a somewhat morbid but relatively lighthearted feature, readers learn very little that is new about Ozwald Boateng, but the undertaking does place his lifelong project of self-fashioning into rather perverse relief. As if to immediately foreclose the possibility that he can be mourned, Boateng predictably begins, "I don't want people to wear black at my funeral." Still, in an act of melancholic self-projection, the fashion designer cum funeral planner is compelled to add: "Everyone should look smart, and all the men should be dressed in Ozwald

Boateng Couture, so that the ceremony will have the feel of a retrospective."[36] Lending itself to an easy psychologism, Boateng's imagined wake lights upon several motifs vital to the designer's self-fashioning and the iconic persona he has spent his career orchestrating: "I'd like to be buried wearing a kante cloth . . . worn by Ashanti chiefs" and "I would want there to be a spectacular bash held in my honour." Boateng does not imagine anyone in particular attending his funeral, save for himself, an inversion of the metaphysical logic of "It's Your Funeral." His wake is oddly "peopled" with "theys" and "thems" and "everyones" and, surprise again, "men," whose expressions of grief he conditionally sanctions: "People are allowed to be in floods of tears if I depart earlier than planned, but I hope that won't be the case." To be sure, the job of designing one's own funeral invariably draws into uneasy tension retrospection and anticipation, not unlike the uncanny temporalities of the moribund Savile Row itself. Yet in a bizarre, self-fulfilling confluence of his interest in fashion, film, and funerary grandeur, in 2010 Boateng decided to "up the ante" on the already glamorous events scheduled for London's Fashion Week by promising an unabashedly extravagant runway show at the Leicester Square Odeon: a "massive event" with "a film-premiere feel, with a red carpet, 1,800 guests including sportsmen, artists and musicians (exactly who is unconfirmed . . .) and a show featuring 100 male models instead of the usual 20 or so."[37] As with his ideal funeral, Boateng's runway spectacular imagined a lot of bodies but nobody in particular.

A Man's Story opens and closes with a dramatic scene from Boateng's personal life, a heated argument over a cell phone with his second wife, Gyunel. In the first iteration, the viewer enters the exchange in medias res, uncomfortably eavesdropping on a conversation by way of an audio track played against a blackened screen, a moment not anchored by any context or detail. The woman sounds muffled, incoherent, and hysterical; the man is calm, collected, and reasonable. The audience can easily comprehend his dismissive retorts but cannot clearly discern what she is saying. When repeated at the end of the film, the audio is accompanied by a shot of Boateng sitting casually, with subtitles now conveying the content of the argument. She asks him, "Are you a man?" He replies, "What does that mean?" In retrospect, the conversation viewers could not make out at the beginning has framed the film as a response to those two questions. The answers it pursues, however, are as conventional as Savile Row itself. To be a man is to be busy, to be successful in business, to be famous, to be wealthy, to take risks, to experience life, to believe in oneself, and to always attend to the minutest of details, without which none of the former are achievable. Gyunel is heard but remains unseen in the concluding return to Boateng's ongoing domestic drama, framing the dispute as symptom and cause, metaphor and metonym, in the deeply homosocial world of men and men's fashion. Women are secondary if not recalcitrant to masculine endeavors; women might aide, but they are as likely to impede or disrupt, if not destroy, the man's story, that is, male self-fashioning. Indeed, while the opening and closing scenes recount the same 2010 confrontation between Boateng and Gyunel, the documentary's timeline is bound by the 1998 divorce from his first wife and the 2010 separation from his second, suggesting not only repetition but also a troubling pattern of exchangability that brings the agonistic temporality of fashion into his conflictual romantic entanglements. Corresponding to what he describes as the low and high points of his career—the loss of his business in 1998 and the wild success of his 2010 fashion show (also titled "A Man's Story") in the frenetic epicenter of London tourism, Leicester Square—the trajectory of Boateng's career, his revolutionary modernization of men's bespoke, rests on little more than a melancholy desire for a return to those conventional attributes of manhood nostalgically haunting Savile Row: taking risks, accumulating wealth, cultivating an appreciation for luxury, and, most importantly, assuming the power of an unshakable belief in oneself. *A Man's Story* offers a fundamentally economic narrative of Boateng's rise in the world of men's fashion, not only because it depicts the transformation of a small bespoke tailory into a fashion empire, or an aspiring fashion designer into a global icon, but because exchangibility underwrites the recursive modus ponens at the core of his modus operandi.

A Dandy on the Underground

"The rules of fashion are a mystery to me," Decca Aitkenhead admits in the opening of her 2012 profile of Ozwald Boateng. "Endlessly changing, apparently arbitrary and frequently contradictory," she adds in a familiar vein, "the fashion industry doesn't fabricate clothing so much as artifice."[38] Fashion is ephemeral; fashion is artificial; fashion is inscrutable: three nearly axiomatic starting points for the popular criticism of clothing as a signifier of the cultural present. As I showed at the beginning of this chapter, with the image of nineteenth-century guild tailors and gentlemanly patron secreted behind closed doors, inscrutability has long served as shorthand for addressing the seemingly inherent idiosyncrasies that follow from the queer temporality of fashion—as both an industry and a set of dictates guiding often unpredictable alterations in mass popular taste.

Perhaps no figure has as persistently represented the inscrutability, ephemerality, and artificiality of modern fashion as the dandy. Since the end of the eighteenth century, the British dandy remained a steadfast trope for the excesses of male modishness, the consequences of compromised masculinity, and the risks of gentlemanliness gone awry. As I demonstrated in the preceding sections, while retooling the tradition of bespoke tailoring into a runway-ready bespoke couture, Ozwald Boateng has maintained an anxious relationship to the overlapping cultural terrain occupied by the gentleman and the dandy. The designer's carefully modulated masculinity often appears to foil the queerness of the traditions of male style on which he most relies, especially the queer relationship to spectacle and spectatorship through which both the fashion icon and the fashion designer, like the dandy, find their audience. To perform such a redirection, however, let me admit to some misdirection, for there is a much more apt figure for the contemporary black British dandy hard at work in another creative field that has likewise undergone a dramatic reorganization as it enters an expansive global economy. What I have in mind is the global market in contemporary fine arts and the black British dandy to whom I refer is Yinka Shonibare.

The ambit of spectacle and spectatorship is the central theme of one of Shonibare's most recognized works, *Diary of a Victorian Dandy* (1998), a series of large-scale photographs that stage the intersections of race, gender, and sexuality within the "domestic economy" of the colonizing nation and the country estate. *Diary* was initially commissioned as a three-day site-specific performance at Somerset House, a stately home in Hertfordshire, in which the artist cast himself in the role of a black dandy inhabiting a nineteenth-century estate. In a set of eight vivid, C-type photographs, Shonibare captures a series of carefully orchestrated domestic scenes reminiscent of Isaac Julien's tableaux vivants (discussed in the preceding chapter) and referencing the satirical depictions of aristocratic society sketched by William Hogarth and appropriated by David Dabydeen (addressed in chapter 3). In these highly stylized set pieces, Shonibare positions himself as the effete gentleman who simultaneously appropriates, hyperbolizes, and challenges nineteenth-century taste. Shonibare's parody of the empty nostalgia of the costume drama so popular in British cinema in the 1980s (one thinks of the films of Ismail Merchant and James Ivory, of the *Jewel in the Crown*, or the BBC's production of *Brideshead Revisited*) reminds us again of the history that graces, indeed haunts, the English country house, as well as the mounting presence and proximity of a legible black British culture in postwar Britain. Like its art-historical precedent, William Hogarth's *Rake's Progress*, *Diary of a Victorian Dandy* highlights the excesses of the aristocracy; but unlike Hogarth, he refuses to simply relegate blacks to their common representation in the background as servants.[39]

Although the series has been reproduced and circulated in a number of high-traffic venues, less remembered today is the public exhibition of one of the photographs from the series on advertising hoardings (billboards) across the platforms at a hundred stations of the London Underground. Commissioned by the International Institute of Visual Art (InIVA), the posters that appeared in the Tube placed the figure of the black dandy in a public cultural context significantly different from the much larger and glossier prints covering entire gallery walls of its various museum settings, underscoring issues of artistic production, commercial reproduction, and public consumption of art generally and the staging of contemporary black Britain within the context of nineteenth-century colonial history in particular (see Figure 28). Rather, Shonibare provides a contrast between the labor and leisure that underscores the excesses made possible precisely through their decentered presence. In Shonibare's piece, the black British subject is brought forward from the periphery and placed in the center of the scene. The photographic series captures a few precise moments in the course of a day, thus they are titled according to the hour in which they are taken. By arresting the time of social transaction, as is apparent in *Diary of a Victorian Dandy: 14.00 Hours*, the black dandy is made both subject and object of the gaze; indeed, he holds his audience spellbound, and thus achieves what every dandy hopes to achieve: he has turned his public life into a private work of art.[40] As the dandy commands attention, so too does he command, and it is perhaps no surprise that *14.00 Hours* should find our dandy in the library, the archiving archive of the domestic sphere, where the law is housed and from where it emanates, in Derrida's formulation. Just as the domestic setting of the series shows once again that the domestic sphere is far from outside public life, so too does the viewer experience as public the private moments that also fall within the regime of biopower.

As with the characters developed in the literary texts I examined in previous chapters, what interests me in this work is the way in which its

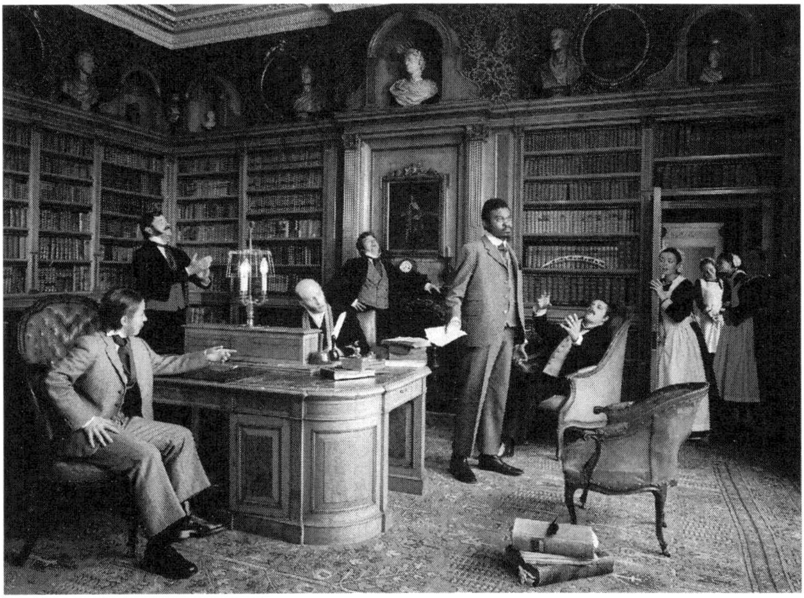

Figure 28. Yinka Shonibare MBE, Diary of a Victorian Dandy: 14.00 hours, *1998. C-type photograph. Copyright by Yinka Shonibare MBE. All Rights Reserved, DACS 2015. Image courtesy of Stephen Friedman Gallery, London.*

meaning—and historiographic significance—is conveyed through a critical figuration. Shonibare appears to be drawing on a number of sources, ranging perhaps from Thomas Carlyle's scathing satire of the figure in "The Dandiacal Body" from *Sartor Resartus* (1833) to Oscar Wilde's very embodiment of him at the end of the century, but surely Charles Baudelaire's passages on the dandy in "The Painter of Modern Life" (1863) must also be counted among them. In that essay, Baudelaire describes the "man who is rich and idle, and who, even if blasé, has no other occupation than the perpetual pursuit of happiness; the man who has been brought up in luxury and has been accustomed from his earliest days to the obedience of others—he, in short whose solitary profession is elegance, will always and at all times possess a distinct type of physiognomy, one entirely *sui generis.*"[41] Like Carlyle's guild of tailors, however, Baudelaire characterizes "dandyism" as "a mysterious institution," one that is "beyond laws" even while its own guilded members follow their own set of "rigorous laws which all its subjects must strictly obey," and a discipline to which they must submit in the manner of the monastic orders, *"perinde ac cadaver,"* that is, with mortification. In *Diary* we find such a figure represented perhaps most emphatically in *14:00 Hours,* the setting used on the Underground poster. But here the dandy looks conspicuously like the Victorian gentleman, and from this side of history it might be difficult to distinguish the two. The dandy does not desire money for its own sake, but "would be perfectly content with a limitless credit at the bank." Money is "indispensible" but should not be aspirational. Rather, Baudelaire adds, the dandy has "no other calling but cultivate the idea of beauty in their persons" and "to satisfy their passions, to feel and to think," a pastime that requires "a vast abundance both of time and money," without which "love is incapable of rising above a grocer's orgy or the accomplishment of a conjugal duty. Instead of being a passionate or poetical caprice, it becomes a repulsive duty." If it is this last that distinguishes the dandy from the Victorian gentleman, then it is also how the viewer can distinguish the figure represented in *14.00 Hours* from one in *3.00 Hours* where our dandy is not only engaged in his own acts of hedonistic pleasure but is determined to share his pleasure beyond any sense of utility, with his friends and with his audience who are, after all, one and the same. Yet dandyism, for Baudelaire as for Shonibare, is neither simply an immodesty nor an immoderateness but rather the achievement of distinction, the acquisition of originality (or singularity), and the provocation of public *astonishment* while being impervious *to* astonishment. The dandy finds strength in "opposition and revolt." To be sure, as Baudelaire insists, Shonibare's dandy also performs a characteristic detachment and reserve, captured in the almost disdainful gaze directed toward the camera.

The dandy is, however, also a walking anachronism, and the black Victorian dandy compounds temporal dissonance with a spatial displacement linked directly to colonial and postcolonial entanglements. So too does the black dandy confound the already subtle distinction between the gentleman and the dandy. James Eli Adams observes that as norms of masculinity become increasingly anchored by economic class rather than social rank, the position of "gentleman" is appropriated by professional middle-class men as a masculine ideal, and the self-discipline necessary to achieve gentlemanly status is reimagined as a democratic opening across class lines.[42] Adams's observation resonates with Baudelaire's assertion that the figure of the dandy "appears above all in periods of transition, when democracy is not yet all-powerful and aristocracy is only just beginning to totter and fall." In contrast to Carlyle's satirical characterization of the dandy as the benign antihero of the Victorian era, Baudelaire celebrates countercultural performances of "dandyism" as "the last gleam of heroism in times of decadence." The condition of crisis—uncertainty, even precarity—attains to the figure of the dandy, especially in a time in which that "limitless credit at the bank" *is* the crisis. And if credit *is* the crisis, the dandy *is* the emergency.

As such the dandy appears as the dangerous, crisis-ridden supplement to gentlemanly security. He haunts the masculine ideals of the emergent middle-class subject as a reminder of impending catastrophe; in his own recourse to spectacle, spectatorship—and indeed speculation—the professional man conjures the theatricality of the dandy as he ascends the ranks of bourgeois society, and portends the coming collapse his performance disavows but that he beautifully embodies nonetheless. As economic changes throughout the nineteenth century enabled more and more middle-class professional men to stake a claim to the moniker of gentlemen—now, according to Adams, unyoked from heritable social rank—there arose a "new moral urgency to the seemingly banal task of distinguishing between sincerity and performance," an imperative to separate "the 'true' gentleman from the aspirant who is merely 'acting' the part."[43] Aspiration, indeed, becomes a "textual mark" of an "inauthentic (because theatrical) simulacrum" of gentlemanliness that the dandy merely performs.[44] In this context one might view Shonibare's necessarily reflexive assumption of dandyism as a way of situating himself in a position historically foreclosed. Historical accuracy, therefore, is of only strategic value; indeed, calculated and tactical inaccuracy is leveraged as a critical means of breaking into and breaking out of racialized social positions. In short, by performing as black dandy, Shonibare plays (with) the exception. Very few blacks in England in the nineteenth century had the kind of access to the public sphere or its domestic sites of articulation that Shonibare's dandy enjoys, just as few command the economic power of the football or pop superstar. The work's disregard of historical veracity, and the knowledge—and acknowledgment—of its incommensurability with what the spectators know is at once the source of its power and the source of its play. Thus, while few blacks could have held sway over a country estate as Shonibare imagines (and images) himself doing, he acknowledges that the history of those few who did remains untold: an unacknowledged exception. *Diary of a Victorian Dandy* fabricates what Gayatri Chakravorty Spivak might call a *catachrestic* exception—a kind of *misappropriation* of the figure or trope of the dandy.[45] Shonibare is clearly referencing Victorian personae like Walter Pater and Oscar Wilde, but popular black dandies of the eighteenth century—such as Samuel Johnson's servant and companion Francis Barber; or Julius Soubise, who began his life as a favorite of his aristocratic mistress and ended it as a Hogarthian rake—also come to mind (see chapter 3). Inasmuch as men like Shonibare's dandy could not have been easily reproduced under the ideological and biopolitical order of eighteenth- or nineteenth-century Britain, his performance adds another sly commentary on the historical record, namely the ways in which those black men who did achieve public notability could never be considered "true" gentlemen, for their performances were ever in excess, ever theatrical, and thus they were always already dandies. Olaudah Equiano's aristocratic pose in the portrait that gazes out from the frontispiece might then serve as an instance of inscrutability with which this section began; but the image of a refined black masculinity—from the absurd excesses of servant livery in the eighteenth century to the era of hip-hop artists decked out in top hats, furs, and bling today—remains one of artifice. It is a stereotype so bound up in the history of modern human bio-cargo dependent on the spectacle of, and speculation on, black bodies as to render its contestation virtually impossible and its appropriation forever profitable.

Fashion Matters

The notion of historical "redress," in the fashion contexts outlined above, is now cleverly inflected by meanings that appear to veer off in wildly different and seemingly unrelated directions: as a matter of clothing and as an object of justice. How might we draw the two back together to reunite what we wear and what we do in the field of everyday public life? In the final sections of this chapter I want to leverage the digressions into matters of fashionability into a provocation for returning to the prospects for a critical redressive historiography, one now attuned to the clothed artifactual bodies on the street and in the home, and the relationship between clothing and fashion and reparation now gathered under the trope of redress. Here the affix—the *im-* of the immaterial—holds in some suspension the play between the material and the immaterial, or the concrete and the affective, particularly when we think about the materiality of historical materialism (what counts as the material?) or the materiality of the historical archive on which material critique relies. As I explored in earlier chapters, the terms *material* and *immaterial* also signify in a legal sense to designate *what counts* or has consequence, say, *in law;* evidence or testimony, for instance, might be deemed immaterial by the prosecution, in a criminal case for instance, but quite material by the defense; that the determination of who has standing before the law and who does not is predicated on a prior determination of what is material and what immaterial to the law. I now want to extend this consideration on the (im)materiality of fashion by returning to the public institutions of the gallery and museum that house the material artifacts of colonial history as they are reflexively engaged in the project of historical redress and the dilemmas any just project entails: historical recoverability, affective sensibility, flexible temporality, and the decidedly unstable materiality that underwrites what gets dressed and what can be materially or ethically redressed.

Yinka Shonibare has long been recognized for his singular artistic engagement with the history of colonialism in West Africa in the aftermath of the Atlantic slave trade. Insomuch as compulsory migration and organized human trafficking, strategic financialization and sustained indebtedness, and calculated political and social instability continue to sustain the reach of global capitalism into the so-called third or developing world, Shonibare's installations and their array of historical citations are reflexively designed to elicit awareness of the historical conditions that shape the present, both inside and outside the West. At the same time, through a series of museum and gallery interventions, Shonibare has interrogated insistently the very institutions of art, that is, the establishments in which he participates and from which he himself profits mightily. In his work, Shonibare quite self-reflexively and ironically maps his own position within the global economic flows of the international art market. In this sense Shonibare's gallery-based works resonate with the wide range of reflexive critical practices and creative forms examined in previous chapters. But as I also show in these chapters, such public history work is fraught with often-irresolvable dilemmas of representation, authorization, and, of course, archivization.

Here I explore how Shonibare responds to these critical issues as he constellates and performs the archive of aristocratic dress and leverages the materiality of fashionable attire as a site of articulation for an (im)material historiography in "spectral fashion." While spectral fashion resists entextualization within the historical archive as such, while nonetheless remaining determinant *of* the archive, the archival events that perform the archive in fashion likewise unhouse fashion as irreducible remainders of global markets and the colonial means of production and accumulation that made them possible. In this sense, Shonibare's appropriation, citation, and indexing of eighteenth- and nineteenth-century aristocratic dress and décor simultaneously encode and decode a set of historical conditions that themselves appear recalcitrant to stylization on a range of textual surfaces, including the artifactual bodies marked otherwise by the colonial and postcolonial past. That is, in Shonibare's creative practice, index and citation function as primary formal techniques for the cultivation of a historical imaginary that is redressive in intent—if not always in execution—as he plays in and with the market in fashion time.

Shonibare's emphasis on the daily lives and households of upper-class society may appear counterintuitive to the project of historical redress, but I suggest that by restaging the milieu of aristocratic social life he is able to demonstrate how sumptuous clothing and opulent accouterments of the wealthy homes themselves come to be haunted by colonial modernity and how fashion and commerce draw the spectral demands of colonial and postcolonial others into contemporary public cultures. Shonibare is best known for his use of African batik/Dutch-wax textiles in an array of African and non-African patterns, which he uses to fabricate a variety of elaborate eighteenth- and nineteenth-century women's and men's fashions (dresses, gowns, suits, hunting outfits, etc.). In an early interview, Shonibare describes his use of these textiles as a reference to his own experience as an African artist, the demands placed upon him to be representative *as* a black artist, and as a response to the art-historical appropriation of the "primitive" in modernist aesthetics. He explains, "I want to incorporate this symptom of commodification into my work . . . [yet] there is a deliberate denial of the authentic in this installation."[46] His subsequent use of batik suggests more than its status as a contemporary commodity designating African identity; rather, while ironically critiquing the reification of identity, his practice also references the imbrication of these fabrics within the history of colonialism and a globalizing capitalism.

Shonibare's installations incorporate both traditional patterns dating back to the nineteenth century as well as contemporary print styles, in effect weaving textual meaning back into textile objects by drawing attention to the sheen of colonial economy diffused across the mantle of eighteenth- and nineteenth-century domesticity and dominant modes of masculinity and femininity produced and reproduced both inside and outside the home. Shonibare replicates a variety of conventional suits and gowns, but they are fabricated in African batiks whose patterns and iconographic details resonate with his critical interest in the material and discursive forms power takes in colonial and postcolonial social life. Displayed on headless shop-window mannequins and professional dress-dummies posed in alienated and alienating physical attitudes, his emphasis on fashionable items associated with upper-class consumption—clothing in particular—these installations provide an uncanny reminder of the spectral remainder through which colonial history might be redressed. Placards accompanying Shonibare's work draw attention to the complicated material history of batik as an "indigenous" technique of dyeing cloth. Initially developed in regions of Southeast Asia and Oceania, batik enters global trade through Dutch colonies in present-day Indonesia; but by the mid-nineteenth century, batik fabrics were being mass-produced in northern Europe, first in the Netherlands and then in Britain, for export *back* to colonial merchants in Indonesia and then in Africa. Only later, after decolonization, did batik begin to be manufactured locally, sold globally, and worn as a signifier for authentic African identity.[47] Although the history of its migration across a number of colonial sites frustrates any desire for an easy return to origins in postcolonial signification, and undermines its status as a recognizable icon of pan-African solidarity, Shonibare's use of batik underscores its easy consumption as a signifier of indigenous "tradition" as well as its commercial appropriation as a visible sign of African authenticity.[48] Thus visibility and display, spectatorship and spectacle, become instrumental for Shonibare's engagements with problems of agency, artifice, authenticity, and self-fashioning, on the one hand, and his imminent critique of the institutions of art that draw the history of capitalist accumulation via colonial exploitation and expropriation into present-day circuits of postcolonial cultural production, on the other.

It is in this context that I consider Shonibare's 2001 public installation *Yinka Shonibare Dresses Britannia,* which was commissioned by the Tate Britain to commemorate the reopening of the museum after an expansion and refurbishment of its galleries and a significant new corporate partnership with British Petroleum (BP).[49] In this intervention the artists draped the iconic statue of Britannia that tops the imposing front portico with Shonibare's (by then) signature African patterned batik (or Dutch-wax), a textile whose historical provenance binds together a chain of colonial and postcolonial signifiers. In this instance, the batik served as a way of constellating a number of historical references and art-historical citations: on the one hand, the Tate itself, which was founded at the end of the Victorian era by the sugar baron Henry Tate (of Tate and Lyle Sugar) and built on what had once been a prison, notably for convicts being deported to Australia; on the other, the economic exploitation that underwrote its construction and that can be said to still underwrite both its edificial and philanthropic "foundations." In lieu of the commission's commemorative context, the piece might be understood as a critique of BP's corporate sponsorship, which connects it to a long history of philanthropy that funneled the wealth generated through colonial exploitation into civic institutions like the art museum. As Divya Tolia-Kelly and Andy Morris acknowledge in their essay on Shonibare's "disruptive aesthetics," "the gesture of Britannia's clothing draws attention to the history of the Tate as an institution, not just in terms of the well-documented wealth generation of its sugar-trading founder Henry Tate but also in terms of its role as a gallery that has historically defined itself through fixed and stable notions of nationhood."[50]

To be sure, the Tate Britain remains a monument to the Victorian era's ideological and political moment of empire, epitomized by the venerated Britannia seated defiantly above her nation and gazing across the Thames, trident held tight in her right hand and shield resting beneath her left. In Shonibare's hands, however, her once-stately body is tempered and contained by flowing swathes of African batik, refashioning her status as emblem of the nation into the very figure of the native over whom she is supposed to rule. Once the personification of the empire—and in 1897, when the statue was installed, a metonym for the far less prepossessing body of Empress Victoria—the redressed Britannia became a transient signifier of colonial and postcolonial entanglement. On the one hand, inasmuch as Britannia's dignified and defiant presence is undermined by the whimsy of Shonibare's colorful fabric, the piece is conventionally iconoclastic. On the other hand, there is an implicit violence expressed in the act of redressing Britannia that sits less comfortably with the already complicated and deeply problematic history of gendering the nation through the figure of a goddess whose irreproachable womanhood is secured through the codes of female masculinity. With the evocation of racialized violence, whose script colonial discourse had so effectively managed to flip, appears the specter of a savage black masculinity once again threatening the sanctity of white femininity. Thus the layering of African batik complicates the way in which the relationship between colonized and colonizer (indeed, their complicity) is predicated on an ambivalent history that simultaneously genders nationhood through the figure of an all-powerful womanhood while insisting on the vulnerability of white femininity and the exclusion of women from the public sphere. By redressing Britannia's female body, Shonibare draws our attention to an equally entangled history of exploitation—sexed, gendered, classed, and racialized—both at home and in the colonies, and to the endless transactions and exchanges that bring the colonies into Europe and take Europe to the colonies.

I suggest that commemorative works engaged in the project of a critical redressive historiography necessarily operate in reflexive engagement with the neoliberal market for the postcolonial that serves as a precondition for institutional commissioning, and that their success or failure hangs on their capacity to transform acts of institutionally sanctioned housing into spectacular *archival events:* performances that constellate archival material in order to consolidate a historically aware and nuanced public culture. As such, Shonibare's 2001 intervention at the Tate Britain anticipated a more ambitious project at the National Gallery in 2007 as one of many black British artists commissioned that year to commemorate the bicentenary of the abolition of the Atlantic slave trade. Throughout his twenty-five-year career Shonibare has, by way of a series of gallery interventions such as this one, quite insistently interrogated the very institutions of art from a postcolonial perspective, the same institutions in which he himself participates and from which he profits mightily.[51] Shonibare has especially been recognized for his singular artistic engagement with the history of colonialism and especially the colonial relation in and to Africa, including the Atlantic slave trade. Inasmuch as human traffic continues to sustain the global reach of capitalism and the mass migrations entailed by capitalist development, Shonibare's batik plays on its material, representational, and affective qualities in order to emblematize the long history of colonial exploitation, a history that winds its way into the very structures of national identity but simultaneously attempts to efface that history in those locations of national consolidation such as the National Gallery.

In collaboration with Jonah Albert, the Inspire Curatorial Fellow at the National Gallery for 2007, Shonibare's *Scratch the Surface* consisted of two distinct sections, each housed in separate galleries in the museum. The first part of the exhibit was located in a small gallery off the main portico where Albert displayed three portraits drawn from the permanent collection: first, Sir Thomas Lawrence's 1790 painting of John Julius Angerstein, whose extensive art collection was purchased by the National Gallery upon his death in 1823 and laid the foundation for the growth of the National Gallery as an institution; second, a large portrait of Mary Oswald (née Ramsay), titled simply *Mrs. Oswald,* painted by Johann Zoffany between 1763 and 1764; and finally, Sir Joshua Reynolds's triumphant *Colonel Tarleton* of 1782, which captures Banastre Tarleton in full military regalia, replete with horses and a suggestively positioned canon.[52] What link together each of these seemingly disparate figures—the accompanying placards inform us—are their various involvements in the slave trade and plantation slavery in the West Indies. Angerstein, for instance, made his fortune with the Lloyds Bank in the insurance of trading ships en route to and from Africa and the Americas, as well as his own extensive land holdings in the Caribbean. Mary Ramsey had been born on a Jamaican plantation but returned to Britain upon her father's death. Having inherited his plantation, however, she married the wealthy Scottish merchant and slave trader Richard Oswald and lived out her life of leisure in a stately home at Auchincruive in South Ayrshire. Banastre Tarleton likewise had inherited his wealth from his father's Liverpool-based trading interests, which included investments in the sugar trade. His father, John Tarleton, had served as mayor of Liverpool and Banastre himself had been one of its MPs following his military career; both Tarletons were vocal proponents of the slave trade and worked tirelessly to foil the efforts of the abolitionists in Parliament.

These portraits were joined by two small contemporary works by the Nigerian British artist Yinka Shonibare, both creative interpretations of the hats worn by the two sitters in the older paintings: Colonel Tarleton's shako helmet with ostentatious plume, and Mrs. Oswald's modest wide-brimmed Leghorn sun hat with silk ribbon. *Colonel Tarleton's Hat* reworks the grand plumage in a colorful, shredded African batik, while *Mrs. Oswald's Hat* replaces the silk ribbon with a simple band of batik. Batik, or Dutch-wax fabric, is a recognizable signature material in Shonibare's oeuvre and a polyvalent signifier for the history that is inscribed just below the surface of the gallery walls or beneath the fabric of period dress. If the portraits by Lawrence, Zoffany, and Reynolds represent a certain type of archival knowledge, we might then understand Shonibare's intervention as a counterarchival insistence on postcolonial knowledge production and embodied practice. In this sense, *Scratch the Surface* in its curatorial logic and Shonibare in his artistic practice both enact and represent the process of decolonization, indeed of decolonizing the archive. Indeed, Shonibare's quite distinguished body of work helps us better understand how creative historical engagement might materialize a demand to rethink the traditional art-historical archive and its exhibition practices through its forceful occupation of a contemporary public and civic space such as the National Gallery.

The historical portraits and Shonibare's detailed reinterpretation of the two hats were displayed alongside mural-sized informational panels offering extensive historical and contextual materials, materials that literally papered the gallery walls. The panels provided a history of colonial slavery and its African trade and explained the role that slavery played in the lives of the three portrait sitters. They also highlighted the relationship between Angerstein, Oswald, and Tarleton and the National Gallery, which has for over a century prominently displayed their portraits with no mention of their involvement with slavery. The panels draw our attention to the economic and social connection between the subjects of the portraits and the artists they commissioned, as well as to the art they collected and the civic institutions they supported. In the now requisite video accompanying the exhibit, Albert repeats much of the information provided on the walls and takes us on a tour of Mrs. Oswald's estate, explaining how her wealth, produced on the backs of generations of enslaved Africans, enabled the construction of her comfortably situated and elegantly appointed home back in Scotland, an estate house now open to the public.[53] Meanwhile, a short presentation by Shonibare emphasized his own career-long interest in aristocratic leisure enabled by the wealth generated by colonialism, slavery, and the slave trade.

Much, of course, has been said in the international art press about Shonibare's career-long use of Dutch-wax fabrics, not least by the artist himself, and critics have generally followed the artist's own interpretive cues when discussing these works.[54] In interviews and on accompanying panels and placards at most of his exhibits, for example, Shonibare recounts how he began experimenting with batik while in art school, after an instructor suggested he try to produce a more "authentic" African art. In an early interview, he describes his use of these textiles as a reference to his own experience as an African artist, the demands placed upon him to be a representative *as* a black artist, and as a response to the art-historical appropriation of the "primitive" in highly commodified modernist and postmodernist aesthetics.[55] But his use of batik suggests more than simply its status as a contemporary commodity designating African identity, as if culture and commodity were essentially exchangeable. Rather, while ironically critiquing the reification of identity, his practice also references the imbrication of these fabrics within the long history of colonialism and an ever-globalizing capitalism. Shonibare reminds the spectator that batik, in fact, has a quite complicated material history, and that its migration across a number of colonial sites frustrates any desire for an easy return to origins in postcolonial signification. Originally a weaving and dyeing practice in Indonesia, batik was subsequently mass-produced by Dutch colonizers and then British manufacturers in the nineteenth century. The British attempted unsuccessfully to trade their batik back in Indonesia, and then later more successfully in Africa. But it was only after decolonization that batik became a recognizable icon of African dress and in turn began to get manufactured locally, sold globally, and worn as a signifier for "authentic" African identity.[56] At the same time, batik is easily consumable *as* African "tradition" and thus Shonibare's pieces also reflexively signify contemporary appropriation of postcoloniality *as* indigenous authenticity.

The second, more prominent, half of *Scratch the Surface* consisted of another commissioned installation by Shonibare located in the National Gallery's stunning grand rotunda. *Colonel Tarleton and Mrs. Oswald Shooting* consisted of two headless mannequins representing our two portrait subjects, dressed in formal attire now fashioned out of batik. The mannequins stood facing one another from across the rotunda, resting on elevated platforms placed in front of the walls on which Tarleton and Oswald usually hang (see Figure 29). Incorporating an array of African and non-African patterns, Shonibare fabricated an elaborate gown, in keeping with his interest in eighteenth- and nineteenth-century women's and men's fashions. The most striking element of the installation, however, is the depiction of the two figures holding guns aloft in the disconcerting act of shooting a pheasant flying overhead. Flayed and bloodied, the pheasant was exquisitely captured in the light falling through the glass rotunda ceiling (see Figure 30). In the accompanying video, Shonibare explained that in the piece he was not trying to compare the violence of game hunting to the violence enacted upon the body of the enslaved but was interested instead in shooting as a trope for the still-violent aristocratic leisure that slavery made possible. Rather than trying to represent the atrocities taking place out in the colonies or along the Atlantic slave routes, he emphasized what might be described as its displaced, spectral presence back home. To be sure, the pheasant under glass, its body blasted across the rotunda sky, like

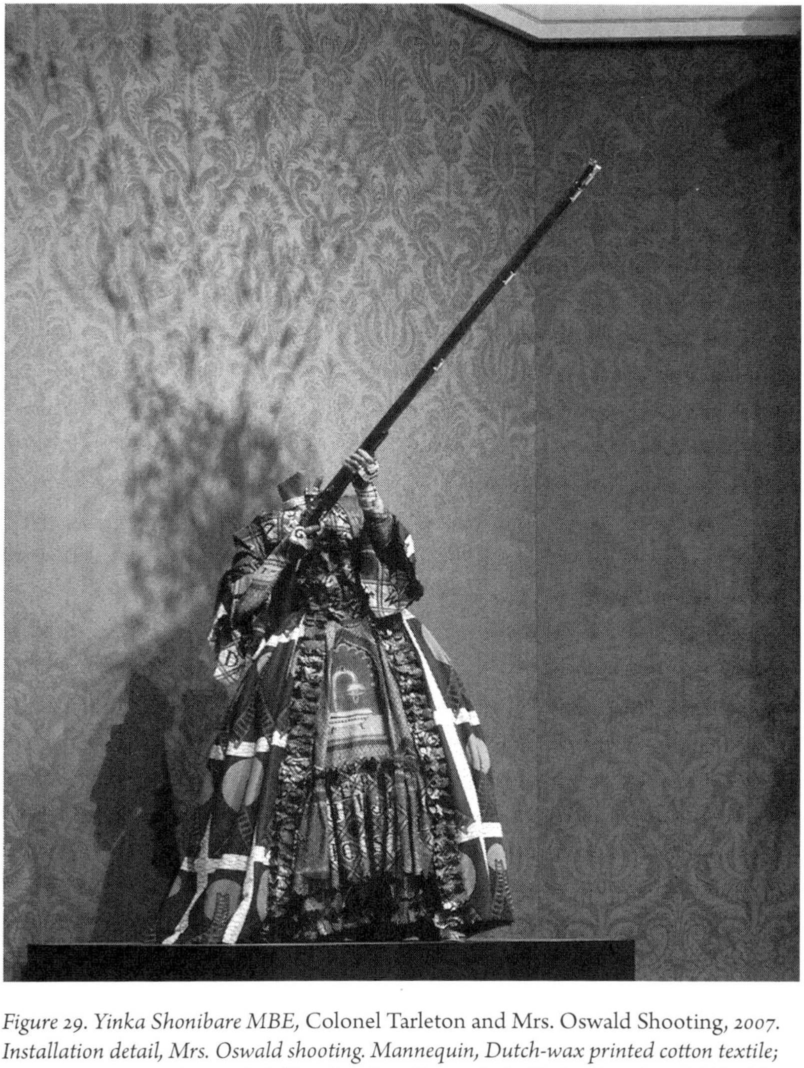

Figure 29. Yinka Shonibare MBE, Colonel Tarleton and Mrs. Oswald Shooting, *2007. Installation detail, Mrs. Oswald shooting. Mannequin, Dutch-wax printed cotton textile; 393 x 192 x 152 cm. National Gallery, London. Copyright by Yinka Shonibare MBE. All Rights Reserved, DACS 2015. Image courtesy of Stephen Friedman Gallery, London.*

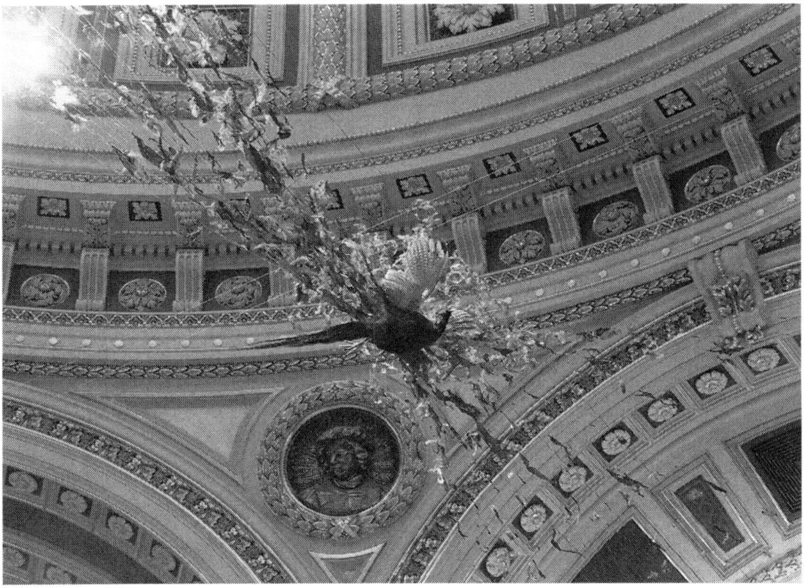

Figure 30. Yinka Shonibare MBE, Colonel Tarleton and Mrs. Oswald Shooting, *2007. Installation detail, pheasant suspended overhead. National Gallery, London. Copyright by Yinka Shonibare MBE. All Rights Reserved, DACS 2015. Image courtesy of Stephen Friedman Gallery, London.*

the batik that clothes the headless mannequins, served as an index for that violence, while also pointing out the ever-shifting, and sometimes immeasurably narrow, line drawn between the human and the animal. Explicitly, but ambiguously, Shonibare is asking the viewer to reflect on contemporary debates about the treatment and rights of, or obligations to, nonhuman animals in our own historical context. Implicitly, he is also invoking the troubling history of the racialized distinctions between the human and nonhuman. Here Shonibare repeats a trope common in nineteenth-century slave narratives: to reverse the script such that spectators are compelled to ask, who in the instance of colonial slavery is truly bestial?

While Shonibare's installation certainly compels reflection on the violence that redounds through the long history of colonial atrocity, he also demands that we confront discomfiting questions about responsibility and culpability in the present. Mieke Bal has recently argued that current exhibition practices have drawn upon literary and performative aesthetic forms in their organization logics. She identifies particularly narrative and poetics (along with theatrics and film) as models or concept metaphors for powerfully innovative and transgressive exhibitions. Here, perhaps, one's attention should be turned back to the curator of *Scratch the Surface*, Jonah Albert, who carefully organizes the movements between the traditional and the new, the historical and the aesthetic, such that the exhibit is both installation and performance. The "poetic model" that Albert constructs, in Bal's words, "attunes the visitor to the various grounds of repetition that, in turn, foreground difference: in style, color, scale, theme, medium, and, indeed, thought" but that also emphasize structural continuities and discontinuities—in aesthetic as well as socioeconomic and political terms.[57] According to Bal, the poetics of the gallery, as a space that is navigated and negotiated by the spectator, draws his or her attention to the rhyme and rhythm of the works on display, such that "the building, or the curator, offers a frame that deviates from the rule the building has established."[58] Indeed, the rhythm of artistic consumption also evokes a narrative form. Here Bal's thinking about the operations of the contemporary art gallery reflects a broader turn in recent museum practice of a reflexively inclusive, historically and politically savvy, institutional critique.[59] Works like *Colonel Tarleton and Mrs. Oswald Shooting* foreground not simply a *critical* aesthetic but also an aesthetic that draws the museumgoer both materially and affectively into such scenes of gross subjection, of absolute bare life and utter contingency—most viscerally felt while looking up at that pheasant. Shonibare registers the genuine viciousness at the very heart of aristocratic leisure, without much of the irony that typically characterizes his artwork. The experience is as corporeal and sensuous as it is cognitive and reflective; indeed, each of Shonibare's installations generate what might be called a *som*aesthetic experience, that is, an experience that brings us back to, and into, the body. At the same time, his gallery interventions place the historical moments or events he references into public circulation; and while there is no guarantee that anyone will walk away with a new sense of obligation or empowerment, Shonibare opens up institutions like the National Gallery for a kind of immanent critique, one that in turn binds its spectators to both its history and their own.

In both interventions Shonibare not only succeeds in making legible the excess (or waste) of the eighteenth-century bourgeoisie, but he is especially apt at bringing into view the complicated relationship between race, class, gender, and sexuality within the domestic scene and the economic and ideological systems that it bears. He also challenges the epistemological and ontological conditions of our own moment of globalization and globalized spectatorship and artistic and historical consumption. Indeed, *Scratch the Surface* marks the almost imperceptible slide of Western liberalism into global neoliberalism. This work also demonstrates how the artist's creative/critical practice begins by isolating archival objects with exceptional historical resonance and following the applications of batik, reintroducing them into popular circulation as citational and indexical objects of public culture. Shonibare endeavors to transform the institutions of art—including the very buildings that house them—available for a critique of both colonial history and the history of commodity exchange that underwrites it. In doing so he is, perhaps, likewise putting the institution to work against itself as a site clearly within the circuits of commodity exchange by acknowledging the need to "redress," in that other sense, the crimes of empire that enabled (and continue to enable) the very institutions of state and civil society and everyday domestic and public life.[60] Shonibare reminds us that colonial and postcolonial lifeworlds cannot be relegated to the historical or archival periphery and that decolonization begins with a rupture at home, no matter where or what that is.

Inasmuch as the notion of redress finds articulation within notions of goodwill, Christian charity, and private philanthropy, it is worth turning to one final installation by Shonibare before returning to Ozwald Boateng in the last section. In *The Victorian Philanthropist's Parlour* (1997), Shonibare decks out an entire sitting room in his signature batik, marking the brutal economic accumulation and material and cultural exploitation upholstering the British manor house and, by metonymic extension, the museum gallery itself (see Figure 31). Not only does *The Victorian Philanthropist's Parlour* appropriate the domestic space of the Victorian sitting room, and designate the domestic as an important site for the consolidation of public life, but, more importantly, Shonibare recognizes that even the biopolitical regime of Victorian philanthropy, as a mode of social command that simultaneously introduced the conditions of the impoverished and disenfranchised into public debate and enabled a handful of elite women access to the public sphere, is also marked by a colonial presence.[61] The installation is also reminiscent of a room in one of the many restored houses managed by the British Council peppering the English countryside, as well as installations in any number of history museums meant to educate visitors and tourists on the everyday lives of the eighteenth- and nineteenth-century

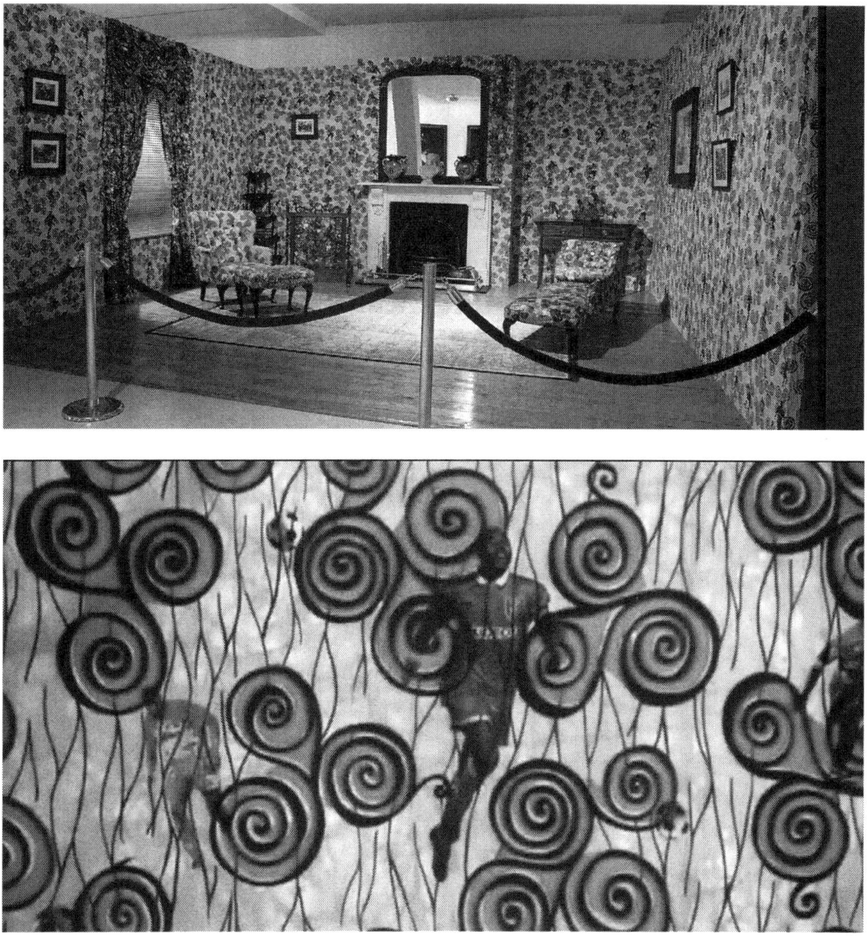

Figure 31. Yinka Shonibare MBE, The Victorian Philanthropist's Parlour, *1997. Reproduction furniture, fire screen, carpet, props, Dutch-wax printed cotton; approximately 260 x 488 x 530 cm. Commissioned by London Printworks Trust. Copyright by Yinka Shonibare MBE. All Rights Reserved, DACS 2015.*

English landed aristocracy and professional bourgeoisie, such as Bristol's Georgian House. *The Victorian Philanthropist's Parlour* incorporates a less traditional, contemporary pattern of batik fabric, which on closer inspection reveals itself to be a series of football (American soccer) players at play. The batik was designed by Shonibare himself—his first original design—and commissioned for production by the London Printworks Trust for an exhibition held in their Brixton arts space. The exhibit *Pledge Allegiance to a Flag?* interrogated the use of national symbols in multicultural Britain. Utilizing the batik as both décor *and* a kind of iconostasis for the projection of colonial fantasy, these contemporary footballers, then, are apposed to a genteel Victorian domesticity, asking the viewer to reflect on the circuits of exchange that bring the colonies into the home, and on the spectatorial economies that place the black male body under the gaze of middle-class consumers. Here he is clearly thinking about the commodification and global circulation of black players from Africa and elsewhere, and football itself as both spectator sport and spectacle of and within global economic flows. The ambivalent demand for public visibility is refracted (troped even) by a self-reflexive insistence on an interrogation of the operations of African spectatorship—Africa as an object of spectatorship as well as Africans as the subject of spectatorship—within global neoliberalism associated with multiple articulations of "development."

The Scramble for "Africa Rising"

In an opinion piece appearing in June 2013 on CNN's online platform, Ozwald Boateng announced the latest expansion of his global brand: his entry into the "new" philanthropy market, or what Matthew Bishop and Michael Bishop unabashedly call "philanthrocapitalism."[62] Just prior to the CNN piece, in May 2013, Boateng guest edited a special issue of the magazine *New African* dedicated to the critical role that this new, market-friendly mode of philanthropic investment would need to play in potentiating rapid economic growth and what has come to be called "Africa rising."[63] The discourse of philanthrocapitalism is, as the word suggests, rooted in neoliberal ideology and trades in business speak and the empty idioms of the market, in which philanthropists "partner" with locally based "social entrepreneurs" to "invest" in "for-profit" and "publically traded" companies that will build the infrastructure and capacity needed in order for the economies of sub-Saharan Africa to reach their full potential.[64] "Trade not aid" is the mantra of philanthrocapitalists, and while the devastating outcomes meted out with development aid have certainly been a regular topic of criticism on the political left, the threat posed by this latest mode of global-scale capitalist expropriation eclipses the failures of direct aid. As I discussed earlier, Boateng is somewhat cagy about his relationship to his African, particularly Ghanaian, identity, largely relegating references to his ancestry to basic biographical facts and a handful of cultural traditions and signifiers—cast in the common tropes of generalized Africanness—but in the mid-2000s the designer, whose company was attempting once again to "go global," began to turn his attention to his native land. In 2006 Boateng set up his Made in Africa Foundation and brought together a selection of Africa's global leaders in 2007 in an event attended by a handful of political and business leaders and a bevy of media celebrities. By the time his CNN article appeared he was well ensconced in the rhetoric of "Africa rising," had embraced the tenets of philanthrocapitalism, and was enthusiastically repeating all the right slogans, catchphrases, and bywords of the movement. In 2012 Boateng's foundation partnered with *Arise* magazine to organize a collaborative fashion event that would feature collections from sub-Saharan Africa's most talented designers. It was inevitable, perhaps, that at this moment, as he begins to "reconnect" with his Ghanaian "roots," Boateng began to incorporate fine Dutch-wax fabrics into his high-end menswear—shirts, pants, jackets, and accessories—that literalized the kind of cultural appropriation Shonibare's work self-reflexively ironized (see Figure 32). More significantly, his new "Africanized" fashions coincided with the introduction of his brand into markets across the continent.

The historical resonances that emerge with the call for a new philanthropy market in Africa are not unexpected, but they are surprising to find uncritically acknowledged in the defenses and celebrations of the movement—like an unconsciously reflexive confession. In the introduction to *Philanthrocapitalism,* for instance, the authors attempt to situate their project within a long and noble tradition of humanitarian generosity, indeed as the very "revival and reinvention" of it, with Warren Buffet and Bill Gates as the second coming of John D. Rockefeller and Andrew Carnegie. Stressing the simultaneous emergence of philanthropy with the rise of capitalism, the authors note that the eighteenth century was a particularly important moment in the history of charitable giving. By way of illustration they identify the founding of Guy's Hospital in London as an important precursor: "In the eighteenth century, philanthropy was embraced by the inventors of

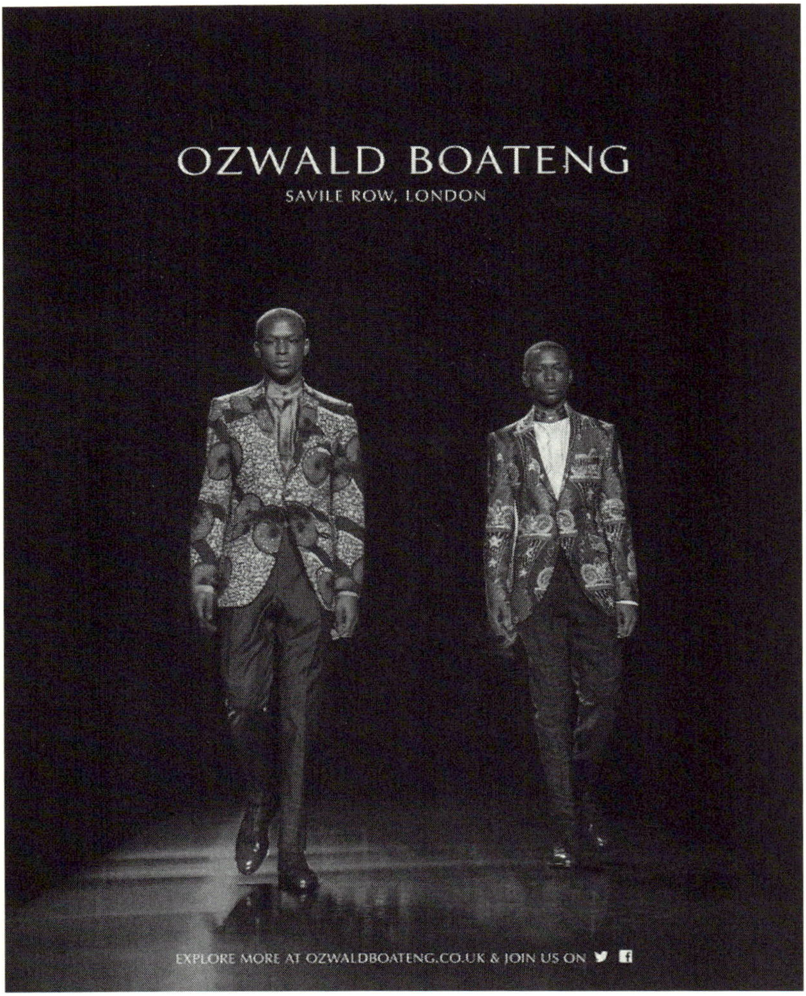

Figure 32. Ozwald Boateng, advertisement, 2013.

the joint stock company and . . . speculators such as Thomas Guy, who sold at the top of the South Sea Bubble and used his profits to found Guy's Hospital in London."[65] The authors here do not connect the South Sea Bubble with the development of colonialism and imperialism, nor do they refer to the economic crisis in the UK that ensued. Rather, they celebrate Guy as a perspicacious investor taking advantage of what Naomi Klein calls "disaster capitalism."[66] The authors do, however, follow the Thomas Guy hospital with what they identify as another key moment in the history of eighteenth-century philanthropy, William Wilberforce and the founding of the Society for the Abolition of the Slave Trade. As their example makes obvious, historical references do not constitute historical consciousness, redressive or otherwise.

I want to place Boateng's CNN op-ed in the context of philanthrocapitalism because he too opens up with historical citation, an assertive call to remember that period of African decolonization in the 1950s. While Boateng's gesture toward remembrance is evocative, it does not offer much in the way of activating that historical moment. It becomes clear that for Boateng, it is proper to remember the past but effective action arises only in the present. "When change comes," he begins his article, "it comes all of a sudden, leaving only a remembrance of the past, a previous present, as its memorial." For Boateng, the past is remembrance, but remembrance is nothing more than memorial, a slender headstone resting supine atop a remarkably shallow grave. Utterly flat, utterly passive, utterly shallow too are history's human actors, who appear to have been caught off guard in their own presentism as the spontaneous exigencies of unseen agents blow in from an elsewhere that has no name. If history is nothing more than a series of "previous presents," unconnected, for Boateng change comes not through collective human agency causally linked by their overdetermination but by a select few who generate the wind. Such a storm is forming across Africa once again, Boateng insists, and when it finally rages it will be

> a moment as sudden as British Prime Minister Harold Macmillan's realization that there was a "wind of change blowing through this continent, whether we like it or not" prior to the granting of independence to so many African people 50 years ago. It is this wind that now blows again over Africa.
>
> This time it is less political than economic but it will be just as permanent and just as shocking. And this time, it will not be awkward majors from disbanded colonial battalions muttering into their beer, it will be our well-meaning liberals that will be left behind, lumpen in its wake like a broken Luddite army.

The rhetoric is unusually heated for Boateng, whose interviews and appearances almost always capture a manner far more measured. But unlike the scorching rhetoric and fierce physical resistance by Africa's anticolonial revolutionaries, which he imagines suddenly seizing the attention of European leaders like Macmillan and leaving a handful of sullen military leaders broken and resentful, Boateng's message is clearly that economic liberalism of the Keynesian variety is as out of date as the call for an African revolution along Marxist lines.

Boateng explicitly endorses neoliberalism's promise of private capital investment by visionaries from abroad, not liberal goodwill coerced by "a million posters showing our babies starving with flies in their eyes" and not with the help of "perpetual funds raised for mosquito nets as a panacea against our ineffective drainage systems." In today's tech-savvy world, change "will come as swift as our Tunisian Spring, a revolution sprung by social media, and as insistent as the ringtone of our mobile phones." Boateng, it turns out, appears as unaware of the driving forces of the so-called Arab Spring as he is the long history of anticolonial resistance that preceded the 1950s. All Africa really needs, he suggests, is a mobile phone: "Between 2000 and 2012, mobile penetration grew in Africa from 1% to 54%. Some predict that by 2014, 69% of mobiles on the continent will have internet access. This virtual infrastructure, plus the commodity boom, has meant that 7 out of 10 of the world's fastest growing economies including, yes, Ethiopia, the poster child of our Live Aid generation, are not in Asia but in Africa." And Asia serves as the go-to model of economic investment and development Boateng imagines not only possible but already happening in an admittedly unevenly distributed set of locales. "Africa is throwing off its 300-year yoke. Much as China did. China, too, suffered its post-colonial period, drunk on nationalism and at best neglected by its dictators. And in many ways, Africa's growth patterns mirror those of the new China's." China, of course, is also currently Africa's biggest investor, though Boateng makes no mention of this fact, or that China is seeding the continent with a proliferation of arms and weapons systems decidedly not intended for a Luddite army but for the private armies of the private owners who have seized or retained control of Africa's enormous wealth. Such enthusiasm brings Boateng back to the mystifying rhetoric of "Africa rising," an expression, Boateng explains, that once "floated like fairy tales" but is "becoming commonplace now in investment circles."[67] Advocating for large-scale investments in energy, transportation, and information technology infrastructure, Boateng describes these projects as "Africa helping Africans—the ultimate trade-not-aid policy." His mantra here, as in his own professional career, is "self-sufficiency," and while much of the advocacy and organizational work is indeed carried out by representatives from across Africa and its diaspora, Made in Africa Foundation's primary capital investors are most certainly not made in Africa, though they stand to make billions through large investment firms specializing in high-risk markets. Taking the lion's share of the credit for a success yet to come, Boateng boasts, "I mixed these great talents from the diaspora and Africa in amongst the finance ministers, bankers and entrepreneurs. This is what a designer looks for: the harmony in contrasts. They find their common desire to make it happen—one group bringing this solution to the global audience, giving it transparency and encouraging investment, and the other group implementing it. That's why I set up Made In Africa Foundation." Of the many red flags present in Boateng's CNN article, this last one should be the most alarming, because the sentence doesn't end there, so let me quote it again in full: "That's why I set up Made In Africa Foundation with the support of a fast-growing Nigerian business, Atlantic Energy."[68]

Using the power of social media across a range of available technologies—from word of mouth to wireless—in the opening days of January 2012, a year and a half before Boateng's op-ed ran on CNN, crowds of protesters gathered in the streets of cities and towns across Nigeria to protest the government's controversial suspension of a long-standing fuel subsidy. Protesters also amassed outside the Nigerian embassy in London. By canceling the subsidy, protesters warned, the government was ending the only universally accessible state-sourced benefit, which had long been vital to keeping the machinery of everyday life and work running, even when its engines sputtered more often than hummed. Facing the threat of rapidly escalating prices, union leaders joined the movement and announced an "indefinite strike," in solidarity with the many quite distinct but allied actions across the world under the banner of Occupy Nigeria.[69] Within days, at least eight protestors had been killed by police and dozens of others injured. Given that Nigeria is one of the world's largest producers of crude oil, it likely strikes one as deeply ironic that the cost of fuel is exceptionally high and that without a subsidy exceeds what most Nigerians can afford to pay. But the situation is anything *but* ironic; it is deeply historical. Government-contracted producers (Shell, Chevron, Exxon-Mobil, among them) export almost all of the oil they pump out of already deeply damaged environment. Of a piece with the acknowledged paucity of transportation and energy infrastructure in Nigeria (as in most of sub-Saharan Africa), there are no significant oil refineries, so petroleum must be imported from elsewhere at a very high cost. Surely this was precisely the kind of problem Boateng's Made in Africa Foundation was intended to address. After all, in an oil-rich nation like Nigeria shouldn't its most basic fuel commodities be made in Africa? Surely Boateng's "strategic partner," Atlantic Energy, was established in order to provide the oil-processing infrastructure Nigeria desperately needs? Atlantic Energy must be a refiner of oil and supplier of local petrol, no? Indeed, no. Atlantic Energy is a local, private crude oil extraction company operating outside the auspices of the state's system of joint-venture incorporation through the Nigerian National Petroleum Corporation (NNPC). Through an agreement with NNPC, independent companies like Boateng's partner Atlantic Energy can operate on oil fields not already under lease to an NNPC partner, about 5 percent of all production land. Since that time a scandal has erupted over Atlantic Energy's receipt of a no-bid contract from the Nigerian government.

There can be no doubt that Boateng's personal commitment to Africa, no matter how well intentioned (and such good intentions have long been the subject of harsh critiques of outside interference in local, national, and regional development) through his Made in Africa Foundation, is little more than a foil for the commitment to global neoliberalism, whether his own or that of his business and celebrity supporters. Nor should one hesitate in exposing their agenda as neocolonial—an instrument for the ongoing economic benefit of interests in the Global North through the rewarded machinations of political and social elites in the Global South, at high cost to the majority of those living and working in the postcolonial nation. Given this, one cannot be surprised by the condescending, lecturing tone Boateng takes in the final lines of his op-ed, in which he aims to once again teach Africa an aesthetic lesson in tailoring a self-sufficient, civilized, bespoke existence in this connected, globalized world: "The peoples and continents of the world are not separate, they are part of the same social and economic system: a system that must return to balance and harmony. But this balance can only occur when Africa itself realizes that it is time for Africa."

I conclude with a selection of striking visual echoes that bring Ozwald Boateng and Yinka Shonibare into closer proximity. I am struck, for example, by the uncanny exchange of style between Boateng and Shonibare in scans of two content pages taken from the May 2013 issue of *New African* that Boateng edited (see Figure 33). The first shows an overly literalized digital graphic of empty, headless "suits" accompanying an article celebrating the rising class of "Africapitalists," like the Nigerian investor and philanthropist Tony Elumelu (pictured left), who "hold the key to Africa's future"; the second features a group of men seated around a conference table discussing the "boundless future of opportunity" that will arise from "investing in Africa."[70] I place these pages side by side with one final gallery

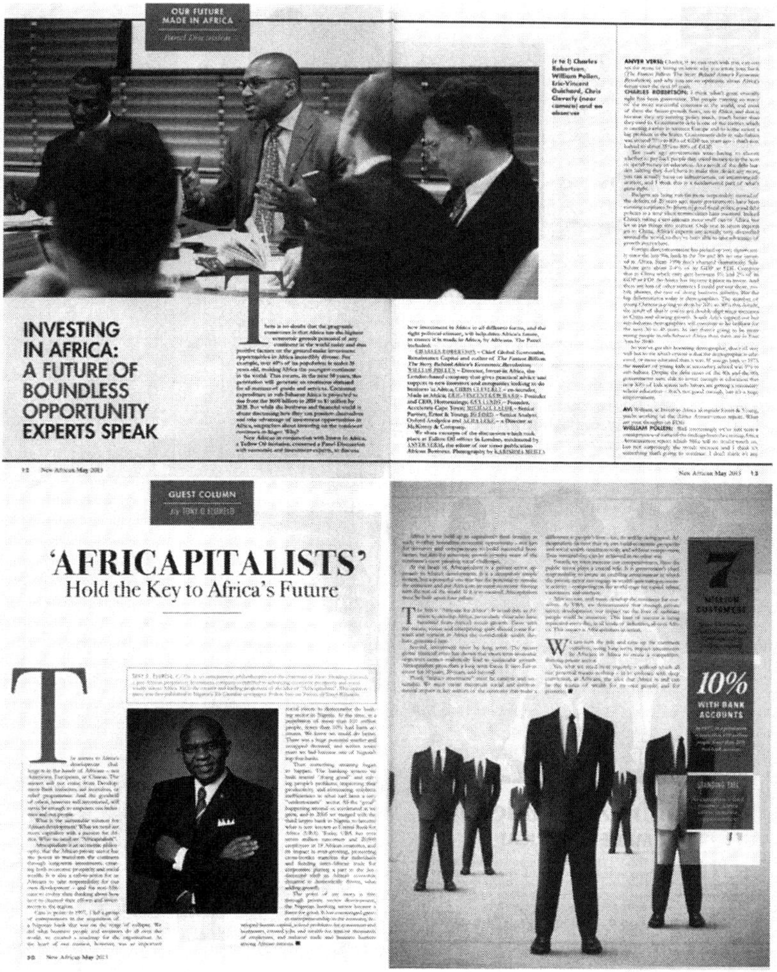

OUR FUTURE MADE IN AFRICA

INVESTING IN AFRICA: A FUTURE OF BOUNDLESS OPPORTUNITY EXPERTS SPEAK

GUEST COLUMN

'AFRICAPITALISTS' Hold the Key to Africa's Future

10%

WITH BANK ACCOUNTS

Figure 33. New African, *May 2013.*

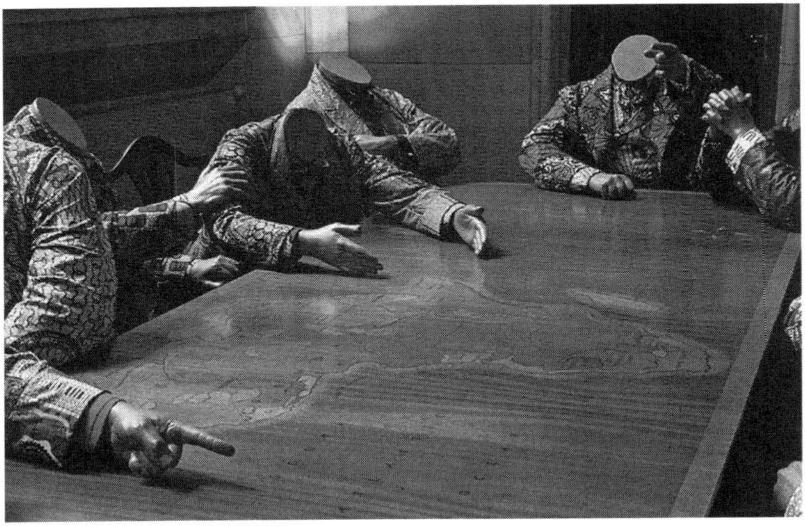

Figure 34. Yinka Shonibare MBE, Scramble for Africa, *2003. Fourteen life-size mannequins, fourteen chairs, table, Dutch-wax printed cotton; 132 x 488 x 280 cm. Commissioned by the Museum for African Art, N.Y. Copyright by Yinka Shonibare MBE. All Rights Reserved, DACS 2015. Image courtesy of the Pinnell Collection, Dallas.*

installation by Shonibare (see Figure 34). *Scramble for Africa* addresses dual, mutually constitutive, ruptures central to understanding postcoloniality: on the one hand, a readily legible historical rupture produced by the redirection of the colonial enterprise into the interior of the African subcontinent at the end of the nineteenth century, which occurred at the Berlin Conference of 1884–85, where European powers gathered to parcel out the remainder of the African continent among competing colonial regimes; on the other, a subsequent, less-theorized, ontological rupture, that is, a breach in the very conditions of being and becoming that "undoes" subjectivity and transforms the spectator into a self-reflexive (and self-reflecting) subject of history. The figures that circle the Berlin conference table are not only ghosted through their uncanny, headless representation, but once again the African textiles with which they are dressed collapse any assumptions about the distinction of colonial center and colonized periphery, or of race itself as a category of knowledge, into a zone of *indistinction.* Shonibare here engages the biopolitical at the very site of its institution (the conference/dinner table in Berlin, 1885), while also gesturing at the manner in which the biopolitical underpins the phenomenological at the site of its institution as art (the gallery space, 2003), and in turn opens history into the political, the singular as a strategy of undoing. It is worth noting as well that the extraction of valuable resources that motivated and constituted the scramble for Africa also made possible the introduction of a variety of African arts, artifacts, and textiles into the great museums of Europe, and led to the explosion in "primitivism" that is so indicative of the modernist (and now postmodernist) aesthetic.

Despite his own cozy relationship to the global art market, Shonibare still helps one understand the ways (or strategies) in which a catachrestic and anachronistic engagement with the past might short-circuit the economy of signs that sustains both historical understanding and the means through which racial, gender, and colonial ideologies get reproduced across time (as diachronic replication) and within the moment (its synchronic instance). Shonibare's figural catachreses and temporal anachronisms haunt the Victorian drawing rooms Shonibare occupies, unlocking them as sites for renarrating and redressing performatively historical violence and the reproduction of violence as a strategy of decolonization. Shonibare inhabits the museum and gallery such that he tags them as colonial *and* postcolonial, as the here and now *and* the there and then, and as indexes of the multiple sites of archival foreclosure, and the possibility of counterarchival disclosure. It is in such a context, such a constellation, that I think pieces such as *The Victorian Philanthropist's Parlour* and *Scramble for Africa* make themselves most felt: they problematize quite ironically, it seems, the notion of *re*dressing the past from within a position of paradoxical or ambivalent complicity with the institutions in which the artist associates, a reflexive awareness utterly lacking from Boateng's own participation.

· CHAPTER 6 ·

@Bristol

Dissident Publics in a Neoliberal City

Banking

I begin with a preliminary excursion, from the tailored runways of the Global North to a threadbare high street in the Global South. In *A Small Place,* Jamaica Kincaid's powerful 1988 broadside on her native Antigua, then ensnared in the contradictions of capitalist development and machinations of political power, the narrator ruminates on the long cycle of indebtedness that structures the postcolonial nation's relation to the West. Employing a forceful polemical tone, the speaker rails against the overseas commercial ventures that have taken command of the economic, political, and social life of the island. As she takes the reader on a demystifying tour of Antigua's most prominent landmarks, institutional reminders of the island's colonial past appear everywhere the speaker turns. "In the middle of High Street," she advises, "was the Barclays Bank."[1] Ubiquitous across the UK and its Commonwealth, Barclays might not appear to be an especially remarkable sign of a lingering British presence, but as an emblem of the rapacious global economy, Barclays represents a crucial historical nexus in the vast infrastructure of finance capital. Describing how the past is both indexed and obscured by the building's façade, the speaker assails the two founders whose name continues to grace this singular enterprise, John and David Barclay:

> The Barclay brothers, who started Barclays Bank, were slave-traders. That is how they made their money. When the English outlawed the slave trade, the Barclay brothers went into banking. It made them even richer. It's possible that when they saw how rich banking made them, they gave themselves a good beating for opposing an end to slave trading (for surely they would have opposed that), but then again, they may have been visionaries and

> agitated for an end to slavery, for look at how rich they became with their banks borrowing from (through savings) the descendants of the slaves and then lending back to them. But people just a little older than I am can recite the name of and the day the first black person was hired as cashier at this very same Barclays Bank in Antigua. (25–26)

As the narrator lays out her trenchant historical indictment, she tries to imagine what might constitute an act of justice capable of disrupting the ceaseless circuits of economic exploitation initiated by the transatlantic slave trade, or of amending the irreparable collective harm experienced by her and by generations of "people like" her. In a rhetorical turn perhaps more shocking today than a quarter century ago, the speaker pictures herself as a suicide bomber. "Do you ever imagine," she asks, "why some people blow things up?"

> I can imagine that if my life had taken a certain turn, there would be the Barclays Bank, and there I would be, both of us in ashes. Do you ever try to understand why people like me cannot get over the past, cannot forgive and cannot forget? There is the Barclays Bank. The Barclay brothers are dead. The human beings they traded, the human beings who to them were only commodities, are dead. It should not have been that they came to the same end, and heaven is not enough of a reward for one or hell enough of a punishment for the other. (26–27)

For a brief moment, the speaker turns away from her historiographic project to offer a troubling reparative vision predicated on expiating violence, a fantasy of spectacular annihilation carried out against this one small outlet in an immense network of the brothers' speculative venture. By standing against the building that bears their name, she compels the Barclay brothers to stand in for the long history of colonialism and its ongoing neocolonial enterprises. Ultimately, the speaker's retributive fantasy affords her no solace and the prospect of her own symbolic sacrifice provides no consolation; nor does she find satisfaction in the prospect of any divine dispensation that sequesters those who are damned from those who are delivered or promises eternal torment to one and everlasting peace to the other. For history is not an afterlife; history is life itself.

Kincaid suggests that the material conditions necessary for accounting for and recounting fully the losses sustained by "people like" her in the long history of colonialism—beginning with its highly speculative and heavily financed trade in human lives—are foreclosed by, if not foreclosed to, institutions like Barclays Bank. Neither the brothers nor the bank can be held to account, even as the evidence of its crimes remain conspicuously present and everywhere visible. While the Barclay name endures as a painful figure for the history of colonial slavery and postcolonial indenture, the prospect of violent retribution against Barclays as an institution is rendered materially inadequate, ethically untenable, and affectively unsatisfying: symbolically meaningful in the abstract, perhaps, but too particularized to count much toward the settling of historical debts. Which makes the speaker's closing remark on Barclays all the more confounding. "So do you see the queer thing about people like me?" she concludes. "Sometimes we *hold* your retribution" (27, emphasis added). Given the speaker's location in the imagined ruins of Barclays Bank, the comment seems to extend the banking metaphor, temporizing historical debt as some kind of future assurance. The word *hold,* however, seems queerer still. For in our moment of finance capital, banking institutions like Barclays "hold" another's debt as a securitized asset of their own, ready to be bundled and resold for even greater financial gain. From the perspective of the lender, debt is yet another instrument of capitalist accumulation.[2] From the perspective of those living under its unbearable weight, Kincaid suggests, there is a greater historical debt—an uncollateralizable and unmarketizable *moral* debt—*owed* by entities like Barclay and *owned* by the speaker and "people like" her. Yet by "holding" retribution—withholding it in the present but retaining it in perpetual reserve—the speaker emphatically rejects the injunction to "forgive and forget." Indeed, as the speaker realizes, retribution appears recalcitrant to the language of debt, since debt—like certain liberal forms of redress and reparative justice I discussed in chapter 1—is founded on the presumption that it *can* be repaid (even if by personal indenture) or otherwise be forgiven. As David Graeber has argued, there simply is no such thing as an "unpayable debt," for something given or taken that cannot be repaid cannot be considered debt in the first place.[3] Thus, the beneficiaries of colonial and neocolonial expropriation cannot be foreclosed upon (they are simply "too big to fail"), while the historical cost to those who appear to own nothing (not even their own debt) continues to accumulate, not as moral debt but as political capital—the accumulating potential of material tribulation.

Kincaid's speaker is not demanding payment but speculating on payback. Historical debt is just another toxic asset.

John and David Barclay, the brothers Kincaid references, were indeed deeply entangled in the Atlantic economy, including the slave trade; but they were not, as it turns out, slave traders in the sense Kincaid suggests. Nor did they transition their enterprise from the business of slave trading to the business of banking upon the abolition of the trade in 1807. But they were, for a time, owners of a Jamaican grazing farm, Unity Valley Pen, on which thirty-two Africans were enslaved, property the brothers "received" when its owner defaulted on a debt. A Quaker and long supporter of slave-trade abolition and, like Granville Sharp, of a "gradual" emancipation, David Barclay asked the overseer to manumit the slaves on his newly acquired plantation, but his request was never carried out. When John Barclay died, David inherited the farm in full and again endeavored to free the Africans still laboring on *and as* his property, but pressure from other slave owners on the island complicated his effort. David Barclay recounts his experiences as a slave owner and frustrated, philanthropic liberator in an 1801 treatise, *An Account of the Emancipation of the Slaves of Unity Valley Pen, in Jamaica.*[4] As the title suggests, the problem of disposing with the thirty remaining Africans was gradually resolved. Barclay had the group, sixteen adults and twelve children (two others were too "infirm" to travel), removed to Philadelphia, where he had business interests. They were placed in the "protection" of the Society for Improving the Condition of Freed Blacks, which was charged with overseeing their apprenticeship in an appropriate trade. While the Barclay brothers may not have been the heartless slave traders Kincaid imagined, their imbrication in the nexus of finance, speculation, investment, debt, and the disposal of human bio-cargo cannot be dismissed.

Barclays is unlikely to ever return any of its unprecedented capital gains to those whose unprecedented losses—accumulated in labor and in lives—made it possible. History is misconstrued, Kincaid seems to be suggesting, when it is recast in the language of redemption. By deciding against "unmaking" Barclays, and herself along with it, is Kincaid "making bank" on the futures of retribution? Or does she want to reframe entirely how one thinks about the strained analogies that arise when speaking the language of finance—between monetary debt and moral obligation, between economic exchange and spiritual redemption, between paying back and payback? Kincaid's narrative device helps illustrate how the life-making, death-letting, and death-meting power of biopolitics extends, extrajuridically, from the state to commercial enterprises, private interests, and the individual and corporate holders of wealth in the long history of capital accumulation under the regimes of colonialism and empire. Ultimately, by refusing forgiveness Kincaid concedes unpayability; but by naming and then holding back retribution, she *holds onto* the aleatory threat of terror posed by the forces assembled against global capital: the accumulating counterpower of human bio-cargo, constantly in circulation, forever in store.

Debt and slavery appear so historically entangled it would be impossible to think them apart, especially at a time in which the global reach of neoliberalism has brought the concerns over the politics of economic development expressed by the "Global South" so intimately in tune with the politics of austerity in the "Global North." In a recent study of 43,000 global corporations, a team of complex-systems analysts identified a "relatively small group of companies, mainly banks, with disproportionate power over the global economy."[5] Of the 147 "super-entities" that control most of the world's wealth, Barclays PLC was number 1.[6] Since its ascendance as a global financial institution, the bank has been shrouded in controversy, maintaining friendly relations with the apartheid government of South Africa and Robert Mugabe's Zimbabwe. It has faced accusations of facilitating money laundering for a rogues' gallery of despots and dictators, and in 2011 was the subject of a WikiLeaks document drop that exposed not only massive accounting irregularities but widespread, systematic, and highly consequential fraud. According to investigators, by fraudulently reporting its interbank lending rates in an effort to shield itself from the discovery of massive undercapitalization during the 2008 banking crisis, Barclays illegally manipulated both the London Interbank Offered Rate (Libor) and the Euro Interbank Offered Rate (Euribor), two critical indexes on which the interest rates of even the smallest borrowers depend.[7] What the Libor scandal shows us is that, even in its most abstract and immaterial appearance as "numbers" on a screen, the orchestration of debt as a mode of capitalist accumulation generates unanticipated consequences that are unevenly felt both individually and collectively. It would appear that the financial crisis of 2008 did little to change how securitized debt operates as a financial instrument or is regulated across global markets. It would be equally fair to say that Barclays, as Jamaica Kincaid long ago realized, remains the perfect emblem of modern global capital.

Although Antigua remains an important site in the network of global financial institutions and Internet ventures spread across the Caribbean—institutions famously engaged in dubious practices of offshore banking and online gambling—there is no longer a Barclays Bank on the island. In 2001 Barclays PLC merged much of its Caribbean operation with the Canadian Imperial Bank of Commerce (CIBC) to form FirstCaribbean International Bank. In 2006 CIBC purchased Barclay's stake in FirstCaribbean (43.7 percent of shares) for just under US$1 billion in cash. But the building on High Street remains, now under the sign of FirstCaribbean. It is right across the street from the Bank of Nova Scotia and the Royal Bank of Canada, and just up the street from the Eastern Caribbean Amalgamated Bank located on the fashionable Heritage Quay, a redeveloped and revitalized shopping area serving tourists from the island's resorts and the cruise ships at port in St. John's Harbour. But the lines of flight that draw a small, bygone branch of Barclays, an institution that inspired Jamaica Kincaid's dreams of violent retribution, into transnational networks of investment banking and global finance also bring it into view here, in a chapter on the redevelopment and revitalization of an English city. For standing in Queen Square, in the heart of the city of Bristol, thousands of miles from that island in the Caribbean, I glance across the street at yet another branch of Barclays Bank and Jamaica Kincaid immediately comes to mind. Because the history of colonialism that made Antigua—the history mapped on the geography of its towns, named on its street signs, stamped atop its buildings, and printed on the placards and hoardings that entice tourists to buy into such a small place—also made Jamaica Kincaid; and the history of modern enslavement that is written on every page of *A Small Place* is the same history that made the port city of Bristol. Just as the colonial past penetrates her everyday life and the lives of every other resident or former resident of Antigua, so too is it relayed here and now, passing into the lives of those who today live and work in the former colonial metropole. What vanishes from one place reappears in another; indeed, it becomes ubiquitous. The global trade in human lives—the extraction of living labor through submission to social death—haunts the orchestration of credit and debt in the current cycle of accumulation. The entire system of modern bio-cargo that continues to link one island to another is conveyed into the present by way of a closed bank and an open book. The relocation with which I began proves to be no relocation at all, for it is all right here in Queen Square, in the district of Redcliffe, in the city of Bristol. "There is the Barclays Bank," I recall to myself. There it is. Here I am. Is it retribution time? Or the day of jubilation?

Holding

Queen Square is a gorgeously restored park in what once was, and is now again, a fashionable city-center district. Named in 1702 in honor of Queen Anne, it was around this square that one would have greeted the now infamous merchants and financiers whose success enabled the town to develop as a major crossroad in global trade and, in the first half of the eighteenth century, Britain's largest slave-trading port. Many of the owners and investors who outfitted merchant ships for the Atlantic trade, or who owned and operated plantations in the colonies—or both—built attractive townhouses around Queen Square. Woodes Rogers remains perhaps its most remembered resident and the Merchant Venturers its most celebrated chartered society. The accumulation of wealth through finance and trade in the eighteenth century powered Bristol's emergence as a viable, competitive, industrial city by the nineteenth century. John Michael Rysbrack's 1733 statue of a triumphant William III, which still occupies the center of Queen Square, may stand as a monument to the city's ascendance, but the statue's neglect in the years following widespread civil unrest in the 1830s serves as an emblem of the cycles of prosperity and decline that continue to define the urban landscape of modern Britain.[8]

Conventionally referred to as the Queen Square riots, the events of the last three days of October 1831 are well rehearsed in the city's history, captured in numerous paintings and prints, described in local chronicles and personal letters, and now presented in tourist brochures and guided walks. Today, the story of the Queen Square riots is often retold as a satisfying sign of the city's tradition of nonconformist attitudes, or as a splash of local color added to an often unattractive picture. After Parliament twice failed to pass the Reform Bill, which would have modestly extended the franchise and eliminated the "rotten boroughs" endemic to Parliament at the time, supporters began to agitate against those politicians in most vocal opposition. When Charles Wetherell, then recorder of Bristol, arrived to open the assize law courts, he was met by a large assembly of outraged citizens hurling both words and refuse. An outspoken opponent of political reform, as well as adamantly opposed to the abolition of slavery and virulently anti-Catholic, Wetherell was also a longtime MP representing at various times constituencies scattered across the country—from Dorset to Sussex, Devon to Oxford, and at the time of the riots, way up in Yorkshire—to which he had only a tenuous connection. He was, in other words, the very face of the corrupt rotten-borough monger. After threatening the raucous protesters with arrest, Wetherell was forced from the law courts and chased through the narrow streets of the city, finding refuge at the Mansion House in Queen Square, residence of the Lord Mayor of Bristol Charles Pinney, a name to which I will return. As the small crowd grew, rioters ransacked the Mansion House and tried to set it ablaze. Wetherell escaped unharmed. With provisions raided from the Mansion House the assembly reveled through the night. On the following day the Mansion House was again attacked and this time burned to the ground, followed by the Custom House, Bishop's Palace, tollhouses, and other buildings representing the entrenched power of affluent merchants who ran the city as a self-elected, "close corporation." The crowd then stormed Bridewell Prison, releasing those arrested the night before as well as those awaiting trial under the ministry of Wetherell, before moving on to the new City and County Gaol and a smaller prison on Gloucester Road; each was destroyed by fire.

Although troops repeatedly confronted the rioters in the square, no clear order of force had been given so the local commander ordered his troops to stand down before retiring for the night. The following day a frustrated lower-ranking commander ordered his troops to attack the demonstrators with force, using sabers rather than munitions, which led to hundreds of casualties gruesomely killed or wounded. Queen Square was utterly destroyed, with almost every building ransacked and burned to the ground. Over a hundred participants were later arrested and, in the following spring, tried by a special commission. Several received long prison sentences while others transportation to the colonies. Five were executed. The riotous scenes that unfolded in Queen Square over the next three days was captured in a series of paintings and etchings by local artists—William James Müller and Thomas Leeson Rowbotham in particular—from the immediacy of celebratory crowds gathered around Rysbrack's monument in Queen Square, to the commanding view of the city afforded by the prospect from the hills near Clifton, to the violent assault on the crowd by the local militia (see Figures 35 to 37). It is a powerful visual archive that competes with the written record left by city officials and political commentators at the time.

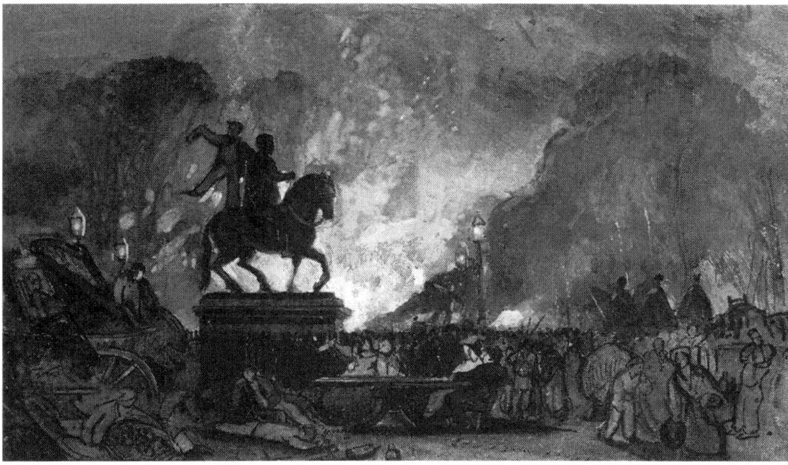

Figure 35. William James Müller, Queen Square during the Bristol Riots, 30th October 1831, *1831. Watercolor on paper, 14 x 22.9 cm. Private Collection/Courtesy of Bridgeman Images.*

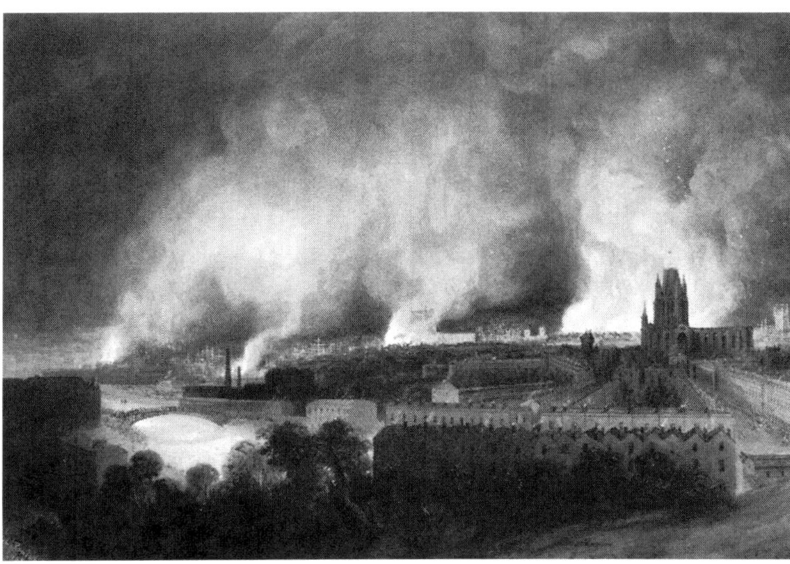

Figure 36. Thomas Leeson Rowbotham, Bristol Seen from Pile Hill on the Night of October 30th, 1831, *1832. Watercolor on paper. Copyright by Bristol Museum and Art Gallery, UK/Bridgeman Images.*

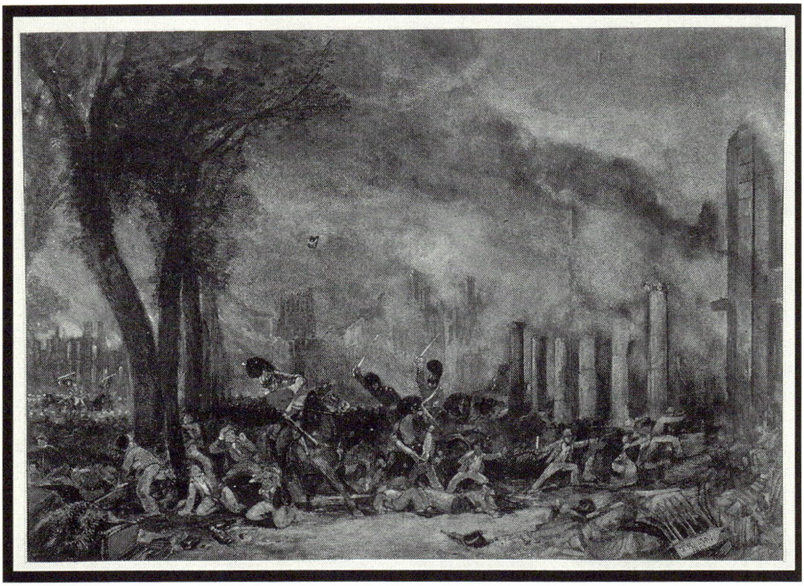

Figure 37. Thomas Leeson Rowbotham and William James Müller, Charge of the 3rd Dragoon Guards in Queen Square, Bristol, Monday 31st October 1831, *1833. Pencil, watercolor, and gouache on paper. Copyright by Bristol Museum and Art Gallery, UK/ Bridgeman Images.*

In a keen observation on the geography of civil disobedience captured in Müller and Rowbotham's depictions of the Queen Square riots, then on exhibit at the Bristol Museum, a group of Bristol historians remarked that, far from appearing as a chaotic expression of "mob" violence, the rioters "had clearly been organised enough to traverse the city, picking targets and dispatching them with precision"—an assessment that runs counter to the authorized history of this and other urban uprisings as instances of unwarranted and uncontrolled violence and indiscriminant destruction. From within the same visual archive that is assumed to represent the disorder of the riot, these viewers detected a powerful record of its *strategic order,* a series of "precision strikes" against the ruling class that left undisturbed "the working class districts south of the river [and] the poorer neighbourhoods local to the fires."[9] Contrasting the conventional assumption of views from "above" and those from "below," depicted from amid the revelers intimately amassed in the square, the scene appears one of chaos, confusion, and criminality; regarded from the commanding view of the hill, however, it appears nothing less than a disciplined and deliberative collective action. This interpretation comports with several nineteenth-century accounts of the riots, some of which distinguish between a smaller, more tactically minded group led by radical reformers, which are nonetheless described as "gangs" of petty criminals let loose upon the largely unguarded town. In a letter composed in the immediate aftermath of the riot, the Reverend J. L. Jackson offers a compelling account of the uprising, describing the scene in strikingly sympathetic terms: not as a riot but a "ferment"; not a mob but a "multitude," a "populace," an "assembly" of the "greater masses"; property is "destroyed," but the people are "slaughtered."[10] Despite his ultimate condemnation, Jackson's letter, like Müller and Rowbotham's paintings, reminds us that the view from below is sometimes surreptitiously captured by, and archived in, those decidedly above.

Queen Square was eventually rebuilt, but in the century that followed this area of Redcliffe would no longer be fashionable. A burst of economic growth between the wars brought about sprawling suburban expansion and in the 1930s Queen Square was virtually paved over. Heavily bombed during World War II, Bristol was rebuilt with an eye toward the infrastructure then most needed in a modern industrial city—roads. For the next six decades the Inner Circuit Road cut a broad diagonal swath across the square, hedged in by forecourt parking along its periphery. After decades of deterioration, in the late '90s Queen Square was once again—and more fully—restored. And while the Queen Square riots continue to be recounted in the modulated inflections of tour guides and travel brochures as a proud, historically remote and socially benign moment in the city's storied past, they also remain lodged in the city's political unconscious as an important touchstone of spontaneous collective action. Surveying the beautifully manicured lawn of today's Queen Square, dotted with lunchtime picnickers and well-rested tourists, I imagine those more raucous working-class revelers who held the city in common for three short autumn days.

In the eighteen years of Thatcherism and thirteen years of Blairism that followed, Britain's urban landscape would be reshaped in sometimes stunning, frequently devastating, and often racialized ways. Government policies valorized private property and rewarded individual property ownership, while actively dismantling many forms of collectivization, which led to deepening poverty in increasingly racially and economically isolated neighborhoods.[11] One cannot reflect on the events of 1831 without now thinking about the riots that broke out "spontaneously" across the UK in 2011, or of the series of disturbances that punctuated the 1980s to which they were compared. While the 1981 Brixton riot is perhaps the most remembered expression of Thatcher-era discontent, that event was preceded by almost a year here in Bristol, only a mile or so north of Queen Square in the district of St. Pauls, initiating a period of violent confrontations across the UK that would continue into 1981 and erupt again in 1985.[12] The St. Pauls riot erupted after a police raid on the popular Black and White Café in the spring of 1980, but like the urban uprising that followed, it was forged in the crucible of racialized deprivation and social exclusion, institutional racism and police brutality, and exacerbated by the prime minister's vocal disdain for antiracist social movements and disparagement of immigrant communities—attitudes well established during the '79 campaign—which did much to antagonize already volatile relations between working-class white and black populations.[13] Indeed, the social agitation that followed from the frustrated efforts at political reform in 1831 echo in the social unrest in the wake of Thatcher's election and the end of the postwar settlement; and do so again after the postcrisis election of the Tory government in 2010, initiating what Prime Minister David Cameron himself called the "age of austerity."[14]

In August 2011, discontent over both the immediate and the long-term consequences of austerity, as well as long-standing anger over systemic racism and racialized police brutality, came to a head in the London borough of Tottenham with the murder of Mark Duggan by the Metropolitan Police. What began as a protest march from the Broadwater Farm social-housing estate to the local police station developed into insurrection on Tottenham High Road. Then came a series of more forceful attacks—organically and strategically coordinated by way of mobile technology and social media—on shops and businesses at the Tottenham Hale Retail Park and in nearby Wood Green. In the days that followed, the upheaval spread across London and to the deindustrialized cities of the west and northwest (among them Bristol, Liverpool, Manchester, and Birmingham) as young people from some of the most impoverished areas in the UK took to the streets. Coinciding with popular efforts to retake the urban commons in cities around the world in 2010 and 2011, however, the riots were situated within a historical moment of massive organized resistance but also at a time in which such efforts were becoming less and less viable as effective actions against state policies; and at a time in which even the most legitimate expressions of opposition were met with shocking levels of militarized suppression by the state.[15] The "age of austerity" is also "the age of riots," to borrow Joshua Clover's expression.[16]

Despite their coincidence with protests against austerity led by student groups and strikes organized by trade unions in the UK, the 2011 riots were regarded in the popular media as isolated and sporadic, the insufficiently motivated action of a handful of malcontents, and outliers to and disconnected from any legitimate concerns raised in the wake of economic crisis. Public condemnation was almost universal.[17] State and corporate media reports duly repeated the general attitude and conventional wisdom of government officials and political commentators: these were riots, not protests; occasions for wide-scale looting and indiscriminate destruction; violent unrest among the urban poor is unrelated to the low-grade discontent expressed by working and middle classes and aimed narrowly at government mismanagement and corporate malfeasance; the latter were led by otherwise respectable students and labor leaders, the former was the work of thugs instigated by gang leaders or other criminal delinquents. "Britain's 2011 riots," lamented the liberal *Guardian,* had "become a defining contest between disorder and order," and "in that contest . . . there is only one right side to be on."[18] Others denied either the legitimacy of the social discontent or the political context in which the rolling attacks occurred. If the rioters could be described as disaffected, critics suggested, they were so by choice, or by a sense of entitlement engendered by the misguided policies of the welfare state. In a time of an acknowledged financial crisis, staggering levels of unemployment, and massive reductions to vital services in health care and housing, those living at the farthest margins of economic and social life were viciously discredited in the same classed and racialized rhetoric that had justified centuries of African enslavement, on the one hand, and forced industrial labor, on the other: the population who rioted were indolent, lacked the initiative to improve their lives, were content to live off the goodwill and charity of others, and were incapable of self-sufficiency, a value, we are told, that resides at the very heart of the true English character. By reframing social unrest and political dissent as either criminally dangerous, laughably absurd, or naïvely fashionable, state and corporate interests set to work containing opposition by reappropriating insurgency as a signifier of the market. Responding on air to massive organized strikes in November 2011, which the Trade Union Congress described as "the biggest in a generation," a notoriously combative Jeremy Clarkson feigned outrage as he declared on BBC, "I would have them all shot. . . . I would take them outside and execute them in front of their families," harkening back to the massacre that concluded the 1831 Queen Square riot and the executions that followed.[19]

The riot, as E. P. Thompson acknowledged long ago, is difficult to reconcile with either liberal or radical politics, the former regarding it as fundamentally anathema, the latter as essentially futile. Yet the spontaneous eruption of collective action exhibited many of the characteristics of political expression.[20] Such popular insurrections, however, often manifest alongside other more formally legitimized political arenas or more recognizable political actions—organized protests, marches, strikes, boycotts, and occupations, itself a contested tactic that synthesizes direct political action and civil disobedience—as a response to the very conditions of exclusion that come to define liberal politics as a site of foreclosure. With rapid deindustrialization in much of the West, the collapse of organized labor, divestment of the welfare state, and intensified forms of urban enclosure—the hallmarks of neoliberalism in the Global North—one can hardly be surprised that a new age of riots, transnational in scope, should appear in response. Rather than viewing the riot as not-quite politics of the disengaged, or the not-yet politics of the disenfranchised—both versions of what Alain Badiou characterizes as a nascent *proto-politics*—the popular uprisings of the 1980s, like those at the two ends of my periodization (1831 and 2011), might be described as the yet-quite politics of the grievously dispossessed, *para-political* eruptions that occur at those times in which the sanctioned institutions of the political are effectively foreclosed to the popular.[21] Referencing Thompson's framework of a preindustrial "moral economy," Clover observes that the riot is not essentially an intervention into the arena of circulation but an action at the site of production as the marketplace displaces the workplace as a staging-ground for action. The "circulation strike," as he calls it, should also be distinguished from protest carried out at the level of consumption, such as the consumer boycott, the generally legitimized but largely ineffectual liberal response to the changing conditions of political economy. Inasmuch as the market is closed to those without the means or resources required to gain entry, it remains a site of political foreclosure. Subsequently, those spaces adjacent to the marketplace offer attractive locations for articulating social, political, and economic exclusion at—and more to the point, across—the thin boundary that separates the public from the private.

The shattered glass, splintered doors, tattered signs, repurposed garbage bin and retooled newspaper racks, and uprooted postboxes that litter the streets in front of the looted shop in the aftermath of a riot represent that material breach through which rioters advance along the local high street. The characterization of the riot as a para-politics to the occupation, then, helps elucidate the relationship between various actions over the course of 2011, wherein there is a shift from the demand to seize the means of production to the drive to occupy those already fully surveilled and heavily policed slivers of the urban common not already fully subsumed by the private holders of the market itself. While they might not add up to a single coherent revolutionary movement—even as they are now often consolidated under the banner of Occupy—these postcrisis upheavals should be understood as a consequence of the same neoliberal policies that have swept postindustrial economies worldwide and that remain in place in the UK today under the leadership of Cameron. They should also be situated within the neoliberal projects of urban redevelopment that, like the uprisings that fomented in the new industrial cities of the nineteenth century, appear as singular articulations in the long, continuous history of public discontent violently expressed when private interests seize the commons and the commonweal of the people.[22]

Trafficking

Standing at the water's edge in the heart of Bristol, one feels long historical concurrencies reverberate across an elegant pedestrian bridge spanning a narrow cut extending north from Bristol Harbour. Pero's Bridge, as it came to be called, links the historical buildings of Redcliffe to leisure and entertainment venues around Millennium Square and along Harbourside, two city-center locations whose redevelopment in the late 1990s and 2000s was fraught with tension and conflict. In late 1998, shortly before the new—and as-yet unchristened—footbridge was scheduled to open, the local politician and member of the European Parliament Ian White proposed that it be named in honor of a long-overlooked figure in Bristol's maritime history, an African who had served in a local residence for over fifteen years in the later part of the eighteenth century but who was known only by the name given by those who enslaved him: Pero. By doing so, White reasoned, the city would officially acknowledge its institutionally unrecognized entanglement with the long history of colonialism, the African slave and plantation slavery trade in particular. The gesture would pay worthy tribute to those enslaved Africans whose lives and labor enabled the emergence of Bristol as a modern, industrial city. White's proposal was not met with enthusiasm by project developers, who wanted a name that "reflects all that is great about Bristol."[23] Helen Holland, then chair of the city's planning committee, suggested that the name should serve as a "symbol for the new Bristol," which, if not quite in contradiction with the developer's equally ambiguous aim, was certainly a complication of it. Anticipating public controversy, a nervous Bristol City Council proposed a citywide poll on potential names. Despite vocal opposition to the name, by the time of its dedication two hundred years after his death, Pero's Bridge it would be (see Figure 38).[24] Dubbed, in a platitude nothing short of cringe-worthy, "the bridge across time," Pero's Bridge does double duty as a commercially functional memorial to the history of the slave trade and, as Holland had hoped, a key "symbol," in the city's rebranding as a tourist destination, appearing in almost every redevelopment brochure and planning document the city has since produced.

The sparsely detailed story of Pero Jones is now well rehearsed in local history, but in the late 1990s his name was largely unknown. According to

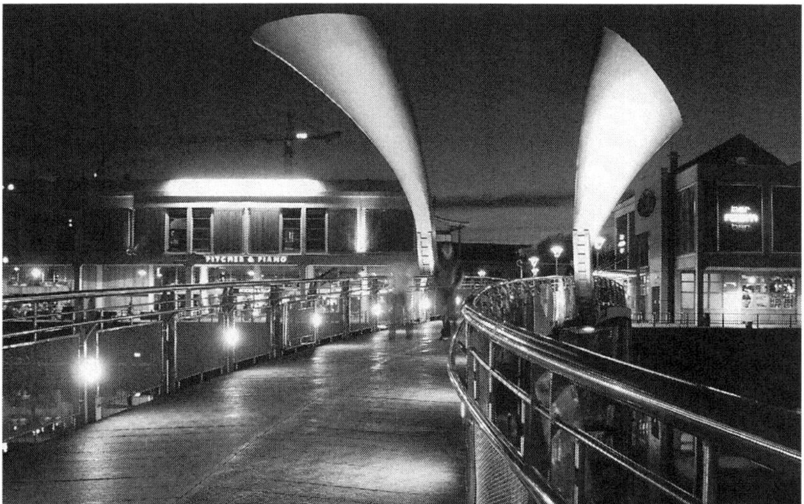

Figure 38. Pero's Bridge, Bristol, UK. Photograph by David Pilgrim.

a handful of extant commercial and private documents, Pero was purchased at age twelve on the island of Nevis by the plantation owner and sugar merchant John Pinney. He was transported to Bristol in 1783, at about age thirty, where he remained in service to the Pinney household until his death in 1798. Until 1999 there had only been one public memorial acknowledging Bristol as a major slave-trading port, a small plaque placed two years earlier quayside on the L Shed building. Donated by Ian White and Philippa Gregory, the author of *A Respectable Trade* (1992), a popular novel set in late eighteenth-century Bristol, it read in part: "In memory of the countless African men, women and children whose enslavement and exploitation brought so much prosperity to Bristol through the African slave trade." If the quayside plaque captures the defensive posture of incalculability—the countless human lives whose enslavement brought immeasurable wealth—Pero's Bridge serves as a singularly ambivalent and ambiguous figure calculation: a metonym for the one slave city history remembers, but a synecdoche for all those nameless others that remain part of its "forgotten" past.

To be sure, Pero's Bridge is stunningly beautiful as it spans St. Augustine's Reach. The two sculptural "horns" gracefully balanced on either side of a double leaf bascule—practical yet elegant counterweights for raising and lowering its central span—evoke the deep melancholy moan of ships navigating through the fog on their way to safe harbor. Designed by the artist Eilis O'Connell and engineered by the renowned British firm Arup, the bridge has garnered extensive media attention and critical acclaim primarily for the poise of its outsized horns and the gentle curve of its three spans.[25] While the horns have certainly contributed to its iconicity, they are also a reminder that the bridge was not designed as a memorial to Pero Jones or anyone else subjected to the atrocities of the slave trade, violence of the plantation, or the outrages of domestic service, registering as they do a much more palatable history of maritime trade in the era of steamships that dominated the seas in the decades following the abolition of slavery in the British colonies and many decades after the abolition of the slave trade. Although Pero's Bridge represents a wonderful orchestration of architectural design and civil engineering, successfully balancing the tension between form and function, the discordance between its purpose as a pedestrian conveyance between two sites of city-center redevelopment and its status as a site of historical reparation signals a number of racial, economic, and ideological conflicts that would soon erupt at the intersection of the commemoration and regeneration. The sound still echoing across

Pero's Bridge turns out to be an old argument over public history, public–private partnership, and shape of the city in postwar, postcolonial, post-Thatcher, multicultural Britain.

While Bristol's historical involvement in the slave trade and plantation system likely comes as no surprise, that city and civic leaders now aspire to regain its status as a "global city" of high-tech engineering, high-finance capital, high-street shopping, high-end real estate, and, most importantly, high-traffic tourism, very well might. In the decades following the turmoil in St. Pauls, Bristol was mostly known for its underground subcultures, alternative vibe, and cutting-edge music scene, which grew out of the reggae and punk movements of the '70s and had, by the '90s, consolidated into a distinct "Bristol Sound."[26] Today, that sound is also associated with a group of graffiti artists, spoken-word performers, and radical activists who define the city's cultural scene. The street artist and global activist icon Banksy—who was born in Bristol and for years treated as a pariah by authorities—is nothing short of a local hero. Many of Bristol's best-known artists grew up in inner-city neighborhoods like Easton, St. Pauls, and Knowle West, working-class communities hard-struck by the changing economic conditions of the city and areas that continue to be identified as some of the most deprived in the UK.[27] Once anathema to the city's sense of order and industry, urban subcultures associated with the Bristol Sound are now celebrated as the source of the frenetic energy the city hopes to sell. Since the arrival of market-led and city-facilitated regeneration in the late 1990s, urban planners have tried to leverage the success of these artists and the popularity of their "sound" into a commercial branding campaign aimed at enticing the industries of the so-called new economies to relocate to its redeveloping urban core. Since the 1990s, the city has embarked on a number of large-scale redevelopment projects that have utterly transformed the built environment and social demographic of its central areas. The dismantling of an old infrastructure of production (factories and power plants; roadways, rail yards, and loading docks, all deemed redundant) has cleared the way for a new infrastructure of consumption (leisure facilities and pedestrian malls; green belts, heritage trails, and tourist sites) and has been hailed as both economic miracle and *aesthetic* improvement.

Bristol's economic resurgence in the areas of finance and trade; aerospace manufacturing and other specialized military technologies; the construction of enormous, and enormously fashionable, shopping outlets and successful expansion of international tourism; the real estate boom that accompanied the rebuilding of its city center—all these have overshadowed the precipitous decline in the overall welfare of those experiencing persistent economic deprivation and entrenched forms of social exclusion. At the heart of Bristol's aspirations, however, resides a powerful nostalgic belief in the splendor of the city's history as a center of global trade, an outsized faith in the market to generate new wealth through unprecedented returns on high-stake investments, and a naïve hope for an easy passage into the high-tech, knowledge-based economy that neoliberal economists had long been promising. Through the gentrification of its core districts, planners and developers strategically relegated the city's history to the background, where it could provide an attractive urban décor suited to an enjoyable shopping experience, valued only to the extent that it accumulates today the promises of a greater return tomorrow. Only in the last couple of decades has Bristol's position as one of Britain's largest slave-trading ports in the eighteenth century begun to receive sustained critical attention and public scrutiny. Indeed, the history of slavery and the slave trade has become a particularly volatile point of local contention. To speak too critically of the city's former status as a powerful engine in the transatlantic slave trade—or about the historical involvement of the same civic institutions that now drive the city's economic rebirth—inevitably leads to public discord and outspoken dissent, two values at odds with the picture of quirky harmony the city tries to project. But given the "coincidence" of the city's commitment to neoliberal redevelopment and the contested debate over how the public should remember the city's violent colonial past, the attempt to restore Bristol's prominence as a global city must be thought back through its long history as a central axis in the system of modern human bio-cargo.

The restoration of Queen Square and the construction of Pero's Bridge coincided with an explosion of urban regeneration in Bristol and throughout the UK, beginning in the late 1990s, which has significantly reshaped and redefined the turn-of-the-millennium city. Subsequently, the city offers a powerful case study in the concurrency of economic redevelopment and the "wrangling and hoarding" of the city's history as a major node in the circuits of human bio-cargo. For those communities left out of the fleeting economic booms of late-century finance capital, who also pay the highest price for the chronic economic busts that follow, the stakes of urban redevelopment are very high. Given the way in which economic risk is now redistributed from private interests to the public coffers—a banner characteristic of neoliberalism that mirrors the privatization of government services and public property—the conflict over access to collective goods and common spaces is hardly unexpected. That this conflict is often staged as a struggle over the very nature of collective memory or the role of public history might be more surprising. As I will show, the city common has reemerged as a crucial venue for staging alternate historiographies of global modernity, a site where history can be performed against commodification. While city planning and development may operate on principles that appear ahistorical, the desire for an urban "renaissance" founded upon city-center "regeneration" is deeply biopolitical; and the vision of the city as a site for the production of human bio-cargo is housed in the archive of urban regeneration.

To get at these concurrencies more fully, I want to situate the market-driven schemes for urban regeneration in the wake of neoliberalization with the projects and performances of public history by a number of artists, activists, and organizations over the last two decades, performances and actions that try to retake the urban commons enclosed by state privatization. Redevelopment schemes and policy proposals turn out to be especially valuable materials for thinking about the processes of housing and unhousing the history of the colonial metropole and the individuals and communities that populate it. They are especially meaningful when brought into relation with the differently constituted publics and counterpublics that are engaged in the concurrent practices of history making and community building in opposition to the neoliberal state and the agents of capital accumulation. In order to unhouse the history and historicity of urban redevelopment, I draw into constellation an archive of institutional planning and an archive of popular dissent as affective as it is performative. That is, I draw upon the mountain of planning documents stored in city archives in order to map out a plan of withdrawal from the archive of urban regeneration already set in motion. Here I aim to show how traces, resonances, intersections, assemblages, and alliances, once brought into constellation, offer new forms of local and global worlding that make powerful claims on the right not only to freely *traffic* in urban space but to *hold* the city in common, and to open the trafficking city up to others as a safe harbor from the storm of global capital and the strain of neoliberalism.

"Regeneration" has been a buzzword for national urban policy since the Thatcher era, but only in the late 1990s did it emerge as an almost transparent code word for the devolution of authority over urban planning and, more crucially, full-on privatization. After the Conservative takeover in

1979, and the launch of their radical program of deindustrialization, urban policy had focused on a half-hearted combination of small, targeted incentives for private investment in areas with the highest concentrations of economic deprivation, reflecting Thatcher's enthusiasm for unregulated business and disdain for the unregulated poor. Urban regeneration was imagined less as a *solution to* the economic despair brought about by radical deindustrialization than as a means of *capitalization on* the ensuing symptoms of national ennui. By exacerbating and then leveraging class resentments—now agonistically racialized—those on the losing end of Thatcherism were brought into sometimes violent conflict, a situation the government cultivated, then publicized. Urban regeneration became synonymous with "slum clearing," the fiscal and social abandonment of the council estates, especially densely populated tower blocks, and the wide-scale dislocation of residents. Since those initial Conservative-led initiatives, the strategy of state devolution—the transfer of management and oversight from the national government to local authorities—has led to continually shifting centers of decision-making, regulation, and control, and policies of "cost-shifting" and "burden-sharing" that, in effect, choke off state funding in order to secure the acceptance of corporate intervention. Established by central-government mandate, a string of regionally and locally "devolved" urban development corporations, nominal "public–private partnerships," orchestrated what would prove to be a wholesale abrogation of the commonweal in favor of an opportunistic seizure of rights and resources by corporate real estate developers and their private investors, who in turn would reshape the built environment of the postindustrial city and reorganize the relationship between individuals, communities, capital, and the state. If council housing—whether in towering inner-city blocks or sprawling suburban estates—represents an unabashed form of big-state biopolitics, "urban regeneration" names its insidious, privatized extension across class lines.

Following the 1997 change in government, urban redevelopment was rebranded an "Urban Renaissance," as aspirational expression for the dramatically scaled-up redevelopment initiatives launched by the market-friendly, image-savvy, bureaucratic modernizers of New Labour. Urban development corporations were replaced by "regeneration partnerships" charged with establishing "core strategies" reflecting a defined national "vision" and "local plans" responsive to market "realities." That government-mandated vision was developed by the Urban Task Force, a body of planning, architecture, and design experts appointed in 1998 by Deputy Prime Minister

John Prescott and led by Richard Rogers, and articulated in its report, *Towards an Urban Renaissance,* a document that would prove remarkably influential in the decade that followed. Ultimately the task force established three core tenets to guide twenty-first-century city planning: "principles of design excellence, social well-being and environmental responsibility."[28] Their broad, three-part mandate is notable for having elevated "environmental responsibility" as a concern for civic life and for placing, rhetorically and causally, "design excellence" ahead and above "social well-being." As a norm, social well-being—like design excellence—hovers in abstraction, and environmental responsibility is reduced to a vague concern over energy use, carbon emissions, and global climate change. In their attempt at ecological worlding, the task force appears oblivious to the relationship between the micro-ecologies of neighborhoods, streets, and homes and the macro-ecologies of region, nation, or world. *Towards an Urban Renaissance* is uncritical of what counts (or matters) as good design for communities already marginalized by both the state and private capital; and uninterested in the implications of persistently uneven access to resources in the norming of energy use. A more historically circumspect vision might have spoken more powerfully to communities locked into a long cycle of economic deprivation and social exclusion, imagined social responsibility as integral to excellent design, or addressed how social excellence might be achieved through the greater well-being of individuals and communities living in and moving through urban environments.

In the collaboratively written *Cities of the Many Not the Few,* the urban geographer Ash Amin and his colleagues describe this "design-led" vision of redevelopment as reminiscent of "the urban environmental determinism of the 1960s" even as it evokes alarming scenes from "the Tory years, when local coalitions of property developers, business executives and development corporations—in blithe contempt of work and welfare—face-lifted city centers, warehouses, waterfronts, and derelict spaces as sites of consumption, play, spectacle and magnets for investment," such as those initial efforts along Bristol Harbour in the late '70s.[29] Although the Urban Task Force outlined nominal provisions for community participation and democratic consensus, their planning strategies explicitly aimed at reshaping the urban core "in the context of a global shift towards a knowledge economy based on intangible goods and communication technologies and knowledge workers," an approach, critics argued, that underestimated the importance of "traditional" economic sectors to the health of local communities and mainstream workers. The urban renaissance, according to Amin's group, sought nothing less than "the gentrification of the economy" itself, predicated on the assumption of "a world which is internationally connected to similar enclaves elsewhere," that "turns on 'global' connection," even while it remains "highly geographically concentrated," in which "the parts of an economy that do not fit the story of a change to 'the new' are conveyed into the dustbin of history" (18). By relying on the unrealized promises of a "knowledge economy" as *the* primary outlet for urban reintegration into the global market, the Urban Task Force produced a new urban imaginary founded on a precarious economic fantasy, one especially perilous for those already at the greatest risk of social exclusion and deprivation. It is not difficult to imagine how or why the rewards produced by the most celebrated features of the new economy—such as "'fast' networked, non-hierarchical forms of corporate organization," "new working practices" and "flexible job situations," "intangible goods" and "weightless" commerce, all enabled by the revolution in digital information and communication technologies—would remain difficult to distribute equitably. While purportedly new "global flows" made possible by "open markets" are presented as an elegantly horizontal mode of immaterial production, they function as an unremittingly vertical mode of capitalist accumulation, redistributing wealth to the increasingly few. Meanwhile, labor markets became increasingly volatile, wages remained stagnant, and a debt crisis of unimagined proportions loomed.

Between the adoption of Bristol's Local Plan at the end of 1997 and its replacement by the Core Strategy for Regeneration in 2011, city leaders have produced a flood of planning documents and strategy papers through which they attempt to identify and "brand" the city's most recognizable and marketable "characteristics," often by instrumentalizing difference, diversity, creativity, and dissent in a vision of the postindustrial city that is dangerously homogenous and utterly banal.[30] Andrew Kelly's *Building Legible Cities* (2001), for example, describes one Bristol focus group convened to help develop an "identity system" suitable for city marketing and promotion. Asked to identify the city's "color," the group settled on blue, as a reminder of both its maritime history and the popular blue glass once manufactured there. Challenged to name its "persona," they selected Michael Palin of Monty Python fame, now a popular travel show presenter: like Palin, they agreed, the city is "quirky but classy," "distinguished but with an edge."[31] Subsequently, Bristol planners have carefully orchestrated the celebration of the city's "distinguished" yet "edgy" heritage as a center of global commerce, while cautiously managing the commemoration of its "quirky" but "classy" legacy as a powerful force in the development and maintenance of colonial slavery.

Heritage-driven redevelopment endeavors to enshrine the city's past in a provincial cultural chauvinism while attempting to revitalize its urban core as a center of global trade, pitting an economy of consumption (shopping and tourism) against an economy of "weightless" production (finance and technology). Against vocal opposition from a number of constituencies across the city, the ruling council has settled on a series of short- and long-term planning strategies for refashioning the built environment, making it more attractive to property developers and more conducive to large commercial outlets into downtown Bristol. As public funding and government-backed private investment began to pour into the initial city-center redevelopment schemes, neighborhoods experiencing the greatest deprivations remained neglected.[32] As I have been arguing throughout this book, such projects are not simply economic; they are biopolitical. The social reengineering, geographic remapping, architectural refashioning, and environmental rehabilitating of lived space through the expansion of the technologies of human bio-cargo is made evident in a city like Bristol—so evident, in fact, that planning requires new strategies of masking older, historical social relations as lives are reshuffled and placed in new hands. Marketing, publicity, graphic design, slick technologies and slicker advertising campaigns, and the surfeit of planning documents circulating in the public sphere: no longer exclusively the purview of the corporate state, urban policy is handed over to corporate interests but always under the banner of strategic partnership, community involvement, and government transparency. By narrowly circumscribing public participation, city officials and corporate investors are able to manufacture consent among communities with significantly divergent interests, and to cultivate a population conducive to new consumer logics. The time and expense agencies have been willing to give to hundreds of strategy papers and planning documents since the late 1990s and throughout the 2000s—beautifully designed, elegantly laid out, carefully worded, and richly produced—suggests their enormous value as guides for not only policy makers and planning technicians but also a range of "strategic partners" in local communities who could then see their future, and know that it is *theirs*, through the orchestration of good graphic design.

Read from this side of the 2008 financial crisis and the long economic downturn that followed—including policies of austerity that helped leverage crisis and collapse into a stunning period of financialized accumulation in the boardroom, on the one hand, and the militarized state response to forceful resistance in the street, on the other—the vision of the city offered in *Towards an Urban Renaissance* proved prescient, as we continue to observe the simultaneous retrenchment and abdication of the security state as it doubles down on technologies of power and control and doubles back on its commitment to social equality and economic well-being, once the foundational values of modern liberalism. We likewise witness the ongoing relocation of biopolitics to the private sphere. In its perverse echo of the vision of the garden city, redevelopment schemes that are "integrated with their surroundings," "maximize their potential by increasing density," "foster . . . a strong sense of community and public safety," and incorporate "the public space between buildings where people meet and move about" sound today like a blueprint for new urban enclosures made possible through the large-scale transfer of public space and community assets into private hands, the aggressive use of compulsory purchase orders by city planners, and, more recently, the continuing devolution of power to local authority mandated in the 2011 Localism Act. Despite the rhetoric of the urban renaissance, the objective of neoliberal regeneration is not easing economic deprivation or ameliorating social exclusion in those communities left at greatest risk following their institutional abandonment by the state. For these communities, urban renaissance means little more than gentrification, dispossession, and enclosure. But the syntagmatic slide from urban renewal to redevelopment to regeneration to renaissance signals something more: as a rather pedestrian rebranding of a historically resonant moment of national ascendency, or a functionally anodyne assurance of a viable future by the continually devolving state, or a portentous sign for neoliberalism's claim on life itself and the reentry of a precarious population into the circuits of modern human bio-cargo.

Harboring

If it is said that a rising tide lifts all boats, it is striking to recall that the city's most ambitious development effort occurred not at the turn of the twenty-first century but in the first decade of the nineteenth century: the construction of the New Cut tidal bypass and the reengineering of Bristol Harbour, a response to shifting maritime economy in the wake of the abolition of the slave trade.[33] With the completion of the Floating Harbour in 1809, the water level along the docks no longer rises and falls with the tide.

Despite improvements to its capacity, by the middle of the nineteenth century, commercial traffic had receded to the cheaper and more accessible docks downriver at Avonsmouth and Portishead. Like many cities associated with shipping and manufacture, Bristol remained in steady decline and the Floating Harbour commercially redundant—that is, until the mid-1970s, when the Arnolfini Gallery moved into a quayside warehouse, initiating the renovation of "brownfield" sites along the docks. In 1978 the city opened the Bristol Industrial Museum in a battery of abandoned "sheds" across the harbor on Prince's Wharf, registering the cornerstone of the "old economy" as a thing of the past. Two additional large art and media complexes followed in the early 1980s, the Watershed to the north along St. Augustine's Reach and Spike Island to the west between Cumberland Basin and the New Cut, both providing work and exhibition space for local artists and artisans. With the arrival of cultural venues along the water's edge, Bristol inaugurated its much-touted "creative" economy. City-center regeneration has been ongoing ever since.

By the late 1990s the entire area around Canon's Marsh was awash in redevelopment schemes as the city aspired to reclaim its international stature by transforming its run-down warehouses into a "tourist and cultural attraction on a global scale."[34] Launched under the banner of Bristol 2000 with a £41 million grant from the Labour government's Millennium Commission, initial Harbourside redevelopment proposals included a new science and technology exploratory branded as At-Bristol, or @BRISTOL, as per its logo. In addition, a proposed £83 million performing arts venue called the Harbourside Centre would represent "the jewel in the crown of Bristol's Harbourside."[35] Although the Harbourside Centre never materialized, a group of private investors, incorporated under the name Bristol Harbourside Sponsor's Group, together with another £18 million public-sector commitment by English Partnerships, proposed a massive, £93 million mixed-use housing, shopping, and entertainment complex that would include a four-thousand-seat Odeon cinema, a health and fitness center, a nightclub and casino, and a complement of trendy restaurants and pubs. Under the leadership of the powerful real estate development firm Crest Nicholson, the "Scene At-Bristol," as they called it, would link the private, commercial enterprises with other public–private sector "At-Bristol" attractions, promising "a hive of activity both day and night, giving the whole area a vibrant, lively feel" that would establish Canon's Marsh as the city's primary entertainment destination.[36] To be sure, by the turn of the millennium, as one area reporter put it, "industry [had] made way for leisure."[37]

Predictably, plans for commercial redevelopment on such an ambitious scale were met with considerable opposition. While the proposal for the science exploratory was largely welcomed by the public, and the performing arts center viewed as sorely needed, the housing and entertainment complex drew immediate criticism from the largely wealthy constituents in nearby Redcliffe, as well as historical preservationists led by the Bristol Civic Society. Dissatisfaction spread quickly to less affluent residents in surrounding areas—some already under threat from gentrification—which in turn led to a revolt within the City Council and a demand for a substantial redesign of the Harbourside scheme.[38] When the City Council failed to secure additional Arts Council lottery funding for the one project that garnered widespread support, the Harbourside Centre arts venue, prospects for city-center regeneration were thrown into disarray.[39] The following year, the revised proposal from Crest Nicholson was met with competition from an unsolicited plan drawn up by a well-respected local architect, George Ferguson—who in 2012 became the city's first popularly elected mayor—at the behest of the same alliance of wealthy locals and preservation groups that scuttled their initial scheme. Ferguson's "Little Venice" quickly gained popular support, while the residents and council members both remained unconvinced of Crest Nicholson's outsized and off-scale vision. As one Bristolian charged in a letter to the press, Crest's Scene At-Bristol was little more than a "vast leisure-box," a "backward-looking hotch-potch of failed ideas," a "sterile exercise in crash commercialism" whose only "bold vision" was "of enormous profits for people with little long-term interest in our city."[40] In a matter of weeks, the conflict over Harbourside regeneration had accelerated from a minor skirmish to an all-out war of words in the press, alarming already nervous investors.[41] By the time Crest Nicholson had produced a third set of revisions, in the midst of the spectacular millennial celebrations of 2000, the consequences of another failure were deemed by market-oriented city planners as potentially catastrophic, and the City Council felt it had little choice but to approve their proposal despite ongoing community protests.[42]

Between the late 1990s and the 2000s, derelict "brownfield" sites across the city's core, such as the sheds along the wharf, were targeted for redevelopment, primarily for leisure and entertainment activities geared toward middle-class residents living in the suburbs and tourists drawn to popular destinations in the west of England. But as controversies raged over regeneration, another conflict was starting to brew, this one over the derelict history housed within these same buildings and redevelopment sites. Redevelopment schemes and planning proposals at the turn of the millennium were met with almost constant protests by a wide range of community activists across the city, primarily over the systematic, institutional neglect of large swaths of the urban poor and the redirection of public resources into projects that would largely benefit those already well-off. Strikingly, these protests included remonstrations over Bristol's marketing campaign, which was intended to draw global attention to an urban renaissance in the making. Concurrent with costly proposals for city-center redevelopment was the growing demand by local activists and organizers that city and civic leaders begin to acknowledge, commemorate, and redress Bristol's historical relationship to members of its black and ethnic minority communities reaching back to the transatlantic slave trade and plantation slavery. The conflict, in short, wasn't about whether Bristol had been significantly involved in the slave trade, since all agreed it had, but about whether emphasizing that history—or history in general—was desirable in or even relevant to the present. Increasingly angry disagreements over the "collective good" of urban regeneration were mirrored in equally heated debates over Bristol's "collective memory."

For those invested in the work of various civic and amenity organizations, historical engagement meant celebrating the city's past and taking pride in its achievements, especially its maritime accomplishments. (That their pride might conceal an unacknowledged "collective shame" hardly seemed possible.) A purportedly "guilt-centered" public history hardly seemed compatible with city-center regeneration aimed at attracting consumers or conducive to selling the city to either locals or visitors. That the history of the slave trade might be repackaged into a commodity had yet to occur to city planners, a failure of imagination soon to be remedied. For those who believed that, an inclusive and unembroidered public history would aid in comprehending the broader legacies of the colonial past, which redounds in the everyday lives in the present. The insistence on a more equitable allocation of development resources, accompanied by calls for an inclusive public history of colonial slavery and the slave trade, led to a number of significant creative interventions—some, ironically, sponsored and/or sanctioned by the state—and powerful performances of the past that restaged Bristol's colonial past as a fundamental part of its postcolonial present. The confluence of development schemes and demands for a redressive public history continued as tensions over the vision and direction of redevelopment mounted, and the history of slavery became a public relations dilemma that city officials and corporate developers hoped the regeneration framework itself might successfully manage. Official, state-sanctioned, and government-sponsored accounts of Bristol's important role in the colonial economy—rehearsed through an array of private institutions, civic societies, and governing bodies—might satisfy the public's interest in the city's history, while containing the implications it might have on the present. To some, legacy appeared oppositional to heritage, which was about honor and dignity; to others, heritage mystified historical legacy.

The full transformation of Bristol from a center of manufacture and trade to one of tourism and consumption reached something like symbolic achievement with the closure of the Bristol Industrial Museum in 2006 and its reopening in 2011, following a £30 million renovation, as M Shed. In the language of urban regeneration, the dockside warehouse had been brought back into "productive use" as an important Harbourside attraction. Managed under the auspices of the Bristol City Museum, the M Shed is housed in the same 1950s transit and storage units as its predecessor—listed as the L and M sheds on Princes Wharf. The industrial museum, which first opened in 1977, had housed an array of objects related to the city's economic story as a center of maritime trade, shipbuilding, and manufacturing; the museum endeavored to preserve the feel of the working docks long after they had ceased to work—emblematized by the four still-functional loading cranes positioned just outside the museum's entrance. Despite the building's exterior, which has been left largely unaltered, the M Shed is as much a monument to gentrification as it is a throwback to the time of industry. The litheness and efficiency of its new name has the feel of corporate branding, while the interior combines a rehabbed loft aesthetic and modern office décor, performing something of a disavowal of its industrial history. At the same time, the restoration of key features of the dockside building marks a nostalgic return to the past, with all the sense of containment and control nostalgia aims to manage.

Before it closed for renovation, the Bristol Industrial Museum (BIM) had been listed as the first stop in the *Slave Trade Trail*, an official guidebook prepared for the Bristol Museum and Art Gallery by the excellent scholars and local historians Madge Dresser, Caletta Jordan, and Doreen Taylor.[43]

Developed in anticipation of a major exhibit set to open at the BIM in 1999, *A Respectable Trade? Bristol and Transatlantic Slavery* (the first local exhibition to address the city's relationship to the slave trade), the tour guide includes an impressive forty-three sites across a little over two square miles of the city center.[44] The walking tour was also the first significant step on the long and contentious road to official acknowledgment and perhaps to a new way of performing urban history. Like the redevelopment schemes discussed in sections above, the *Slave Trade Trail* serves as an aperture to both the uncomfortable relationship the city has with its past and to the relationship of city history to regeneration and the urban renaissance. Gathering just outside the museum, slave-trade tourists would follow a path that meandered along the quay, through Guinea Street and up to the Quaker burial grounds in Redcliffe; the walk then turned toward Queen Square, where it paused at the former homes of the eighteenth-century elite, now housing the offices of expensive solicitors and private physicians, as well as a small branch of a certain global financial powerhouse already mentioned; then from Queen Square to King Street and a large, modern office block where the historic Merchants' Hall (eighteenth-century headquarters of the Society of Merchant Venturers) once stood, a victim of the Blitz. The Merchant Venturers Almshouses building next door, however, remains; then on to Victoria Street, Seven Stars Pub, and Corn Street, where the important business of the trade was once conducted; more monuments, period homes, and historic churches would follow, until the tourist arrived in College Green, at the doorstep of the Georgian House Museum.[45]

Long a feature attraction of the city, the Georgian House Museum is owned by the city and administered through the Bristol City Museum. The home was built in the eighteenth century by one of the city's most prominent merchants. Since 1937, the Georgian House has been open to the public, serving as a proud, if subtle, showpiece for an important period in local history. Today it might be viewed as an emblem of the postindustrial city struggling to become a tourist destination, but in October 1998, the same year the City Museum introduced the *Slave Trade Trail* walking tour, the low-grade conflict over how the city remembers its past erupted into a fever of controversy when a protest was staged at the Georgian House: a site-specific performance intervention in the tradition of guerrilla theater. That prominent Bristol merchant, as you have probably already guessed, was the slave trader and plantation owner John Pinney, and the Georgian House the place where Pero had served.[46] The protesters were the all-male,

African American cast of David Feldshuh's 1993 play *Miss Evers' Boys,* then in performance at another of Bristol's renowned institutions, the Old Vic Theatre, which was also a stop on the slave trade trail.

If the Georgian House Could Speak, as the performance came to be called, was a one-time engagement. Partially planned, somewhat improvised, the play was developed and executed as a kind of occupation and an impromptu scene of historical and ideological contestation.[47] The purpose of the intervention was to provide a powerful counternarrative to the history on offer in the museum's guided tours or on its informational panels, both of which—according to the protesters—failed to provide an adequate or honest account of John Pinney's investments in the slave trade, the extent of his slave holdings, or the number of slaves held at his plantation on the island of Nevis, or by extension the intensity of the city's own debt to the institution on which its economic gains were established, and which its redevelopment continued to leverage. The popular upstairs/downstairs-style reenactments offered by museum volunteers did not mention the conditions of slavery on Pinney's plantation, Mountravers, nor did those other actors bother to tell visitors about the slaves Pinney brought home to Bristol. Pero, the only domestic slave whose name we know, was brought from Nevis to serve in the household, which he did for over thirty years. What information there was about Pero, or about the enormous holdings Pinney maintained in the West Indies, was provided in a set of five informational panels placed virtually out of sight in a small, cramped, uninviting and easily overlooked room off of the second-floor landing. In a prosecutorial tone, the performers expressed outrage over the way in which the history of Pinney's involvement in the slave trade and plantation slavery was, like that of the city as a whole, diminished and distorted—if not entirely obscured—by the official history printed on the small set of panels, which the museum's curators and administrators seemed almost too embarrassed to display. "This house is a testimony to the inhumanity placed upon my people," one performer intoned, but "it *should* be an indictment."[48]

Quartering

In late September 2008, on the eve of the global financial crisis, then characterized as a "credit crunch," a group of anticorporate activists hoisted a large banner atop the central tower of Bristol's latest regeneration scheme, partially obscuring—but also resignifying—a massive advertisement already wrapped around the top of the project's signature building. Timed to coincide with opening day of the massive outdoor shopping center Cabot Circus, their "subvertisement" read crunch cabot credit circus. The chaotic scene below indeed felt like a circus—an opening-day theme intended to play on the center's controversial name—with chockablock activities and performances staged to christen the 1.5 million square-foot and £500 million expansion of the Broadmead pedestrian mall. Also riffing on the circus theme, the banner underscored the spectacle of overconsumption fueled by the overextension of credit, the folly of city-center development driven by the accumulation of debt, and the recklessness of unrestrained speculation that would soon unravel into a full-blown economic recession. (The coming austerity would rip away much of what remained of an already frayed social safety net.) Within a week, the "credit circus" had lost its first retailer, the luxury men's clothing boutique Hardy Amies.[49]

As far as large-scale shopping centers go, Cabot Circus is certainly stunning. Encompassing three multilevel pedestrian streets that terminate at a striking, glass-domed central hub, the facility comprises over a hundred mostly corporate retailers, anchored by the high-end department store Harvey Nichols and serviced by a 2,500-space car park. In addition to its shopping and recreational attractions, Cabot Circus includes two hotels and a block of luxury flats. To avoid the drawn-out debacle that marked the Harbourside development, in late 2002 a consortium of corporate developers called the Bristol Alliance pitched their proposal to city officials in advance of statutory planning meeting and local consultations, securing their support well ahead of any public scrutiny. Over the objections of a number of community leaders and civic organizations, and with little public debate, the City Council moved quickly to approve the scheme. Disquiet continued into early 2003 as property owners living or operating along Broadmead received notices warning that compulsory purchase orders would be issued to those who failed to reach a sales agreement with the Bristol Alliance. Meanwhile, residents living in adjacent neighborhoods feared that the introduction of corporate retailers would force the closure of small locally owned shops, that the reorientation toward large commercial outlets would deplete much-needed social and community services, and that encroaching gentrification ultimately would force residents to relocate.[50] Major media outlets like the *Bristol Evening Post*—which had long proven loyal to the economic interests of property developers—rarely reported on local opposition to the Broadmead development.[51] Fueled by an appetite for hot-button issues and sensationalized controversy—and constrained by an aversion to substantive investigation and legitimate debate—the *Bristol Evening Post* found their scandal in an unanticipated dispute over a proposal by the Bristol Alliance to rename the Broadmead district in order to signal its "more cosmopolitan look."[52] According to the Bristol Alliance project director Philip Vaughan, because the "new city quarter" would bring together "Bristol's rich trading heritage with forward-looking retail opportunities," it was "essential that the name and brand identity reflect this." Vaughan added that the Bristol Alliance was "looking for an *evocative* name that creates a strong sense of identity—appealing not only to existing customers but also to visitors from outside the city."[53] The name they concocted: Merchants' Quarter.

In their zealous campaign to "rebrand" Broadmead—a name they viewed as obsolete, reminiscent of the area's shabby, unfashionable storefronts and outdated, postwar office blocks—the developers failed to consult with local constituents and interested "stakeholders." It therefore came as a surprise to the Bristol Alliance and their well-paid communication professionals that the name that emerged from their market-tested, focus group–driven exercises in product branding turned out to be more provocative than evocative. What Merchants' Quarter evoked, for many, was a long history in which wealthy local merchants profited from human cargo quartered in slave factories along the African coast, quartered on board slave ships crisscrossing the Atlantic, and quartered on plantations in the West Indies and the Americas. What the name provoked was frustration and outrage over the inability of city officials and planners to comprehend the connotations of their chosen terms or to understand why they mattered to residents living in surrounding neighborhoods, areas increasingly marginalized by the forces of regeneration; over the way in which city planning and development schemes continue to sanction ignorance of the colonial history of maritime trade and the path it cut toward Bristol's industrialization; over the disregard of the legacy of transatlantic slavery inscribed in social attitudes, policies, and practices that have left so many mired in a system of deprivation; over outrageously expensive redevelopment schemes that neglect the interests of neighborhoods and communities like theirs; over government policies and housing proposals that guarantee generations of the urban poor, both the deep-rooted and the newly arrived, will continue to be quartered in the inner-city wards and outer-borough estates now abandoned by the state. Like Bristol's corporate media and members of the City Council, Bristol Alliance was mystified by these protests. In public hearings and media reports, supporters of Merchants' Quarter fulminated against what they saw as the excesses of multiculturalism and political correctness, if not the excesses of immigrants and immigration policies themselves, launching invectives against the perceived "sensitivity" of protesters from black and ethnic minority communities. As Merchants' Quarter became a media circus, the city's proud heritage was making a farce of its shameful legacy.

The inability of so many elite stakeholders to comprehend why the naming of a massive mid- to high-end shopping venue would matter to so many speaks volumes about the failure of the proponents of the urban renaissance, including the original members of the Urban Task Force, to acknowledge how, as Amin's group insists, "space and power are intimately interconnected" in the "geographical organization of a city," and that acts of naming more than reflect the power to appropriate, they enact it. The name itself, Merchants' Quarter, like Pero's Bridge, exemplifies how power in and over space operates over long stretches of time. Few understand this as well as those living in communities adjacent to the city center. Unsurprisingly, perhaps the most forceful and successful opposition to the Broadmead expansion, and in particular to the name Merchants' Quarter, was led by a small community association working in Cabot neighborhoods adjacent to the north. St Pauls Unlimited, once the St Pauls Residents Group, would prove effective not only in securing the change in the center's name but in organizing the community in response to the threats that city-center regeneration posed to sustaining their own. Following their protests against Merchants' Quarter, the public was given a limited and highly managed opportunity to chime in on a more desirable name for the outsized complex through an informal referendum sponsored by the Bristol Alliance with the assistance of the *Bristol Evening Post.* Ultimately, participating Bristolians elected to honor—with abundant irony—a celebrated "local hero," the turn-of-the-sixteenth-century Italian explorer John Cabot (born Zuan Chabotto), who had come to Bristol in 1497 in order to prepare his historical voyage to Newfoundland under the flag of Henry VII. The alliance, however, was solely responsible for appending Circus to his name. To be sure, the new name aimed to evoke those frenzied centers of London tourism and retail—Oxford and Piccadilly Circuses—as well as Plymouth's Drake Circus, a similar large-scale redevelopment project that opened in 2006. The whimsy of the latter part of its name may have been at odds with the seriousness of its former name—and incongruent with its upscale retailers and promise of uptight patrons—but it certainly captured the tone of the spectacle surrounding the project's development.

The new name, Cabot Circus, gave developers an apt theme for the opening-day events filling the surfeit of open-air space beneath its crystalline dome: a more literal and thematically congruent spectacle: "Thousands of people packed Bristol's new £500m Cabot Circus shopping centre for its official opening ceremony," announced the BBC. "Drummers, dancers and high-wire performers entertained the crowds, until a circus master announced the opening of the stores at noon."[54] The previous day, the center's anchoring high-end department store, Harvey Nichols, featured a routine by the well-known burlesque artist Dita Von Teese, "who performed a striptease on a jewelled full-size carousel horse to an audience of about 100 VIPs." While the circus atmosphere surrounding its opening-day events belied the financial crisis unfolding across the globe, the Cabot Circus marketing director Julia Bowe remained publically unfazed, "confident people would spend money despite the economic slump." Bowe reassured reporters that while the "effects of the credit crunch are yet to be felt," and acknowledged that they "will affect all levels of society and of the high street," she nonetheless insisted that retailers like Harvey Nichols "are very good at adapting to changing retail conditions."

The choice of the "circus" as a name and theme is suggestive in other ways. As an area simultaneously *opened up* and *enclosed by* a bounded ring or arena, the circus is both an *aporetic space*—a zone of indistinction where the boundary between what is open and what is closed collapses—and a *heterotopic* space. The name *circus* gestures toward the circuitous paths of its itinerary, the transient encampments of its troupe, and the peripatetic lives of its performers—the equestrians, jugglers, clowns, acrobats, animal tamers, and the menagerie freaks and geeks who had long proved popular attractions for European audiences.[55] The traveling circus occupies another('s) space—by invitation, through rent—which it deterritorializes for the purpose of entertainment but also profit. Despite its potential as a model for ad hoc, improvisational communities of care, the historical circus possessed many of the same structural attributes as the slave ship; the circus functions as a mode of bio-cargo, and as deterritorialized space needed to produce and realize surplus value.[56] After regeneration, this stretch of Broadmead is deterritorialized space, enclosed for the purpose of profit in the name of pleasure.[57] Reterritorialization by local activists and community members found short-lived expression in the riots in August 2011 and the Occupy Movement in the months that followed. In the longer term, we find instances of reterritorialization by groups like St. Pauls Unlimited, which has reclaimed the process of regeneration from corporate interests by developing its own neighborhood plan, leading to the establishment of a much-needed Family and Learning Centre, a facility they recently defended against closure as the city planned to eliminate all public funding.

For the sake of resonance, however, I want to note another reterritorialization only blocks from Cabot Circus, the Circomedia Centre for Contemporary Circus and Physical Theatre located in St. Pauls Church in Portland Square. I mention it here in order to contrast the logic of the circus ascribed to the Broadmead regeneration. In this context we might recall that old circus form, explicitly evoked at the grand opening of Cabot Circus, relied on an empty public spectacle orchestrated by the owner-impresario, who simultaneously staged the nonnormative body as social pathology and masked the brutal exploitation that made the spectacle possible. The aesthetic and ethical principles of the contemporary circus *(cirque nouveau)*, which underlie Circomedia's teaching and performance philosophies, reject the ringmaster as author-orchestrator, relocate creative license to performers, reorient the spectator's gaze onto remarkable new possibilities of movement and embodiment, and recast spectacle as the kind of theatricality that makes for captivating storytelling. While the spectacle of the former traded on misdirection, the theatricality of the new circus draws the spectator's attention to its own narrative apparatuses and conditions of performative possibility. I conclude this section with Circomedia in order to point forward to the final, and perhaps unanticipated, site of concurrency between regeneration and historical legacy: the church sanctuary. What we are seeing in the new urban enclosure is the global-scale privatization of the biopolitical itself and the transfer into private hands of the organization and management of new bio-cargo.

Enclosing

Once known for its countercultural attitudes and subcultural vibe, Bristol's history of defiance was one of the characteristics leveraged to attract tourists. In the city's effort at rebranding, organized defiance became quaint idiosyncrasy, a kind of resistance more charming than alarming. Given the city's somewhat anarchic, sometimes playful, occasionally violent, but always steadfast tradition of performative protests and practices of civil disobedience, co-opting its tradition of dissent, and the history against which popular opposition erupts, required particular emphasis on one of the city's most unruly neighborhoods, an area known locally as the People's Republic of Stokes Croft. Situated at the edge of St. Pauls, Stokes Croft is demographically distinct—more racially and ethnically mixed, and socially, economically, and culturally diverse—a population of long-term anti-establishment, antistate, anticapital residents; alternative, small-scale businesses; squatters and urban nomads. Stokes Croft has also been the site of incendiary actions against regeneration in 2011, most forcefully in the days after Bristol police assaulted a peaceful squat on Cheltenham Road. On 21 March 2011—months before the August upheavals that began in the council estates outside London and rapidly spread to cities across Britain—an estimated 160 police officers clad in riot gear stormed the long-occupied squatter's residence called Telepathic Heights, from which only four squatters were evicted.

Telepathic Heights is remarkable for the stunning graffiti murals that cover two exterior walls of this four-floor building and for its role as an important hub in neighborhood life; it is noteworthy here, however, because it happened to sit opposite a Tesco Express that had opened only two weeks prior to the police raid. That particular Tesco had been the target of petitions, protests, and civil-disobedient occupation by local activists for over a year ahead of opening. According to the group No Tesco in Stokes Croft, when an "inquisitive local" discovered that Tesco had secretly submitted an application under a pseudonymous corporate entity to take over a vacant storefront on Cheltenham Road, a hastily organized community meeting brought over two hundred residents out in protest. Despite a massive write-in campaign, unprecedented turnout at subsequent planning meetings, and a survey showing 96 percent of those living in Stokes Croft opposed the proposal, the council approved Tesco's proposal. As one activist quipped, "So much for the community engagement stuff on their website," referencing either Tesco's stated corporate mission or the promise of locally driven regeneration.[58] Beyond their concerns about this particular business—Tesco is notorious for its corporate misdeeds—No Tesco in Stokes Croft was also protesting the way in which "the Planning Process favours big business and leaves people with little power to influence development in their local area." By mid-March 2010, after a six-week occupation of the future Tesco storefront, protesters were removed from the site, leading hundreds to gather in demonstration of their eviction. With a remarkably heavy-handed show of force, that police action would be repeated a year later just across the street from the newly opened Tesco Express.

In a sign of sweeping historical contingency—not coincidental but dialectical—before the eviction of protesters from Tesco, before the eviction of squatters from Telepathic Heights, before the Battle of Stokes Croft, a local artist was busy at work on an enormous mural on Bath Road celebrating the 1831 Bristol riots and commemorating their violent suppression so powerfully preserved in William James Müller's much-reproduced lithograph. It is hardly surprising, then, that the popular memory of Queen Square preserved in Müller's lithograph should reappear in an enormous mural on Bath Road by Scott Buchanan Barden (see Figure 39). Inspired by the massive public demonstrations and popular uprisings that shook North Africa and the Middle East in 2010, Barden completed the mural as residents of Bristol anticipated the disturbances that would erupt across the UK in the remaining months of 2011. Dubbed the "Battle of Stokes Croft," the April 2011 confrontation began when police raided a long-occupied squat called Telepathic Heights, purportedly on the word of informants claiming the squatters were preparing petrol bombs. The "riots" that broke out on 21 April may have begun with a long-standing dispute over city planning, but the violent confrontation between riot police, squatters, activists,

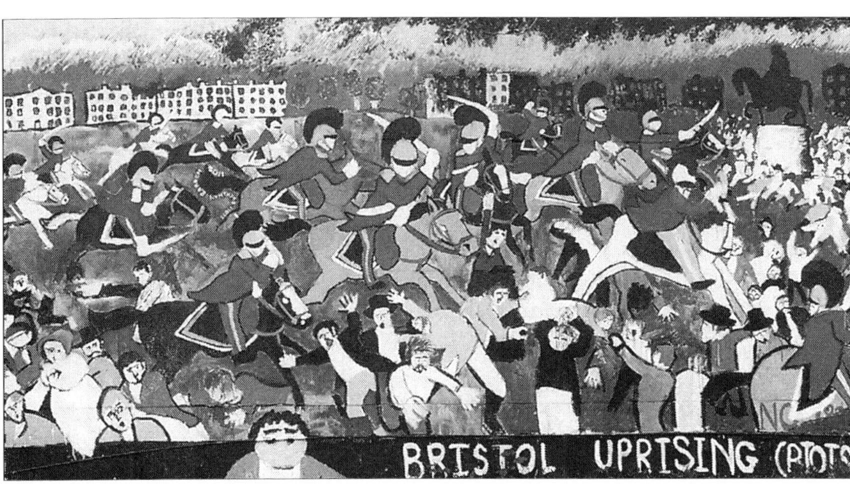

Figure 39. Scott Buchanan Barden, Bristol Uprising (Riots) 1831, *2013. Outdoor mural, Bath Road, Bristol. Courtesy of Scott Buchanan Barden.*

and hundreds of local residents presaged the unrest that would erupt across the country in August, taking an oblivious media and its largely white, middle-class viewers by surprise. Communities left behind in the frenzied schemes for large-scale redevelopment in city centers were now confronting an implacable neoliberal model of public–private partnership driving small-scale planning in already disadvantaged neighborhoods. Despite its rhetoric of goodwill and local collaboration, these projects showed little concern for community input or local interest.

As proposals for regeneration spread from Bristol's city center to the broader designation of central Bristol, the urban core is being remapped, neighborhoods renamed, and redevelopment zones branded. Stokes Croft has been specifically targeted as a promising area for commercial growth, near enough to city center to attract the kind of residents, consumers, and even tourists at the center of the new urban imaginary. Once considered the high-street section along the edge of St. Pauls, in 2011 Stokes Croft was designated as a distinct redevelopment zone separate from St. Pauls. The city's 2012 Central Area Action Plan identified the neighborhood as "a major route into the city centre for walkers, cyclists, cars and public transport" but also as an area that "has struggled to retain conventional high street businesses." Nevertheless, the report goes on, "the neighbourhood has emerged as a vibrant cultural quarter in its own right, being a breeding ground for alternative businesses and community-led regeneration and a focus for street art within the city centre."[59] Further, "Stokes Croft is an area that divided stakeholders between those who sought to promote its unorthodox, multicultural and creative nature and those who were keen to see new development in the area as a driver of regeneration" (132). One can hardly overlook the condescending and dismissive attitude toward the residents of the neighborhood, who are portrayed as having failed in the struggle for "conventional high street businesses," which they paradoxically did not seem to want, even though the area has (also paradoxically) "emerged" as a "vibrant cultural quarter"; nor can one overlook the disdain expressed for "community-led regeneration" and the "alternative businesses" and "street art" when the authors describe the neighborhood as a "breeding ground" in need of new or enhanced access points and improved surveillance" (139).

Once embedded in planning policies and project proposals, renaissance and regeneration name the continuing enclosure of public access and local control. The document goes on to outline two (and only two) possible approaches to redevelopment that emerged from those meetings: the city could pursue either "conventional, market-led regeneration" or "community-led regeneration with a flexible approach to planning control" (135). Drawn into the framework of city-center legibility, Stokes Croft is remapped to ensure routes of way-finding and place-making that link commercial zones rather than community neighborhoods. Stokes Croft is subsequently designated a gateway to Broadmead and Cabot Circus, providing pedestrian and cycling routes that might draw consumers into commercial city-center destinations. The rhetorical strategy the document seems to adopt, like the general tactics the public–private partnership approach aims to deploy, bifurcates stakeholders, interests, objectives, and possibilities into "traders" and "residents," placing them into a productive tension that can only be resolved by the market. Severing one of the few thriving districts of St. Pauls and annexing it to the adjacent Broadmead shopping—including Cabot Circus—Bristol signals the continuing isolation and exclusion of black and ethnic minority communities from its vision of an economically and culturally vibrant city. While Stokes Croft has been absorbed into the city-center redevelopment framework, St. Pauls has been rendered illegible as a vital city-center neighborhood, and thus largely abandoned by the public–private partnerships that now control the flows of capital investment.

Since the 1990s, as national government "modernized" its ministries—abandoning funding priorities, reorganizing regional and local planning agencies, and "devolving" administrative authority—the promise of the "global city" appeared as a new urban ideal for the deindustrialized metropolis. This *new* "new urbanism" leveraged the tenets of neoliberalism—the unassailable commitment to unfettered, deregulated, "open" markets at its core—into an attractive, prepackaged model for city-center regeneration oriented toward tourism, retail, and entertainment, on the one hand, and the trappings of the "creative economy," on the other. At the same time, the idea of the global city rested on long historical geographic connections and economic relationships that could not—despite best attempts—be flattened into a singular horizontal network operating in the empty homogenous time of the present. Cosmopolitanism, the ethos of world citizenship, and global belonging founded on the undisclosed colonial imaginary of the Enlightenment had erupted into a contentious cosmo*politics* demanding the renewal of hospitality and stranger sociality as fundamental principles.[60] The aspiration to regain global standing—and economic and cultural relevance—demanded that cities like Bristol wrestle with unresolved debates over which parts of the city were to remain open and which parts were to remain closed to the various "flows" on which the new global city relied, whether commodities and consumers, information and technology, media outlets and online markets, and—most critically—capital, including marketized debt. But the circulation of these things entailed other flows more difficult to transform into glossy brochures: displaced populations, post-sovereign forms of power, as well as new possibilities for anticapital resistance, anticolonial struggle, and powerful insurgencies against the state.

Taking | Sanctuary

I arrived at the Church of St. Thomas the Martyr on a late summer afternoon, overheated and overrushed, having miscalculated the walking distance from the Spike Island exhibition space back to Redcliffe. I had come on the recommendation of the friend of a friend who had curated a traveling exhibit of young artists from across the UK sponsored every five years by the Arts Council. He had spoken enthusiastically of a young artist, a rising star in the art world, who was concurrently exhibiting several pieces in a Bristol church. On the day I attended, tables and chairs had been crowded into the small chancel just beyond the church sanctuary. The artworks were propped up against the walls beneath the clerestory windows or leaning against the columns along the apse. The positioning was somewhat awkward, not conducive to easy viewing or circulation, and the space itself felt a bit cluttered. Behind the mahogany communion rail a large potluck dinner had been laid out, organized to inaugurate the opening of the exhibit and to honor the artist himself, and while the dinner was open to all in attendance, the formality of the church—along with the stage-like elevation of the chancel and solid rail barrier that separated it—lent an unintended sense of exclusivity. Yet the convivial interactions and festive chatter between diners suggested a familiar, even familial, circle of friends, acquaintances, colleagues, and collaborators, an overcrowded Last Supper from which I stood apart, neither faithful apostle nor apostate disciple. For me, at least, the sanctuary of St. Thomas offered little comfort.

The church itself was surprisingly modest and nondescript for having once been the Redcliffe parish church. Completed in 1793, and serving some of Bristol's wealthiest merchants, the church did not aspire to the size and elegance of Bristol Cathedral, its medieval predecessor whose physical scale and visual sightlines proved crucial to scuttling the earliest proposals for Harbourside redevelopment. According to an early nineteenth-century observer, "The architecture of the present church contains little that will offend a correct taste, though it combines nothing to excite admiration . . . a specimen of what has been denominated the modern style of ecclesiastical architecture."[61] Following an 1879 restoration, however, its gloomy interior was brightened up and now "the combination of high barrel vault ceiling and clerestory windows with painted plastered walls contribute to the spaciousness and light of the interior, leading the eye to the richness of the reredos at the altar." Like much of central Bristol, the area surrounding St. Thomas suffered heavy damage during the Blitz, and the neighborhood was redeveloped as a commercial rather than residential district in the postwar years. By the 1970s, its congregation in steady decline, the diocese determined the church had "no viable future" and St. Thomas the Martyr was declared redundant. The building is now administered by the Churches Conservation Trust, maintained through the Redundant Churches Fund, and made available for hire. Given the city's storied past, the terminal decline of the church, and the competing revisionary accounts of contemporary Britain I had been tracking, it was only fitting that the series of four large-scale, mixed-media, photography-based installation works by Hew Locke on display at the Church of St. Thomas the Martyr should bear the title *Restoration.*

Restoration was a site-specific project engaging directly with the institutional history of Bristol and celebrated the city's most noble patrons while effacing the ignoble means through which they gained their power and wealth. To do so, Locke had taken as the subject of the series four historical monuments erected in the Bristol city center, each commemorating a local or national hero: Edward Colston, Bristol's most famous eighteenth-century merchant, whose prominence in the monumentalizing of the city's history has been the subject of heated debates; Edmund Burke, the social conservative and economic liberal who also served as MP for Bristol between 1774 and 1780, who eventually lost his seat for being simultaneously pro-Catholic and pro–free trade; Samuel Morley, a parliamentary radical and MP for Bristol from 1868 from 1885, who was largely honored for being a model of civic duty, the "merchant philanthropist" who supported adult education, opposed slavery, and championed the Canadian abolitionist campaigner Josiah Hensen (the purported inspiration for Harriet Beecher Stowe's *Uncle Tom's Cabin*); and finally, King Edward VIII, the

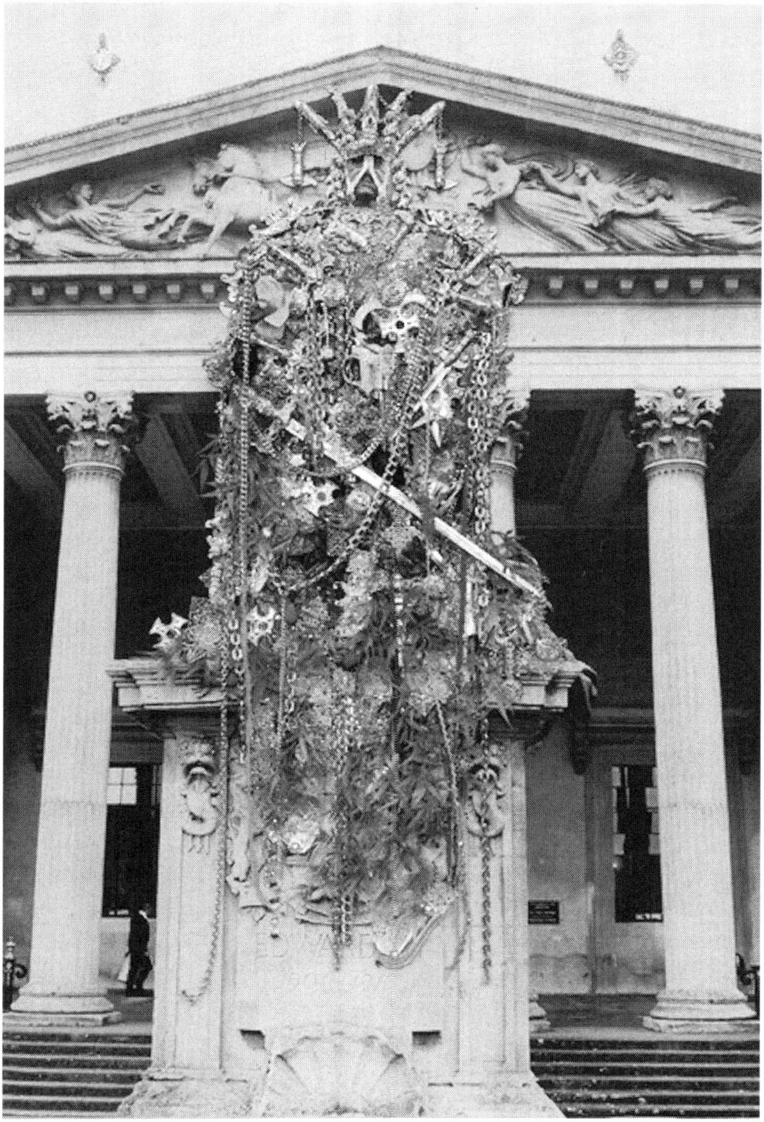

Figure 40. Hew Locke, Restoration*, detail: King Edward VIII, 2006. Series of four C-type photographs with mixed media, 112 x 244 x 15 cm. Commissioned by Spike Island and first shown at St. Thomas the Martyr Church, Bristol. Copyright by Hew Locke. All rights reserved, DACS 2015. Photograph by Stuart Bunce.*

Prince of Wales who put the "apparent" in heir apparent, here graciously depicted in his long-awaited coronation robes (see Figure 40).

The pieces on display at St. Thomas, like much of Locke's work, were reminiscent of the installations of Yinka Shonibare discussed in the previous chapter. But rather than dressing his subjects in historically resonant fabrics, Locke encrusts his surfaces in a thick amalgam of miniature curios, colorful trinkets, and plastic baubles, such as one might find at a Poundland variety store or purchase from a capsule toy machine: beads, charms, chains, and other jewelry; fake plants, leaves, and flowers; animals and creatures of numerous species; dolls and figurines in various states of dismemberment; and, crucially, an assortment of toys, with particular fondness for toy weapons, including knives, swords, daggers, handguns, and hunting rifles, and an arsenal of military firearms and munitions. The contrast of subject matter and creative materials is certainly whimsical, but their decorative fancy is also surprisingly beautiful at the right distance, say, from across the room. In an op-art tradition, Locke toys with how we see and what we see (and how we see what we see); he plays with the exhibition space in a way that leads the viewer from a dissembling appreciation to a diffident recognition, which eventually gives way to a visual amusement marked by the discomfiting realization of the persistence of violence alongside the banality of beauty.

As a site-specific conceptual installation, *Restoration* proposed to recapture the publicness of space and the statues and monuments erected there. In its concrete execution, *Restoration* aimed to reinstate an iconoclastic and idiosyncratic history to the public spaces these landmarks index but obscure. It would be a mistake to detach the biographies of Locke's subjects from the complex, intersecting histories of their monumentalization; or from their relation to the public spaces these statues occupy; or from the relationship to the individuals and communities who inhabit these spaces, or have done so in the past; or from the valences of meaning expressed by the glittering baubles and gewgaws that encase these photographic images, tourist-grade snapshots that capture, record, and frame—or archive—the city's history. Leaving St. Thomas, I am urged to visit the Seven Stars Inn, which has operated next door to the church since the late seventeenth century. It was at the Seven Stars that, disguised as a local miner, Thomas Clarkson clandestinely collected interviews and evidence to use in his antislavery campaign. Thinking about these two buildings, and the kind of publics they organize and represent, I am led to see a somewhat hazy but still important difference between sanctuary and hospitality: not one of conditionality but one of social convention, shared practice, and collective performance.

On the other side of Broadmead, now Cabot Circus, stands Bristol's parish church, St. Stephens. Following the Abolition200 events in 2007, the church established a series of programs to carry on with the work of commemoration honored that year, including a project called the Reconciliation Laboratory, "a facilitated public listening circle in the space before the *Bristol Reconciliation Reredos,* for an honest sharing of the issues which might divide us in Bristol."[62] If the fundamental message of the *Reredos* altarpiece is about finding sanctuary through Christian forgiveness, the church's Reconciliation Project is meant to put that faith into social practice. Thus, the *Reredos,* created by the artist Graeme Mortimer Evelyn, operates in tandem with the local project of social regeneration, which itself must remain open and concurrent with other projects of urban redevelopment. While the Reconciliation Project gestures toward the necessity of historical consciousness for collective action—without quite naming the historical particulars as just so many examples—the *Reredos* panels themselves remain beguilingly abstract as they depict sanctification through forgiveness at the site of divine consecration. In the language of modern "reformed" iconography, benediction is conveyed through colorful rays of light emanating from above as the eyes of the iconic head beam toward the heavens. According to the artist's statement, St. Stephens provided a unique site for thinking about the city's past and the possibility of a resolution going into the future:

> St Stephen's is one of the oldest churches in Bristol and is significant in the history of the city as the church that blessed every ship that left the port, including every merchant slave vessel that left the city. The Reconciliation Reredos is a contemporary artwork of universal reconciliation that responds to the church's past, reflects the voices of the city today while representing the potential of the future.[63]

The development of Evelyn's thinking about the presentness of the past is perhaps better understood through the altarpiece studies leading up to the completed *Reredos.* One such study, titled *christus rex versus christus victor* (2010), combines two rough sketches of Christ in acrylic alongside an arrangement of small, white, plastic military figurines arranged in battle formation, and a series of Afro pick combs all arrayed across a fiberboard (MDF) surface. The title references two competing biblical images of Christ—one as sovereign, the other as sacrifice—and a range of competing theories of atonement, that is, the way in which humankind is redeemed through the suffering and death of Christ. For instance, according to a 1925 Catholic encyclical written by Pope Pius XI, Christ the King is not a figure of sovereign violence but rather one of divine order, but the kingdom of Christ will only arrive after Christ's return. Quoting from Cyril of Alexandria, Pope Pius writes, "Christ has dominion over all creatures, a dominion not seized by violence nor usurped, but his by essence and by nature."[64] Likewise, more recently Pope Benedict XVI distinguished the power of Christ the King from earthly kingdoms, saying that Christ's authority is not derived from "criteria of efficiency and of human power" but from "love and service to others." "The Cross is the 'throne' from which He demonstrated the sublime regality of God-love." But Benedict's words were undermined by the language of belligerence that followed, in which the Kingdom of Christ will be achieved here on earth until "all enemies—and in the last instance, death—have been defeated."[65] Thus, Christus Rex appears both messianic and militaristic and is deeply bound up with problems of state sovereignty in relation to divine authority.

But Christus Victor evokes a quite particular interpretation of the crucifixion established by first millennium Christian theologians that viewed the sacrifice of Christ as the final victory over worldly sin and allegiance to death inaugurated by the fall of Adam and Eve. Redemption comes through the experience of human embodiment—including pain and suffering, alienation and vulnerability, precarity and death—by God through Christ, and the experience of the divine virtues of righteousness and transcendence by mankind through faith. If the resurrection represents the moment of spiritual rebirth, the ritual of the sacrament of the altar figures one's bodily identification with Christ's incarnation, suffering, death, and eternal love and life. Anselm renounced the Christus Victor theory of atonement in the eleventh century, although it continued on in the Eastern Orthodox Church. Rather than atonement as "participation"—a bodily identification mutually achieved by God through the incarnation of Christ, and by Christian believers through the Holy Sacrament—Anselm and subsequent theologians of the Western Church favored a theory of atonement as "penal satisfaction," in which Christ "pays" for the accumulated sins of humankind through a punishing crucifixion, just as the debtor satisfies an economic debt that cannot be repaid through punishment by the law. It is a model of atonement far more resonant with the emergence of the feudal economy and far more conducive to the logic of exchange fundamental to capitalist development.

The *Reredos* commissioned by St. Stephens resonates with a number of projects Evelyn has completed across Bristol and the UK, such as *The Stations of the Cross* (2006–7), commissioned for the nearby Gloucester Cathedral, in which the fifteen moments of Christ's passion are reimagined along the vectors of historical resonance and social currency. Like Hew Locke's *Restoration* installation, Evelyn's *The Two Coins: Meditations on Trade* (2007) was another site-specific multimedia intervention intended, according to the artist, as "a contemporary response to monuments erected in memory of 18th century traders, presenting an unprejudiced historical legacy while highlighting collective responsibility to prevent negative forms of 21st century trade, which often create new forms of modern slavery."[66] In a commissioned work for the opening of the M Shed, *Reading the Riot (Act)* (2009), "an uncompromising and challenging piece of the long history of dissent within the city, which in retrospect, since the riots in Stokes Croft, Bristol, democracy protests internationally, unrest in Greece/Spain and especially the recent riots in London . . . seems strangely prophetic." *Reading the Riot (Act)* appears as a permanent work under the theme of "Challenging" in the Bristol People gallery, alongside those images of the public rioting from 1831 and 1980 with which this chapter began. In each of these commissioned works Evelyn emphasizes the ways in which the historical systems of colonial exchange that created human bio-cargo remain implicated in the economic and social transactions of everyday life in the postcolonial city. Like the story of the Passion, they ground the metaphysics of salvation by depicting the materiality of bare life.

The site-specificity of the church-based installation works by Locke and Evelyn, as part of a larger project of critical and creative interrogation of city history, foreground the way in which efforts to "reconcile" community conflicts continue to draw upon the two dominant paradigms for thinking about the politics of inclusion and belonging: the law of hospitality, the imperative to welcome the stranger into the home, and the principle of sanctuary, the authority delegated to the church to offer refuge to the displaced and dispossessed, or provide asylum to anyone in need of safe harbor. Much has been written about the laws of hospitality and practices of sanctuary as guiding tenets for social policy, in particular as counterforces to the power and violence of the state. While not universal, practices of hospitality and sanctuary, refuge and asylum, have been traced to the early histories of many societies both ancient and modern, in the Global South as well as the Global North, as perhaps two of the most humane safeguards against state violence or collective retribution. The discourse of hospitality analogizes the spaces of social belonging—the neighborhood, the district, the city, the nation—to the home. The civic duty to shelter and protect—to house the unhoused—consolidated into the cities of sanctuary movement in the later part of the twentieth century in response to repressive states, violent regimes of law enforcement, and inhumane policies toward asylum seekers, political and economic refugees, the displaced and the homeless. The right to provide sanctuary pits the authority of the church against the authority of the government, and the power of local communities and councils against the power of the state. Juxtaposed with the explosive energy of the riot or the spirited intransigence of the occupation, the promise of asylum, like the rituals of reconciliation, might appear little more than symbolic pretense or liberal validation. It would not be hard to imagine how a sanctioned campaign to be named a city of refuge might be used to quell the riot and disburse the crowd. But the efficacy of institutionally unsanctioned actions carried out by the agents of the church or activists in the community under the aegis of sanctuary are difficult to gauge using the political calculus by which collective action is measured. While the riot and the occupation endeavor to retake public space for the common good, sanctuary often leverages private space for the benefit of clandestine publics.

Sanctuary shelters, the riot lets loose; sanctuary takes in, the riot takes out; sanctuary protects, the riot threatens; sanctuary houses, the riot unhouses. Sanctuary preserves life in the shadow of death, the riot risks death for the preservation of social life. Sanctuary bestows asylum and grants immunity; but it also demands confession, requires atonement, accepts penance, and guides contemplation. Sanctuary forgives. Should sanctuary be granted to history? Or is sanctuary simply another way of housing it? Not only can I not dismiss the political potential in either movement, but I suspect there is a point at which they converge into a more singular enterprise. If hospitality, sanctuary, and forgiveness name distinct but complementary ethical and political principles, each operates in particular locations where the public and private collapse into indistinction. Might the sacred space of the church and the secular space of the public house provide complementary, perhaps mutually necessary, places of shelter? The church sanctuary and the local pub are unique spaces of accommodation for those who are, for whatever reason and for whatever period of time, unhoused. Given their singular social functions, can the church and the pub provide a model for a broader ethic of accommodation that deregulates public–private space and facilitates movement in an environment of mutual care? If the practices of sanctuary or the performances of hospitality house those who are unhoused, can they themselves be unhoused from the sites with which they are conceptually enshrined? How might such performances gain practical footing outside their sanctioned spaces of enactment? And how might sanctuary and hospitality be leveraged in the organization of public life and the orchestration of new public cultures?

I end this chapter and the book not in the ruins of a branch of Barclays Bank, not on the frontlines of forceful resistance, not in the sanctuary of a church. Instead I take refuge in an "other" space: the graveyard of the Congregationalist dissenters in the Brunswick Square Chapel Cemetery, for which in 2010 the Bristol City Council commissioned a permanent public art installation. In Hew Locke's *Ruined,* ten large cast-iron grave markers "commemorate" the kind of economic ventures that made the city, though not all of the corporations monumentalized here have links directly to Bristol. Grave markers are dedicated to W.D & H.O. Willis, The West Indies Sugar Corporation, The Persian Bank Mining Rights Corporation, Pan Am Airlines, Enron, and, not surprisingly, the Society for Merchant Venturers. More surprising, perhaps, is the inclusion of a monument to Ducrow's Circus (see Figure 41), which was founded in Bristol and is associated with the black equestrian Pablo Fanque, a circus impresario in his own right famously remembered in the Beatles hit "Being for the Benefit of Mr. Kite!" from the album *Sgt. Pepper's Lonely Hearts Club Band.* For the art historian Claire Doherty, the information inscribed on these rusty corporate emblems "is enough to set off a potent set of associations" that "alludes to the persistence of historical forms in contemporary Bristol." But if the inclusion of the Merchant Venturers is intended to suggest historical continuity, perhaps Ducrow's points to the possibility of change by referencing the repurposing of nearby St. Paul's Church for the "decidedly non-conformist" Circomedia.[67]

Other than its shape, Brunswick Square has little in common with Queen Square, either in the profile of its residents—current and historical—or the economic forces that brought them there. Nor does it resemble

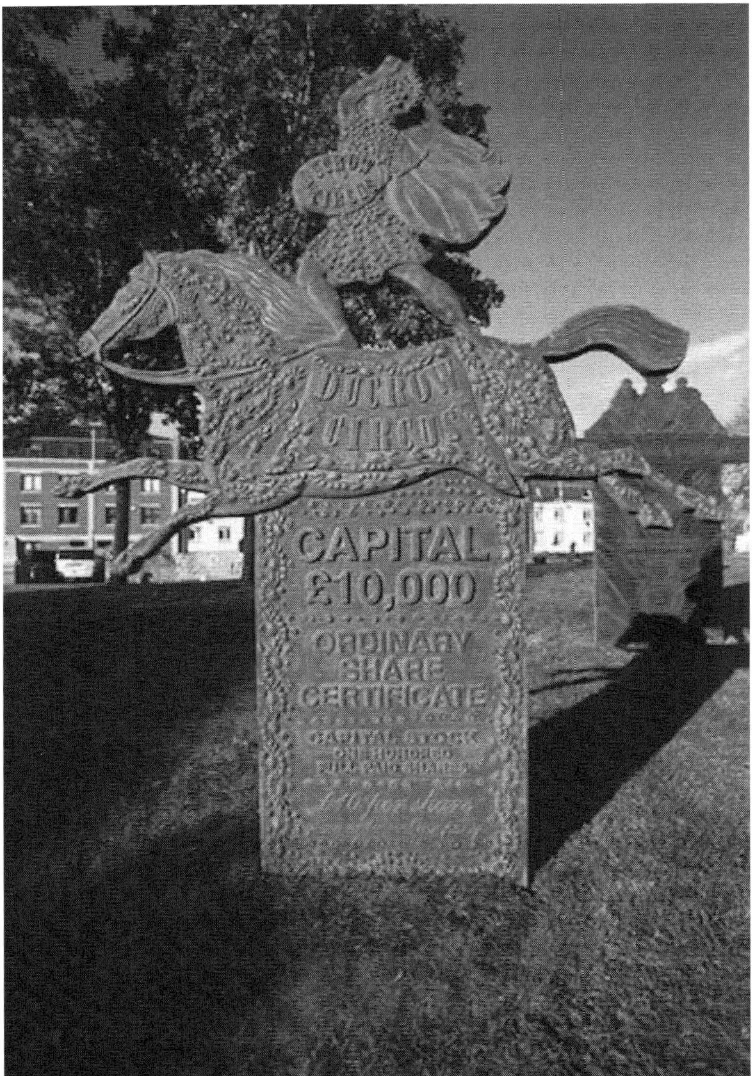

Figure 41. Hew Locke, Ruined*, detail: Ducrow's Circus, 2010. Permanent public art project consisting of ten cast-iron markers, average height above ground 1.5 m. Commissioned by Bristol City Council for Brunswick Square Cemetery Gardens. Copyright by Hew Locke. All rights reserved, DACS 2015. Photograph by Jamie Woodley.*

Cabot Circus, variant geometry aside. In many respects I am both closer to and farther away from that small island in the Caribbean and the ruins of Barclays Bank that Jamaica Kincaid so powerfully envisioned. Like Kincaid's speaker, Locke's installation is in equal measure playfully clever and morbidly hopeful. One senses a certain satisfaction in imagining the demise of these notorious institutions, whether already realized or yet to come. Without returning to Antigua or circling back to Queen Square, I have arrived at the beginning; or perhaps the beginning of a nonmelancholy end. For suddenly, a small chapel cemetery in the St. Paul's district in the city of Bristol feels like a place to dance.

Acknowledgments

Thanks go first and foremost to Bishnupriya Ghosh, who has been nothing less than remarkable from this project's rough beginnings through its mad rush to completion. Bishnu has remained a steadfast mentor and wonderful friend for more than a decade, well beyond her institutional role; no individual has shaped this book as fundamentally or profoundly. David Simpson deserves special acknowledgment for offering expertise in an astonishingly wide range of historical and disciplinary fields, and for providing a close and careful reading of early draft chapters.

My primary scholarly interlocutors are now scattered far and wide, from the office across the hall to campuses across the United States and cities around the world. In the academic diaspora, I thank Nathaniel Cadle, Nandini Dhar, Greg Dobbins, Elizabeth Freeman, Neville Hoad, Annie McClanahan, Brenna Munro, Jason Pearl, Heather Russell, Tim Watson; I also thank Whitney Bauman, Heather Blatt, Maya Boutaghou, Phillip Carter, Sudipto Chatterjee, Joshua Clover, Caroline Faria, Pamela Geller, Jenni Halpin, Jarrod Hayes, Jessica Johnson, Proshot Kalami, John Marx, Carmela McIntire, Linda Morris, Timothy Morton, Vrushali Patil, Yvette Piggush, Riche Richardson, Christopher Schaberg, Scott Shershow, Laurie Shrage, Andrew Strycharski, Donna Weir-Soley, and Cia White. For helping me manage the everyday challenges of life in South Florida, I thank Maya Bell and Robert Nolin; for regularly checking on me with care and concern from the opposite coast, I thank David Do.

For help in securing institutional support from Florida International University for travel and research assistance, I thank James Sutton in the Department of English, Jean Rahier in the Program in African and African Diaspora Studies, and Nicol Rae (now at Montana State) in the College of Arts and Sciences. Early support was provided by the Department of English at UC Davis, as well as the Humanities Institute, Office of Graduate Studies, and Graduate Student Association. Thanks to Denika Mays and Parker Phillips for research assistance.

For assistance securing images and permissions, I thank Jasmine Michaels, along with Kathryn Gile at Alexander and Bonin, Sophie Greig at White Cube, Daniel Tsai at Jack Sherman, Maria Elena Murguia at ARS, and Leslie Wong at Bridgeman. I thank Roger Malbert at the Hayward Gallery and Pauline de Souza at Diversity Arts Forum, as well as Dorothea Smartt, Olumide Popoola, and Mita Datta, who all took time out of their busy schedules to discuss their work and guide me around London. I also thank the staff at the Institute for International Visual Arts, Diversity Arts Forum, the Hyman Kreitman Research Centre at the Tate Britain, the British Library, the Bodleian Library, and Rhodes House Library at Oxford.

Lastly, I thank the two anonymous reviewers for the University of Minnesota Press for the care and attention they gave the manuscript; their insightful comments and astute suggestions for revision have made this a much better book. I especially thank Richard Morrison for ushering the manuscript through the review process, and Danielle Kasprzak, Anne Carter, and Erin Warholm-Wohlenhaus for taking it through production.

Notes

Introduction

1. Foundational texts in archive theory include Jacques Derrida, *Archive Fever: A Freudian Impression,* trans. Eric Prenowitz (Chicago: University of Chicago Press, 1996); Michel Foucault, *The Archaeology of Knowledge and the Discourse on Language,* trans. A. M. Sheridan Smith (New York: Pantheon Books, 1972); Giorgio Agamben, *Remnants of Auschwitz: The Witness and the Archive,* trans. Daniel Heller-Roazen (New York: Zone Books, 2002). There is now also a large body of scholarship on the archive that follows and diverges from this genealogy, including Thomas Richards, *The Imperial Archive: Knowledge and the Fantasy of Empire* (New York: Verso, 1993); Michel-Rolph Trouillot, *Silencing the Past: Power and the Production of History* (Boston: Beacon Press, 1997); Carolyn Steedman, *Dust: The Archive and Cultural History* (New Brunswick, N.J.: Rutgers University Press, 2002); Diana Taylor, *The Archive and the Repertoire: Performing Cultural Memory in the Americas* (Durham, N.C.: Duke University Press, 2003); Ann Cvetkovich, *An Archive of Feelings* (Durham, N.C.: Duke University Press, 2003); and Anjali Arondekar, *For the Record: On Sexuality and the Colonial Archive in India* (Durham, N.C.: Duke University Press, 2009). Edited volumes worth noting: Francis Blouin and William Rosenburg, eds., *Archives, Documentation, and Institutions of Social Memory* (Ann Arbor: University of Michigan Press, 2007); Antoinette Burton, *Dwelling in the Archive: Women Writing House, Home, and History in Late Colonial India* (Oxford: Oxford University Press, 2003); Antoinette Burton, ed., *Archive Stories: Fact, Fictions, and the Writing of History* (Durham, N.C.: Duke University Press, 2006); Carolyn Hamilton et al., eds., *Refiguring the Archive* (Cape Town, S.A.: David Philip, 2002). The following articles and book chapters were especially helpful: Achille Mbembe, "The Power of the Archives and Its Limit," in Hamilton, *Refiguring the Archive;* Sandhya Shetty and Elizabeth Jane Bellamy, "Postcolonialism's Archive Fever," *Diacritics* 30, no. 1 (Spring 2000): 25–48; and Ann Laura Stoler, "The Colonial Archives and the Arts of Governance," *Archival Science* 2 (2002): 87–109.

2. This is Arondekar's wonderful opening sentence. *For the Record,* 1.

3. Taylor, *The Archive and the Repertoire,* 10.

4. I continue to find Stuart Hall's notion of "articulation" essential to understanding the complex and uneven entanglements of "relatively autonomous"

social, cultural, religious, ideological-discursive (etc.) formations with the economic, broadly construed. Articulation helps describe the intricate array of determinations at work within particular social formations with regard to the economic plane, each array representing a singular but unevenly consequent "articulation" within a total constellation of historical determination. See Hall, "Race, Articulation, and Societies Structured in Dominance," reprinted in *Black British Cultural Studies: A Reader,* ed. Houston A. Baker, Manthia Diawara, and Ruth H. Lindeborg (Chicago: University of Chicago Press, 1996), 16–60. Other works by Hall crucial to my project include: "Encoding/Decoding," in *The Cultural Studies Reader,* ed. Simon During (New York: Routledge, 1993), 90–103; "Notes on Deconstructing the Popular," in *Cultural Theory and Popular Culture: A Reader,* ed. John Storey (Upper Saddle River, N.J.: Prentice Hall, 1998), 442–53; "Cultural Identity and Diaspora," in *Identity: Community, Culture, Difference,* ed. Jonathan Rutherford (London: Lawrence & Wishart, 1990), 222–37; and Hall et al., eds., *Policing the Crisis: Mugging, the State, and Law and Order* (London: Macmillan, 1978).

5. For a survey of the variety of approaches to rethinking the materialism beyond the "textualist" orientation of postrstructuralism, see Diana Coole and Samantha Frost's edited volume, *New Materialisms: Ontology, Agency, and Politics* (Durham, N.C.: Duke University Press, 2010). "Materiality is always something more than 'mere' matter: an excess, force, vitality, relationality, or difference that renders matter active, self-creative, productive, unpredictable" (9). Like several of the contributors to this collection, Sara Ahmed and Pheng Cheah in particular, I do not view the reconsideration of materiality and the experience of the material to be at odds with the "cultural turn" generally or poststructuralism and deconstruction specifically. My hope is that my project responds in some measure to Jason Edward's call, in the concluding chapter to the volume, "The Materialism of Historical Materialism," to show how the material practices of everyday life constellate/articulate the operations of global capital. On "feeling historical," see Elizabeth Freeman, *Time Binds: Queer Temporalities, Queer Histories* (Durham, N.C.: Duke University Press, 2010).

6. See Arjun Appadurai, *Modernity at Large: Cultural Dimensions of Globalization* (Minneapolis: University of Minnesota Press, 1996), especially chapter 2, "Disjunction and Difference in the Global Economy," 27–47. See also Benedict Anderson, *Imagined Communities: Reflections on the Origin and Spread of Nationalism* (New York: Verso, 1991).

7. Appadurai, *Modernity at Large,* 7.

8. See Giovanni Arrighi, *The Long Twentieth Century: Money, Power, and the Origins of Our Times* (New York: Verso, 1994). Arrighi demonstrates how the *longue durée* of modern globalizing capitalism is comprised of a series of "overlapping stages" or "long centuries" that mark transitions in the modes of production and cycles of accumulation.

9. I am thinking specifically of historiographic, archivally engaged literary works by black writers in the United States and Canada such as Toni Morrison, M. NourbeSe Philip, and Edward P. Jones; or visual artists such as Kara Walker, Glenn Ligon, Renée Cox, and Suzan-Lori Parks, to name but a few.

10. I am thinking of Aihwa Ong's *Flexible Citizenship: The Cultural Logics of Transnationality* (Durham, N.C.: Duke University Press, 1999); May Joseph's *Nomadic Identities* (Minneapolis: University of Minnesota Press, 1999); Timothy Brennan's *At Home in the World: Cosmopolitanism Now* (Cambridge, Mass.: Harvard University Press, 1997); essays collected in Carol A. Breckenridge et al., eds., *Cosmopolitanism* (Durham, N.C.: Duke University Press, 2002); and Bishnupriya Ghosh, *When Borne Across: The Literary Cosmopolitics of the Contemporary Indian Novel* (New Brunswick, N.J.: Rutgers University Press, 2004).

11. In the United States, the field of transnational cultural studies is associated with the Society for Transnational Cultural Studies and its house journal, *Public Culture*. See Arjun Appadurai and Carol Breckenridge, "Editor's Note" and "Why Public Culture?," *Public Culture* 1, no. 1 (Fall 1989): 1–9.

12. See Appadurai, *Modernity at Large*, and Aihwa Ong, *Flexible Citizenship*.

13. For such an analysis of transnational literary "cultures of circulation," see Ghosh, *When Borne Across*.

14. For earlier critical theoretical approaches to the public sphere and civil society, as loci of deliberation and communicative reason, see Hannah Arendt, *The Origins of Totalitarianism* (New York: Harcourt Brace Jovanovich, 1951), and Jürgen Habermas, *The Structural Transformation of the Public Sphere* (Cambridge, Mass.: MIT Press, 1991).

15. See David Palumbo-Liu, "Introduction: Unhabituated Habitués," in *Steams of Cultural Capital: Transnational Cultural Studies*, ed. David Palumbo-Liu and Hans Ulrich Gumbrecht (Stanford: Stanford University Press, 1997), 1–21.

16. This is Gayatri Chakravorty Spivak's expression, used as the title of the concluding chapter in *A Critique of Postcolonial Reason* (Cambridge, Mass.: Harvard University Press, 1999).

17. My conceptualization of "public history" and "public history work" builds on the articles appearing in the 2008 special issue of *Public Culture* that considered the politics of recognition on which historical or historiographic practices rely but rarely acknowledge. Brian Attwood, Dipesh Chakrabarty, and Claudio Lomnitz, "The Public Life of History," Guest Editors' Letter, *Public Culture* 20, no. 1 (2008): 1–4.

18. On the theoretical concepts of the dominant, emergent, and residual, see Raymond Williams, *Marxism and Literature* (Oxford: Oxford University Press), 121–27.

19. Taylor, *The Archive and the Repertoire*, xvi–xvii.

20. For an excellent discussion of archive and affect, see the final chapter of Cvetkovich, *An Archive of Feelings*, 239–71.

21. On postcolonial historiography, see especially Dipesh Chakrabarty, *Provincializing Europe: Postcolonial Thought and Historical Difference* (Princeton, N.J.: Princeton University Press, 2000), and David Lloyd, *Ireland after History* (Notre Dame, Ind.: University of Notre Dame Press in association with Field Day, 1999). In addition to postcolonial historiography, my thinking about historicism, the philosophy of history, and the experience of historical time is influenced by the work of Reinhart Koselleck, in particular *Futures Past: On the Semantics of Historical Time*, trans. Keith Tribe (New York: Columbia University Press, 2004). Hayden White and Paul Ricoeur likewise remain useful for thinking about the rhetorical tropes though which history enters into public discourse. See White, *Tropics of Discourse: Essays in Cultural Criticism* (Baltimore: Johns Hopkins University Press, 1978) and *The Content of the Form: Narrative Discourse and Historical Representation* (Baltimore: Johns Hopkins University Press, 1987); and Paul Ricoeur, *Time and Narrative*, 3 vols., trans. Kathleen McLaughlin and David Pellauer (Chicago: University of Chicago Press, 1984–88).

22. See, for instance, Ian Baucom, *Out of Place: Englishness, Empire, and the Locations of Identity* (Princeton, N.J.: Princeton University Press, 1999).

23. Peter Fryer's *Staying Power: The History of Black People in Britain* (London: Pluto Press, 1984) remains perhaps the most influential survey of postwar immigrations in the context of the longer history of black residence in the UK. See also Folarin Shyllon, *Black Slaves in Britain* (London: Oxford University Press, 1974) and *Black People in Britain, 1555–1833* (London: Oxford University Press, 1977); and Gretchen Gerzina, *Black London: Life before Emancipation* (New Brunswick, N.J.: Rutgers University Press, 1995). For a study of the demographic transformation of England since the war, see Anthony D. King, *Global Cities: Post-Imperialism and the Internationalization of London* (New York: Routledge, 1990), 71–155.

24. Tom Nairn had already predicted that as a consequence of this sense of "national decline" following the collapse of the Empire, Britain would continue to fracture along the fault lines of older ethnic identity formations and that Scotland, Wales, and even Northern Ireland were destined to break away. See Nairn, *The Break-up of Britain: Crisis and Neo-nationalism* (London: NLB, 1977). In the introduction to its third edition (Altona, Victoria: Common Ground, 2003), Nairn maintains this position, despite the continued participation of these three regions in the British national enterprise. The September 2014 national referendum on Scotland's independence suggests that Nairn may have been right all along.

25. See Paul Gilroy, *"There Ain't No Black in the Union Jack": The Racial Politics of Race and Nation* (Chicago: University of Chicago Press, 1987) and *The Black Atlantic: Modernity and Double Consciousness* (Cambridge, Mass.: Harvard

University Press, 1993). The former serves as a touchstone to periodizing the years leading up to and just following Thatcher's Prime Ministry. The latter was written from a more circumspect position, allowing Gilroy to see the transnational orchestration of global capital as a systemic and long historical phenomenon.

26. The filmmakers comprising the Sankofa Film and Video Collective included Isaac Julien, Martina Attille, Maureen Blackwood, Nadine Marsh-Edwards, and Robert Crusz. The Sankofa artists should be considered alongside a wider group of young black British artists who came into prominence in the early 1980s, including members of the BLK Art Group, Keith Piper, Marlene Smith, Eddie Chambers, and Donald Rodney, as well as those associated with the Black Arts Movement more broadly, such as David Bailey, Sonia Boyce, Rotimi Fani-Kayode, Lubaina Himid, and Eugene Palmer, among many others. Chris Ofili and Yinka Shonibare are more typically associated with the infamous and market-driven YBAs (Young British Artists). See Kobena Mercer, *Welcome to the Jungle: New Positions in Black Cultural Studies* (New York: Routledge, 1994); and David A. Bailey, Ian Baucom, and Sonia Boyce, eds., *Shades of Black: Assembling Black Arts in the 1980s* (Durham, N.C.: Duke University Press, 2005). I do not intend my mention of the transnational financing or global release of the film *Sankofa* as a criticism per se, but it does suggest shifting conditions in the means of film production indicative of the 1990s. Sankofa, it is important to note, is an Akan word for returning to the past ("go back and get it") and the name of an Adrinka storytelling symbol associated with the proverb "It is not wrong to go back for that which you have forgotten" *(Se wo were fi na wosankofa a yenkyi)*. The Sankofa symbol "depicts a mythical bird flying forward with its head turned backward. The egg in its mouth represents the 'gems' or knowledge of the past upon which wisdom is based; it also signifies the generation to come that would benefit from that wisdom." See the Spirituals Project of the University of Denver, "African Tradition, Proverbs, and Sankofa," *Sweet Chariot: The Story of the Spirituals,* http://www.spiritualsproject.org/sweetchariot/Literature/sankofa.php.

27. See Mercer, *Welcome to the Jungle;* Baucom, *Out of Place;* and Bailey, Baucom, and Boyce, *Shades of Black.*

28. See James Proctor's *Dwelling Places: Postwar Black British Writing* (Manchester, UK: University of Manchester Press, 2003); Mark Stein's *Black British Literature: Novels of Transformation* (Columbus: Ohio State University Press, 2004); John Clement Ball's *Imagining London: Postcolonial Fiction and the Transnational Metropolis* (Toronto: University of Toronto Press, 2004); John McLeod's *Postcolonial London: Rewriting the Metropolis* (New York: Routledge, 2004); and Ashley Dawson's *Mongrel Nation: Diasporic Culture and the Making of Postcolonial Britain* (Ann Arbor: University of Michigan Press, 2007).

29. Two other monographs come closer to identifying the history of slavery and the slave trade as particular concerns for recent black British writing: Lars

Eckstein's *Re-Membering the Black Atlantic: On the Poetics and Politics of Literary Memory* (New York: Rodopi, 2006) and Abigail Ward's *Caryl Phillips, David Dabydeen and Fred D'Aguiar: Representations of Slavery* (Manchester, UK: University of Manchester Press, 2011). Neither of these works, however, addresses the broader questions of historicization and periodization, or the intersection of creative expression, public culture, and state governmentality, and neither looks across creative forms and genres, preferring to reside within the purview of the literary.

30. See Michael Warner, "Publics and Counterpublics," *Public Culture* 14, no. 1 (Winter 2002): 49–90.

31. See Stephen Best and Saidiya Hartman, "Fugitive Justice," *Representations* 92 (Fall 2005): 1.

32. I am referring here to a number of studies in recent years on the broader projects of reparative and transitional justice, all of which try to imagine programs for amending historical injustice within both liberal and radical democratic frameworks. See, for instance, Elazar Barkan, *The Guilt of Nations: Restitution and Negotiating Historical Injustices* (Baltimore: Johns Hopkins University Press, 2001); Mark Amstutz, *The Healing of Nations: The Promise and Limits of Political Forgiveness* (Oxford: Rowman & Littlefield, 2005); John Torpey, *Making Whole What Has Been Smashed: On Reparations Politics* (Cambridge, Mass.: Harvard University Press, 2006); and Ruti G. Teitel, *Transitional Justice* (Oxford: Oxford University Press, 2000). I am also indebted to discussions held at the Redress Symposium in fall 2005 under the auspices of the Redress Project, a UC–Berkeley working group. As noted above, several of the papers presented that day have been published in a special issue of the journal *Representations* 92 (Fall 2005), edited by Stephen Best and Saidiya Hartman. Eve Kosofsky Sedgwick famously proposed reparation in its most deeply psychoanalytic sense as a viable antihegemonic critical practice. See "Paranoid Reading and Reparative Reading," in *Novel Gazing: Queer Readings of Fiction,* ed. Eve Kosofsky Sedgwick (Durham, N.C.: Duke University Press, 1997). I will return to the complicated conceptual and etymological history of redress in chapter 1.

33. See Bishnupriya Ghosh, "The Postcolonial Bazaar: Thoughts on Teaching the Market in Postcolonial Objects," *Postmodern Culture* 99, no. 1 (September 1998).

34. Without belaboring the contested causes, characteristics, or consequences of neoliberalism here, I take my cue from David Harvey, *A Brief History of Neoliberalism* (Oxford: Oxford University Press, 2005). "Neoliberalism," Harvey writes, "is in the first instance a theory of political economic practices that proposes that human well-being can best be advanced by liberating individual entrepreneurial freedoms and skills within an institutional framework characterized by strong private property rights, free markets and free trade. The role of the state is to create and preserve an institutional framework appropriate to such practices" (18).

35. My three main conceptual sources for thinking about the biopolitical are Michel Foucault, *"Society Must Be Defended": Lectures at the Collège de France, 1975–1976*, ed. Mauro Bertini and Alessandro Fontana, trans. David Macey (New York: Picador, 2003); Giorgio Agamben, *Homo Sacer: Sovereign Power and Bare Life*, trans. Daniel Heller-Roazen (Stanford: Stanford University Press, 1998); and Achille Mbembe, "Necropolitics," *Public Culture* 15, no. 1 (2003): 11–40.

36. Social death is, of course, Orlando Patterson's well-known expression. See *Slavery and Social Death: A Comparative Study* (Cambridge, Mass.: Harvard University Press, 1982). For a critique of the "vitalist ontologies" and "organismic metaphors" assumed by the expression "social life," on which both critical and nationalist discourses have relied, see Pheng Cheah, *Spectral Nationality: Passages of Freedom from Kant to Postcolonial Literature of Liberation* (New York: Columbia University Press, 2003), 1–18, 381–95. The two theoretically freighted terms of my title—"living" and "cargo"—attempt to hold in tension the life-making, death-letting, and death-meting forces of modern biopolitics and the precarious existence that follows, without reducing life lived as human bio-cargo to the condition of social death but, likewise, without reinstating the vitalist assumptions of social life.

37. There are, of course, all kinds of life forms that circulate as bio-cargo, following the rise of industrialized farming, new medical technologies, and genetic engineering. Chapter 4 addresses the continuities between older and newer medicalized forms of human bio-cargo as they intersect with a renewed interest in family genealogy and the possibilities opened up by the genetic mapping of human populations, which are then leveraged into new biohistoriographies of the African Atlantic. A much fuller consideration of the emergence of posthumanism in the academic humanities is necessary here but unfortunately remains beyond the scope of the current project.

38. The *Brookes* diagram is also central to Kevin Dalton-Johnson's *Captured Africans* (2005), a monument commissioned by the Slave Trade Arts Memorial Project (STAMP) for the city of Lancaster in advance of the 2007 commemoration of the two hundredth anniversary of the abolition of the slave trade in 1807. Likewise, in his large gallery installation *La Bouche du Roi* (1997–2005), Romuald Hazoumé arranged 304 plastic petrol cans into the shape of the central diagram of the *Brookes* plans, each can representing one of the Africans enslaved onboard. Titled after the coastal slave factory in present-day Benin, where Hazoumé was born, the installation was purchased by the British Museum in 2005 for the commemoration of the 1807 abolition of the slave trade and toured across Britain in 2006–7. As with many of the artists my book addresses, Hazoumé aims to show that "slavery has not ended; it has merely changed its form," saying in an interview, "My piece is not talking about old slave ships; it's about what happens today." See Michael White, "Carrying the Past into the Present: Romuald Hazoumé, 'La

Bouche du Roi," located on the event website, "1807 Commemorated: The Abolition of the Slave Trade," http://www.history.ac.uk/1807commemorated/exhibitions/art/labouche.html.

39. In one of its campaign posters, also from 2007, the Anti-Slavery Society, the same organization that helped produce the image en masse in the years leading up to the 1807 abolition of the trade, filled the outline of the fuselage of a modern passenger airliner with the same image used by Hank Willis Thomas. To be sure, the *Brookes* diagrams resonate with the present interest in "info-graphics" and "data visualization," both presentational forms that rely on the representational "icon" and both conducive to the neoliberal marketization of statistical information, leading to a series of controversial appropriation. A number of casual comparisons of the *Brookes* to conditions of modern air travel, none far removed from the 2007 Anti-Slavery Society poster, have been roundly criticized. But so were a group of well-meaning students at Durham University when, again in 2007, they performed a commemorative living re-creation of the *Brookes* on the Durham Cathedral Palace Green, an enactment also carried out at York Castle Museum that same year. See "Palace Green Transformed into a Slave Ship," https://www.dur.ac.uk/durham.first/winter07/slaveship/.

40. I am not the first to consider Hatoum's body of work within the context of modern biopolitics. See, for example, Jaleh Mansoor, "A Spectral Universality: Mona Hatoum's Biopolitics of Abstraction," *October* 133 (Summer 2010): 49–74.

41. I want to thank Mona Hatoum for taking time to read, comment on, and correct the details of my description of both installations.

42. Quoted in Mary Acton, *Learning to Look at Modern Art* (London: Routledge, 2004), 84.

43. Janine Antoni, "Interview: Mona Hatoum," *Bomb* 63 (Spring 1998): 54–61.

44. Agamben, *Homo Sacer*, 144.

45. Michel Foucault, *Discipline and Punish: The Birth of the Prison,* trans. Alan Sheridan (New York: Vintage Books, 1977), 297.

46. Betty Joseph, *Reading the East India Company, 1720–1840: Colonial Currencies of Gender* (Chicago: University of Chicago Press, 2004), 5. Arondikar also cites this passage from Joseph in *For the Record,* 13.

1. Beautiful Remnants, Brutal Remains

1. See, for example, Stephen Best and Saidiya Hartman, "Fugitive Justice," and the other articles collected in the special issue on redress in *Representations* 92 (Fall 2005).

2. For an excellent summation of and engagement with the notion of Afro-pessimism, see Jared Sexton, "The Social Life of Social Death," *Intentions* 5 (Fall/Winter 2011). For debates within African American studies, largely from within

the fields of literary and performance studies, over the politics of optimism and pessimism in black radical traditions, Sexton cites the work of Frank B. Wilderson III, Saidiya Hartman, Fred Moten, Alexander Weheliye, and José Muñoz, among others. In *Habeas Siscus: Racializing Assemblages, Biopolitics, and Black Feminist Theories of the Human* (Durham, N.C.: Duke University Press, 2014), Alexander Weheliye identifies Hortence Spillers as a foundational theorist in critical reconsideration of black life lived in the wake of social death.

3. David Dabydeen, *A Harlot's Progress* (London: Vintage Books, 1999), 156. Further citations appear in text.

4. See Walter Benjamin, "Left-Wing Melancholy," in *Selected Writings,* vol. 2, ed. Michael W. Jennings et al., trans. Rodney Livingstone (Cambridge, Mass.: Harvard University Press, 1999), 423–27. In addition to Hartman and Best, subsequent political configurations of melancholia appear in Paul Gilroy, *Postcolonial Melancholia* (New York: Columbia University Press, 2006); Anne Chang, *The Melancholy of Race* (New York: Oxford University Press, 2000); Judith Butler, *The Psychic Life of Power* (Stanford: Stanford University Press, 1997); Ranjana Khanna, *Dark Continents: Psychoanalysis and Colonialism* (Durham, N.C.: Duke University Press, 2003); and Ian Baucom's *Specters of the Atlantic: Finance Capital, Slavery, and the Philosophy of History* (Durham, N.C.: Duke University Press, 2005), which I will address later in the chapter.

5. Hortence Spillers, "'All the Things You Could Be by Now, if Sigmund Freud's Wife Was Your Mother': Psychoanalysis and Race," *Boundary 2* 23, no. 2 (Autumn 1996): 78.

6. Walter Benjamin, "Theses on the Philosophy of History," in *Illuminations,* ed. Hannah Arendt, trans. Harry Zohn (New York: Shocken Books, 1968), 253–64.

7. David Smith, "Blair: Britain's 'Sorrow' for the Shame of the Slave Trade," *Guardian,* 26 November 2006.

8. Tony Blair, "The Shame of Slavery," *New Nation,* 27 November 2006.

9. UNESCO had selected 23 August in recognition of the uprising in Saint-Domingue, which began on that day in 1791, led by Toussaint L'Ouverture. See UNESCO, "Breaking the Silence: Transatlantic Slave Trade Education Project," http://portal.unesco.org/education/en/ev.php-URL_ID=27835&URL_DO=DO_TOPIC&URL_SECTION=201.html.

10. Hugh Muir, "Livingstone Weeps as He Apologises for Slavery," *Guardian,* 24 August 2007.

11. Ken Livingstone, "Why I Am Saying Sorry for London's Role in This Horror," *Guardian,* 21 March 2007.

12. Granville Sharp, "Extract of a Letter (dated 3rd Oct. 1806) on the Extreme Wickedness, and Total Illegality of Tolerating Slavery in Any Part of the British Dominions," appended to *"The System of Colonial Law" Compared with the Eternal Laws of God; and with the Indispensible Principles of the English Constitution*

(London: Richard Edwards, 1807), 13–20. If the language sounds familiar, it is because the letter reproduces almost verbatim the argument of his much earlier and more familiar essay, *The Just Limitation of Slavery in the Laws of God, Compared with the Unbounded Claims of the African Traders and British American Slaveholders* (London: B. White and E. C. Dilly, 1776).

13. Sharp, "Extract of a Letter," 19. Scriptural arguments circulated on both sides of the slave-trade debate. See, for example, Rev. R. Harris, *Scriptural Researches on the Licitness of the Slave Trade, Shewing Its Conformity with the Principles of Natural and Revealed Religion Delineated in the Sacred Writings of the Word of God* (London: John Stockdale, 1788); or the anonymously written *Letter To Philo Africanus, upon Slavery; In Answer to His of the 22nd of November in the General Evening Post,* signed Candidus (London: W. Brown, 1788). Both tracts use their own biblical exegesis to dispute the theological argument put forth in Sharp's *Just Limitation.*

14. One might properly begin with a linguistic un-housing by turning to that remarkable archive of language, the *Oxford English Dictionary.* A survey of the term's etymology reveals a stunning array of meanings, both religious and secular; a list of synonyms would need to include amendment, atonement, correction, satisfaction, along with a sting of "re-" words: redemption, reformation, relief, remedy, reparation, and restitution, among others. In its earliest usage, redress meant the "satisfaction" of a wrong committed against or sustained by an individual, yet it also described an appeal against an unjust ruling by a judge or court, suggesting an *aporia* in which justice and injustice are housed together under the sign of the law. In another discursive register, however, redress means the correction of an individual's ethical direction or society's moral course. In its ameliorative sense, an act of redress might require the recovery or restitution of various kinds of property lost or stolen, including the "property" of human life. Indeed, in all its meanings, the word suggests a sense of something "proper" (or something owned or held *as* property) that has been lost and demands recovery. The term's polysemy is surprisingly broad, touching also on matters ranging from physical health to spiritual redemption. See *Oxford English Dictionary,* s.v. "redress" (n., v.1, and v.2.).

15. Best and Hartman, "Fugitive Justice," 1, emphasis added.

16. Derrida writes that one must "calculate with the incalculable" in order to come to a decision from which justice might emerge, despite the absolute undecidability of justice itself, which forever exceeds calculability. See "Ethics and Politics Today," in *Negotiations: Interviews and Interventions,* ed. and trans. Elizabeth Rottenberg (Stanford: Stanford University Press, 2002), 305. Derrida repeats this conception of justice in a number of his later works, including "Force of Law: The 'Mystical Foundation of Authority,'" in *Acts of Religion,* ed. Gil Anidjar, trans. Mary Quaintance (New York: Routledge, 2002), 230–98.

17. It is worth contrasting the divergent titles of the first and second editions of Cugoano's narrative. The first reads in full: *Thoughts and Sentiments on the Evil*

and Wicked Traffic of the Slavery and Commerce of the Human Species, Humbly Submitted to the Inhabitants of Great-Britain, by Ottobah Cugoano, a Native of Africa (London, 1787). The subsequent edition alters the second half of the title significantly, reading in full: *Thoughts and Sentiments on the Evil of Slavery; or the Nature of Servitude as Admitted by the Law of God, Compared to the Modern Slavery of Africans in the West Indies; In an Answer to the Advocates of Slavery and Oppression. Addressed to the Sons of Africa, by a Native* (London, 1791). The problems of calculability performed so concisely in Cugoano's initial title points toward the intimately material as well as expansively discursive relationship between law and commerce—indeed, the law of commerce—that is the subject of this and the following two chapters. The latter circulates within the scriptural debates identified above.

18. Saidiya Hartman, *Lose Your Mother: A Journey along the Atlantic Slave Route* (New York: Farrar, Straus and Giroux, 2007), 138. Further citations appear in text.

19. Saidiya V. Hartman, *Scenes of Subjection: Terror, Slavery, and Self-making in Nineteenth-Century America* (New York: Oxford University Press, 1997).

20. See Jacques Derrida, *Specters of Marx: The State of the Debt, the Work of Mourning, and the New International,* trans. Peggy Kamuf (New York: Routledge Press, 1994). On ethical spectrology in postcolonial discourse, see Bishnupriya Ghosh, "On Grafting the Vernacular: The Consequences of Postcolonial Spectrology," *boundary 2* 31, no. 2 (Summer 2004): 197–218.

21. For an excellent overview of English laws governing slavery and the slave trade, see E. V. Goveia, *The West Indian Slave Laws of the 18th Century* (Barbados: Caribbean Universities Press, 1970); and Lord Bingham of Cornhill, "'The Law Favours Liberty': Slavery and the English Common Law," in *Essex Law Lecture: The First University of Essex and Clifford Chance Law Lecture* (Essex: University of Essex and Clifford Chance, 2007). For a sense of the eighteenth- and early nineteenth-century debates over the increasingly convoluted status of slavery and law, see the abolitionist tract *A Summary View of Negro Slavery, as It Existed in Our West India Colonies; With a Few Cases Shewing the Cruel and Defective Operation of Colonial Law* (Hull: Hull and East Riding Anti-Slavery Association, 1824).

22. While a footnote reveals that Hartman consulted several (though not all) printed versions of the trial, she does not otherwise distinguish or contextualize their variants but conflates details from each.

23. In her own effort at an ongoing self-reflexive engagement, Hartman has revisited, even redressed, her earlier narrative reconstruction, in particular what she sees as a repetition of the violent erasure of the second woman killed aboard the *Recovery,* whom the crew referred to as Venus. See Hartman, "Venus in Two Acts," *Small Axe* 26 (June 2008): 1–14. Hartman develops her notion of "critical fabulation" as a mode of narrative historiography, with narrative form resonant with but not identical to what I have described as a critical redressive historiography.

24. See *An Abstract of the Evidence Delivered before a Select Committee of the House of Commons, in 1790 and 1791; On the Part of the Petitioners for the Abolition of the Slave Trade* (London: James Phillips, 1791). Initially printed by the important antislavery campaigner James Phillips, the *Abstract* was subsequently reprinted and distributed widely by the Glasgow and Edinburgh Societies for the Abolition of the Slave Trade, among others, and remained in print well into the nineteenth century in both the UK and the United States. Similar summaries of evidence presented in Parliament or in local colonial assemblies were published by both sides of the slave trade debate to bolster their arguments.

25. Hartman offers an excellent analysis of Cruikshank's illustration, on which my brief reading builds. It is worth noting that Cruikshank's illustration appears in the current edition of Cugoano's *Thoughts and Sentiments on the Evil of Slavery,* ed. Vincent Carretta (New York: Penguin Classics, 1999).

26. Hortence Spillers, "Mama's Baby, Papa's Maybe: An American Grammar-book," *Diacritics* 17, no. 2 (Summer 2007): 68.

27. Uncertain Commons, *Speculate This!* (Durham, N.C.: Duke University Press, 2013).

28. Granville Sharp attended the second trial between the insurers and investors and is credited with relentlessly publicizing the events on board the *Zong* as an instance of brutal atrocity against which the abolitionists fought. See *Memoirs of Granville Sharp,* ed. Prince Hoare (London: Henry Colburn, 1820), 236–47. It was Olaudah Equiano, however, who brought the legal case of the *Zong* to Sharp's attention on 19 March 1783, after having seen a report on the first trial in the *Morning Chronicle and London Advertiser* the previous day.

29. The implications of Baucom's argument against speculation are far ranging and beyond full consideration here. His suggestion that modes of critical speculation are variably but inevitably caught up in the "actuarial" logic of exchange is essentially an argument against what he describes as "High Theory," structuralism and deconstruction specifically. For an antidote to Baucom's construal of speculation, I refer once again to *Speculate This!,* which argues for an affirmative speculation that operates outside the economic logic to which speculation has been harnessed.

30. Fred D'Aguiar, *Feeding the Ghosts* (New York: Ecco Press, 1999), 4. Further citations appear in text.

31. The story of the survivor who, after being thrown overboard, manages to scale the side of the *Zong* and hide away for the duration of the voyage also comes from Sharp's *Memoirs.* On the case's legal ramifications for insurance law, see also Shyllon, *Black Slaves in Britain,* 184–209.

32. See Jacques Derrida, with Anne DuFourmantelle, *Of Hospitality,* trans. Rachel Bowlby (Stanford: Stanford University Press, 2000), 21–25.

2. Living Rough

1. A growing body of scholarship situates the structural and historical development of the carceral in the context of global neoliberalism, the replacement of the social welfare state with a privatized and militarized "security state," the expansion of clandestine operations—indefinite detention, black sites, torture, drone warfare—and the intensification of coercive labor migrations and human trafficking. For a useful overview, see Lucia Zender, *Security* (London: Routledge, 2009), and Mark Neocleous, *Critique of Security* (Edinburgh: Edinburgh University Press, 2008). For a useful discussion of security in the context of British law, see Peter Ramsay, *The Insecurity State: Vulnerable Autonomy and the Right to Security in Criminal Law* (Oxford: Oxford University Press, 2012). For a longer historicization, see James Hevia's recent *The Imperial Security State: British Colonial Knowledge and Empire Building* (Cambridge: Cambridge University Press, 2015). In a U.S. context, see Michelle Alexander's *The New Jim Crow: Mass Incarceration in an Age of Colorblindness* (New York: New Press, 2012), and Douglas Blackmon, *Slavery by Another Name: The Re-Enslavement of Black Americans from the Civil War to World War II* (New York: Doubleday, 2008); and in a transnational one, see Paul Amar, *The Security Archipelago* (Durham, N.C.: Duke University Press, 2012), and Ken Bales, *Disposable People: New Slavery in the Global Economy* (Berkeley: University of California Press, 2012).

2. Caryl Phillips, *Higher Ground* (New York: Vintage International, 1995), 88.

3. Caryl Phillips, *Cambridge* (New York: Vintage International, 1993).

4. Caryl Phillips, *Crossing the River* (New York: Vintage International, 1995).

5. Caryl Phillips, *Foreigners* (New York: Alfred A. Knopf, 2007).

6. Phillips has discussed his narrative strategies in a number of interviews. See, for instance, Lars Eckstein, "The Insistence of Voices: An Interview with Caryl Phillips," *ARIEL: A Review of International English Literature* 32, no. 2 (April 2001): 33–43; Renee Schattemann, "Disrupting the Master Narrative: An Interview with Caryl Phillips," *Commonwealth Essays and Studies* 23, no. 2 (Spring 2001): 93–106; Maya Jaggi, "Interview with Caryl Phillips," *Brick: A Literary Journal* 49 (Summer 1994): 73–77. For a critical assessment of the novel's narrative techniques, see Paul Sharrad, "Speaking the Unspeakable: London, Cambridge and the Caribbean," in *De-Scribing Empire: Post-Colonialism and Textuality*, ed. Chris Tiffin and Alan Lawson (London: Routledge, 1994), 201–17.

7. Phillips, *Crossing the River*, 35. Further citations appear in text.

8. Fredric Jameson, *The Political Unconscious: Narrative as a Socially Symbolic Act* (Ithaca, N.Y.: Cornell University Press, 1981), 17–43. On Phillips's particular engagement with colonial history, see Andrew Armstrong, "bloody history! Exploring a Capacity for Revision, Restaging History in Wilson Harris's *Jonestown* and Caryl Phillips' *The Nature of Blood*," *Jouvert: A Journal of Postcolonial Studies* 6, no. 3

(Spring 2002); Angeles de la Concha, "The End of History: Or Is It? Circularity versus Progress in Caryl Phillips' *The Nature of Blood*," *Miscelanea: A Journal of English and American Studies* 22 (2000): 1–19; Kathie Birat, "A Shameful Intercourse: Meaning and Signifying in Caryl Phillips's Novels of the Slave Trade," *GRAAT: Publication des Groupes de Recherches Anglo-Americaines de l'Universite Francois Rabelais de Tours* 20 (1999): 33–47, and "'Re-Visionary Strategies': History and Fiction in the Novels of Caryl Phillips and Wilson Harris," in *Theory and Literary Creation / Theorie et Creation Litteraire,* ed. Jean-Pierre Durix (Dijon: Éditions Universitaires de Dijon, 1999), 21–31; Claude Julien, "Surviving through a Pattern of Timeless Moments: A Reading of Caryl Phillips's *Crossing the River,*" in *Black Imagination and the Middle Passage,* ed. Maria Diedrich, Henry Louis Gates Jr., and Carl Pedersen (Oxford: Oxford University Press, 1999), 86–95; Benedicte Ledent, "Remembering Slavery: History as Roots in the Fiction of Caryl Phillips and Fred D'Aguiar," in *The Contact and the Culmination,* ed. Marc Delrez and Benedicte Ledent (Liège, Belgium: L3, Liège Language and Literature, 1997), 271–80, and "'Overlapping Territories, Intertwined Histories': Cross-Culturality in Caryl Phillips's *Crossing the River,*" *Journal of Commonwealth Literature* 30, no. 1 (1995): 55–62.

9. The speaker's comment—"There are no paths in water. No signposts. There is no return"—challenges Édouard Glissant's notion of a "submarine network" linked by "underwater signposts" of African bodies discarded at sea. See Glissant, *Poetics of Relation,* trans. Betsy Wing (Ann Arbor: University of Michigan Press, 1997), 6.

10. Carol Margaret Davison, "Crisscrossing the River: An Interview with Caryl Phillips," *Ariel* 25, no. 4 (October 1994): 91–99.

11. See Homi Bhabha, *The Location of Culture* (London: Routledge, 1994), 85–92.

12. See A. C. Carmichael, *Domestic Manners and Social Condition of the White, Coloured, and Negro Population of the West Indies* (London: Wittacker, Treacher, 1833); Maria Nugent, *Lady Nugent's Journal of Her Residence in Jamaica from 1801 to 1805,* 4th new rev. ed. (Kingston: Institute of Jamaica, 1966); and Monk Lewis, *Journal of a West Indian Proprietor* (London: Murray, 1834). Evelyn O'Callaghan usefully identifies several of Phillips's sources, including Carmichael, Nugent, and Lewis. See O'Callaghan, "Historical Fiction and Fictional History: Caryl Phillips's *Cambridge,*" *Journal of Commonwealth Literature* 28, no. 2 (1993), 34–47: In an interview with Graham Swift, Phillips also names Janet Schaw's *Journal of a Lady of Quality* (New Haven, Conn.: Yale University Press, 1921). See Swift, "Caryl Phillips Interviewed by Graham Swift," *Kunapipi* 13, no. 3 (1991): 96–103.

13. In addition to the sources identified above, my reading is informed by a wide range of historical documents representing debates between pro- and antislavery forces in the colonies and in Britain, including but not limited to David

Collins, *Practical Rules for the Management and Medical Treatment of Negro Slaves, in the Sugar Colonies by a Professional Planter* (London: Printed by J. Barfield for Vernor and Hood, 1803); Thomas Roughley, *The Jamaica Planter's Guide, Or, A System for Planting and Managing a Sugar Estate, Or Other Plantations in That Island* (London: Longman, Hurst, Rees, Orme, and Brown, 1823); Thomas Cooper, *Facts Illustrative of the Condition of the Negro Slave in Jamaica* (London: J. Hatchard, 1824); J. E. Alexander, *Transatlantic Sketches: Comprising Visits to the Most Interesting Scenes in North and South America, and the West Indies; With Notes on Negro Slavery and Canadian Emigration* (London: R. Bentley, 1833); and articles printed in the pages of *The Anti-Slavery Monthly Reporter* (London: Society for the Mitigation and Abolition of Slavery in the British Dominions, 1825–30), retitled *The Anti-Slavery Reporter* (1830–36).

14. John Newton's *Journal of a Slave Trader,* ed. Bernard Martin and Mark Spurrell (London: Epworth Press, 1962), is the only source Phillips explicitly acknowledges in the book's front matter.

15. In an interview, Phillips rejects the charge of pessimism, insisting on the capacity to "grow" through the experience of suffering, especially suffering the following from dislocation: "*Cambridge* is to some extent optimistic. Emily grows. Okay, she suffers greatly, but she still grows. It's the price of the ticket, isn't it? The displacement ticket. Displacement engenders a great deal of suffering, a great deal of confusion, a great deal of soul-searching. It would be hard for me to write a comedy about displacement." See Swift, "Caryl Phillips," 103.

16. In addition to O'Callaghan, see Timothy Bewes, "Shame, Ventriloquy, and the Problem of the Cliché in Caryl Phillips," *Cultural Critique* 63 (2006): 33–60.

17. As I noted in the introduction, Achille Mbembe demonstrates how the slave ship and slave plantation operated under the structural logic Agamben describes, long before the concentration camps of Nazi Germany, Agamben's paradigmatic example. See Mbembe, "Necropolitics," 21–23.

18. Colin [Joan] Dayan, "Legal Slaves and Civil Bodies," *Nepantla: Views from the South* 2, no. 1 (2001): 3.

19. Lewis, *Journal of a West Indian Proprietor,* 87. Verene A. Shepherd describes acts of bodily defiance practiced by enslaved women as "gynaecological resistance." See Shepherd, "'Petticoat Rebellion?': The Black Woman's Body and Voice in the Struggles for Freedom in Colonial Jamaica, in *In the Shadow of the Plantation: Caribbean History and Legacy,* ed. Alvin O. Thompson (Kingston: Ian Randle, 2002), 17–38.

20. The artist Yinka Shonibare makes visible the regime of the corset in many of his gallery installations, a topic I take up in chapter 5.

21. Henry Nelson Coleridge, *Six Months in the West Indies, in 1825* (London: John Murray, 1826), 331.

22. Phillips considers the similarities between the experiences of African and Jewish diasporas in several works, but most extensively in *The Nature of Blood* (New York: Vintage International, 1997).

23. Ranjana Khanna reminds us of Octave Mannoni's gloss on the distinction between denial and disavowal, *"Je sais bien, mais quand meme"* (I know very well, but even so . . .). See Khanna, *Dark Continents,* 147.

24. Bhabha, *The Location of Culture,* 66.

25. On cultural hybridity in Phillips's novels, see Brad Buchanan, "Caryl Phillips: Colonialism, Cultural Hybridity, and Racial Difference," in *Contemporary British Fiction,* ed. Richard J. Lane, Rod Mengham, and Philip Tew (Cambridge: Polity Press, 2003), 174–90.

26. On legal limitations placed on the admissibility of testimony provided by blacks, whether enslaved or free, see Goveia, *West Indian Slave Laws,* 34.

27. Agamben, *Homo Sacer,* 81–86.

28. Goveia, *West Indian Slave Laws,* 25.

29. Although Dayan neither uses biopolitics as a theoretical framework nor cites Foucault's work, my use of these terms is consonant with her description of carceral society.

30. This part of the narrative is loosely based on George Jackson's *Soledad Brother: The Prison Letters of George Jackson* (New York: Coward-McCann, 1970). On the literature of antiracism in the post-Thatcher era, see Dave Gunning, "Anti-Racism, the Nation-State, and Contemporary Black British Literature," *Journal of Commonwealth Literature* 39, no. 2 (June 2004): 29–43.

3. Compound Fractures

1. Judith Butler, *Frames of War* (London: Verso, 2009), 11. Butler plays on the wide-ranging polysemy of the word *framed,* contrasting the way in which a painting is "framed" with how a criminal is "framed." Butler regards the frame as a precursor to apprehension; the frame cordons off a set of signs that are then contained (or detained) for interpretation while it consigns (or banishes) others to an outside it likewise defines (8–9). Butler's frame articulates well with Derrida's theory of the archive as a way of thinking about the function of the law.

2. Fred Moten, "The Case for Blackness," *Criticism* 50, no. 2 (Spring 2008): 177–218.

3. It should be noted that Dabydeen is himself a Hogarth scholar, having written a definitive study of African figures in the artist's work, *Hogarth's Blacks: Images of Blacks in Eighteenth-Century British Art* (Athens: University of Georgia Press, 1987), a topic on which he also presented in his film *Art of Darkness* (New York: Filmmakers Library, 1996). For a concise overview of Hogarth's body of work, see the catalog for a major exhibition compiled by Mark Hallett and

Christine Ridin, eds., *Hogarth* (London: Tate, 2006). Ronald Paulson remains the foundational scholar of Hogarth, beginning with his first study, *Hogarth: His Life, Art, and Times*, 2 vols. (New Haven, Conn.: Yale University Press, 1971), followed by *Hogarth*, 3 vols. (New Brunswick, N.J.: Rutgers University Press, 1991–93), and *A Harlot's Harlot: Sacred Parody in Enlightenment England* (Baltimore: Johns Hopkins University Press, 2003), which provides a sustained analysis of *A Harlot's Progress* as an example of the way in which Hogarth engages with religious themes through what Paulson calls "sacred parody." His argument proves useful for my reading of atonement, redemption, and salvation as dominant themes in the novel later in this chapter.

4. See Robert B. Stepto, *From Behind the Veil: A Study of Afro-American Narrative*, 2nd ed. (Urbana: University of Illinois Press, 1979); William Andrews, *To Tell a Free Story: The First Century of Afro-American Autobiography, 1760–1892* (Urbana: University of Illinois Press, 1986); and Frances Smith Foster, *Written by Herself: Literary Production by African American Women, 1746–1892* (Bloomington: Indiana University Press, 1993).

5. On the South Sea Company and the economic bubble with which it is most remembered, see Richard Dale, *The First Crash: Lessons from the South Sea Bubble* (Princeton, N.J.: Princeton University Press, 2004). The name "War of Jenkins's Ear" was coined by Thomas Carlyle, suggesting yet another creative anachronism. See N. A. M. Rodger, *The Command of the Ocean: A Naval History of Britain, 1649–1815* (New York: W. W. Norton, 2005), 240.

6. I will return to the analogies of redemption and repair, redress and regeneration, in chapters 4 and 6.

7. Olaudah Equiano, *The Interesting Narrative of the Life of Olaudah Equiano, or Gustavus Vassa, the African; Written by Himself*, ed. Vincent Carretta (New York: Penguin Classics, 2003). James Walvin's critical biography, *An African's Life: The Life and Times of Olaudah Equiano, 1745–1797* (New York: Continuum, 2000), provides a useful publication history for *The Interesting Narrative*, as does Vincent Carretta's *Equiano, the African: Biography of a Self-Made Man* (Athens: University of Georgia Press, 2005). See also Carretta's critical introduction to the Penguin Classics edition of Equiano's narrative.

8. Mungo's account of his relationship with Saba appears to reverse a memorable moment in *The Interesting Narrative*, in which he recounts "a trifling incident which surprised [him] agreeably." Then twelve years old and briefly stationed on the Isle of Wight, long since removed from Africa, Equiano encounters another black child about his own age: "This boy having observed me from his master's house, was transported at the sight of one of his own countrymen, and ran to meet me with the utmost haste. I not knowing what he was about, turned a little out of his way at first, but to no purpose; he soon came close to me, and caught hold of me in his arms as if I had been his brother, though we had never seen each other

before" (85). The trope of recognition as "mirroring" is ambivalent—Equiano turns away but is nevertheless embraced—but it is worth noting that Mungo or Saba might stand in for either Equiano or the "back boy about [his] own size," so frequent are the reversals between them.

9. Mungo's account of the katran bush, and his recollections of mother more generally, resonates with Equiano's description of his mother's offering of ancestral "oblations" in *The Interesting Narrative,* 40.

10. Dabydeen takes the name of the infamous plantation owner and overseer Thomas Thistlewood, whose diary meticulously recorded in agonizing, sadistic detail the physical and sexual abuse of slaves at Egypt Plantation in Jamaica. Note that Mungo names Thistlewood as the captain of the slave ship that transported him to England rather than a plantation owner in the West Indies, a strategic historical catachresis in his performance of the archive. Although the fictional Thistlewood does not follow the historical Thistlewood's biography, his name serves as a powerful trope for the agents of colonial atrocity and a figure for those who perpetrated and perpetuated brutality on which the slave economy depended. Thistlewood operates like the "example" discussed in the first chapter, a figure that stands beside itself as both singular and exceptional. The use of his name also plays on historical time; a specter of a future that is now past, the name Thistlewood simultaneously produces the anxiety of anticipation and the nausea of remorse. See Douglas Hall, *In Miserable Slavery: Thomas Thistlewood in Jamaica, 1750–86* (New York: Macmillan, 1999), and Trevor Burnard, *Mastery, Tyranny, and Desire: Thomas Thistlewood and His Slaves in the Anglo-Jamaican World* (Chapel Hill: University of North Carolina Press, 2004).

11. Walter Benjamin, "Critique of Violence," in *Reflections: Essays, Aphorisms, Autobiographical Writing,* ed. Peter Demetz, trans. Edmund Jephcott (New York: Schocken Books, 1986), 300.

12. Lars Eckstein, "Getting Back to the Idea of Art as Art: An Interview with David Dabydeen," *World Literature Written in English* 39, no. 1 (2001): 29–30.

13. The expression "cash nexus" is derived from Thomas Carlyle's lament, his essay *Chartism* (London: Levey, Robson, and Franklyn, 1840), over the effects of laissez-faire economics on the "lower classes" of British society: "O reader, to what shifts is poor Society reduced, in epochs when the Cash Payment has become the sole nexus of man to men" (61). Carlyle valorized the guiding hand of the feudal aristocracy over the invisible hand of the market, the retracted hand of the state, and their substitution by the "hand outs" of philanthropy, here represented by Pringle and the Abolitionist Society. It is worth noting that the word *nexus* has its root in ancient Roman law, where it named a system of contractual debt-bondage in which the body and person of the borrower was offered as material collateral for the money borrowed. While the nexi were not considered slaves in the modern sense, they were held in contractual bondage. This form of indenture, in which the

obligation that binds the debtor to his creditor is guaranteed by a promissory note "signed" by the debtor's body or a body that substitutes for the debtor, such as a child, as collateral, suggests a similar juridical imaginary that sanctioned the property logic of human bio-cargo. This sense of bonded obligation was still clearly at work in Carlyle's use of the term, and it continues to haunt the word's meaning in the "virtual" explosion of its use in the last quarter century. Beyond the cash nexus described by Carlyle, and much later by Dabydeen, the nexus itself binds human life to personal debt; it is thus the economic configuration we most associate with neoliberalism. Livy recounts the abolition of the nexum in the fourth century BCE, which followed the attempted abuse of a young man at the hands of a lecherous master, a story with strong resemblance to Mungo's relationship to Thistlewood. See Livy's *History of Rome (Ab Urbe Contita Libri),* book 8, chapter 28, The Latin Library, http://www.thelatinlibrary.com/livy/liv.8.shtml. A recent translation appears as Livy, *Rome's Italian Wars: Books Six to Ten,* trans. J. C. Yardley (Oxford: Oxford University Press, 2013), 146.

14. See Simon Gikandi, *Slavery and the Culture of Taste* (Princeton, N.J.: Princeton University Press, 2011).

15. William Hogarth, *The Analysis of Beauty: Written with a View of Fixing the Fluctuating Ideas of Taste* (London: J. Reeves, 1753), 33. Further citations appear in text.

16. Mungo is perhaps misremembering Michel Adanson's *Voyage to Senegal, the Isle of Goree, and the River Gambia* (London: J. Norse, 1759), which appeared in English translation in 1759. Some catalogs list the author as Michael Adamson.

17. The most infamous promulgator of this theory was C. G. Seligman in *The Races of Africa* (London: Oxford University Press, 1930).

4. Blood Pressures

1. I am here also drawing on what Lauren Berlant calls the "intimate public sphere." See Berlant, *The Queen of America Goes to Washington City* (Durham, N.C.: Duke University Press, 1997), 1–24.

2. Elizabeth Povinelli, *The Empire of Love: Toward a Theory of Intimacy, Genealogy, and Carnality* (Durham, N.C.: Duke University Press, 2006), 206.

3. Melinda Cooper, *Life as Surplus: Biotechnology and Capitalism in the Neoliberal Era* (Durham, N.C.: Duke University Press, 2007), 3.

4. *African American Lives,* hosted by Henry Louis Gates Jr. (Arlington, Va.: PBS, 2006). As most readers are likely aware, Gates worked with professional genealogists, academic historians, and population geneticists in order to limn the heretofore "lost" family lineages of a handful of African American celebrity participants, perhaps most notably the talk-show personalities Oprah Winfrey and Whoopi Goldberg. Given the long history of violently separating black families and erasing

family lineages, Gates's project offered a way in which African Americans today could reconnect with their ancestors and reestablish a sense of family and collective belonging to Africa. Subsequent programs and companion volumes include *African American Lives II* (Arlington, Va.: PBS, 2008); *Faces of America* (Arlington, Va.: PBS, 2010); *Finding Your Roots* (Arlington, Va.: PBS, 2012); as well as companion volumes authored by Gates: *In Search of Our Roots: How 19 Extraordinary African Americans Reclaimed Their Past* (New York: Crown, 2009); *Faces of America: How 12 Extraordinary People Discovered Their Pasts* (New York: New York University Press, 2010); and *Finding Your Roots: The Official Companion to the PBS Series* (Chapel Hill: University of North Carolina Press, 2014).

5. Claudia Kalb, "In Our Blood," *Newsweek,* 6 February 2006. The confidence of Kalb's assertion reminds us of the easy, often unwitting, slide from the language of family trees and genetic tracking to the trope of blood.

6. Henry Louis Gates Jr., "We Are All Africans: Genealogical Research and DNA Testing Can Reveal Your African Roots," *Ebony* (December 2007), 133.

7. Ibid., 134.

8. Ibid., 135.

9. Kalb, "In Our Blood."

10. Toni Coleman, "Regaining a Lost Heritage," *Issues in Higher Education,* 8 February 2007. Coleman highlights the gap between the expectations proponents of DNA testing produce and the very limited information such testing actually supplies.

11. Alondra Nelson, "Henry Louis Gates's Extended Family," *Chronicle of Higher Education,* 12 February 2010. Further quotations in this paragraph are from this source. Nelson's *Social Life of DNA: Race, Reparations, and Reconciliation after the Genome* (Boston: Beacon Press, 2016) appeared as *Living Cargo* went into production, so I was unable to address it here.

12. Quoted in Nelson, "Henry Louis Gates's Extended Family." Duster likewise refers to DNA tests as "a disturbing sleight of hand," in which the limits of technology narrow sharply the lines of descent that can be traced. "What an arbitrary 'choice' of a branch on the family tree!" he declares. Companies offering genetic testing are often limited to the only DNA samples collected in their own databases, as proprietary interests keep companies from sharing information with one another. For instance, African Ancestry, Inc., the company that Gates co-founded with Dr. Paul Kittles, a geneticist at the University of Chicago, claims to have the most extensive database of African and African American DNA, and has been criticized for not sharing that information with other organizations. Gina Paige, a consumer product specialist who was the founding president of African Ancestry, insists, "Really, the community created the company by demanding the service"; they have simply "commercialized" their research in order to "make it available to the world." See Coleman, "Regaining a Lost Heritage."

13. Gates, "We Are All Africans," 136.

14. Ibid.

15. Ibid.

16. Ibid.

17. Elizabeth Povinelli, "Notes On Gridlock," *Public Culture* 14, no. 1 (2002): 215.

18. Ibid., 216.

19. The incorporation of a family genealogy, of course, is not unique to this novel and certainly has significant precedent in a number of historical genres. Andrea Levi's *The Long Song* (New York: Picador, 2010) might be considered in this context, with particular attention to the relationship between the first-person metanarrative voice and the conventions the speaker is both aware of and expressly violates.

20. Bernardine Evaristo, *Lara,* new ed. (Tarset, Northumberland: Bloodaxe Books, 2009), 17. The lines quoted below are also from this poem. The new edition varies significantly from the original publication, which appeared as *Lara* (Turnbridge Wells, Kent: Angela Royal Publishing, 1997). All quotations from this work are from the 2009 edition.

21. Its Latin source suggests the one who is cut, severed, scarred. Severina is also the name of the Roman emperor Aurelian's wife, who was herself perhaps the first empress to have ruled over the entirety of the Roman Empire. Her name is yet another instance in which the naming of slaves follows a cruel history of giving the most powerless the names of the most powerful. We might recall Evaristo's interest in the history of Roman occupation of the British Isles in Andrea Levy's *Emperor's Babe: A Verse Novel of Londonium, 211 A.D.* (New York: Viking, 2001).

22. Dorothea Smartt's original chapbook appeared under the title *Samboo's Grave—Bilal's Grave* (London: Peepal Tree Press, 2007). Further citations appear in text and refer to the revised collection published as *Ship Shape* (London: Peepal Tree Press, 2008).

23. Although Lancaster is not often associated with the slave trade, it was in fact the fourth largest slave port in the UK, behind Liverpool, London, and Bristol. About two hundred slave ships departed from Lancaster in the eighteenth century. For more information on Lancaster and the slave trade, see Slave Trade Arts Memorial Project (STAMP), "Commemorating Abolition: The Slave Trade Arts Memorial Project, Lancaster," available at the Wayback Machine Internet Archive, https://web.archive.org/web/20100415055249/http://www.uclan.ac.uk/ahss/journalism_media_communication/literature_culture/abolition/stamp.php.

24. Information on the work's commission and composition was provided in a conversation with the poet conducted in London, 22 August 2007.

25. STAMP, "Commemorating Abolition."

26. See Dabydeen, *Hogarth's Blacks.*

27. A note at the end of the poem explains that "grocer" was "a popular Lancastrian misnomer for those involved in the buying and selling of goods resulting from the trans-Atlantic slave trade." Smartt, *Ship Shape,* 10.

28. The title of the poem is a play on the proverbial phrase "ship-shape and Bristol fashion," which was used to describe a sailing vessel in good order and prepared for departure, its cargo tied down and secure. The expression was the subject of some controversy in 2005 when a training session on workplace diversity suggested that the phrase originated in a derogatory saying associated with the slave trade. Incredulous journalists jumped at the opportunity to discredit the "politically correct" atmosphere promoted by the session organizers by tracing the expression back to the geography of the Bristol Harbor, though not definitively so. Smartt seems to want to draw attention to the way in which the phrase itself, regardless of its origin, is necessarily linked to the broader history of the triangular Atlantic economy. See Richard Savill, "Thought Police Go Overboard," *Telegraph,* 20 May 2005.

29. A note in the text tells us that the term Maafa is the Kiswahili word for "disaster" or "terrible occurrence" to describe the "African Holocaust of the slave trade."

30. Homi Bhabha, *The Location of Culture,* 66.

31. Derrida, *Archive Fever,* 16–17. Further citations appear in text. The book's subtitle, *A Freudian Impression,* draws our attention to the central role that psychoanalytic theory plays in Derrida's theory of the archive.

32. See Foucault, *The Archaeology of Knowledge,* 126–31.

33. Inge Blackman, dir., *Legacy,* 17 min., DVD recording (San Francisco: Frameline, 2006).

34. See the entry on "Kumina" in "History Notes: Information on Jamaica's Cultural Heritage," National Library of Jamaica, http://www.nlj.gov.jm/jamaican-history-notes#kumina.

35. Luce Irigaray, *This Sex Which Is Not One,* trans. Catherine Porter (Ithaca, N.Y.: Cornell University Press, 1985), 171–72.

36. See Elizabeth Freeman, *Time Binds: Queer Temporalities, Queer Histories* (Durham, N.C.: Duke University Press, 2010), 95–135.

37. Hilton Als, "The Sojourner: The Elusive Langston Hughes," *New Yorker,* 23 February 2015.

38. See Lynda Hart, *Between the Body and the Flesh: Performing Sadomasochism* (New York: Columbia University Press, 1998).

39. Freeman, *Time Binds,* 144.

40. These comments were made in a talk organized in 2001 at the Tate Britian for artists nominated for that year's Turner Prize. See "Turner Prize 2001 Artists: Isaac Julien," archived on the museum website, http://www.tate.org.uk/whats-on/

tate-britain/exhibition/turner-prize-2001/turner-prize-2001-shortlisted-artists/turner-1.

41. David Orgeron, "Re-Membering History in Isaac Julien's 'The Attendant,'" *Film Quarterly* 53, no. 4 (Summer 2000): 33.

42. Isaac Julien, "Confessions of a Snow Queen: Notes on the Making of *The Attendant*," *Critical Quarterly* 36, no. 1 (Spring 1994): 120.

43. Julien misidentifies the title of the painting as *Scene on the Coast of Africa.* See "Confessions of a Snow Queen," 120.

44. *Dido and Aeneas* was first performed in 1689 with a libretto by Nahum Tate. Joseph Roach calls Purcell's *Dido and Aeneas* "a representative event in the genealogy of circum-Atlantic performance," that is, an "enactment of encounter, rupture, and dynastic establishment" linked to both a diasporic rather than autochthonous origin myth of Englishness and to its own moment of economic production and consumption (42). See Roach, *Cities of the Dead: Circum-Atlantic Performance* (New York: Columbia University Press, 1996).

45. It is in the use of these tableaux, in particular the way in which the camera is able to move through the mise-en-scène depicted in the painting, that the influence of Raoul Ruiz's *L'hypothèse du tableau volé* (1979) is most felt.

46. Julien, "Confessions of a Snow Queen," 122.

47. Ibid., 120.

48. Orgeron, "Re-Membering History," 35.

49. Ibid., 36.

50. Julien, "Confessions of a Snow Queen," 122–23.

51. Ibid., 123.

52. Ibid.

53. The criminal case was decided under anachronistic British laws and precedents, namely the 1861 Offences Against the Person Act and a 1934 precedent for applying that law to heterosexual S/M practices. Although the Law Commission has recommended changes to the law regarding S/M, it remains in place today. This information is taken from the excellent online archive "Spanner on the Web," hosted by David Barnsdale, which archives not only materials related to the court cases but also information for S/M activists in the UK and abroad. See www.barnsdle.demon.co.uk/span/span1.html.

54. Julien, "Confessions of a Snow Queen," 125.

5. Bespoke History

1. My thinking about forms of queer time is influenced by Elizabeth Freeman, especially *Time Binds.*

2. James Sherwood, *The London Cut: Savile Row Bespoke Tailoring* (Venice: Marsilio, 2007), 12.

3. The expression "empty homogenous time" is from Walter Benjamin, "Theses on the Philosophy of History," 261.

4. Roland Barthes, *The Language of Fashion,* ed. Andy Stafford and Michael Carter, trans. Andy Stafford (New York: Berg, 2006), 115–16.

5. Decca Aitkenhead, "Ozwald Boateng: Does My Head Look Big in This?," *Guardian,* 9 March 2012.

6. Barthes insists that we consider the particular way in which the fashion industry and fashion journalism work together to produce a mutual self-authorization, thus my analysis of Boateng leans heavily on his ubiquitous media presence. Barthes, *The Language of Fashion,* 115–16.

7. Aitkenhead, "Ozwald Boateng."

8. In reading Boateng as a persona and self-nominated fashion icon, I am influenced by new theoretical terrain explored in Bishnupriya Ghosh, *Global Icons: Apertures to the Popular* (Durham, N.C.: Duke University Press, 2011).

9. Lola Ogunnaike, "Is This Man the Next British Invasion?," *New York Times,* 29 June 2006.

10. Suzy Menkes, "Ozwald Boateng: Jazzy Givenchy," *International Herald Tribune,* 13 July 2004.

11. Courtney Colavita, "Boateng's Balancing Act," *DNR: Daily News Record* 33, no. 50 (December 2003): 1.

12. Aitkenhead, "Ozwald Boateng."

13. Colavita, "Boateng's Balancing Act."

14. William Ham Bevan, "A Passion for Structure and Elegance," *Daily Telegraph,* 13 October 2010.

15. Aitkenhead, "Ozwald Boateng."

16. Natalie Graham, "Tailor Likes to Cut a Dash in a Fast Car," *Daily Telegraph,* 3 August 2003.

17. Ghosh, *Global Icons,* 3.

18. Jane Mulvagh, "Bewitchingly Besuited," *Irish Times,* 6 September 1993.

19. John Walsh, "Waiter, Waiter, There's a Fly in My Suit," *Independent,* 1 June 1998.

20. Ibid.

21. Gary Cotterell, "A Cut above the Rest," *Business Day* (South Africa), 13 May 2011.

22. Graham, "Tailor Likes to Cut a Dash in a Fast Car."

23. John Walsh, "What Ozwald Did Next," *Independent,* 3 February 2004.

24. Ranjana Khanna characterizes disavowal as a psychic act lodged between unconscious repression and conscious expression, a truth known but tenuously denied, with refusal and repetition its hallmark dynamic. See Khanna, *Dark Continents: Psychoanalysis and Colonialism* (Durham, N.C.: Duke University Press, 2003), 147–78.

25. Damian Thompson, "'It's Time for Blair to See Me for a Suit,'" *Daily Telegraph,* 18 September 2002.

26. Robin Givhan, "Unbuttoning Stuffed Shirts: Tailor Ozwald Boateng Shakes Up Savile Row," *Washington Post,* 22 October 1998.

27. Monica Miller, *Slaves to Fashion: Black Dandyism and the Styling of Black Diasporic Identity* (Durham, N.C.: Duke University Press, 2009). Miller provides an extraordinarily useful contribution to the history of black fashion in the United States and the broader diaspora generally, and a particularly powerful argument for the significance of the dandy tradition within it, concluding with a chapter on black cosmopolitanism centered on the artist Yinka Shonibare.

28. Thompson, "It's Time for Blair."

29. Martin Bentham, "'Role Models' Scheme to Boost Young Black Men," *Evening Standard,* 15 July 2008.

30. Walsh, "Waiter, Waiter."

31. Givhan, "Unbuttoning Stuffed Shirts."

32. Carola Long, "Boateng Out to Show He's a Cut above the Rest," *Independent,* 17 September 2010.

33. Hadley Freeman, "Under 35, Slim, and Feels Comfortable at a White Cube Opening," *Guardian,* 10 December 2003.

34. Thompson, "It's Time for Blair."

35. Gary Cotterell, "A Cut above the Rest," *Business Day* (South Africa), 13 May 2011.

36. Celia Walden, "It's Your Funeral: Ozwald Boateng Wants the Men at His Funeral to Wear His Couture Range, But He'll Be in a Traditional Ashanti Robe," *Mail on Sunday,* 18 May 2003.

37. Long, "Boateng Out to Show."

38. Aitkenhead, "Ozwald Boateng."

39. Dabydeen, *Hogarth's Blacks.*

40. For a discussion of the black dandy as a historical figure, I refer again to Miller, *Slaves to Fashion.*

41. Charles Baudelaire, "The Painter of Modern Life," in *The Painter of Modern Life and Other Essays,* ed. and trans. Jonathan Mayne (London: Phaidon, 1995), 26–29. All quotations are from these pages.

42. James Eli Adams situates the Victorian dandy within a handful of modes of masculinity available to middle- and upper-class men, specifically the gentleman, prophet, dandy, priest, and soldier. See Adams, *Dandies and Desert Saints: Styles of Victorian Manhood* (Ithaca, N.Y.: Cornell University Press, 1995).

43. Ibid., 53.

44. Ibid., 54–55.

45. Gayatri Chakravorty Spivak, *Outside in the Teaching Machine* (New York: Routledge, 1993), 161.

46. Yinka Shonibare, quoted from unpublished interview with Clémentine Deliss, 6 March 1992, cited in John Picton, "Yinka Shonibare: Undressing Ethnicity," *African Arts* 34, no. 3 (Autumn 2001): 69.

47. John Picton identifies two nineteenth-century patterns, "Staircase to Heaven" and "Staff of Kingship," along with a cheaper "Fancy Print" fabric likely manufactured in Japan. See Picton, "Yinka Shonibare," 70–71.

48. Shonibare is here reminding readers of the global trade in cotton fabrics that links a variety of colonial sites with European industrial centers. By politicizing this history in his contemporary artistic practice, the reader is also reminded of a previous moment in the history of decolonization when *khadi,* a rough homespun cotton fabric, indeed famously handspun by Gandhi himself, became iconic of economic resistance in the Indian freedom movement. For a discussion of Gandhi's political deployment of the tradition of *khadi* weaving, see Emma Tarlo's *Clothing Matters: Dress and Identity in India* (Chicago: University of Chicago Press, 1996). For a good overview of Shonibare's use of batik, see Pernilla Holmes, "The Empire's New Clothes," *ARTNews* (October 2002): 118–21.

49. The piece commemorated the success of the "Centenary Development" plan and the expansion of the museum. It also celebrated the rebranding of the Tate Britain and its satellite institutions in the wake of the opening, in 2000, of the Tate Modern. The expansion included a new gallery space and a research library and archives. BP continues to be one of the museum's largest and most visible sponsors.

50. Divya Tolia-Kelly and Andy Morris, "Disruptive Aesthetics? Revisiting the *Burden of Representation* in the Art of Chris Ofili and Yinka Shonibare," *Third Text* 18, no. 2 (2004): 155.

51. Shonibare's contemporary cachet as a global art icon is perhaps nowhere made clearer than in his being awarded the Member of the "Most Excellent Order of the British Empire" (MBE), a moniker he now wears ironically as a kind of trademark or brand, for example, in the major international retrospective titled *Yinka Shonibare MBE* (2008–9). In 2008–9, Shonibare was the subject of a major survey, titled *Yinka Shonibare MBE,* which opened at the Museum of Contemporary Art in Sydney before traveling to the Brooklyn Museum and to the Museum of African Art at the Smithsonian Institution, in Washington, D.C. See also the artist's website at www.yinkashonibarembe.com.

52. Images of each of these paintings are available in the National Gallery digital archive, http://www.nationalgallery.org.uk/artists/.

53. The video accompanying the installation also features an interview with the conservator of Oswald House at Auchincruive, now itself a sightseeing destination, who gives us a tour of the lands and the famous Oswald Temple, an estate teahouse built by the architect Robert Adam in 1778.

54. For a good discussion, see again Picton, "Yinka Shonibare."

55. See Nancy Hynes, "Yinka Shonibare: Re-Dressing History," *African Arts* 34, no. 3 (Autumn 2001): 61–62.

56. Picton, "Yinka Shonibare," 66.

57. Mieke Bal, "Guest Column: Exhibition Practices," *PMLA* 125, no. 1 (January 2010): 11.

58. Ibid., 13.

59. On recent general turns in museum studies and gallery display, see Peter Vergo, ed., *The New Museology* (1989; repr., London: Reaktion Books, 2000), and Elizabeth Mansfield, ed., *Art History and Its Institutions* (London: Routledge, 2002). For works on the intersection between museum display and cultural memory, see Didier Maleuvre, *Museum Memories: History, Technology, Art* (Stanford: Stanford University Press, 1999), and Susan A. Crane, ed., *Museums and Memory* (Stanford: Stanford University Press, 2000). For a superb and theoretically savvy example of art criticism attentive to the relationships between art institutions, creative practices, and spatial arrangement, particularly as they also relate to issues of race, class, gender, and sexuality, see Jennifer Gonzalez, *Subject to Display: Reframing Race in Contemporary Installation Art* (Cambridge, Mass.: MIT Press, 2008).

60. Shonibare might almost be said to be playing with the double meaning of redress his works evoke, though he never explicitly says so.

61. Judith Walkowitz, writing on nineteenth-century women charity workers, explains that "increasingly, female philanthropists constituted themselves as people who saw more than men, because they saw the domestic side of poverty. In their effort to moralize the poor into paragons of domestic virtue, they came to recognize the centrality of women to family and neighborhood." *City of Dreadful Delights: Narratives of Sexual Danger in Late-Victorian London* (Chicago: University of Chicago Press, 1992), 55.

62. Ozwald Boateng, "New Wind of Change Is Blowing through Africa," *CNN*, 7 June 2013; see also Matthew Bishop and Michael Green, *Philanthrocapitalism: How Giving Can Save the World* (New York: Bloomsbury, 2006).

63. Ozwald Boateng, ed., *New African* 528 (May 2013).

64. "The Birth of Philanthrocapitalism," *Economist*, 23 February 2006.

65. Bishop and Green, *Philanthrocapitalism*, 2.

66. Naomi Klein, *The Shock Doctrine: The Rise of Disaster Capitalism* (New York: Picador, 2007).

67. Boateng's enthusiasm, as well as his political and economic perspective on the emerging African economy, can be traced to a self-described "seminal new book," *The Fastest Billion: The Story behind Africa's Economic Revolution* (London: Renaissance Capital, 2012), which was authored by the management team of Renaissance Capital, a major Russian-based global investment banking firm now controlled by the even larger ONEXIM Group. According to its own press release, the book is "aimed to accelerate the world's realisation that the economies of most

African nations have transformed beyond recognition, and are set to surpass the growth seen in Asia and India over the past 30 years." Renaissance Capital, press release, 22 November 2012, https://www.rencap.com/Media/PressReleases/?id=421. Charles Robertson, the Global Chief Economist of Renaissance Capital and a major author of *The Fastest Billion,* is the only economic expert Boateng names in his article, where he cites Robertson's estimate that "Africa's GDP will increase from $2 trillion to $29 trillion in today's money by 2050." It is at this point in the op-ed that the network of private capitalist interests that shrouds the piece becomes most visible. Dishearteningly, Boateng appears to be little more than a shill for Robertson, Renaissance Capital, and ONEXIM's global economic agenda. The book gains a measure of legitimacy by including a foreword by the respected economist and top World Bank official Ngozi Okonjo Iweala, who in 2010 was the top non-U.S. contender for World Bank President in its first contested election. She is currently Nigeria's powerful Finance and Economy Minister and a member of the nonpartisan but decidedly neoliberal U.S. think-tank the Brookings Institution. The ONEXIM Group, it may be worth mentioning, is another large investment firm that, until recently, was led by the Russian billionaire, political puppet, and sports dilettante Mikhail Prokhorov, who is also majority owner of the Brooklyn Nets and minority owner of its controversially named arena, the Barclays Center. I talk briefly about the history of Barclays PLC in the opening of the final chapter.

68. Atlantic Energy, which operates solely in Nigeria, describes itself as "a private upstream oil and gas company founded by Nigerian and international Exploration & Production executives with an extensive track record, market-leading insight and experience in the Nigerian independent E&P sector." The company website is no longer online but is available through the Wayback Machine Internet Archive, http://web.archive.org/web/20140115052554/http://www.atlanticenergy.com/. The company was cofounded by the oil magnate and close Boateng associate Kola Aluko, himself most known for his extravagant, jet-setting lifestyle. Boateng appeared in a photograph on the company's online home page in a statement touting its partnership with the Made in Africa Foundation. On its "Sustainability" tab the company added, "Our new partnership with Ozwald Boateng's 'Made in Africa' foundation will set a new paradigm for developing Africa. The Made in Africa Foundation, focuses on supporting and funding power and infrastructure projects that would not get off the ground without such support. The Foundation will provide the support necessary for high-impact power and infrastructure projects to access funding by providing feasibility studies as well as developing the management teams and business plans." Atlantic Oil is currently embroiled in a number of financial scandals related to its no-bid contracts with the Nigerian government, and Aluko himself was, as of this writing, a fugitive from prosecution, along with Atlantic Energy chairman Jide Omokore and former

Nigerian oil minister Diezani Alison-Madueke. While an arrest warrant was issued in 2015, Aluko awaits extradition from Switzerland.

69. Here is how the movement initially described itself on its Facebook page: "Occupy Nigeria is a people-powered movement that began on October 17, 2011. Occupy Nigeria is fighting back against the corrosive power of major banks and multinational corporations over the democratic process, and the role of politicians in creating an economic collapse that has caused the greatest recession in generations. The movement is inspired by popular uprisings in Egypt and Tunisia, and the USA and aims to expose how corrupt politicians & bankers are writing the rules of an unfair global economy that is foreclosing on our future."

70. This panel of "economic and investment experts" was convened at Tullow Oil's London offices for a wide-ranging roundtable discussion of Africa's economic future, which was moderated by Anver Versi, editor of *African Business* magazine. The panel included Charles Robertson, chief global economist for Renaissance Capital; William Pollan, director of Invest in Africa, an initiative of Tullow Oil; Chris Cleverly, cofounder with Boateng of the Made in Africa Foundation; Eric-Vincent Guichard, founder and CEO of Homesprings; Guy Lundy, founder of Accelerate Cape Town; Michael Lalor, a senior partner at Ernst and Young; Jo Ford, an analyst for Oxford Analytica; and Acha Leke, director at McKinsey and Company. A total of eleven photographs, all essentially like the ones included here, accompanied the article.

6. @Bristol

1. Jamaica Kincaid, *A Small Place* (1988; repr., New York: Farrar, Straus and Giroux, 2000), 25. Further citations appear in text.

2. In the lead-up to the 2008 financial crisis, undercollateralized debt obligations were bundled, repackaged, and traded in the high-risk and highly speculative securities trade, one of the most volatile forms of capitalist accumulation. These new investment instruments and their role in the spectacular implosion of financial markets that year further confound this passage.

3. David Graeber, *Debt: The First 5,000 Years* (Brooklyn: Melville House, 2011).

4. David Barclay, *An Account of the Emancipation of the Slaves of Unity Valley Pen, in Jamaica* (London: William Phillips, 1801).

5. Stefania Vitali, James B. Glattfelder, and Stefano Battisto, "The Network of Global Corporate Control," *PLOS ONE* 6, no. 10 (26 October 2011): e25995. See also Andy Coghlan and Deborah MacKenzie, "Revealed: The Capitalist Network That Runs the World," *New Scientist Online,* 24 October 2011.

6. In the early days of the financial crisis Barclays maneuvered to buy several divisions of Lehman Brothers—one of the world's largest investment banks then facing liquidation—cleansed of its toxic asset. See "Barclays Buys Core Lehman

Assets," *BBC News,* 17 September 2008. Like the Barclays, brothers Emanuel and Mayer Lehman were merchant bankers who immigrated to the United States from Bavaria in the mid-nineteenth century. In 1844 they established a dry-goods store in Montgomery, Alabama, which in 1850 became a commodities trading firm capitalizing on the southern cotton trade. Thus the Lehmans likewise built their firm on the backs of the enslaved. See Joseph Wechsberg, "The Lehman Brothers: Magic Magicians," in *The Merchant Bankers* (Boston: Little, Brown, 1966), 279–319.

7. See Stephanie Flanders, "Inconvenient Truths about Libor," *BBC News,* 4 July 2012.

8. While 1831 saw widespread social turbulence across Britain, it ended with the largest slave insurgency to arise in a British colony: the Baptist War, often called the Christmas Rebellion, broke out on 25 December and continued to 4 January 1832. I offer this digression on the Queen Square riots in order to situate a longer history of forceful, labor-based opposition to the propertied interests secured through colonial slavery, interests that continue to define the city of Bristol as it does former colonies like Antigua or Jamaica. On the history of the Reform Act, see Edward Pearce, *Reform! The Fight for the 1832 Reform Act* (London: Jonathan Cape/Random House, 2003). On the Baptist War, see Michael Craton, *The Economics of Emancipation: Jamaica and Barbados, 1823–1843* (Chapel Hill: University of North Carolina Press, 1995).

9. Roger Ball, "1831, and All That," *Bristol Radical History Group,* 10 December 2006.

10. Jackson's letter appears in the published journals of C. B. Wollaston's antireformist half sister, Mary Frampton. See Frampton, *The Journal of Mary Frampton, from the Year 1779, until the Year 1846,* ed. Harriot Georgiana Mundy (London: Sampson Low, Marston, Searle and Rivington, 1885), 384–85.

11. See Jayne Mills, *Deprivation in Bristol* (Bristol: Bristol City Council, March 2011); Mills draws upon data from the Department for Communities and Local Government (UK), *Indices of Deprivation 2010.*

12. See Joshua Harris and Tina Wallace, *To Ride the Storm: The 1980 Bristol Riot and the State* (London: Heineman, 1984), and the Centre for Contemporary Cultural Studies, *Empire Strikes Back: Race and Racism in 70s Britain* (London: Routledge, 1992).

13. In a 1978 television interview Thatcher had declared, "People are really rather afraid that this country might be rather swamped by people with [or of] a different culture and, you know, the British character has done so much for democracy, for law and done so much throughout the world that if there is any fear that it might be swamped people are going to react and be rather hostile to those coming in." Her rhetoric harkened back to Enoch Powell's infamous "Rivers of Blood" speech a decade earlier. See Margaret Thatcher, interview by Gordon Burns, *World in Action,* Granada Television, 27 January 1978.

14. David Cameron, "The Age of Austerity," speech, Conservative Party Spring Forum, Cheltenham, UK, 26 April 2010.

15. See Richard Wolff and David Barsamian, *Occupy the Economy: Challenging Capitalism* (San Francisco: City Lights Open Media, 2012), and Noam Chomsky, *Occupy,* Occupied Media Pamphlet Series 1 (Westfield, N.J.: Zuccotti Park Press, 2012).

16. The expression comes from Joshua Clover's paper "World-Systems Riot," presented to the Social Science History Association 37th Annual Meeting, 2 November 2012. A revised version of the essay will appear in *Riot.Strike.Riot* (New York: Verso, 2016).

17. For a short account of state and corporate media responses to these popular actions, see David Harvey, "London 2011: Feral Capitalism Hits the Streets," in *Rebel Cities: From the Right to the City to the Urban Revolution* (London: Verso, 2012), 155–58.

18. "Urban Riots: The Battle for the Streets," *Guardian,* 9 August 2011.

19. Clarkson immediately disavowed this comment as a joke, and he was later forced to apologize. See "Jeremy Clarkson Apologizes over Strike Comments," *BBC News,* 1 December 2011; "Jeremy Clarkson One Show Exchange Transcript," *BBC News,* 1 December 2011. On leadership reactions to the strikes, see "Public Sector Strike Proving a Damp Squib—David Cameron," *BBC News,* 30 November 2011; and "Public Sector Strike Rallies Held across the UK," *BBC News,* 30 November 2011.

20. E. P. Thompson, "The Moral Economy of the English Crowd in the Eighteenth Century," *Past and Present* 50 (February 1971): 76–136. On his idea of the "moral economy," see especially 78–79.

21. See Alain Badiou, *The Rebirth of History: Times of Uprisings and Riots,* trans. Gregory Elliott (London: Verso, 2013), 5.

22. Such disturbances are typically attributed to long-standing social and economic deprivation, the continued application of "sus" laws, and the conflicted relationship poor and minority communities had with the police. See Cindi John, "The Legacy of the Brixton Riots," *BBC News,* 5 April 2006. For early cultural studies analysis of racialized policing, see Stuart Hall et al., *Policing the Crisis;* see also Paul Gilroy, *"There Ain't No Black in the Union Jack,"* in particular chapters 3, "Lesser Breeds without the Law," 72–113, and chapter 6, "Conclusion: Urban Social Movements, 'Race' and Community," 223–50.

23. "Let People Name New Horn Bridge Say Builders," *Bristol Evening Post,* 20 May 1998.

24. Bristol City Councilor Stephen Williams castigated the decision as "daft" and an example of "gesture politics." It is worth noting that Pero was not, however, the first choice of most respondents to the *Bristol Evening Post* poll, who preferred the then still-living local businessman and philanthropist John James. See Ian

Onions, "Slave Bridge Attack; New Name a Snub to City Benefactor," *Bristol Evening Post,* 17 November 1998.

25. O'Connell herself objected to the name, which she worried was "a bit political." See Onions, "Slave Bridge Attack."

26. The Bristol Sound is notable for its collaborative spirit and political edge—as well as for its often slow, moody, desolate style—represented by groups such as The Wild Bunch, Way Out West, Massive Attack, Up Bustle and Out, Portishead, and Reprazent, as well as the individual artists who comprised them: Tricky, 3D, Inky, Roni Size, Dynamite MC, and Onallee. See Peter Webb, *Exploring the Networked Worlds of Popular Music: Milieu Cultures* (New York: Routledge, 2007), 41–59.

27. Mills, *Deprivation in Bristol.*

28. Urban Task Force, *Towards an Urban Renaissance: Final Report of the Urban Task Force* (1999; repr., London: Department of the Environment, Transport and the Regions, 2002).

29. Ash Amin, Doreen Massey, and Nigel Thrift, *Cities for the Many Not the Few* (Bristol: Policy Press, 2000), 3. Further citations appear in text.

30. See *Bristol Local Plan,* prod. Strategic and Citywide Policy Team and the Directorate of Planning, Transport and Development Services (Bristol: Bristol City Council, 1997), and *Bristol Development Framework Core Strategy* (Bristol: Bristol City Council, 2011). The latter identifies no agency authorship but was produced "in regards to" the *Bristol 20:20 Plan* (Bristol: Bristol Partnership, 2009) developed separately by the Bristol Partnership, a public–private initiative operating in coordination with—but formally outside—the Bristol City Council through which corporate-sector interests have gained unprecedented access to and responsibility for city planning. As a City Council document, the *Core Strategy* satisfies the statutory mandate by the national government for a binding "development framework," applying the official imprimatur of the state on a development strategy fashioned largely by the city's corporate partners.

31. Andrew Kelly, *Building Legible Cities* (Bristol: Bristol Cultural Development Partnership, 2001), 36.

32. The picture of urban regeneration—and community responses to it—that I develop in this chapter is drawn from a review of dozens of state and local government documents (policy statements, task force reports, long- and short-term planning strategies, action plans, and project descriptions and assessments), tourist brochures, shopping guides and other promotional materials, as well as hundreds of mainstream and alternative media reports. Although my approach to thinking about the intersection of colonial history and contemporary urban regeneration follows a cultural studies tradition, I have consulted current scholarship on urban planning and design relevant to Bristol in particular and global trends more generally.

33. The Floating Harbour was intended to keep Bristol competitive with Liverpool and London in the wake of the abolition of the slave trade by allowing newer and larger vessels to dock there. It was completed at a cost to the public of around £600,000, the equivalent of around £34 million today; or, as a percentage of GDP, an outlay of £2 billion. See "Bristol Harbour Reaches 200 Years," *BBC News*, 1 May 2009; see also the "Bristol Floating Harbour" webpage, http://www.bristolmuseums.org.uk, maintained by Bristol Museums, Galleries and Archives, an independent, nondepartmental ("devolved") trust contracted by the Bristol City Council.

34. "Europe's Largest Project," *Bristol Evening Post*, 15 October 1997.

35. Chris Starkie, "Harbourside Wins 4,000-Seat Cinema," *Bristol Evening Post*, 28 October 1998.

36. Nigel Dando, "Welcome to the Pleasuredome . . . Work, Rest and Play at Harbourside," *Bristol Evening Post*, 30 October 1998.

37. "Docks Are Becoming the Cultural Heart of City," *Bristol Evening Post*, 3 September 1998.

38. See Jerry Hicks, MBE, "Harbourside Development," Soapbox, *Bristol Evening Post*, 5 March 1999.

39. Neil Fraser, "Docks May Lose Lottery Millions," *Bristol Evening Post*, 27 July 1998.

40. "Harbourside Development," Letters, *Bristol Evening Post*, 28 October 1999.

41. See "Harbourside Development," Soapbox, *Bristol Evening Post*, 21 September 1999; Ian Onions, "Harbourside Heaven: Public Backing for Canon's Marsh Scheme in Survey," *Bristol Evening Post*, 10 December 1999; Ian Onions, "Protest over Poll on Harbourside," *Bristol Evening Post*, 20 December 1999; and "Poll Gets Vote: Harbourside Bias, Claim Is Rejected," *Bristol Evening Post*, 22 January 2000. It should be noted that while opposition was voiced in the opinions section of the *Bristol Evening Post*, and opponents were often quoted in news reports, the newspaper itself was a strong supporter of large-scale redevelopment and an advocate for property developers, as in the opening sentence of the following news item by its city reporter Chris Drucker, which could easily have appeared in a press release by Crest Nicholson: "Most people would agree Bristol has got its Harbourside development just about right, providing a glittering cultural and leisure facility for the new Millennium." Drucker, "The Battle of Temple Quay," *Bristol Evening Post*, 5 February 1998.

42. "Less Talk, More Action on City's Harbourside," *Bristol Evening Post*, 25 February 2000.

43. Madge Dresser, Caletta Jordan, and Doreen Taylor, *Slave Trade Trail around Central Bristol* (Bristol: Bristol Museums and Art Gallery, 1998).

44. Following the closing of *A Respectable Trade?*, the city curated a small, permanent exhibit drawn from its holdings in the industrial museum. The Bristol and Transatlantic Slavery Gallery would serve as the city's only significant display of materials pertaining to slavery until the 2007 bicentenary of the abolition of the slave trade and the opening of the much more comprehensive exhibit mounted by the British Empire and Commonwealth Museum (BECM) under the title *Breaking the Chains: Bristol and the Slave Trade.* The BECM, located in the historic nineteenth-century Temple Meads railway station designed by Brunel, was itself a redevelopment project. The museum was short-lived, however, closing in 2008 with the announcement that it would be relocating to London, a plan that has since been abandoned.

45. Barb Drummond's self-published *The Bristol Slavery and Abolition Trail* (Bristol: Barb Drummond, 2006) celebrates the role of local abolitionists in ending the slave trade rather than pursuing the longer and more difficult history of the city's relationship to colonial slavery and the trade. The BBC's guide "The Bristol Abolition Walk" follows Drummond's path. See "In the Footsteps of Bristol's Abolitionists," *BBC News,* 16 March 2007.

46. For an excellent discussion of the development of the slave trade trail walking tour, see Elizabeth Kowaleski Wallace, *The British Slave Trade and Public Memory* (New York: Columbia University Press, 2006), 43–65. For her account of the protest at the Georgian House, see 49–50. Wallace is critical of the intervention, which, she claims, "polarized, rather than united, a community committed to the full story of Pero's life."

47. Jeremy McNeill et al. "If the Georgian House Could Speak," 1998, http://jeremymcneill.tripod.com/georghouse.html.

48. Ibid., emphasis added.

49. "Wow?," *Bristol Evening Post Watch,* 28 September 2008; "Cabot Crunch," *Bristol Evening Post Watch,* 3 October 2008.

50. Several of these neighborhoods are identified by the Department for Communities and Local Governments as experiencing persistent, long-term economic deprivation and social exclusion, and include the districts of St. Pauls, St. James, and St. Agnes (in Cabot and Ashley), and Easton Road, Barton Hill, Old Market, and the Dings (in Lawrence Hill).

51. Alternative media and neighborhood publications certainly did report on this opposition. *Bristol Indymedia* and *Bristol Evening Post Watch* proved invaluable for tracking the opposition and the actions against the Broadmead scheme.

52. "'Offensive' Centre Name Changed," *BBC News,* 20 April 2006.

53. Ibid., emphasis added.

54. "New £500m Shopping Centre Opens." *BBC News,* 25 September 2008.

55. The circus began in more permanent settings, such as Astley's Amphitheatre (est. 1773), but following its introduction to the rural geography of North

America, the circus returned to Britain in the mid-nineteenth century as a largely itinerate operation, such as the black British showman Pablo Fanque's Circus Royal, which toured the Isles heavily in the second half of the nineteenth century. See George Speaight, *A History of the Circus* (San Diego: A. S. Barnes, 1980); and in a U.S. context, see Janet M. Davis, *The Circus Age: Culture and Society under the American Big Top* (Chapel Hill: University of North Carolina Press, 2002)

56. It would be irresponsible to valorize the circus as a site of progressive occupation or collective belonging given the well-documented ruthlessness and cruelty endemic to such historically unregulated ventures: systematic abuse, a practice of capture and removal, and shocking levels of exploitation—all consequent to the almost unchecked power of the owner-impresario over the lives of the most acutely disadvantaged and marginalized groups of itinerate workers and performers.

57. For many living in nearby St. Judes, Cabot Circus was viewed as an enormous, and enormously impractical, imposition, its shops ill suited to the needs of residents of the council estate located across from its main entrance. Cabot Circus could offer a place to purchase an expensive designer handbag but, as one local complained to BBC News, "nowhere to buy a simple pint of milk or loaf of bread," thus leading the BBC reporter to conclude, "Despite having a shopping mall on their doorsteps the people of St Judes will have to pay serious money for gourmet grub in the Circus or walk half a mile to the Horsefair or one of the convenience stores in Stapleton Road." "Cabot Circus: The View from St Judes," *BBC News*, 25 September 2008.

58. No Tesco in Stokes Croft, "The Campaign So Far," February 2010, https://notesco.wordpress.com/thecampaign/the-campaign-so-far/.

59. *Central Action Plan: Options Consultation* (Bristol: Bristol City Council, February 2012), 130. Further citations appear in text.

60. See Derrida, *Of Hospitality*.

61. The observer is the historian Dr. John Evans, quoted in a brief synopsis written by the current administrator of the building under the Bristol Churches tab of the *About Bristol* website, http://www.about-bristol.co.uk, also quoted later in this paragraph.

62. "Saint Stephen's Reconciliation Laboratory," 7 February 2011, http://www.saint-stephens.com/2011/02/saint-stephens-reconciliation-laboratory. The Reconciliation Laboratory was discontinued after the retirement of Canon Tim Higgins, Priest in Charge, at St. Stephen's, in 2014. Reference to the Reconciliation Laboratory no longer appears on the church's website but can be found through the Wayback Machine Internet Archive.

63. The quotation is from Graeme Mortimer Evelyn's CV and biography, as included on his website and now archived at the following website: https://www.londonart.co.uk/sales/cv.asp?artist_id=7358.

64. Pope Pius XI, Quas Primas, 11 December 1925, http://w2.vatican.va/content/pius-xi/en/encyclicals/documents/hf_p-xi_enc_11121925_quas-primas.html.

65. "Christ's Kingdom Not Based on Human Power, Pope Says," *Catholic World News,* 27 November 2006.

66. Evelyn, CV and biography.

67. Claire Doherty, "Hew Locke," http://www.hewlocke.net/ruined.html.

Index

STEVEN BLEVINS is a writer and teacher in northern California.